100 GREAT SCIENCE FICTION SHORT SHORT STORIES, ed. by Isaac Asimov, Martin Harry Greenberg, and Joseph D. Olander. Doubleday, 1978. 270p 77-76221. 8.95 ISBN 0-385-13044-9. C.I.P.
In the introduction to his and Groff Conklin's anthology, *Fifty short science fiction tales* (1963), Isaac Asimov suggested that because of the speculative nature of science fiction, the SF short short story, when it succeeds, offers the reader more than the usual joke-like concentration of thematic intent and ambuscade of narrative outcome characteristic of conventional short short stories. It offers the additional and refreshing intensity of an exotic background that is not required at all in conventional fiction but mandated in fantastic fiction. Most of the "tales" included in the 1963 volume seemed to bear Asimov out, but not convincingly. They were simply not that successful as stories. However, the selections in this present volume, which includes, significantly, only one story from the previous collection, are successful, and the "great" of the title is not hyperbole. Established practitioners of the full-length science fiction novel such as Larry Niven, Roger Zelazny, Frederick Pohl, C. M. Kornbluth, and Laurence Janifer are included in the collection along with equally renowned primarily short story writers and essayists such as Alfred Bester, Damon Knight, and Martin Gardiner.

Continued

100 GREAT SCIENCE FICTION SHORT SHORT STORIES

The result of such heterogeneous inclusion is the elicitation of the short stort story format itself at its most successful. An enjoyable volume, it merits consideration in the critical assessment of a literary form. All libraries should own a copy.

BORN SECRET

Pergamon Titles of Related Interest

Cannizzo   THE GUN MERCHANTS
DeVolpi   PROLIFERATION, PLUTONIUM AND POLICY
Edmonds   INTERNATIONAL ARMS PROCUREMENT
Golden   SCIENCE ADVICE TO THE PRESIDENT
Jolly   DISARMAMENT AND WORLD DEVELOPMENT
Laszlo/Keyes   DISARMAMENT: The Human Factor
Long/Reppy   THE GENESIS OF NEW WEAPONS
Mroz   BEYOND SECURITY

Related Journals*

FUTURICS
HABITAT INTERNATIONAL
HEALTH PHYSICS
NUCLEAR & CHEMICAL WASTE MANAGEMENT
WORLD DEVELOPMENT

*Free specimen copies available upon request.

BORN SECRET
The H-Bomb, the <u>Progressive</u> Case and National Security

A. DeVolpi
G.E. Marsh
T.A. Postol
G.S. Stanford

Pergamon Press
NEW YORK • OXFORD • TORONTO • SYDNEY • PARIS • FRANKFURT

Pergamon Press Offices:

U.S.A.	Pergamon Press Inc., Maxwell House, Fairview Park, Elmsford, New York 10523, U.S.A.
U.K.	Pergamon Press Ltd., Headington Hill Hall, Oxford OX3 0BW, England
CANADA	Pergamon Press Canada Ltd., Suite 104, 150 Consumers Road, Willowdale, Ontario M2J 1P9, Canada
AUSTRALIA	Pergamon Press (Aust.) Pty. Ltd., P.O. Box 544, Potts Point, NSW 2011, Australia
FRANCE	Pergamon Press SARL, 24 rue des Ecoles, 75240 Paris, Cedex 05, France
FEDERAL REPUBLIC OF GERMANY	Pergamon Press GmbH, Hammerweg 6, Postfach 1305, 6242 Kronberg/Taunus, Federal Republic of Germany

Library of Congress Cataloging in Publication Data
Main entry under title:

Born secret.

  Bibliography: p.
  Includes index.
  1. United States, appellee. 2. The Progressive.
3. Liberty of the press--United States. 4. Atomic
weapons information—Law and legislation--United States.
5. Hydrogen bomb. I. DeVolpi, Alexander, 1931-

KF228.U5B67 1981   342.73'0853'0264   80-28841
ISBN 0-08-025995-2   AACR1

Printed in the United States of America

I know that's a secret, for it's whispered everywhere.

- William Congreve

Contents

PREFACE   xi
ACKNOWLEDGMENTS   xiii

CHAPTER

I: THE NUCLEAR AGE: POINT OF NO RETURN   1

    The Beginnings of the Progressive Case   3
    Chronology of Events   4
    Press Reaction   9
    Historical Perspective   11
    The Underlying Issues   12

II: THE CHANGING MEANING OF DEFENSE   15

    Technical Information and Modern Political Affairs 17
    Strategic Arms Control   20
    The Shell Game: MX   22
    Summary   23

III: SOCIETY'S NEED TO KNOW   24

    Secret Decisions During World War II   26
    The Right to Know Versus National Security   31
    Misinformation About Nuclear Power   42
    Environmental Issues   45
    The Progressive Case and the CTBT   46
    The Relevance of H-Bomb Information   48
    Need-to-Know as Seen by Progressive Case Participants 49
    Overview   53

IV: THE OPPOSING LEGAL ARGUMENTS IN THE PROGRESSIVE CASE   57

    Filings for a Temporary Restraining Order   58
    Filings for a Preliminary Injunction   63
    Motion to Vacate the Injunction   73
    Arguments on Appeal   76
    Summary of Legal Issues   81

V: TECHNICAL DISCUSSION   82

    Fission Versus Fusion   83
    Types of Nuclear Weapons   84
    The Ideas in Morland's Article   89
    Deducibility of Morland's Ideas   91
    The Article Should Have Been Ignored   97
    Public Information Sources   98
    Mistakenly Declassified Documents   103
    The Glenn Letter   105
    The Hansen Letter   106
    Authoritativeness   107
    Conclusions: Deducibility of the Three Concepts   108

VI: PROLIFERATION RISK   110

    Proliferation Risk from Morland's Article   110
    Five Nuclear-weapons States   115
    Industrial States   117
    Espionage   118
    Nuclear Weapons Testing   119
    Nuclear Test Bans   122
    Proliferation Concerns   126
    Disincentives to Proliferation   127
    Conclusions Regarding Proliferation Risk   129

VII: GOVERNMENT SECRECY   131

    The Atomic Energy Act of 1954   132
    Declassification   137
    Executive Order on National Security Information   137
    What the Government has been Classifying   140
    Volume and Costs of Classification   142
    Secrecy and Technology Denial   144
    Deducibility and Classification Policy   149
    Metastable Nature of Secrets   152
    Restrictive Effects of Secrecy   154
    Summary: Secrecy and Government Institutions   156

VIII: MISUSES OF SECRECY 158

Misuse for Political Purposes 158
Selective Classification 168
Acquiescence to Classification Abuse 170
Selective Declassification in the Progressive Case 172
Overclassification of Research Data 176
Implications 177

IX: OFFICIAL INFRACTIONS OF SECURITY GUIDELINES 179

Legal Action 179
Affidavits that Spilled Secrets 180
Classification of the Glenn Letter 181
Challenges to the Atomic Energy Act 183
Government Weapons Documents 184

X: LEGAL CONSIDERATIONS 188

The Temporary Restraining Order 188
Judge Warren's Decision on the Preliminary Injunction 189
Factual Disputes 190
Statutory Conflicts 192
Constitutional Arguments 195
The Pentagon Papers Test of Harm 198
Advisory Procedures 206
The Appeals 208
Dismissal of the Suit 210
Legal Precedents 211
Sequel 212
Congressional Hearings 214
Hollow Victory? 216

XI: REMEDIES 217

The Cost of Litigation 218
Reform Principles 218
Information Sources 220
Classification Review 221
Decision-Making Processes 223
The Judicial Process and Technical Issues 224
Dealing with Classified Information 227
Atomic Energy Act Reforms 229
Oversight of the Classification System 233
Summary of Suggested Remedies 233

EPILOGUE   235

COMMENTARIES   238
     Howard Morland   238
     Samuel Day, Jr.   239
     Erwin Knoll   240
     Charles Sims   240
     Hugh DeWitt   242

APPENDICES

A: MORLAND'S ARTICLE AND ERRATUM   245
B: THE GLENN LETTER   256
C: SELECTED PASSAGES FROM THE ATOMIC ENERGY ACT   258
D: EXECUTIVE ORDER ON NATIONAL SECURITY
        INFORMATION   262

NOTES   266
GLOSSARY   286
ACRONYMS AND ABBREVIATIONS   289
PROGRESSIVE CASE LEGAL REFERENCES   290
GENERAL REFERENCES   297
INDEX   299
ABOUT THE AUTHORS   305

TABLE AND FIGURES

Table I.   Summary of nuclear weapons tests through 1979   116

Fig. 1.   Design configurations for four types of nuclear
            weapons   85

Fig. 2.   Encyclopedia Americana version of H-bomb conceptual
            design   92

Fig. 3.   Merit Students Encyclopedia version of H-bomb
            conceptual design   100

Fig. 4.   The most significant "Greenglass Diagram" used as
            evidence in the Rosenberg case   163

Preface

It was with mixed emotions that we became involved in the <u>Progres-</u><u>sive</u> case -- a legal conflict between government secrecy and the First Amendment. We found ourselves caught between those who felt that to preserve national security our constitutional institutions would have to yield, and those who thought that the constitutional protections were more important than what they saw as remote risks to national security. We felt squeezed between our public duty, as we saw it, and the views of the agency that funds our employer. Caught in a controversy among scientific colleagues, we found ourselves submitting testimony to courts, giving technical advice (solicited) to defendants, offering advice (unsolicited) to legislators, communicating with reporters, and generally contributing to the cacaphony raised by various people and groups in their diverse efforts to make nuclear war less likely.

The opinions we express in this book are our own -- not those of the U.S. Department of Energy nor those of our employer, Argonne National Laboratory, which is under contract to DOE. Nevertheless we acknowledge with admiration and gratitude the forbearance of those two organizations. In the best democratic tradition, they have let us have our say -- with some indications of disappointment, perhaps, but with no hint of pressure to cease and desist. Indeed, the classification branches of Argonne (which is not a weapons laboratory) and DOE have been actively helpful in granting the security clearances needed by two of us in assisting the defendants, and in making special arrangements for the local security and storage of pertinent classified documents. In being frankly critical of some of the things DOE has done, we are doing our best to enhance national security. We are all on the same side.

The book does not dwell on our personal reactions, but rather attempts to assemble in one place material that will help foster an understanding of the events surrounding the <u>Progressive</u> case. We hope it provides insights into the broader underlying technical, social, and legal issues for which the episode is but a paradigm.

The work was not sponsored by the government, and the book contains no information from classified sources.

We use four notations for references. Documents from the
Progressive case are indicated by numbers in brackets (thus, [1]);
they are listed at the end of the book. Names of legal cases are
underlined (Progressive, or New York Times); no full reference is
given because that would be outside the scope of this book. One-of-a-
kind references to articles and books are expressed in full when
mentioned; repeated references are cited by initials and date of
publication in brackets (thus, [F&W-74]). These references are
tabulated at the back. Notes containing extended remarks or references
are listed separately according to chapter; thus [Note IV-3] is the
third note for Chapter IV   Notes for all chapters follow the
appendices.

Throughout we have made reference to the "government." We use this
term in a generic sense to refer to the executive branch of U.S.
federal government as a political entity. Its use is not necessarily
confined to any particular presidential administration, nor do we mean
to single out or exclude any particular department, branch, or agency.

A glossary of technical terms and a list of acronyms and
abbreviations are near the end of the book. Also, some documents that
are freqently referred to but are not readily available, including the
contested article about the H-bomb, are reproduced in appendices.

Acknowledgments

We are indebted to The Progressive Foundation for supplying us with copies of all the case documents in their possession, and to Marshall Perlin for providing an extensive file of documents regarding the Rosenberg case.

The American Civil Liberties Union, particularly Bruce Ennis and Chuck Simms, helped us make our way through the legal thicket. We appreciate their legal support throughout the case and their review of drafts of the manuscript.

Howard Morland has permitted us to reproduce his article. From Sam Day and Erwin Knoll we have received continued encouragement, as well as constructive remarks about our manuscript. Much-appreciated suggestions have also come from Hugh DeWitt and Ray Kidder.

Material from a column by Rear Admiral H.C. Eccles is reprinted by permission of The Christian Science Monitor: ©1980, The Christian Science Publishing Society, all rights reserved.

Excerpts from The Myths of National Security, ©1957 by Arthur Macy Cox, are quoted by permission of Beacon Press.

We also appreciate permission to quote passages from Secrecy and Foreign Policy, edited by Thomas M. Franck and Edward Wiesband, ©1974 by Oxford University Press.

David Kellogg, our editor from Pergamon Press, reviewed the manuscript at several stages, and has been a constant source of editorial ideas and congenial guidance.

1 The Nuclear Age: Point of No Return

In nuclear warfare, mistakes are irretrievable.
- H. C. Eccles, Rear Admiral, U.S. Navy

When the atomic bomb was dropped on Hiroshima in 1945, the most revolutionary weapon ever to be introduced into warfare destroyed not only a city and much of its population, but also all classical concepts of warfare. It was no longer possible to defend industrial centers, territories, or populations. The concept of defense became an anachronism, to be replaced by deterrence -- the threat of retaliation. In an attempt to prevent other nations from getting the atomic bombs against which there is no defense, the government created a superstructure of secrecy around nuclear technology.

Because information and programs protected by secrecy are effectively removed from public view and discussion, secrecy and the democratic process are fundamentally inconsistent. Any benefits of secrecy claimed for a given program must be carefully balanced against the costs. As secrecy becomes more pervasive, it increasingly threatens social, political, economic, and democratic institutions in fundamental, if subtle, ways.

During and after World War II the extraordinary power of science and engineering in military affairs was manifested in the form of radar, aircraft, the proximity fuse, fire-control systems, ballistic missiles, submarines, and the most destructive weapon of all time, the nuclear warhead. The great military and economic benefits of giant, well-organized, and protected (by secrecy) government projects were recognized, and many such projects became permanent institutions. Allied war operations were revolutionized by the technology created in these massive and impressive efforts. However, the national security implications of the war-born technologies have been immeasurable, and the existence of large programs behind veils of secrecy is a matter of growing concern.

One danger in large, institutionalized secret programs is that they can develop significant political undercurrents that have an important impact on our lives. As an example, consider the original decision, shortly after the atomic (fission) bomb was developed, to proceed with

1

work on the thermonuclear H-bomb. The decision to develop a thermonuclear (fusion) weapon, the "super" as it was then known, was debated behind closed doors. Declassified only in 1974, an October 30, 1949, report of the General Advisory Committee to the Atomic Energy Commission contains warnings, by knowledgeable scientists, that should have had a public airing. A statement by James B. Conant and others noted that the super would be in a totally different category from the atomic bomb, and that if such weapons would work at all there would be no inherent limit to their destructive power. They believed that such a weapon should never be produced. To the argument that the Russians might develop one, they responded that our own stock of atomic bombs would be able to assure national security. The final paragraph states:

> In determining not to proceed to develop the super bomb, we
> see a unique opportunity of providing by example some
> limitations on the totality of war and thus of limiting the
> fear and arousing the hopes of mankind.

Enrico Fermi and Isador Rabi, two prominent scientists, also submitted a statement in opposition to the development of the super, and they included the moral dimension:

> The fact that no limits exist to the destructiveness of
> this weapon makes its very existence and the knowledge of
> its construction a danger to humanity as a whole. It is
> necessarily an evil thing considered in any light.

Had the issue been publicly debated, the decision to develop the super might very well have been delayed, without compromising the security of the country. But it was not openly debated, and the chance to reach international accords prohibiting such weapons was missed. The specter of damage to national security was of course raised to justify keeping the debate secret -- under the assumption that scientists in the Soviet weapons program would not independently recognize the possibility of constructing fusion-based devices unless it were called to their attention by public discussion in the United States. The Soviets were expected to forget that the power in the stars comes from fusion reactions made possible by high temperatures and pressures, conditions duplicated in a fission explosion.

As should have been predicted, the Soviets did independently recognize that thermonuclear weapons might be feasible. The secrecy around discussion of the super merely kept the American public from getting the information it needed in order to exercise its democratic right to debate the decision to develop or not to develop. Citizen participation at one of the most important crossroads in the history of human affairs was forestalled.

The Role of Secrecy

Secrecy can be valuable in retarding the use and abuse of potentially dangerous technologies. Slowing the spread of fission and fusion weapons, for instance, as well as blunting efforts by terrorists or nation-states to divert special nuclear materials or to fabricate fission explosives, is clearly in the interest of national (and indeed international) security. At the same time, there is also a national (and global) need for productive diplomatic, economic, and industrial programs -- endeavors that thrive on the free flow of information. To what extent are these two goals incompatible? That is a question that we examine in this book. It is one of the issues surrounding nuclear weapons, and those issues are the most critical that the human race has yet faced.

The problem has been effectively shielded from public scrutiny for more than thirty years. In that context, the Progressive case should not be viewed as an isolated dispute over H-bomb secrecy between a magazine and the U.S. Department of Energy. As a confrontation between concerned citizens and a government whose policies they call into question, it exemplifies the critical human issues that emerge along with the growth of technical knowledge -- issues that encompass far more than the H-bomb. Although the main focus in this book is on the dangers to national security from too much secrecy about thermonuclear weapons, the principles discussed carry over to other areas (fission weapons, for example) where excessive secrecy can also be harmful.

THE BEGINNINGS OF THE PROGRESSIVE CASE

The Progressive is a crusading monthly that focuses on political analysis and opinion. It is published in Madison, Wisconsin, and has a circulation of about 40,000. Founded in 1909 by Robert LaFollette, it has developed over the years a more or less respectful following among people to the left of the political center.

The editor since 1973 has been Erwin Knoll, who had been its Washington editor since 1968. He has had a thirty-year career in journalism, working for Editor and Publisher, the Washington Post, and the Los Angeles Times-Washington Post News Service. For a time he was White House correspondent for the Newhouse newspapers. In addition to writing for many leading magazines, Knoll has lectured on problems of journalism. Here is how he sees part of his magazine's mission [43]:

> One of the major editorial concerns of The Progressive throughout its 70-year history has been the prevention of international military conflict. In recent years, it has focused attention on the nuclear-arms race. The Progressive has published many articles on the dangers of nuclear war and on the steps that might be taken to reduce or eliminate those dangers. For several years, almost every issue of The Progressive has contained articles or editorials dealing with one aspect or another of the nuclear-arms race.

The managing editor of The Progressive was Sam Day, Jr. The authors of this book knew Sam from his time as editor of the Bulletin of the Atomic Scientists, for which all of us have contributed at one time or another. The Bulletin is edited near us -- at the University of Chicago -- and our contacts over the years stemmed from our common interest in bringing nuclear armaments under control. It was Day who initiated The Progressive's inquiry into the role that government secrecy plays in suppressing public awareness of the nuclear arms establishment in America.

In 1978, The Progressive's editors asked Howard Morland, a free-lance writer who had been specializing in energy and nuclear weapons issues, to research and write an article about government secrecy. He did, and an unexpected tempest ensued. The Progressive, the U.S.

government, the American Civil Liberties Union, and many lawyers, scientists, and journalists became embroiled in a dispute that swirled around the First Amendment, thermonuclear weapons and proliferation thereof, and government-restricted data. Although the article (Appendix A) was eventually released, there was a court-imposed half-year delay, the longest period of prior restraint of publication in U.S. history.

Morland did not have an extensive background in technology, having taken only a few undergraduate courses in science. He graduated from Emory University, Atlanta, in 1965, and served in the air force during the war in Vietnam. After leaving military service (as a captain) in 1969, he worked as a commercial pilot, carpenter, and freelance writer. Morland now lectures widely on the subject of nuclear weapons and energy, and has produced and distributed a slide show entitled "Atomic Power and the Arms Race," and more recently one entitled "The H-bomb Secret," oriented toward thermonuclear weapons and arms control.

CHRONOLOGY OF EVENTS

Morland prepared for his H-bomb article by spending six months in 1978-79 reading and talking to people. He interviewed DOE officials, made visits to nuclear weapons production facilities and museums, studied the Congressional Record, and asked questions. His research and train of thought are exhaustively documented in his first affidavit filed with the court. Among the people he contacted were two of us (Alexander DeVolpi and Theodore Postol), whom he knew to have technical expertise in the physics associated with nuclear and conventional weapons. Because we had had no access at the time to secret information on thermonuclear weapons (and therefore could reveal nothing classified), we were free to comment on the plausibility of some of his technical findings, and make suggestions for improvements in accuracy.

Late in 1978 the authors received for review from Sam Day a draft of the first article written by Morland for publication. It was on the hazards of tritium, a radioactive isotope of hydrogen that is used in H-bombs and luminous watch dials. We made suggestions for various corrections of fact and perspective, some of which were acted upon.

Then in February 1979 Day mailed us, for technical review, a draft of the H-bomb article that later became notorious. Because of our background in physics, nuclear technology, weapons proliferation, and arms control, the four of us were able both to understand the article's technical content and to judge its political component. Our reactions were not unanimous, but there were some things we agreed on.

One was that the article contained insights into possible features of hydrogen bomb design that had not occurred to us -- in particular a couple of new concepts. That does not mean much, though, because none of us had made any effort to figure out how to go about making a fusion weapon, or had worked in nuclear weapons development, or had any classified knowledge of the fusion part of thermonuclear weapons.

We all could see, on the basis of fundamental physical principles, that there were serious technical errors in the draft, as well as ideas that seemed to have some technical merit.

It was our consensus that the ideas new to us were plausible, would probably be deduced by any competent physicist who set his mind to working on the problem, and would certainly occur to any well-qualified research group that was given the task.

We agreed that we could not tell how near the mark Morland's diagrams were -- how closely they corresponded to actual warheads, or even to warheads that would actually work. All we could tell was that the general layout seemed reasonable.

We could not tell what was missing -- what other ideas one would have to implement in order for the fusion reaction to proceed.

We saw that there was no quantitative information: none of the numbers (sizes, proportions, precise shapes) that would be essential in order to make the thing work. It was clear to all of us that a multibillion-dollar development effort would be needed if Morland's article were to be the starting point for an H-bomb program -- an effort that could be undertaken only by a large nation with advanced technology.

We also were agreed on this: Many of Morland's details did not seem particularly relevant to his case. At that time, we felt that Morland could make his points against excessive government secrecy with comments on H-bombs that were far less specific.

Our comments and criticisms were combined and returned to The Progressive with a recommendation for extensive revision of the article. Most of us thought that no harm would be done by publishing it, because the weapons-related technical information was either wrong or easily deducible by anyone who could make use of the information. At least one of us (George Stanford), however, had reservations. In a phone call to Sam Day, he expressed the view (long before the government had taken any public action) that publication of the article might take some of the mystique out of the H-bomb business, perhaps triggering research or development that would not otherwise have been begun.

Day would not accept that argument, which he had also gotten from others; he saw the puncturing of the secrecy mystique surrounding design and production of the H-bomb as a principal value of the article. The mystique does not deter other governments that have the scientific/industrial base and the desire to build H-bombs, he reasoned. The real function of the mystique, he felt, was to keep the public from knowing about the H-bomb and its effects, thereby giving vested interests a free hand to continue the nuclear arms race. In fairness, his argument that the Morland article would not significantly enhance proliferation was not unreasonable. Given sufficient resources and the desire for fusion bombs, "mystique" cannot reasonably be expected to stand in the way of other countries for long. Further, Day could have pointed out that H-bombs would be of no military value to most small countries, since the simpler A-bombs offer more than enough destructive power.

Government Intervention

It was in late February or so, 1979, that the Department of Energy (DOE) learned of The Progressive magazine's intention to publish an article about secrecy in the hydrogen bomb program. Drafts of the article had previously been sent to three reviewers [Note 1-1]. One of them -- Ron Siegel, a graduate student -- turned over his draft copy to George Rathjens, a political scientist at MIT. Rathjens phoned The

Progressive to urge that it not be printed, giving, in part, arguments similar to Stanford's. When his arguments were rejected, Rathjens turned the draft over to classification authorities at the Department of Energy and notified the magazine's editors of his action.

There was no immediate response from DOE. Early in March, faced with the rapidly approaching deadline for the April issue, The Progressive's editors decided to submit their final version to DOE themselves, with a request that it be checked for accuracy. Thereupon, DOE, in phone calls and in a visit to the magazine's editorial offices, objected to publication on the grounds that the article included secret, still-classified data. This was clearly in conflict with the desires of the article's author and editors, who wanted to dispel the mystique and bring discussion of nuclear weapons policy into the public arena where it belonged.

The first legal action in the case took place March 8, 1979, when the government moved to suppress the article by asking the Federal District Court of the Seventh Circuit (in Milwaukee) to issue a preliminary injunction restraining publication. The government claimed that the article contained "Secret Restricted Data" as defined by the Atomic Energy Act of 1954. The next day the court issued a temporary restraining order (TRO) prohibiting publication or other disclosure. Subsequently a protective order was issued to safeguard sensitive information filed in the case. The legal scene then shifted to the mandatory hearings on a preliminary injunction.

Very high officials took an interest in the case. The Secretary of Energy, James R. Schlesinger, assumed a personal role. Robert Gillette of the Los Angles Times, in an article printed September 30, 1979, reported that on Saturday, March 10,

> Schlesinger sought both to assuage an alarmed press and head off end-run publication of the article elsewhere, in telephone calls to editors at the Los Angeles Times, the New York Times, the Washington Star and the Washington Post.

Asked by Anthony Day, editor of the Los Angeles Times's editorial pages, whether "it was because of the importance of the precedent or because of the thing itself," Schlesinger replied, "Both. Either would be sufficient."

The Progressive saw the actions of the government as a particularly intolerable form of censorship -- an ironic example of the very policy of overreliance on secrecy that the magazine was attacking. Constitutional rights were also involved. In the words of Erwin Knoll, "Rights exist only when they can be exercised. If there is no First Amendment for The Progressive, there is no First Amendment for anyone." Lawyers for the magazine contested the issuance of an injunction.

The situation was unusual. Only a few people had read the article before it was classified, and a lot of misinformation came out. Many who filed affidavits or made public statements had not read it, and many of those who had were not technically qualified to evaluate it. Our opinion at the time (it hasn't changed) was that representatives of the government were exaggerating the effect that publication might have on proliferation risk.

At the request of The Progressive, Ted Postol filed two affidavits that demonstrated the existence in the public domain of certain concepts that, as it turned out, were considered by the government to be classified. Three of us (Gerald Marsh, George Stanford, and Alexander DeVolpi) later entered an affidavit on behalf of the American Civil Liberties Union as "friends of the court" (amici curiae). That affidavit supported the ACLU's suggestion that the court set up an independent panel of experts to advise it on the actual sensitivity of the information contained in Morland's article. In addition, DeVolpi filed an individual affidavit that challenged some assertions by the Secretaries of Defense and State.

On most of the legal issues we found ourselves in agreement with The Progressive and the American Civil Liberties Union (ACLU). In particular, we saw that the government had not met the "heavy burden of showing justification for [prior] restraint" that the Supreme Court had called for in connection with the Pentagon Papers and other cases; it had not shown that publication of the Morland article would surely result in direct, immediate, and irreparable damage to the nation.

We also were sympathetic with the concerns of the press about possible erosion of First Amendment rights. However our involvement on the side of the defendants does not imply that we would advise abandoning the system for classifying official data. On the contrary. As will become clear, one of our aims is to promote constructive changes that will both strengthen the protection of truly sensitive data and permit public access to information needed in policy debate.

Sam Day, in a trip to California, obtained supportive affidavits from over half a dozen prominent scientists, including Hugh DeWitt and Ray Kidder, two physicists at the Lawrence Livermore nuclear weapons laboratory. Dr. Kidder once had extensive thermonuclear weapons design responsibilities, and Dr. DeWitt has been active in the statistical mechanics of dense plasmas, a subject relevant to thermonuclear fusion.

Because of its obvious First Amendment implications, the Progressive case immediately attracted the attention of the press and received rather heavy coverage. Any legal precedent that was set would surely be far-reaching. Adding to newsworthiness was the charge that the article could potentially further the proliferation of hydrogen weapons, with the implied conflict between national security needs and the public's right to be informed.

Subsequent events, which we discuss more fully later on, attracted continuing public attention. One had to do with a letter (Appendix B) that we sent to Senator John Glenn, Chairman of the Senate Subcommittee on Energy, Nuclear Proliferation and Federal Services. We were bothered by the outright government assertions, in public affidavits, that the Morland H-bomb description was essentially a correct, if incomplete, description of U.S. fusion weapons -- a fact that neither we nor anyone else could have deduced from public information. Our letter detailed this apparent government breach of security, and raised the possibility that the public confirmation of Morland's information was deliberate. The letter was not treated with urgency by the Glenn committee. In five or six weeks they sent it for comment to DOE, whose response was to classify it. It came to public attention, however, when a student newspaper, the Daily Californian at Berkeley, defied a government order and published it.

Legal maneuverings followed a decision by Federal District Judge Robert Warren of Milwaukee to grant the preliminary injunction. After he denied a motion to vacate his injunction, both the Seventh Circuit

Court of Appeals and the Supreme Court were asked for expedited hearings. The motions, which were turned down, were based on the claim that technical information about thermonuclear weapons could be found in the open literature: In particular, there was a revealing nuclear weapons progress report, UCRL-4725, that had inadvertently been declassified by the government. By the time the appeal was heard, by a three-man panel of the Court of Appeals in Chicago on September 13, the public-domain issue became prominent.

Government Retreat

If UCRL-4725 was the mortal wound for the government's case against The Progressive, the coup de grace was the Hansen letter. Charles Hansen, a thirty-two-year-old computer programmer in Mountain View, California, had run a design-your-own H-bomb contest as a hobby. In that contest, he solicited designs based on public information, and submitted them to DOE to be cleared for publication. The winner was to be the first design to be classified.

From his reading and the material sent to him, Hansen pieced together his own H-bomb design, and included it in a letter to Senator Charles Percy, who was on the Governmental Affairs Committee. Hansen had become concerned about the Progressive case as it might affect the First Amendment, and also about apparent release of truly sensitive information by certain prominent figures who had been privy to highly classified weapons details. His letter had two purposes -- first, to show how much he, as an amateur, could deduce about fusion weapon design (in support of Morland, whose H-bomb description he had not seen), and second, to ask why those prominent government figures had not been prosecuted for revealing what he claimed they did.

The Hansen letter was classified by the DOE, which also obtained a TRO prohibiting publication by the Daily Californian. However the letter was promptly published (September 16, 1979) by the Madison [Wis.] Press Connection. It was at that point that the government -- with an almost audible sigh of relief -- withdrew its prior restraint case against The Progressive, claiming that the Hansen letter had let the cat out of the bag.

Allegation of Criminal Violations

We suspect that certain people in the government were left smarting from their traumatic tangle with The Progressive. They perhaps could not admit to themselves that official blunders had destroyed their case. The "Teller diagram," a crucial element that we will discuss in due course, had appeared in the Encyclopedia Americana without being cleared for publication; a warning by Postol that some of the references in his unclassified affidavit might point to classified concepts in college textbooks was ignored; and there had been the erroneous declassification of UCRL-4725. Not willing to make even a de facto admission that the sensitive information in the Morland article had been gleaned from the public domain, the DOE apparently started looking for a scapegoat. On September 20, 1979, the Chicago Tribune carried a story entitled "U.S. probing H-bomb leaks by own scientists":

A [Justice] department spokesman, Robert Havel, confirmed [that a criminal] inquiry was under way after the Washington Post published a story reporting that [DOE] officials suspect government scientists, allegedly including some from Argonne National Laboratory...are responsible for leaking classified secrets [to the authors of stories on the hydrogen bomb].... One source said Energy Department officials found significant similarities between sections of the [secret] government briefs and parts of the 18-page Hansen letter.... The Post said it was not clear why scientists from Argonne and Livermore were under suspicion....

The Argonne "government scientists" mentioned could only be the authors of this book. Two of us with the appropriate clearance, DeVolpi and Marsh, were unable to find the alleged "significant similarities" in the Hansen letter. On September 4, 1980, about a year after the original allegations, the Justice Department publicly announced that "no prosecutive action will be taken for alleged violations of the Atomic Energy Act and the court orders in the Daily Californian and the Progressive Magazine cases." Although litigation was terminated [180] on that date, after agreement had been reached on disposition of certain materials that had been sealed by the court, some of the broader issues were unresolved and continue to simmer.

PRESS REACTION

When the government asserted that an article The Progressive wanted to publish contained information whose release would damage national security, the press at first reacted with caution. Although editors tend not to take suppression of speech or publication lightly, the knowledge that no freedom can be absolute led most of them to support the temporary restraining order on the strength of the government's claims. The New York Times editorial of March 11, 1979 is representative:

The Federal courts have long recognized that suppression before publication is the gravest possible denial of free speech and press.... [We] feel a touch of sympathy for United States District Judge Robert Warren of Milwaukee, who...is being told the article would help smaller nations make a hydrogen bomb, or make it sooner, and thus wreck the anxious effort of the United States to halt the spread of these weapons....

This seems to be a legitimate contest of concerns. Under the circumstances, a week or two of enforced restraint for a monthly journal seems a tolerable price.

By March 25, the day before Judge Warren issued his preliminary injunction, the situation had changed considerably. In its editorial "Public Bombs, and Minds Born Secret" of March 25, the Times had a very different tone:

The Government is doing its best to intimidate the Milwaukee judge and to incite the public against the magazine....

The case against the Progressive...turns out to be a case against the national interest -- against free speech

and free inquiry.... On the available evidence, the
Government has failed to prove a sure, grave, direct,
immediate and irreparable harm to our nation -- the only
conceivable justification for censorship.... The article
may be an embarassment and inconvenience: it may even be
harmful to policy. But those are not judgments that
Government may impose on editors. They plainly do not
justify suspending the First Amendment.

And, in their March 29 lead editorial:

[Judge Warren] yielded in the end to the authority of
distinguished Government witnesses whose policy judgments
he felt too ignorant to dispute....

What the Government really aims to protect is a system
of secrecy, which it seeks now to extend to the thought and
discussion of scientists and writers outside Government.

Consistent with the early ambivalence of the press, the Freedom and
Information Committee of the American Society of Newspaper Editors,
then holding its annual convention in early May in New York City, was
initially reluctant to make any recommendation to the ASNE board that
would indicate wholehearted support for The Progressive. But after a
day to consider, and without addressing the merits of the article, the
board voted unanimously to join in the appeal. The basis was their
feeling that the government had failed to meet the heavy constitutional
burden of proof needed to justify prior restraint of publication, as
defined by Justice Potter Stewart in the Pentagon Papers case.

By the time of the appeals hearing on September 14, 1979, any
hesitation the press may have earlier felt about supporting The
Progressive had vanished. The discovery of much information in the
public domain -- including the 1956 secret Los Alamos laboratory
weapons report, UCRL-4725 -- convincingly demonstrated that the
information in the Morland article was publicly available. The
government had in fact now shifted its argument away from the Pentagon
Papers standard, and instead introduced the novel argument that
technical information is not protected by the First Amendment. This
argument was strongly questioned by the press. In a September 9
editorial, the Chicago Tribune stated:

In a technological age in which the quality of our lives
and the dangers that threaten us often turn upon highly
technical disputes, the government's contention that
technical information should be given second-class treatment under the First Amendment is particularly disturbing.... It should be especially troubling to the scientific community, though its implications touch us all.

When it received a copy of Charles Hansen's letter to Senator
Charles Percy, the Chicago Tribune notified the federal government that
it planned to print portions of the letter, and challenged the
government to try to stop it. The Tribune had no chance to make good
its threat, because the letter was published first by the Madison
[Wis.] Press Connection. The Chicago Tribune is not known for having a
liberal point of view, and its intention to directly violate the
Atomic Energy Act (technically it did so subsequently by publishing the
letter before it had been officially declassified) dramatically
illustrates the depth of opposition by the press to the government
actions.

Commenting on the implications of the Hansen letter, and the government's attempts to suppress it, the Tribune used some rather strong language in a September 16 editorial:

> About the only "unique" thing about the Progressive article is that the government made the foolish and dangerous decision to try to censor it....
>
> The only real purpose the case against the Progressive serves is to draw attention away from the government's own failure to protect its secrets over the years. And for this meager purpose, the government would prostitute a constitutional protection as important today as it has ever been.
>
> If the government refuses to stop this dangerous business, the courts should do it themselves by requiring the government to try to justify its bizarre and unconstitutional conduct.

By then the government's position was clearly becoming untenable, and it dropped the case. The Hansen letter, and the press by publishing it, had given the government a way to get out while retaining, undamaged, the "born secret" interpretation of the Atomic Energy Act. That the fundamental issues of the case remained unresolved was clearly understood by Anthony Lewis of the New York Times, who wrote in his September 20 column,

> A prior restraint actually operated for six months. Even though the Government's lawsuit is now dismissed, the fact of that restraint will remain: a dangerous precedent ready for use by other Administrations and other courts.

HISTORICAL PERSPECTIVE

Immediate forerunners of the Progressive case include the Pentagon Papers and Marchetti proceedings. Those cases differed from Progressive in that the dispute was over the right to publish information that had an official origin, whereas Morland had developed his information from public sources.

The Nixon administration's attempt to enjoin publication of the Pentagon Papers was the first case of its kind. Those papers revealed a consistent pattern of deception of the Congress and people of the United States by the administrations involved in the Vietnam war. Even though the contents would prove embarrassing to many high officials, the government did not succeed in its attempt to suppress publication -- although the New York Times was temporarily restrained by a court order from publishing material in its possession.

In the suit brought against Victor Marchetti in April 1972 to prevent publication of a nonfictional account of CIA covert intelligence gathering and political operations, the government obtained not only a temporary restraining order, but also a permanent injunction that was subsequently upheld on appeal.

The historical legislative basis for classifying nuclear information is the Atomic Energy Act, originally passed in 1946 and revised in 1954 (Appendix C). Material classified under that act is called "Restricted Data." There is confusion in the classification system stemming from the fact that there is an overlapping category of secret data called

"National Security Information" (NSI) (Appendix D). NSI consists of data, nuclear and otherwise, classified under the authority of various presidential executive orders. The current Executive Order, 12065, explicitly says that information may be "considered for classification [if] it concerns...weapons...[or] scientific, technological, or economic matters relating to the national security." It also defers to the Atomic Energy Act by stating, "Nothing in this order shall supersede any requirement made by or under the Atomic Energy Act of 1954, as amended."

Nuclear weapons data is unique under the law, in that all such information is inherently classified as a form of Restricted Data. The Atomic Energy Act of 1954 grants responsibility for protecting Restricted Data to the Atomic Energy Commission and its successor agencies. The executive order apparently grants similar classification authority with respect to nuclear weapons to designated administration officials. Because the enforcement provisions are different, the legal origin of the classification authority invoked in a given case is not a mere academic point.

It was in this historical context that Federal District Judge Warren issued his protective order on March 14, 1979, and his preliminary injunction against The Progressive magazine on March 26. Unlike the Pentagon Papers and Marchetti cases, here the heart of the issue was not the publication of (properly or improperly) classified information, but rather the "born secret" interpretation of the Atomic Energy Act. Under the born secret doctrine, a writer or researcher working from unclassified sources could combine information in such a way as to produce concepts that are "classified at birth." The constitutionality of including privately generated information under classification authority derived either from the Executive Order or the Atomic Energy Act is far from clear.

The category "Restricted Data" is an administrative construct resulting from the Act. Data stamped SECRET are not necessarily secret. Many classified principles of atomic processes are not protectible as secrets (for they are "whispered everywhere"). Even if they are "born secret" in government research, they cannot be kept secret if deducible by others without classified information.

THE UNDERLYING ISSUES

One of the foremost problems highlighted by this case is the role of government secrecy in preventing the spread of a sensitive technology such as the art of making nuclear weapons. Another is the extent to which secrecy is misused in order to satisfy political objectives, such as winning support for administration policies or avoiding embarrassment. Secrecy, even if sometimes necessary, is inherently in conflict with the public need for the information that permits technology to be understood and controlled. A particular example of such conflict arises in the growing dispute over whether there are better policies than present ones for limiting the proliferation of nuclear weapons and controlling the competitive arms race.

Explicit technical issues arose concerning the principles of thermonuclear weapons design. Did Morland's article actually contain "the secret" of the H-bomb? We think not. Chapter III is devoted to a technical analysis of his work and the available, open sources of information. We conclude that Morland gathered mostly conceptual information, and speculated on some additional concepts. He had no confirmed, quantitative details. Lacking official verification, this material had essentially no potential value to another nation. Thus we differ both with The Progressive, which asserted that the "the greatest secret of them all, the H-bomb," is really no secret at all, and with the government, which acted as though there had been little erosion, over the years, of supposedly safeguarded knowledge.

The possibility of chronic abuse of the security classification system has been brought into focus by the Progressive case. The frightening nature of the Morland article's subject matter -- H-bombs -- and the surrounding ignorance born of secrecy seem to have been exploited by the government to elevate the apparent level of sensitivity of the article, perhaps to help get a court decision that would put the classification system on a firmer legal footing. There have been other, similar instances of misuse of secrecy, which will be documented later in this book.

In the legal battlefield, there was a clear conflict between national-security needs, as the government presented them, and the constitutional rights of the press. The litigation also brought into question the constitutionality of the Atomic Energy Act -- in particular the doctrine that ideas may be "born secret." The major constitutional issue was the extent to which prior restraint can be justified.

A particularly relevant point is whether there are national-security reasons why the Act should extend to data simply deduced from public information. We conclude that there are not, and go into the reasoning later. In reviewing events that have taken place, we have found cause for concern over the processes associated with classification and declassification. Whether or not particular technical data should be restricted would appear to be a matter of technical judgment, yet we find that the Department of State strongly influenced government action in the case, without the benefit of qualified in-house technological expertise.

The intention of The Progressive to publish an article on secrecy and the hydrogen bomb may have looked to the government like an opportunity to obtain a clear legal license for imposing prior restraint, as well as a chance to resolve the born-classified issue. Because of the indeterminate outcome of the case, however, the legal precedent is yet to be established.

Of the three legal areas of dispute in the Progressive case -- factual, statutory, and constitutional -- the third raised the most profound questions. Is there a constitutional right and a societal need for the public to know the type of H-bomb information contained in Morland's article? A full answer requires an understanding of the law and of technology, as well as perspective regarding the political facets of proliferation. In due course we go more deeply into the legal (Chapter IV) and technical (Chapter V) issues that were important to the Progressive case. First, though, we set the stage, to see what the conditions were that caused such a case to arise. Feelings and facts about "national security" were important, as were feelings and facts about constitutional rights. Some saw a conflict between those two concerns, a conflict denied by others. In the next two

chapters we question the realism of certain current ideas about
defense, and then examine the type and extent of the information that
the public needs if policy decisions are to be made in the light of
informed public debate.

Although not everyone agrees, we start from the position that policy
decisions made in secret have a greater chance of being wrong than if
they are made in the light of public scrutiny. Revolutionary implements of war have been brought in without the public or even Congress
having the chance to appreciate the consequences of possible
alternatives. Intelligent debate must be based on adequate, sound
information. Underlying the issues raised by the Progressive case
is the fact that extensive application of any technology has far-
ranging political, social, economic, and moral reverberations. Society
cannot prevent abuse of a technology without first knowing something
about its fundamental technical concepts. Only then can we understand
how the technology can be applied and constrained, and identify our
possible choices. While we hope that each new technology can be
controlled, there can be no turning back.

2 The Changing Meaning of Defense

The men in the nuclear weapons laboratories of both sides
have succeeded in creating a world with an irrational
foundation, on which a new set of political realities has
in turn had to be built.
- Lord Zuckerman, chief scientific advisor
to the British Government

For most of man's existence, people believed that the sun and stars had
been created to rotate around the earth. Early in the sixteenth
century Copernicus, with profound insight, showed otherwise -- sparking
a transformation of scientific awareness. Although advances in
scientific knowledge are usually expected to have a major social
impact, the Copernican displacement of the earth from the center of the
universe had little immediate effect on the structure of Western
society. Certainly the issue of whether the sun moves around the earth
does not affect the daily business of the average person. However, the
birth and development of the scientific method have left untouched no
facet of modern life. The Copernican revolution played an instrumental
role in the evolution, not only of celestial mechanics, but of the
scientific process itself. Pure reason as an isolated tool for
determining the nature of the universe was rejected, and the Western
world was reorganized and industrialized. A fusion of empirical
evidence with rational theory, devoid of theological motive, became the
mainstay of the scientific approach.

In 1945 there was an equally profound scientific discovery, whose
implications are yet to be fully comprehended and whose impact has
still only been partially felt. It was shown that runaway multiplication of neutrons in a piece of fissionable material could be made to
continue long enough for a nuclear explosion to occur. The energy was
so great, and released in such a short period of time, that it was
hotter (briefly) at the center of the explosion than at the center of
the sun. Suddenly physical conditions could be achieved on earth that
formerly had existed only in the interiors of stars. In effect, we
were able to bring a piece of the sun down to earth, for whatever
purposes we chose.

15

Human ingenuity in inventing new techniques and discovering and applying new science far exceeds the ability socially and culturally to adapt those inventions or insights unless they have a direct impact on daily life. (We seem in some respects to have assimilated the automobile far better than we have the A-bomb.) Because weapons of mass destruction are small, compact, and unobtrusive, and do not affect daily routine, to the average American they seem to be considerably less significant than baseball scores. Nevertheless, the impact of the new weapons on human affairs will probably be more profound than the four hundred years of thought and innovation that followed the insights of Copernicus. In what is perhaps the final step of the evolutionary endgame, we have produced something that is so destructive and alien to human experience that there is no assurance that society will learn how to control it.

The prospect is bleak. Nuclear weapons now exist in such great numbers, are deployed in so many diverse ways, and can be delivered so promptly on a decision to go, that the miracle is not that two atomic bombs have been used, but that only two have been used. Even though they are the most serious threat faced by humanity, the species has been unable to work them into its thinking. The inability to adapt as fast as it can invent could very well be the human animal's Achilles heel. Intelligence is perhaps a lethal mutation.

The lag between means and attitudes is sharply demonstrated when issues of what is euphemistically called defense arise. No longer appropriate are certain cultural attitudes that are rooted in classical military realities. Thousands of years of experience have left most peoples of the world with a deeply felt notion of how to protect tribe, country and family. Defense is traditionally related to the idea that one is protecting the homeland from invasion. Intuition says that it is always prudent to build more, better, and newer weapons. The visceral reaction of people faced with an adversary of uncertain military strength is to buy insurance by increasing their own forces; they have been taught by historical experience that they will thereby increase their ability to repel military aggression or protect vested interests. While there undoubtedly still are limited circumstances where this reaction is appropriate, it is dead wrong when applied to the military strategy of a modern superpower.

Nowhere is the conflict between unrevised cultural values and modern technical realities more striking than in much of the classically trained political-science community. Discussions there revolve around whether certain actions of national restraint might appear weak or indecisive. There is, the thinking goes, some optimum degree to which one ought to appear reckless, unpredictable, and irrational (just enough to be convincing). Political "signals," how the "other side" might perceive or interpret a given act or stated policy position, and other traditional issues are solemnly considered in a contextual void. We presume that the same discussions occur on the "other side," wherever that happens to be at the moment. Hidden behind such abstrusness is the inability (or unwillingness) to confront and analyze the changed circumstances -- to examine the consequences of retaining old attitudes in the face of new technical realities.

And policymakers play the posturing game. "Won't shun A-war, Haig warns Soviets" was the page one headline of the Chicago Sun Times, January 10, 1981:

WASHINGTON -- Secretary of State-designate Alexander M. Haig Jr. said Friday that U.S. foreign policy must be based on the premise that "there are things worth fighting for," even if it means using nuclear weapons. That tough stand means letting the Soviet Union know that the United States is willing to engage in nuclear war if push comes to shove....

The same message, of course, comes back from Russia from time to time. Haig went on to say, "Our deterrent achieves its credibility by the perception of our willingness to do whatever is necessary to protect our vital interests." (Emphasis added.)

TECHNICAL INFORMATION AND POLITICAL AFFAIRS

Where human values come into play, different people faced with similar choices react differently. This is especially true when risks must be weighed against benefits (which should be most of the time). Even if much solid background information is available, and even if the debaters consider it, there is often much uncertainty and a lot of room for subjective judgment. Consider the problem of balancing the benefits of a comprehensive nuclear test ban against the risks of someone managing to cheat. (We discuss the matter of test bans later in the chapter.) Is, for instance, the feasibility of clandestine nuclear tests on (or under) the surface of Mars realistic enough, and is the advantage to the Soviets great enough, to outweigh the nonproliferation benefits that a test ban would bring? There are those who would answer yes, in spite of the growing list of potential nuclear-weapons states (currently Argentina, Brazil, Iraq, Israel, Pakistan, South Africa, South Korea, and Taiwan, and maybe others). Or, how does one balance the risks of continuing to develop and deploy new nuclear weapons against what might happen if no new ones were developed or deployed? Opinions on such questions are inevitably influenced by vague, culturally induced feelings.

While it is not new that technical information has played a role in human affairs, it is new that this information has brought about revolutionary changes in the way risks and benefits have to be balanced against each other. Militarily, prudent commanders have always had to carefully assess the potential for loss of life and equipment that goes with any contemplated operation. In the past, however, a general merely had to decide how to deploy cavalry, mounted armor, troops, fortified barriers, and the like. Military technology was such that the potential loss in any given battle was confined to the size of the armies in combat. Although the consequences of the loss of an army could be rather serious, the possibility for rapid escalation of military commitment was limited by the technology of the period. World War II gave perhaps one of the firt examples of losses that, for technological reasons, spread beyond the immediate military participants.

Current military thinking, based on the availability of modern aircraft, ballistic missiles, and other technologies, has to take into account the ability of both sides to strike deep into rear areas of supply, support, and communications. The use of long-range destructive weapons is conditioned not only by immediate military effectiveness, but also by considerations of escalation and retaliation, and the military commander must now think far beyond the narrow (and by itself demanding) problem of protecting forces. In modern times, an ill-conceived military action might not cost just thousands of lives, but hundreds of millions.

Implications of Nuclear Weapons Effects

No weapon is less discriminating than a nuclear explosive. Any political theory of power based on the limited or extended use, or the threat of use, of nuclear weapons for tactical, strategic, or "surgical" purposes must not ignore that fact. The smallest "strategic" nuclear weapon the United States deploys, the Poseidon warhead, has a yield of 40 kilotons (kT) TNT equivalent, which is two or three times as big as the bomb that destroyed Hiroshima. The largest of the U.S. warheads, the Mk9, has a yield of 9 megatons and is capable of setting fires more than twenty miles from ground zero. The Soviet Union deploys hundreds of high-yield warheads in the 18 to 25-megaton range, and thousands of warheads in the low megaton range.

The lethality of a high-yield nuclear weapon is so great that an intuitive grasp of its scale is probably beyond anyone's abilities. Consider radioactivity alone. The Castle-Bravo detonation of February 28, 1954 (which was designed to produce 8 megatons but yielded 15) contaminated 7,000 square miles (18,000 square km) to such an extent that unprotected individuals anywhere in that area would have died or suffered serious chronic disabilities. If a bomb that size were to hit the largest power reactor currently built or contemplated (3,000 megawatts thermal), the reactor and its protective containment would become part of the fireball -- but it would not make much difference in added public harm. One minute later, the radioactivity from the weapon would be about 10,000 times greater than that from the reactor (both of which would now be part of the radioactive cloud). An hour later, the reactor's share of the fallout is still only a thousandth part.

Even "tactical" nuclear weapons have yields in the range of at least 0.1 to 1 kT. For perspective, some of the largest chemical-explosive accidents that have occurred have been on the order of 0.1 kT. In addition to blast and fireball effects, nuclear weapons leave a radioactive residue in the atmosphere, and create local fallout if they are detonated low enough for the fireball to touch the ground. The same is true for "neutron" bombs, which have enhanced gamma and neutron radiation for a given blast yield.

There is no possibility of discriminating military use of a weapon whose immediate "collateral damage" could extend hundreds of miles downwind -- a matter that must be borne in mind by anyone trying to weigh the pros and cons of keeping alive the option to use such weapons, or of policies that could precipitate their use. Although a small neutron bomb whose fireball did not touch the ground could be used in ways that many would consider relatively "discriminating," there would still be extraordinary damage and radioactivity. Because rear echelon commanders of forces that have been destroyed with neutron weapons are unlikely to be able to distinguish the damage from that caused by other types of tactical nuclear weapons, a neutron warhead attack is likely to be considered the beginning of a general nuclear attack. The first use of a tactical nuclear weapon runs the risk of retaliation in kind and escalation to strategic nuclear war.

Nuclear Realities

Rational, technically informed people have come to comprehend that the transformation in the nature, scale, controllability, and predicta-bility of warfare has been so radical that the traditional use of military force (or the threat thereof) to augment political power no longer works. That realization, however, has yet to permeate the world's major military and political establishments.

Some of the fundamental changes brought about by the availability of unlimited destructive force are useful to keep in mind. One of the revolutionary consequences is that it is now possible to design and deploy offensive weapons systems for which no defense exists (a point that is expanded upon in some detail in Chapter III). All conceived-of defensive measures are much more complex, expensive, and uncertain than quickly and easily implemented offensive countermeasures that can nullify them. Anyone who has studied the various anti-ICBM systems that have been proposed -- antimissile missiles, particle-beams, ground-based lasers, and even the currently touted space-based lasers -- can show how these complex, expensive, and technologically dubious systems can be circumvented by fairly trivial tactics or minor adaptations of existing and inexpensive (by comparison) off-the-shelf technology.

Another distinctive property of nuclear bombs is that they are weapons of offense (or retaliation or preemption), with virtually no defensive role (although using them on one's own territory to attack an invading army might be considered defensive). A country that acquires nuclear weapons may soon find itself less secure than before. (Before 1945, nobody would have seriously thought that Washington, New York, or Los Angeles could be destroyed by foreign military action.) The ease of delivery and the destructive power of these weapons not only makes their possessor an adversary to reckon with, but enhances the posses-sor's importance as a military target.

Nonnuclear states, even if bystanders, also stand to suffer in any nuclear exchange. Those in central Europe could be the primary victims of a war limited to tactical nuclear weapons. A large-scale strategic exchange could affect global weather patterns, causing shifts in the world's deserts, altering the migrations of insect populations, destroying many plant and animal forms, and even changing the level of the oceans. The Third World's people already live at the brink of famine, and any ecological deterioration could be disastrous. To them, the failure of the weapons states to develop a less parochial attitude toward nuclear weapons is a legitimate source of fear and irritation.

It may very well be true (but is by no means obvious) that the existence of these weapons has so far prevented a war between the major world powers, and perhaps some takeovers of small countries by large neighbors. However, even if this is true, to conclude that the current situation is so stable that it can be expected to go on indefinitely requires considerable imagination. The attitude is like that of a driver who has never been killed running red lights, and therefore thinks of running red lights indefinitely.

Adding to existing arsenals of these unprecedented, revolutionary weapons does not enhance strength and security.

STRATEGIC ARMS CONTROL

The advance of technology makes it reasonable to consider arms control or arms limitation, phrases that refer to efforts to stop the super-powers' nuclear arms race. It might or might not be a practical idea, and certainly will not be easy. It can only begin when each partici-pating nation can feel assured that the others are not secretly violating the agreements. Effective verification of treaties is needed, and that is now possible because of technological advances in optical, infrared, and microwave remote-sensing techniques, seismic sensing, satellite observation, and the like. By proper attention to different monitoring capabilities, treaties can be formulated to be verifiable in considerable detail.

Photoreconnaissance capabilities, for instance, are impressive, as exemplified by some interchanges in the SALT II negotiations. Satel-lites had observed enough details about ICBM silos at the Soviet testing center at Tyuratam to permit the U.S. to raise pointed ques-tions pertaining to whether the silos were for testing or were part of an operational system. Similarly, the United States was queried by the Soviet Union about "weather covers" that were used during modernization of ICBM silos in the deserts of the Southwest; the covers interfered with satellite monitoring of the activities.

The object of arms-limiting agreements is not to eliminate all military conflicts. Arms control is merely a way to try to limit the potential for violence. It is based on the practical recognition that shared restraint in armaments is likely to promote international stability by reducing uncertainty and insecurity. Mutual and balanced control of forces, weapons systems, and related technologies is sought.

Underlying this modern diplomatic approach to technology control is the slowly growing recognition of what we have been saying in this chapter -- that defense against a strategic nuclear attack has become impractical or impossible. For an arms control treaty to be effective it must achieve a balanced, unambiguous, and verifiable military standoff. Here are some stabilizing things that a carefully negotiated arms control treaty might do:

* Ease international fears and tensions that create incentive to strike first.

* Create formal diplomatic channels to provide increased opportunity for discussion, cooperation, and exchange of information among potential military adversaries.

* Free national resources that might otherwise be committed to military activities.

* Channel the developing military technologies into directions likely to be less unbalancing, thereby making crisis management more stable.

* Help to limit the extent of hostilities and scale of destruction if diplomacy breaks down and military actions are precipitated.

* Ban the military technologies that are the most indiscriminate and therefore likely to affect noncombatants most heavily.

As an example of the last point, the nerve agent GB, a lethal dose of which is about a thirty-thousandth of an ounce, can be countered by proper military gear. Unprotected civilians 50 to 100 kilometers downwind from a concerted GB attack could suffer death or serious health impairment from exposure to this insecticide-related chemical. The U.S. Army currently has about 8 million pounds (3,500 tonnes) of GB stored in drums on the desert in Utah. A negotiated ban of these chemicals could remove serious risks to noncombatants thousands of miles from an actual battle zone -- risks from a substance whose approach they could not even know of.

The Hitch: How and What to Negotiate

The political problems of implementing realistic arms control treaties should not be underestimated. First, there are legitimate differences of opinion between honest, thoughtful people as to what should be negotiated, what can be negotiated, and how to balance different risks against each other. Second, there are deep-seated cultural prejudices against negotiating with potential adversaries. The fact that the treaties would be of mutual benefit (which must be true of any treaty if it is to succeed), and would be carefully negotiated so that both sides can verify treaty compliance, does not seem to impress a significant fraction of the political world.

Partial recognition that we can no longer defend ourselves is implicit in the Strategic Arms Limitations Talks (SALT). These negotiations have been going on with the Soviet Union since the late 1960s, and have so far resulted in one treaty -- an interim agreement that limits certain strategic weapon systems. (SALT I went into effect in May 1972 and expired in October 1979). Ratification of SALT II has been stalled in the U.S. Senate, and has apparently even been repudiated (as of this writing) by the incoming Reagan administration. SALT has, unfortunately, been the focus of almost all public debate on arms control, distracting public attention from questions far more fundamental than the largely issue-skirting topics considered at the SALT negotiations. Perhaps SALT has plumbed the depths of the politically possible, but that does not make the larger issues go away: Is there perhaps a way that we could pull out of the arms race with the Soviet Union, regardless of what they try to do? Is there such a thing as superiority at all, given the destructive force now available?

The SALT negotiations are evidence of lip-service to the thought that unrestrained development of certain technologies may threaten all parties, regardless of political or ideological differences. But that recognition is clearly not profound enough to lead to meaningful progress. In principle, for instance, it is more or less agreed that the United States and the Soviet Union will have to settle for parity, or "equivalence," in military power. But just what constitutes equivalence is a hotly debated matter, complicated by the need to compare apples with oranges (for example, large, inaccurate Soviet missiles with smaller but very accurate U.S. warheads). How many weapons of what types should each side be allowed? How does one discriminate between a tactical nuclear weapon and a strategic one? When is a weapon acceptably dismantled? When do improvements to old weapons make them new ones? What means of technical verification and cooperation will be allowed under the provisions of the treaty? It seems that many similarly detailed questions must be resolved if there is to be a treaty that favors arms limitation.

Such questions are perceived by the SALT participants to be important. To many observers, however, including us, there are no

single, optimum answers to most of them. Compromise anywhere within
very broad ranges would be to the advantage of both sides, and the
interminable, solemn debating of fine points is a stalling tactic put
on for show. Failure to agree on meaningful arms-reduction measures
indicates lack of genuine desire to do so -- fundamental failure to
comprehend the consequences of the delay. The U.S. Senate's foot-
dragging over ratification of an almost do-nothing SALT II treaty is
merely symptomatic of the myopia that afflicts us.

The irrationality of the cultural resistance to arms-control
measures is clearly demonstrated in political debates over control of
nuclear weapons. Complex and tedious arguments, often technically
incorrect, attempt to show how the other side might manage to cheat.
Claims are made that the other side is irrational and cannot be
trusted. Two central facts are missed: (1) as a treaty must be
verifiable, trust is not an issue; and (2) the way things now are, only
the other side's rationality (and ours) keeps small disputes from
growing into global destruction. Humanitarianism aside, nothing
prevents one side from attacking except the rational understanding
that the other can strike back.

THE SHELL GAME: MX

Meanwhile the arms race goes on. Currently, as the next step in the
quest for the Holy Grail of security through strength, the MX missile
system is being promoted. The Air Force sees in it a cure for the
vulnerability of land-based ICBMs. Since it is being seriously
considered in Washington, it is a timely example.

MX would be a major undertaking. The missile itself weighs about
190,000 pounds (85,000 kg). The proposal is that 200 of them be
deployed in 4,600 "hardened" (blast-resistant) structures. Thus each
missile would have 23 launching sites, and would be moved from one
launch tube to another in a way that the Soviets presumably could not
monitor. The intent is to have more sites than there are Soviet
warheads, so that the 200 missiles could not be destroyed even if the
Soviets committed their entire arsenal to doing so.

A necessary feature is that the 4,600 launch sites must be connected
by roads, and the sites would have to be far enough apart that an
incoming missile could not destroy more than one. About 10,000 miles
(15,000 km) of roadway would have to be constructed. The roadbed must
support the missile and a transporter vehicle that by itself would
weigh more than the missile. The system of roads would be one-fourth
as long as the entire federal highway system. It has been said that
the MX system would be the largest single project ever undertaken by
man.

The issue of where military technology is taking us has increasingly
troubled military and civilian thinkers alike. Concern over whether
the MX would work, tied to the broader issue of nuclear deterrence, was
voiced by Rear Admiral H.C. Eccles, who pointed out that
> even a relatively small nuclear exchange would produce
> catastrophic long-range harm.... The concept of counter-
> force nuclear warfare as a means to assure national secur-
> ity is being challenged.... [There is the] fallibility of
> the presidential decision process. The reliability of the

operation of the command and control system under stress is seriously questioned.   The cumulative effect...is to diminish rather than enhance...national security.
We find the fuller quotation [Note II-1] interesting reading. The military perspective is clear, yet the usefulness of levels of force beyond those already achieved by the superpowers is called into question.

CONCLUDING REMARKS

Perhaps the greatest challenge facing the modern world is recognizing how to adjust to the constantly shifting costs and benefits that come with changing technology.   Some policies that were reasonable a generation ago are now hopelessly unrealistic. A dramatic example is national defense. If adversaries have large numbers of deliverable nuclear weapons, defending population and industry is something that is no longer practical. Defense has given way to deterrence.

Society can react to the situation in one of three ways: try to ignore it, try to turn technology off and return to "the simple life," or try to make institutional and attitudinal changes that might have a chance of coping with the situation. Obviously, ignoring it will not help. As for the simple life, that certainly has its appeal, at least in the abstract, but it might not be a practical solution. Most of the people in the world are already forced to live a simple life, and it tends to subject them to famine, disease, overcrowding, and a short life expectancy. Further, the nuclear bombs and know-how exist. We shall have to adapt as best we can.

The most serious attitudinal lag is in the area of arms control. We already have the wherewithal to destroy everything, and have shown distressingly little inclination to face up to it. Failure to achieve a comprehensive nuclear test-ban treaty, when there is much to gain and nothing to lose, is a symptom that emphasizes the magnitude of the problem. Lack of public pressure for ratification of the largely symbolic SALT II treaty, so that serious SALT III talks might begin, is striking evidence that the public is suffering from a case of apathy that could prove terminal.

The issues are of transcending importance. Lack of informed public participation in the Soviet Union adds to the urgency of the need for full and open discussion in the United States. In place of a paternalistic attitude that tends to obscure a danger to the American people and the world, the government should take an active lead in providing the basis for intelligent discussion.

3 Society's Need to Know

We live in a complex society with a government of immense powers that a democratic public can hope to control only if it is able to learn the facts in some depth and detail. Accountability, the principle at the heart of the American Constitution, more than ever requires information.
— Anthony Lewis, columnist

Society's need for information takes many different forms. Private citizens need information for discussion of national policy. Business and industry need information to plan new ventures and maintain efficient performance of existing ventures. Scientists, technologists, and industrialists need data to develop new and less expensive ways of providing goods to more and more people. Researchers in science and industry create new information by building on the accumulated knowledge of the past (old information). New information, in turn, rapidly becomes old and leads to the creation of still more. Thus scientific, industrial, and managerial innovation are intimately tied by a fabric of data woven from diverse activities. Information is not only essential to the functioning of democracy, it is also essential for the physical health and economic well-being of society.

Technology that has hazardous overtones needs to be carefully controlled, and in order to control it one needs to understand it, and for understanding one needs information -- basic information that might sometimes even seem rather detailed. How much help might that information be to someone who would misuse the technology? It is easy to overestimate. A racing bicycle, for instance, appears to be mechanically simple, but a modern bicycle would not be possible without modern metallurgy. A transistor radio circuit may appear uncomplicated, but transistor manufacture not only takes a great deal of specialized proprietary information, but equally specialized and quite expensive equipment as well. Knowledge that a particular aircraft cannot fly a transatlantic distance or be aerially refueled permits one to conclude accurately that it cannot be used for transatlantic bombing missions -- but that general knowledge is no help in trying to copy the aircraft.

24

Consider the F-15 fighter airplane. Impressively detailed structural drawings of the F-15 have been printed in unclassified books on aviation. Is that irresponsible publication? Is news media responsibility lacking if the drawings are reproduced on the front page of a daily newspaper? At first glance the answer might be yes, but really it is no. Could it encourage some group to build an F-15 in a garage and use it in acts of terrorism against commercial aircraft? Obviously not. Structural drawings contain almost none of the design information needed in making high-performance aircraft. Materials composition, metallurgical processes and alloying techniques, binding methods, avionics, power plant specifications, tolerances, and other proprietary details are far more significant than a mere diagram. And even with all those details, "tricks of the trade" would still be important, not to mention access to materials from production facilities that cost billions of dollars.

Where is the greater risk to public safety: in publishing a largely useless structural diagram of an F-15? Or in not publishing it, thereby missing a chance to let people know more about the national security implications of the technology?

Technological innovation is spurred on by a number of personal motivations, the prospect of wealth being only one of them. Many in the technological forefront are driven by need for peer recognition, by fascination with their subject, and by strong wishes to contribute to society in a lasting way. Highly alluring opportunities often appear, for which there have never been legal or moral norms. For instance, revolutionary uses of genetic engineering may be able to eliminate birth defects and cancer, or regenerate injured limbs and organs. But this and related biological discoveries can also be used to make disease organisms so lethal that even the current generation of nerve agents, lethal on contact in minute quantities, might seem harmless by comparison.

Society must collectively participate in evaluating and debating each new technology. If sound policy is to result, technical information is essential in the debate. To be sure, technical information alone is not sufficient. In the real world many political and economic factors compete with one another, and technologies can always serve dual purposes. A consequence is that policies aimed at preventing the misapplication of a technology may involve tradeoffs or compromises that might, on the surface, appear prudent, but which instead could be counterproductive.

Denial of technology to the "wrong people" sometimes might have a parochial usefulness, but it also can have unexpected consequences. Example: The Soviet Union refines about eleven million barrels of oil a day, but does not yet have the technical knowledge to exploit its extensive Siberian oil and gas reserves. Denying the Soviets access to the appropriate technical information is therefore tantamount to denying them these resources. This policy would appear to achieve the (possibly desirable) goal of weakening the Soviet economy by refusing them access to critical resources. However, the result of such a policy, if successful, might be to drive the Soviets to desperation, inducing them to attempt to take the Iranian or Saudi Arabian oil fields by force. Only far-ranging debate on policy issues can bring to light and evaluate such possibilities.

Examining policies may therefore require not only technical information in the widest sense of the term, but also serious discussion and
input from diverse non-technical sectors of society.

The sort of benefits that can come from widespread public discussion
can be illustrated by considering some momentous decisions from the
recent past that were made without public participation.

SECRET DECISIONS DURING WORLD WAR II

When people first produced (in an exploding A-bomb) an environment more
extreme than the center of the sun, a new capability was born. Perhaps
its destructive use was not inevitable. The atomic bomb was of course
created secretly under the impression that the very capable German
scientific establishment, directed by Werner Heisenberg, was moving
just as feverishly and with the same level of support (which turned out
not to be the case, although there was some German activity). It would
still be difficult to argue that the Manhattan Project should have been
public. That would have told the German scientists how seriously the
Americans took the possibilities. (Many of the Manhattan participants
were not certain until the project was well along that such a weapon
was truly possible.) However, once Germany had been removed as an
adversary there were two choices: (1) never tell anyone that such a
weapon existed, or (2) use the weapon in some fashion, thereby
broadcasting the critical and most important piece of information
that other interested scientific communities would need -- an atomic
device is realizable!

It is hard to imagine that the weapon could long have been kept
secret. Many thousands of people had been involved in the project. In
any event, the decision to try to do so would have to have been made
before the first one was tested at Alamogordo, because the fact that
the explosion had taken place would sooner or later have become known
through disclosure by participants, leaks from official sources, or
spying.

Also, the underlying information about the potential for fission
weapons was known to scientists in Europe (and also in the Soviet Union
and Japan). In an unpublished paper written in 1939, Leo Szilard had
indicated the possibility of fission chain reactions. He voluntarily
kept it secret because he immediately understood the military implications. However, equivalent, independently derived conclusions had
been published that same year in Nature by the Paris group led by M.
Joliot-Curie. By early in the summer of 1939, the New York Times had
carried a report quoting Niels Bohr on the potentialities of a uranium-
235 bomb. In Germany, Flugge had published his now-famous detailed
description of the uranium chain reaction in the July issue of Natur-
wissenschaften, and shortly thereafter had published an account for
laymen in the widely circulated journal Deutsche Allgemeine Zeitung.

In Russia, A.I. Leipunskii had published an account of the theory of
nuclear chain reactions early in 1940 in the Proceedings of the Academy
of Sciences of the USSR (Izvestiya Akademii Nauk SSSR, Seriya Fiziches-
kaya). By November 1940 the Soviet scientific work on fission had
advanced rapidly. In the face of all that, to believe that the
existence of the American weapon could have been kept secret for very
long would require an extraordinary leap of faith.

Since there was no hope of keeping secret the feasibility of fission bombs, a significant opportunity was missed by not releasing certain conceptual, deducible information after the fall of Germany. This would have enabled public participation in the forthcoming decision on whether to open the atomic age with a bloody hand. The technical details of implementation could still have been protected (thereby forcing any interested party to develop a project on the same scale as the American effort, which the Soviets immediately did anyway), so there would have been no additional risk to American national security.

The Atomic Attacks on Japan

There were a number of alternatives to the atomic destruction of Hiroshima and Nagasaki. Each branch of the armed forces advocated the military position that increased its importance, hardly a unique situation. The Navy, for instance, was opposed to the atomic bombing strategy because it had estimated that Japan could be blockaded and brought to its knees within a year. (Even today, Japan imports all of its oil and most of its food.) The Army wanted to invade Japan in order to punish them on their own territory, estimating the cost at one million American casualties. This is where one of the most popular justifications for the atomic attacks on Japan comes from. However, to contend that it was necessary to weigh those high estimates of American combat losses against civilian Japanese losses is to misrepresent what people knew and debated in closed circles of government.

The Army's invasion plans were not militarily necessary, nor could they have been effected until several months after the atomic bombs were detonated: The bombs were dropped in August, within three days of each other; the Army assault was not expected to be possible until November. Also worthy of note was the fact that Japanese codes had been broken, and messages indicating that the Japanese were sending out peace feelers had been intercepted.

Proposals to drop the weapon at night in sight of the Imperial Palace over Tokyo Bay or in a heavily forested area not far from Tokyo were put forth. Since there would have been enough light from the fireball to blind viewers tens of miles away, the Tokyo Bay proposal would presumably have left Hirohito and his general staff with a suitable impression. The advantage of the forest proposal was that the instantaneous destruction of five square miles of healthy adult trees could have been conveniently contemplated by the Japanese leaders. As it turned out, when Hiroshima was bombed the Japanese authorities were so out of touch with the city and with scientists who could interpret the event that it took them several days to comprehend what had happened and its implications.

Understanding was not helped by the Japanese armed forces, which controlled communications. A poignant account of the situation faced by Toshikazu Kase, a former member of the Japanese Foreign Office, is given in his book, Journey to the Missouri [Archon Books (1969)]:

> When the atomic bomb was dropped on Hiroshima on August 6
> we could not make out at first what it actually was. The
> next day the San Francisco broadcast carried an announce-
> ment by President Truman that it was an atomic bomb. We
> were staggered. If a single bomb was equal in destructive

power to the mass raid of a fleet of two thousand B-29's, with this lethal weapon the Allies could exterminate all life in Japan in less than a week! Further continuation of the war was mass suicide. Togo immediately went to the palace. The Emperor, showing deep concern over the fate of the helpless victims, said that since it was obviously impossible to defend the homeland any longer we had better conclude peace immediately without wasting time arguing about terms. That was common sense. But the Army, as ever, was a stranger to common sense....

It...even went to the length of forbidding the press to mention the atomic bomb lest it affect the people's morale.

So for some time the press referred to the atomic bomb as merely a "new type of bomb" while all the world was agog at the new terror. But the nation could not for long be left in ignorance, as the enemy radio widely disseminated the news.

The authorities tried in vain to drown out the powerful enemy broadcasts from adjacent bases such as Manila and Okinawa. These broadcasts, in excellent Japanese, exercised a great influence on the minds of the people. When it became no longer possible to suppress the truth, the Army attempted to minimize the destructive power of the bomb.

It is certain that we would have surrendered in due time even without the terrific chastisement of the bomb or the terrible shock of the Russian attack. However, it cannot be denied that both the bombs and the Russians facilitated our surrender. Without them the Army might still have tried to prolong resistance.

While the Japanese army would presumably have wanted good news to travel fast, they did not want the bad news to travel at all. This "good news, bad news" syndrome is not entirely peculiar to the Japanese armed forces. In the United States we have created a system that is inimical to public safety (not to mention democratic institutions) by giving the armed forces far-reaching information-classification powers. Malfunctions of weapons systems, mistakenly interpreted missile attacks, aircraft accidentally dropping nuclear bombs, nuclear weapons tests that irradiate civilians with fallout hundreds of miles downwind, accidental releases of nerve gas that were denied by government officials while populations were still at risk and should have been evacuated, and other "minor" oversights have, under the "national security" provisions of the classification system, been allowed to be completely protected from public review. These incidents conjure up the image of a George C. Scott asking his President, "You wouldn't condemn the whole system just because of one mistake, would you, sir?" -- as a B-52 wing has gone beyond the point of recall into Soviet territory. One wonders how many times some variation of this disturbingly funny scene has occurred in Omaha, Washington, Cheyenne Mountain, or any of the other command-and-control points hidden from public view, in this country and the Soviet Union.

The critical influence of the decision to destroy Japanese cities with atomic weapons cannot be overstressed. As historian David

Holloway [HOL-79] has pointed out, the entire direction of history
after 1945 was affected by it:

In August 1945, after the American attacks on Hiroshima and
Nagasaki, the Soviet Union launched a full-scale effort to
develop the atomic bomb. This effort was undertaken in a
competitive spirit, as a response to the challenge which
American possession of the atomic bomb was seen to pose to
Soviet security and to Soviet interests. From August 1945
it was Soviet policy to destroy the American atomic monopoly in the shortest possible time. The launching of this
atomic effort marked the entry of the Soviet Union into a
nuclear arms race with the United States, and is therefore
one of the key decisions in the history of Soviet-American
strategic arms competition.

While a nuclear arms race could have started in other ways, no
decision stands out so clearly as the one to atom-bomb Japanese cities.
There followed a clear and frightening progression of lesser, though
significant, decisions -- a series that still continues.

Development of Thermonuclear Weapons

Momentous recommendations regarding thermonuclear weapons and the
future of mankind were made in secret by the General Advisory Committee
of the AEC [YORK-76]:

The first Soviet A-bomb and the U.S. determination to react
to it led...to a doubling of the size of the American
nuclear weapons development program.... This particular
episode, like the history of the super[bomb] itself, can be
seen as an illustration of just how...technological
momentum can determine the course of the arms race....

The main body of the GAC report makes a plea for low-
ering as much as possible the barriers of secrecy that surrounded the whole process of deciding what to do about the
super. This same plea was echoed over and over in statements made by other scientists in this same context, and
Oppenheimer returned to it often in subsequent articles and
speeches. The committee recognized that certain technical
details should be kept "secret," but they felt a very large
part of what they were discussing could be made available
without endangering the national security. They obviously
felt very strongly that such momentous decisions affecting
all mankind should not be made by a tiny elite in-group
exclusively privy to all of the relevant facts, even though
in this case they were themselves included in it.

AEC Chairman David Lilienthal made a...comment concerning secrecy:

In part, the news [of the first Soviet atomic bomb
explosion] means, to me, that we should stop this
senseless business of choking ourselves by some of
the extremes of secrecy in which we have been
driven, extremes of secrecy that impede our own
technical progress and our own defense....

However, preceding this soul-searching by the GAC, some decisions of
great consequence had already been made. Foremost was the initiation

of the Manhattan Project. In view of the "clear and present danger" that spurred the undertaking, it is difficult to criticize that choice even with hindsight. President Truman's order to use the atomic bombs on Japan may be viewed more questioningly, as we pointed out earlier. Also, although the GAC counseled delay in proceeding with development of the "super" thermonuclear bomb, they did promote development of much larger fission weapons (more than 500 kT) and the fusion-boosted fission weapons (single-stage devices ten or more times as powerful as the bombs dropped on Japan). All this was decided in secret.

In a biography of Edward Teller [B&O-76], one issue is identified that found both Teller and J. Robert Oppenheimer on the same side: the overuse of secrecy. Oppenheimer is quoted as suggesting

candor on the part of the officials of the United States government to the officals, the representatives, the people of their country. We do not operate well when the important facts, the essential conditions, which limit and determine our choice are unknown. We do not operate well when they are known, in secrecy and fear, only to a few men....

Teller's "powerful voice against secrecy" is also discussed and quoted:

His goal was at least partial removal of secrecy. "Purely scientific data -- that is, facts concerning natural phenomena -- must not be kept secret.... Scientific facts cannot be kept secret for any length of time. They are readily rediscovered."... The only justifiable secrecy, in Teller's opinion, was that which dealt with technical details. And the policing of security regulations, he suggested, should be largely entrusted to the people who themselves engage in the work.

Concurrence came from the renowned Soviet physicist and dissident, Andrei D. Sakharov, who has consistently argued for openness. In 1973 he observed that "genuine and lasting detente requires a candid and open world." [B&O-76]

In 1955 physicist Ralph Lapp wrote an article to call attention to how thermonuclear weapons had "dramatically altered the very dimension of warfare." The article, intended for the New York Times, was classified by the Atomic Energy Commission and never published. Lapp recently commented:

In the early 1950's I considered that it was vitally important to provide the American public with essential information about thermonuclear weapons...introducing as [they] did the potential for radioactive fallout lethality. I was also concerned about the health effects of nuclear testing.

Looking back over more than three tormented decades of nuclear secrecy, I believe that the late Leo Szilard was correct when he observed "The SECRET stamp is the greatest weapon ever invented." I'm sure he had our democratic freedoms in mind.

THE RIGHT TO KNOW VERSUS NATIONAL SECURITY

The public's awareness of its stake in military matters is growing. Fear and frustration are bred by the spreading realization that the government can no longer protect the population in a nuclear war. In the past it has been possible to safeguard almost all citizens by risking or sacrificing the lives of a few. Today, in a nuclear war the country's weapons could protect no citizens, while risking or sacrificing the lives of most. Technology has transformed the situation from one in which mostly military personnel would be killed in a war to one in which the casualties would be mainly civilian. American security shrinks as the stockpiles of nuclear weapons expand.

The past few decades have seen the most profound changes in technology yet experienced. Less than thirty years ago the first detailed numerical calculations on thermonuclear ignition (performed at Los Alamos under the brilliant guidance of the famous Polish mathematician Stanislaw Ulam) took teams of clerical people weeks to perform. Today any home hobbyist with a few hundred dollars can buy a microcomputer that can do such calculations in minutes; modern centralized facilities can do them in seconds. Current ability to process digital information would have boggled the minds of the most imaginative innovators of even a decade ago. The invention of minicomputers and advances in communications, materials science, rocketry, and aircraft have affected us in many direct and subtle ways.

The problem that most threatens the survival of our society is the unfettered growth of military technology. Lack of restraints on the numbers of nuclear weapons and on the ability to deliver them accurately, and the implicit use of these weapons, by various countries, as instruments of foreign policy, are political failures of unparalelled importance.

The inner circles having failed so dismally in finding security for us, perhaps greater hope lies in hastening the expansion of public awareness -- which requires that the relevant knowledge be accessible. To illustrate the nature and role of the needed technical information, we will consider a number of current or recent defense issues. While perhaps impressive, the array is far from exhaustive.

Two Arms-Control Issues

For any arms control treaty to be acceptable and useful, the parties to it must have confidence that cheating can be detected. Modern technology can be applied to the verification problem. Although such an application is not military in purpose per se, the relevant technical capabilities are still caught in a web of military secrecy.

Photoreconnaissance. Since much of the verification of the arms control treaties currently under discussion comes from satellite observation, the public cannot have well-based confidence in such a treaty without access to knowledge about what the satellites can and cannot see.

Government policy [Note III-1] in this regard has not been consistent even with the desire that has been professed (by the Carter administration) to get SALT II ratified. It is possible to show -- from public information, known technological capabilities, mathematical analysis, and general physical principles -- that objects inches across can be optically discerned from a hundred miles in space. Until quite recently, however, government officials have not been allowed even to confirm that satellite photoreconnaissance is used by the United States. But the Soviets know about photoreconnaissance, and anyone with sufficient knowledge of optics can deduce its theoretical capabilities. Only the public was being kept in the dark, and open discussion was inhibited.

When Government officials are not allowed to tell people about basic verification technology, it is easy to see why so many members of the public feel that, while arms control might be a good idea in principle, it is unrealistic because "you can't trust the Russians."

Test bans. Both the limited and comprehensive test bans involve important features of nuclear weapon design and test verification technology. How much radioactivity is released in the tests? Must weapons be frequently tested for reliability? Is it adequate to test only the nonnuclear components? What size weapons must be tested? To prevent development of large thermonuclear weapons, where should the test ban threshold be set? Will such a threshold prevent testing of fission triggers for fusion weapons? (We address some of those questions in Chapter VI.) To take part knowledgeably in the debate, one must know a lot about the concepts behind both fission and fusion weapons.

Strategic Offensive and Defensive Systems

The public has a legitimate and vital interest in the nation's nuclear weapons systems and defense possibilities. Current issues are: the sea-based ballistic missile forces (Polaris-Poseidon-Trident), the land-based ballistic missile forces (ICBMs), antiballistic missile defenses (ABMs), civil defense (CD), multiple-warhead missiles that can attack more than one target with a single ballistic missile (MIRVs), political attempts to control the qualitative and quantitative growth in offensive strategic weapons systems (SALT), attempts to reduce perceived uncertainties in the capability of the strategic bomber force as a credible deterrent (B-1), nuclear test bans (CTBT), and the growing fear that the land-based missile force could be preemptively destroyed if the basing mode and missile characteristics are not modernized (MX).

Missiles are increasingly reliable and accurate, modern nuclear weapons are compact and light, and crucial combat decisions can, and therefore must, be made in very short times -- in a matter of minutes. In a war, human decision-making must play a smaller and smaller role. The only place left for human intervention is in the debate as to what to deploy, how to deploy it, and what the alternatives to deployment are.

For each of those weapons systems and political initiatives, we shall now show the type of technical information that has been essential for an informed assessment of alternative policies. In many cases, concepts paralleling classified information have been derived and explained to the public by independent citizens. This has helped to clarify the different technical choices, to the benefit of national security.

Polaris-Poseidon-Trident. The United States has ballistic missile submarines for attacking the Soviet Union and Eastern Europe in case of war. This is one of three separate nuclear strike forces for deterring the somewhat similar Soviet forces. According to current military thinking, each of the three -- submarines, strategic bombers, and land-based intercontinental missiles -- must alone be able to obliterate the Soviet Union. Some experts say publicly that this doctrine has been oversold. The nuclear-armed submarines are sufficient, the claim is, because (for a long time at least) they will be impossible to detect and destroy.

To support or refute such claims, an honest advocate must give technical information. But in that field many of the technical details are closely guarded, leaving uncertainties about important points: range and accuracy of the submarines' missiles, evasive capabilities of submarines under wartime conditions, degree of operational readiness, detectability at sea, communications capabilities, yield of the nuclear warheads -- and the safety of those weapons when the submarines are in port.

Before being willing to put all their deterrence eggs in one basket, people will understandably want to be sure that the basket is sound. The debate must go on in light of knowledge of the technical concepts that would let one assess the effectiveness and degree of invulnerability of undersea missile systems. Unless there is sufficient information available, public appreciation of the invulnerability of the naval deterrent will not be realistic. Even with no access to classified sources, anyone with the requisite technical background who carefully sifts through the scientific literature and the military data that have been released is likely to reach conclusions that duplicate classifed information. Are such conclusions legitimately classifiable? Unless critical information is uncovered that would make U.S. submarines easier to find and destroy, the answer is no.

ICBMs. Intercontinental ballistic missiles constitute another of the three strings to the United States' nuclear bow. This force currently consists of 1,000 solid-propellant Minuteman IIs and IIIs, and 53 storable liquid-propellant Titans. All of these missiles are housed in vertical underground concrete and steel structures called silos, "hardened" at great cost to make them less vulnerable to attack by Soviet nuclear missiles.

The United States is currently debating whether to modernize or phase out its land-based missiles. Advances in missile guidance, reliability and lifting capability have raised doubts that the land-based missile force could survive a determined attack by Soviet nuclear ICBMs. That such an attack could really succeed is by no means certain. The ambiguity has, however, led to much discussion about how to preserve what is often considered (perhaps erroneously) the most important component of the strategic nuclear forces.

The disturbing thought that an attack on our missiles might even be contemplated has resulted in a set of elaborate and exotic proposed remedies. One suggestion, for instance, is that a new type of missile, the MX (discussed in Chapter II), be deployed with "multiple structures" (more silos than missiles): The missiles would be shuttled between the silos to confuse the attacker. Another is that existing ICBM silos be further hardened against nuclear attack. Rows of gigantic towers have been suggested, to intercept nuclear warheads far enough away from silos that a detonation would be ineffective. Nuclear explosives in the ground near the silos have been proposed, to create giant clouds of debris that would destroy incoming warheads. It has also been argued that the land-based missile forces are more of a liability than an asset and should be abandoned altogether.

The range of technical analysis needed to evaluate the various proposals spans a large number of subjects: military strategy, civil and electrical engineering, environmental protection, economics, naval architecture, physics, and the politics of arms limitation. At the heart of the debate is the unresolved technical question, How vulnerable to a pre-emptive nuclear attack is a missile force deployed in the various suggested ways?

In order to determine the likelihood that a target will be destroyed, it is necessary to know how blast-resistant the target is (the target's hardness), how large a warhead is being used to attack the target (the warhead's yield), and how near the target the warhead is likely fall (the accuracy, expressed as a "circle of equal probability," or CEP). Obviously a warhead with just enough power and accuracy to destroy a suburb will not be able, with the same probability, to destroy a hardened military structure. Using elementary mathematical modeling and scientific principles, it is possible to calculate the likelihood that different attack strategies will succeed under a wide range of assumptions about missile accuracy, weapons yields, number of available warheads per target, and target hardness. Such studies could substantially duplicate and encroach upon the results of classified work. There has even been reason to believe that unclassified studies have been somewhat more complete than those performed within the defense establishment, a situation that should not comfort citizens, regardless of their point of view.

MX. Debate on the MX missile has been going on for some time. Needless to say, a number of technical and environmental questions have already been raised about a project of such scale. Here are some of them: Is it needed? Are the fixed sites and the other elements of the deterrent triad really vulnerable? Could the missile locations be reliably hidden from Soviet surveillance? How much danger would result from MXs shuttling between launch points? Could the warheads explode spontaneously? What is the environmental impact where they would be deployed? The proposed sites are in dry-climate states: How much water is required to mix the millions of tons of concrete? Would a land-locked submarine fleet (for example, in Lake Michigan) do as well or better? Would it be better to deploy the system on shallow-diving submarines off the continental shelf? Could a different missile instead be deployed on short takeoff and landing aircraft that would be widely and randomly dispersed at different airfields?

ABM. A major national debate took place in the 1960s and early 1970s over antiballistic missile (ABM) systems. Because a city-defense ABM system would mean "A-bombs in the backyard," there was considerable public interest, and local opposition developed wherever sites were proposed. Government proponents and civilian opponents traveled around the country debating the merits of the various ABM concepts.

The proposals stemmed in part from the concern and frustration of military planners over their inability to defend either military or civilian targets against nuclear attacks. As the technology of radars and rockets has advanced, a variety of ambitious, exotic, and technically dubious proposals have been put forth for intercepting ICBMs, to try to protect at least the more important targets. Because accuracy of the interceptors would not be good enough to do the job with chemical explosives, nuclear warheads would have to be used in the ABM warheads. Some citizens questioned whether planning to explode nuclear warheads over American cities, even to try to fend off a nuclear attack, would result in a net gain -- especially since the mere existence of the system might cause the attack to be much heavier.

It was shown technically that even the most sophisticated of antiballistic missile defenses could be easily overwhelmed by relatively simple countermeasures (among which were decoys to draw the ABM fire, and precursor nuclear explosions to blind the defensive radar). Nevertheless, the drive to regain the ability to defend American cities was very strong, not to mention the drive for lucrative military contracts. It is likely that, in spite of straightforward factual demonstrations that the system would not work, the ABM would have been deployed -- at great cost, and possibly danger, to the public -- had there not been public uproar, supported by the cogent technical arguments of scientists outside the defense programs. Deployment was stopped, and the ABM treaty of 1972 followed.

The American debate over the ABM embraced such issues as siting near cities, "collateral damage," radar detection, launch velocities, nuclear weapons yields and effects, weights of warheads and missiles, targeting accuracy, intercept probabilities, countermeasures, and weapons safety. The opponents of ABM deployment found it necessary to independently derive critical weapons system concepts in order to counter government assertions about how well the system would work [Note III-2]. All such information, of course, in the detail needed for the discussion, was available to the Soviets. At the same time, the government selectively released classified information in order to justify ABM performance claims.

An interesting postscript to the ABM debate is brought out by Halperin and Hoffman [H&H1-77], in their discussion of the importance of congressional access to information:

> The defense budget considered by Congress in late 1974 included a request for funds to complete a ballistic missile defense site. This was the only ABM installation that the United States was permitted to have under the revised Strategic Arms Limitation Treaty. Now Congress had been informed in secret that the Pentagon planned to dismantle the site as soon as it was completed. However, a vote against the ABM site would appear to the naive public to be directed against a serious military program. Because the plan to dismantle was secret, it was difficult for a member of Congress to vote against the appropriation. It was even difficult to bring this classified information to the attention of all members of Congress.

Recently the ABM issue has been revived because of improved accuracy of interceptors. It now is claimed that conventional explosives could be used if the incoming missiles were intercepted above the atmosphere. The difficulties of launching interceptors on short notice and reliably hitting ballistic missiles at long distances remain as serious obstacles to effective missile defense, and the basic arguments against the ABM remain valid.

MIRV. The introduction of multiple independently targetable reentry vehicles (MIRVs) was not as widely debated as was the ABM. The

rationale used to promote the MIRV was that the Soviets might develop
an effective ABM system, thereby nullifying the United States' ability
to retaliate against Soviet cities if American cities were attacked.
We argue that lack of public concern over MIRV has resulted in the
dilemma we now face with the MX -- a dilemma that could have been
avoided if MIRV (both here and in Russia) had been forestalled.

"MIRVing" increases the efficiency of an existing ballistic missile
without requiring major design changes, except in the warhead. In
place of the single warhead in a ballistic missile, it is sometimes
possible to mount a small rocket-powered vehicle. On this small "bus"
sit several nuclear warheads, like eggs in a carton. The main rocket
launches the bus toward a set of targets to be attacked. While the bus
(also called the "postboost vehicle") drifts through space it can make
small changes in velocity and direction, each time releasing one or
more warheads aimed toward one of the targets.

Before MIRVs were developed, more than one land-based ICBM had to be
committed to each of the adversary's land-based missiles if an attack
against those missiles was to be mounted. Because of the inaccuracy
and unreliability of ICBMs, one warhead targetted for each missile silo
would not be sufficient to provide high assurance of a hit. If both
sides had equal numbers of missiles, for either side to attacked the
missile forces of the other it would have to effectively disarm itself,
except for a few nuclear weapons held back for use against the cities.
This was a standoff that compelled each side (assuming rationality) to
have a wait-and-see policy in the event of an international crisis.
However, with MIRVs in place things change. More than a dozen nuclear
warheads have been fitted into large land- and sea-based missiles. It
becomes theoretically possible to try to destroy the opposing land-
based missile force by committing only a small fraction of one's own
missiles. Each attacking missile might, in principle, be used to
destroy three, five, or ten of the adversary's missiles, depending on
the capabilities of the MIRV system and on whether the enemy's missiles
remain in their silos long enough.

The invention, development, and deployment of the MIRV, without much
public discussion, has resulted in a situation that faces decision
makers with the problem of whether to "launch on warning." Without
MIRV there was no need to rush ahead and launch our missiles if it was
mistakenly thought that a missile attack was underway, since in any
event there would be plenty of missiles left for retaliation. With
MIRV, we (or they) would have no more than fifteen or twenty minutes to
decide whether to launch our land-based missiles or risk having them
destroyed by warheads that might be on their way.

As things actually are, of course, submarine-based ballistic
missiles remain invulnerable. We could let our planes and land-based
ICBMs be largely destroyed while waiting to be certain, and still have
ample retaliation. Whether we or the Soviets have that fail-safe
policy is an open question, as is whether it would work in a time of
crisis.

Although some of the MIRV technology came from the space program,
where there was an interest in launching many small satellites with a
single rocket, most of its development required a considerable amount
of specialized guidance, control, and data-management technique that
was not needed for satellites. Implementing MIRV also required
extensive flight testing in ballistic trajectories at intercontinental

distances, which was easily monitorable by the Soviet Union. It would therefore have been possible to reach a mutually verifiable agreement with the Soviets that we would not employ MIRVs if they also refrained.

In assessing MIRV's value as an attack system, the government's analysts did not factor in strongly enough the destabilizing effect of adding large numbers of increasingly accurate warheads to the U.S. arsenal. During the very limited public debate, some used arguments in favor of the system that were based on the technical assessment that the Russians would not be able to deploy a similar system rapidly -- while others, for a less sophisticated audience, were claiming that we had to get there first, because the Russians were going to do it regardless. These arguments, while largely irrelevant, served to confuse question of MIRV's utility, and created doubt in the minds of the government as well as the public.

Doubt is the ally of the strong-defense advocate. Adequate information about the nature and difficulty of developing MIRV buses and their accompanying compact, high-yield nuclear warheads would have considerably altered the then-prevailing opinion that the Soviets would take ten years to do it. The ten-years-to-do-it argument is like the one now being used in favor of the cruise missile, which may also be reproduced by the Soviets in only five years. The chance to stop the incremental creep to MIRV was missed. Now the U.S.-originated concept has been mimicked by the Russians, and the security of both nations has suffered.

Civil defense. Two or three attempts have been made in the United States to introduce shelters and other defensive preparations against nuclear attack. Proponents have argued that civil defense would save lives in a nuclear war. Opponents say it would merely stimulate a compensating growth in the size of the arsenals so that both sides could be assured that deterrence was being maintained -- pointing out that it would be much cheaper to get more bombs than to implement even a modest civil defense program. Thus the security of both nations would be lessened by increasing the potential destructiveness of a nuclear war and raising doubts about whether deterrence would keep on working.

If the civil defense opponents' arguments are valid, the net result could easily be a greater cost in life and property, rather than a saving. To be able to discuss such matters productively, the public needs to know a lot about fission and fusion processes, explosive yields and destructive capabilities of nuclear warheads, and important aspects of early warning systems and delivery methods for offensive and defensive weapons.

Bombers. Our discussion so far has largely focused on systems that deliver nuclear weapons by ballistic means. (Warheads that travel to a target without being powered are ballistic, whether they get their initial velocity from a cannon or from the brief, high acceleration imparted by a rocket.) There are, of course, other means of delivering those light, portable devices of mass destruction. The oldest is the manned bomber. In spite of the continuing developments in radar, signal processing, noise reduction and discrimination techniques, guidance and infrared technology, air-to-air missiles, surface-to-air missiles, and the like, bombers have remained a reliable delivery platform. This is a consequence not only of new penetration strategies (low-level terrain following), but also of the mapping of Soviet fixed, land-based radars by satellites. This allows bombers to proceed to their targets with confidence that they can avoid being directly exposed to the most capable of the Soviet radar systems. In addition, bombers need no longer fly over a target in order to successfully attack it. This is due to the availability of light, long-range, nuclear-armed missiles that can be carried instead of gravity bombs.

Currently, the United States maintains a force of over 300 B-52 G and H bombers ready to attack the Soviet Union. There are an additional 200 of these capable and versatile aircraft in mothballs, which could be activated if the need arose.

B-52's are armed with short range attack missiles (SRAMs), which can be used to attack targets within 45 to 125 miles (70 to 190 km) from the aircraft with 200-kiloton warheads. A single B-52 G or H can carry up to twenty SRAMs in addition to four gravity bombs. Thus, if a fully armed B-52 were to penetrate Soviet air defenses to an area 100 miles (150 km) southeast of Moscow, it could simultaneously deliver nuclear weapons against Moscow, Smolensk, Serpukhov, Kirov, Kaluga, Kalinin, Ryazan, and Vyazma. It would still have sixteen weapons available for additional attacks on airfields, radar, and military installations in that region. If such a plane penetrated to an area fifty to seventy-five miles (75 to 110 km) northwest of Chicago, it could simultaneously destroy Milwaukee, Madison, Beloit, and Racine in Wisconsin, Gary and South Bend in Indiana, and Rockford, Joliet, and Aurora in Illinois. It would still be able to deliver eleven additional warheads against Chicago with its attack missiles, before its ten-minute trip to Chicago to drop its four gravity bombs.

Do we really need a new, advanced bomber? The Carter Administration decided not, and vetoed the Air Force's proposed B-1. Many have objected to that decision, citing against the current B-52s their susceptibility to countermeasures, low state of readiness, structural aging of the airframes, lack of speed, vulnerability to nuclear detonation, slow acceleration (making it difficult to get away from airfields in a surprise attack), and a host of other highly technical but potentially significant criticisms. To evaluate their validity and relevance takes technical data and analysis.

Cruise missiles. The cruise missile has been proposed, and is expected to be deployed, as an alternative to a new manned bomber. This missile has roughly the same weight and dimensions -- about 2,200 pounds (1,000 kg), length 18 to 22 feet (5 to 7 m) -- as the currently deployed SRAM, and carries an equally potent 200-kT warhead. Thus these missiles can be easily mixed with or used to replace the SRAMs, with only minor modifications to the B-52. The cruise missile, unlike the SRAM (which is supersonic and rocket-propelled), is an air-breathing, subsonic winged weapon with a range of 1,500 to 2,500 miles (2,200 to 3,700 km), ten to fifteen times the range of the SRAM. It is constructed largely of non-radar-reflecting materials, and flies so low that ground radars cannot see it behind terrain features or man-made objects. Airborne radars cannot see it because they are blinded by reflections from the ground below; finding a cruise missile from an airborne radar is roughly comparable to finding a white matchhead in freshly fallen snow from the top of a hundred-story building.

Cruise missiles need not carry only nuclear warheads. On-board electronic spoofing equipment can detect the faint signal of a radar installation, record the signal, introduce a time delay, change the shape of the signal, and transmit it back to the radar installation. The installation could be fooled into thinking it was observing a low-flying B-52 or other aircraft, at a distance different from that of the cruise missile.   If interceptors were used to triangulate on the missile, it would be difficult to locate it but eventually possible, assuming there is enough time to figure out what is actually happening and enough radars to simultaneously track the ghost images of the missile. The missile could be set to detonate if it were intercepted before reaching its target, destroying all aircraft within miles.

Cruise missiles will clearly extend the effectiveness of bombers. In fact, bombers would not be needed to deliver such missiles. Because almost all targets in the Soviet Union could be covered without ever penetrating Soviet airspace, large transport aircraft could be used to carry seventy or eighty missiles to launchpoints hundreds of miles outside the Soviet Union, to retaliate in case of war. A question that might next be raised is, When this technology is duplicated by the Soviet Union (as it almost certainly will be), how much will it have enhanced our security?

Missile accuracy.   The ability of nuclear-weapons states to discourage a missile onslaught is rooted in the deterrence principle: Invulnerable nuclear weapons can be launched in retaliation against the population centers of any nation that attacks first.   As long as population and military/industrial centers are the target -- this is known as a "countervalue" policy -- there is a high degree of confidence in the ability of the ballistic missiles to carry out their assigned task.   However, if a first strike -- "counterforce" -- philosophy reigns, the question of missile accuracy (and reliability) comes to the fore. A Carter Administration policy decision, known as Presidential Directive 59, was leaked in the summer of 1980.   It acknowledged that official attention has been given to limited-nuclear-war scenarios that would include "surgical strikes" and "flexible response," and it did not exclude counterforce possibilities.

Counterforce takes for granted that "a missile fired 6,000 miles can land within 600 feet of a target no more than 50 yards in diameter" [C&C-80]. However,

> data about the accuracy of US missiles, and hence many of the suppositions about the performance of their Soviet equivalents, are drawn from test results which -- along with codes -- are among the most highly classified secrets of the government....

> The predictions of missile accuracy cited above are impossible to achieve with any certainty, hence...the premises behind "vulnerability," the MX, and Presidential Directive 59 are expensively and dangerously misleading.

If the concept of selected military targetting, intended to permit a "limited" or "controlled" nuclear war, is successfully challenged by critical evaluations of accuracy and reliability, then the entire military strategy of the United States would need to be altered. It could become necessary to place much more emphasis on the conventional, non-nuclear elements of national defense. The public should be in a position to assess the argument that nuclear war could become unavoidable without a dependable structure of conventionally armed mobile forces that have modern capability to withstand armored attack.

SALT. While quite possibly SALT II would have been for both parties, if ratified, the most important treaty negotiated to date, no treaty in the history of the United States has been accompanied by more confusion, misunderstanding, and misinformation. Not only has it been hampered by lack of technical expertise in the Congress and executive branch, but there are even indications that the original negotiating team had poor technical support (a defect that appears later to have been remedied). Sensitive negotiating positions were prematurely released to the public, while general information about well-known, deducible, technical capabilities in such fields as photoreconnaissance, over-the-horizon radar, and missile-monitoring techniques have been artificially excluded from the government's program of public information. The result has been a pathetic and disturbing set of flaps, such as incorrect charges that the Soviets have been violating agreements, and reinterpretation by each side of provisions that had supposedly been agreed upon. There is now the apparent determination of the Reagan administration to renegotiate the treaty -- perhaps not much of an additional setback, in view of the Democrat-controlled Senate's failure to ratify it.

With the Strategic Arms Limitation Talks in mind, the Defense Department Task Force on Secrecy [DSB-70] had this to say:

> Some members of the Task Force are inclined to the view that, as a nation, we would have more to gain in the long run by pursuing a policy of complete openness in all matters. For example, the Strategic Arms Limitation Talks (SALT) might be more realistic if they were accompanied by a full and open public disclosure of knowledge of weapons capabilities and state-of-the-art developments, preferably by both sides, but at least on our part -- especially what we know about Soviet systems. In this way, the Congress and the general public would be better informed regarding the significance of the SALT discussions.

The United States, of course, is not the only country to have problems with government secrecy. They are considerably worse in Russia, for instance. Andrei Sakharov has commented on the lack of public information in Soviet society. Sakharov, believed to have led the successful Soviet H-bomb effort, won the Nobel Peace Prize in 1975 for his efforts toward disarmament. He was quoted in the Perspective section of the Sunday Chicago Tribune, June 15, 1980 as saying that

> in order to assess the [international] situation properly, it is imperative to take note of the Soviet Union -- a closed totalitarian state with a largely militarized economy and a bureaucratically centralized control, all of which make the growing might of such a country even more dangerous. In more democratic societies, every step in the field of armaments is subjected to public budgetary and political scrutiny and is carried out under public control. In the Soviet Union, all decisions of this kind are made behind closed doors and the world learns about them only when confronted by the accomplished facts. Even more ominous is the fact that this situation applies also to the field of foreign policy, involving issues of war and peace.

Unfortunately, Sakharov's assumptions regarding public visibility in democratic societies are more valid in principle than in fact, as shown farther on. Sakharov also discussed suppression of dissidents in the Soviet Union and the very ill-advised (in his opinion) Soviet invasion of Afghanistan. He said that NATO should modernize its medium-range nuclear missile forces to balance the already accomplished Soviet modernization, and deplored the state of the Vienna disarmament negotiations (for whose failure he blamed primarily the Soviets). Having expressed these severe criticisms of his government, he viewed them in light of the danger from nuclear weapons:

> Despite all that has happened, I feel that the questions of war and peace and disarmament are so crucial that they must be given absolute priority even in the most difficult of circumstances. It is imperative that all possible means be used to solve these questions and to lay the groundwork for further progress.
>
> Most urgent of all are steps to avert a nuclear war, which is the greatest peril confronting the modern world. The goals of all responsible people in the world coincide in this regard, including, I hope and believe, the Soviet leaders -- despite their dangerous expansionist policies, despite their cynicism, dogmatic conceptions and lack of confidence that often prevent them from conducting more realistic domestic and foreign policies.
>
> Therefore I hope when there is some easing of the present crisis in international relations, caused mainly by the Soviet invasion of Afghanistan, there will be a revival of efforts in regard to SALT-II, a technologically progressive treaty that provides the essential foundations for SALT-III.

Weapons Safety, Command and Control

The proposed ABM system discussed previously relied on two types of nuclear missiles, the long-range Spartan and the short-range Sprint. The latter was a "point defense" weapon, and had to be sited near the city it was to defend. Although the Spartan ("area defense") could have been located more distantly, the Department of Defense did not want to do that, because it would have meant some loss of efficiency. The proposed local siting focused the interest of a large part of the public on issues of nuclear weapons safety, "hair-trigger" responses, and presidential control. In view of the potentially catastrophic consequences of inadequate steps to prevent accident, or of improper control over unsanctioned use, the public perceived a possible threat to its safety.

The problem, however, is not limited to ABMs. Nuclear weapons are fabricated, transported, and deployed throughout the United States. They are stored in some forty-three states, and perhaps 100,000 people have access at some stage or another to the weapons or their fissile components. They are moved through populated cities. Nike nuclear-tipped anti-aircraft missiles were once stationed in and near cities [Note III-3]. In the past, aircraft have routinely flown over the United States laden with nuclear bombs. Hydrogen bombs have been accidently released from such aircraft, either in flight or upon crashing -- in North Carolina, Spain, and Greenland, for example. It is said that only one of six safing devices remained untriggered to prevent a thermonuclear weapon from exploding over North Carolina when it was jettisoned from a SAC bomber [Note III-4]. Moreover, according to a Reuters dispatch quoted in the Chicago Tribune (December 22, 1980), U.S. agencies might have admitted to only about half of the accidents ("Broken Arrows") involving nuclear weapons.

There is no civilian agency with oversight over the safety of nuclear weapons. Furthermore, under the sweeping and vague secrecy provisions of the Atomic Energy Act (see Chapter VII), effective civilian oversight might be difficult. Any oversight agency would have to be provided with information about weapons and safing principles, if it is to determine the extent to which safety is being compromised in favor of operational readiness (hair-trigger response).

Various reports have surfaced regarding the degree of security associated with nuclear weapons. One person alone is supposed to be unable to activate a nuclear device; can two persons in concert do so? Is it true that at one time foreign nationals at forward-storage depots overseas were qualified to be one of the two activators? Could the American counterpart have been overcome or have conspired to turn over effective control of nuclear weapons to a foreign state? These are questions of deployment practices; they are also questions that require an understanding of arming principles, including the permissive action link (PAL), which is designed to require active command concurrence before a nuclear warhead is detonated.

Some false alerts of U.S. strategic nuclear forces in 1979 and 1980 have publicized the risk of accidental triggering of a nuclear war by "computer error" -- doomsday by short circuit [Note III-5]. The military doctrine of "launch on warning" places a premium on technological reliability and human infallibility. There is no way to compensate for a mistake that leads to nuclear warfare, as Rear Admiral Eccles has so cogently concluded [Note II-1]. The public clearly has a substantial interest in understanding the underlying principles of our current system of weapons safeguards, as well as many details that would be pertinent to an effective system of oversight.

Some have argued that independent scrutiny is the only way to guarantee the public safety in these matters. Because some weapons information is in the grey area between what is sensitive and what is not, an intermediary civilian agency would be needed, with access to classified information. It would have to protect legitimately sensitive data, while assuring that relevant, non-sensitive details were available. The DOE and its predecessor, the AEC, do not have a good record in fulfilling such responsibilities. Their past disregard of public safety with the handling and testing of nuclear weapons has contributed to public mistrust of the civilian nuclear establishment. The benefit of a separate agency to oversee weapons safety, by helping to restore trust that the public interest was being protected, could extend considerably beyond the weapons dimension.

MISINFORMATION ABOUT NUCLEAR POWER

Recent experience by Alexander DeVolpi, in preparing his book Proliferation, Plutonium and Policy [DEV-79], illustrates the need for detailed, independent knowledge of the concepts underlying fission weapons. In 1977 De Volpi undertook a study of the potential for denaturing plutonium -- ways to make it less useful for weapons but still suitable for a reactor fuel. International interest in this topic had arisen because of various public pronouncements, mostly from the U.S. government, that plutonium could not be denatured. Denaturing of fissile isotopes is not a new idea, having been considered under the Baruch Plan, immediately after World War II. Although isotopic dilution is known to reduce the potential explosive yield from uranium, its effect on plutonium, being somewhat more complicated, is less well recognized.

According to government announcements in the latter half of the 1970s, supported by the release of selected technical information, "any 'grade' of plutonium can be used as the fissile material for a credible nuclear explosives program." "Credible" was left undefined. All forms of plutonium, including that created in commercial power reactors, would be suitable as a fissile component in fission explosives: so went the argument.

On the other hand, if that argument were incorrect, if plutonium could be denatured, then a properly managed nuclear fuel cycle involving plutonium would not necessarily contribute to additional proliferation of nuclear weapons. The U.S. government had made far-reaching energy policy decisions that were based to a large extent on belief in the nondenaturability of plutonium. If that assumption was wrong, the policy decisions were likely to be wrong.

Certainly a policy that depends so heavily on a single assertion should have that assertion thoroughly documented. Yet no public substantiation existed; the data were classified! Despite the repeated government claims that plutonium cannot be denatured, DeVolpi's initial calculations and evaluation suggested otherwise. In order to place the calculations on a firm basis, he proceeded to scour the literature for unclassified data on concepts underlying fission weapon design and characteristics. The explosive yield of plutonium weapons as a function of denaturant concentration had to be estimated, as did yields for uranium weapons. Other characteristics of nuclear weapons, such as size, weight, spontaneous heat generation, spontaneous neutron and gamma output, mechanism for operation (gun-barrel or implosion), and high-explosive velocities were essential elements in the assessment. Although it is laborious for one person to dig out the information, all of it is available in many countries.

Those who argued that reactor-grade plutonium is "suitable" as a fuel for a nuclear weapon avoided definition and quantification. When the issue was broken down further, two particular bones of contention were revealed: What would be the explosive yield as a function of plutonium fissile fraction, and was there a minimum size of explosion that was always achievable? Clarification of those points required generic calculations that run parallel to classified data -- even if accomplished, as they were, without restricted sources.

The results indicated that, as plutonium becomes diluted by extraneous isotopes and other constituents, it rapidly degrades in explosive quality. At 20 percent enrichment, uranium-235 is considered impractical for weapons use. Plutonium can be diluted so that it is equally poor for sustaining a fission explosion (and in addition has other drawbacks).

There are, to be sure, fuel cycle stages where it is at least theoretically possible to divert spent fuel for weapons use, although it is not as simple as some would make it appear. Proper institutional and technological safeguards will always be necessary for both plutonium and uranium in all forms and grades. Moreover, there are severe limits to the amount of plutonium that can be isotopically denatured in a given time.

In addressing the point about minimum yield, issue had to be taken with a variety of categorical, unproven public assertions. The official suggestion was that the minimum yield would always be in the range of 1 kiloton (TNT equivalent), a rather large burst. Those who supported this contention would apologetically say that they, the cognoscenti, were hampered by security restrictions -- the implication being that they knew more than they could tell. When pressed, they would all refer to some hoary quotations from J.Robert Oppenheimer and General Leslie Groves. In a recent book from the Stockholm International Peace Reasearch Institute [SIP-79], the assertions are repeated once more, again without proof.

The numbers in the original quotations were examined by DeVolpi and analyzed with classical statistical methods. It turned out that the available data are consistent with a Poisson distribution in yield, for a suitable choice of parameters. The statistical approach accounts for the inferences drawn by Oppenheimer and Groves and does not sustain the threshold theory. Thus the information cited in support of a minimum plutonium-weapon yield appears to have been misinterpreted.

Undoubtedly, independent derivations of fission-explosive yields are congruent with at least some data originally determined at the classified weapons laboratories. Under a literal interpretation of the Atomic Energy Act, DeVolpi's entire book would have been Restricted Data -- in spite of the fact that all of his information and results were derived from unclassified sources and fundamental principles. Before reaching his final determination of relevant fission-weapon characteristics, DeVolpi had been challenged (properly) to show conclusive evidence in support of his contention that plutonium could be denatured. Under a strict born-classified regime, it would not have been possible to call attention to these shaky foundations of U.S. non-proliferation policy.

On the other side of the argument, Amory Lovins, in an article in Nature [LOV-80] concludes that denaturing plutonium is not a valid concept. He asserts that "power reactors are not an implausible but are rather potentially a peculiarly convenient type of large-scale military Pu production reactor." To reach that position, he had to review a substantial body of literature and examine various parametric relationships involved in weapons physics, technology, and design. Lovins placed particular emphasis on the ability of various adversary groups to reach certain levels of technological sophistication. Each level was defined by how rapid an implosion the organization could achieve for compressing the fissile material in a bomb. (High compression leads to high reactivity insertion and a large explosive yield.) Regardless of the merits of that analysis, Lovins, too, had to use deducible data regarding fission weapons, and it is in light of such data that the dispute will eventually be resolved.

Laser Enrichment of Fissile Isotopes

Fission weapons work best with fuel that has been highly enriched in fissile isotopes. New isotope separation processes that utilize laser excitation of atomic or molecular resonance levels of natural uranium are under development, and any possible enrichment shortcut is a matter of proliferation concern. If laser enrichment becomes inexpensive (as it might under extensive government-supported development) and widespread, it could lead to cheap and easy production of fissile materials for nuclear weapons. Laser enrichment is, properly, a restricted, classified subject. To evaluate its potential for proliferation, one nevertheless needs to understand the process. While there is no need to publish detailed data on resonance levels, there should not be and need not be restrictions on discussing the underlying concepts.

Thermonuclear Power

There are very large government and private research efforts aimed at fusion power reactors. For a number of years a valid inquiry has been conducted into the extent to which fission reactors might be sources of fissile materials for diversion, or might contribute technology for proliferation of fission weapons. In a similar vein, would fusion reactors contribute to the spread of thermonuclear weapons? Are the fuels for fusion power suitable for direct application to fusion weapons? Would the technology of fusion power aid thermonuclear weapons design? Because the destructiveness of thermonuclear weapons is so much greater than that of fission weapons, the significance of these questions possibly reaches a higher level of importance. Unless enough is known of the concepts surrounding small and large fusion weapons, it is not possible to make independent evaluations of the risks of thermonuclear weapon propagation resulting from fusion reactor development and deployment.

Classified laser research reenters the debate in the thermonuclear context. The current basis for classification in the fusion program is the possibility that hydrogen bomb information might be released in the course of developing a technique known as "inertially confined fusion" (ICF). In view of that risk and the one just noted (successful development of laser techniques for isotopic enrichment could lead to cheaper A-bombs), what should government policy be in those two laser areas? Can the public be satisfied that safeguards against abuse of laser technology are adequate? To answer, the public must have access to the concepts associated with using lasers in those sensitive applications.

ENVIRONMENTAL ISSUES

Perhaps the 1970s will be considered by history a decade in which environmental concerns and the need for energy appeared to be in conflict. The 1980s may see the world coming to grips with the necessity of balancing these diverse objectives. To do so will require adequate public access to knowledge about the influence of technology on the environment and on policies that affect the environment.

Many environmental abuses have been hidden under the cloak of national defense. Consider the environmental effect of worldwide testing of nuclear weapons. Not only is there local damage, but the results of atmospheric testing are visited on the entire earth. For purely military reasons, nations that tested nuclear weapons on the earth's surface created whatever rationale and coverup was necessary to get the job done. Maximum secrecy reduces attention, information, and prior notice to the minimum. The less said about nuclear-weapons testing, the less risk that there would be that the public would understand the adverse effects, and the more chance that sanitized statements that fail to reveal the entire possible impact would be accepted at face value.

All military systems have potential environmental impact. That is recognized by Congress, which requires that each arm of the military file with the Arms Control and Disarmament Agency an environmental impact statement. Unfortunately, the services have chosen to evade the intent of the law, providing only cursory statements (a few paragraphs for the B-1 bomber) to be made public. A somewhat larger, but apparently still evasive, impact statement is filed in secret, thus perhaps obscuring issues of significant public concern.

THE PROGRESSIVE CASE AND THE CTBT

Some conceptual information that came out during the Progressive case is both valuable and necessary for public evaluation of the technical (and, as it turns out, spurious) arguments that have been used against the comprehensive test ban treaty (CTBT: Chapter VI). In this regard there may be a silver lining in the government's disclosure of hitherto secret information.

Because of the complexity of the design of thermonuclear weapons there are uncertainties that can only be removed by nuclear explosive testing, as Chapter VI explains. There are conflicting claims, however, about whether further testing is needed to check reliability, once the prototype of a particular design has been proven to operate. There are many ways to evaluate the subsystems without detonating a full weapon. This matter should be open to public debate, in view of its important implications. It is not satisfactory to accept at face value what might be a marginal, tainted assessment by those who have a vested interest in the continuation of nuclear testing.

Nuclear explosions for ostensibly peaceful purposes (such as canal building or oil recovery) could be weapons tests in disguise. In recognition of this, both of the superpowers are now willing to forego peaceful explosions -- perhaps, a cynic might say, because practical peaceful applications have turned out to be only marginally useful, at best.

It was in 1977 that the Soviet Union agreed to cancel its program of peaceful nuclear explosions. The agreement eliminated what the United States had previously claimed was a major obstacle to a comprehensive ban on nuclear testing. It removed a significant compliance ambiguity, because any detonation detected seismically or otherwise would constitute a clear and unambiguous violation of the treaty. President Carter responded by instructing American negotiators to seek a five-year comprehensive test ban with the Soviet Union. In reaction, the

Secretary of Energy, James Schlesinger, the director of Lawrence Livermore, Roger Batzel, and the director of the Los Alamos Laboratory, Harold Agnew, visited the White House and reportedly spent an hour and a half attempting to dissuade the President from seeking a CTBT. One of the arguments used against the treaty was that it would eliminate certain tests needed to maintain confidence in the existing U.S. stockpile.

Also, in public testimony before the House Armed Services Committee, the DOE Assistant Director for Defense Programs, Donald Kerr, (now the director of Los Alamos National Laboratory), told the committee that random sampling of warheads in the stockpile occasionally turns up problems that cannot be precisely assessed on the basis of past tests. In this situation, he claimed, an additional test might be required before the weapon could be returned to the active inventory. A comprehensive ban on testing could result, according to Kerr, "in entire weapons systems [being] deleted from the force structure."

Kerr's testimony was apparently marked by quarrels and angry reactions to his failure to submit written testimony prior to the hearings. In response to his testimony, the Federation of American Scientists (FAS) made public a letter (August 15, 1978) signed by Norris Bradbury, former director of Los Alamos, J. Carson Mark, head of Los Alamos's Theoretical Division from 1947 to 1973, and Richard Garwin, a long-time consultant to Los Alamos. The letter stated, regarding tests of the type referred by Kerr, that it has been "rare to the point of nonexistence for a problem...to require a nuclear test for its resolution." Wolfgang K. H. Panofsky, appearing before the Senate Foreign Relations Committee on September 15, 1977, had declared unequivocally that "it has been amply demonstrated that stockpile verification can be carried out without the benefit of nuclear testing."

Dr. Robert N. Thorn, head of the weapons program at Los Alamos, was one of the earliest expert government witnesses in the Progressive case to confirm Morland's speculations, saying [26A] that the article contained discussion "perhaps as suggestive of the process used in thermonuclear weapons as the original outline on the subject by Teller and Ulam." Dr. Thorn apparently agreed with the government that the information presented too great a proliferation risk to to be published. Yet Dr. Thorn has consistently opposed that most meaningful of proliferation preventives, the CTBT. For instance, in hearings on August 15, 1978, before the House Armed Services Committee [Science, 201:1106 (September 22, 1978)], he objected to the CTBT, in part because the Russians might gain advantage by clandestine testing on Mars.

Thorn disputed the FAS letter, indicating that there were weapons-component remanufacturing problems caused by the unavailability of certain materials. When asked for examples, he said that certain adhesives have been declared carcinogenic and other materials of a classified nature are no longer on the market. On the strength of Thorn's vague statements about carcinogenicity (hardly a serious threat, in this case, to public health) and secret materials (perhaps particular alloys of aluminum, stainless steel, and so on), the United States passed up still another opportunity to slow the growing danger of the vertical arms race between the Soviet Union and the United States -- thereby frustrating further the increasingly impatient signatories of the Nuclear Non-Proliferation Treaty.

Having headed off a step that could have had a major antiproliferation impact, Schlesinger, Batzel, and Thorn subsequently all filed
affidavits claiming that grave and irreparable harm would be done to
the cause of nonproliferation if The Progressive were allowed to
publish Howard Morland's (deducible) information.

THE RELEVANCE OF H-BOMB INFORMATION

Public apprehension (well justified) about the consequences of a
thermonuclear war seems to have spawned a reluctance to scrutinize
nuclear weapons policy. Certain aspects of the subject appear to be
"off limits." That is unfortunate, because the matter is vital and
public understanding is needed. The pertinent technical information
about hydrogen bombs is already out: The Morland article and subsequent
events have shown that the concepts are indeed public, either explicitly or because they can be independently deduced.

We do not, of course, suggest that detailed H-bomb data have to be
part of open discussions. The details of H-bomb design are still
relatively secure, though at least four other nations have worked them
out. Certain purists take the position that all data belong in the
public domain. We do not share that view. Thermonuclear weapons are
for mass destruction, and, like even lesser public hazards, should be
amply safeguarded.

As we explain more fully later, there is an important difference
between deducible and nondeducible information. Consider the
experimental data (nondeducible) from nuclear weapons tests. That sort
of data is inaccessible without an expensive and visible program of
nuclear weapons testing (unless, of course, it is divulged, as perhaps
happened when the sensitive progress report on nuclear weapons, UCRL-
4725, was mistakenly declassified). That kind of detailed,
nondeducible information is rarely, if ever, needed for public
discussion.

National security concern over nuclear weapons proliferation is
legitimate, and there is more that could be done to make it very hard
for new nations to get A- or H-bombs. Some of the possibilities would
involve changes in government policy. The various claims and counterclaims about what would or would not work can only be understood in
light of the fundamental physical principles of nuclear weapons.
Derivation of these principles does not require access to classified
data, yet the exchange or publication of such derived information, so
that others can check the work, is discouraged by the potential for
prior restraint. Some of the thoughts in Morland's article, for
instance, are indispensable in a debate about different political
approaches to the control and spread of nuclear weapons. If censorship
of the article had been upheld, the executive branch would have established a precedent for putting a damper on valid public discussion.

Discouraging public dialog on these issues can be harmful to
national and international security -- contrary to intentions. Because
there various possible technological and institutional ways to resist
proliferation, some more promising and realistic than others, current
approaches should not be frozen without full consideration of alternatives. Could the United States, for example, improve its security by a
unilateral moratorium on production and testing of nuclear weapons?

With conflicting answers from knowledgeable people, independent examination of the technical design concepts and their implications (requiring specialized but unclassified knowledge) is needed.

NEED-TO-KNOW AS SEEN BY PROGRESSIVE CASE PARTICIPANTS

The editor of The Progressive, in justifying publication of Morland's article, said [43]:

> Secrecy [surrounding the nuclear weapons program] withholds from the public information that is essential to an understanding of the many public policy questions that program presents -- environmental protection, occupational safety and health, arms control, and Federal spending priorities, for example. In the absence of such information, it is difficult if not impossible for the people to arrive at informed decisions on public policy.

Additional examples were given by Thomas Emerson on behalf of Scientific American magazine [175]:

> Speech delayed is tantamount to information denied. On some occasions the public need for information is immediate, and to withhold it is to effectively frustrate the process of self-government. The Bay of Pigs may have been such an instance where a disastrous policy could have been averted by the immediate dissemination of information....
>
> The effect [of a classified-at-birth concept] on the right of the public to know could be...devasting. The solutions to all of the pressing problems of this technological society depend upon access to information. Much of this information involves knowledge that could affect our national security. This is true, not only of the decisions that must be made with respect to nuclear energy, arms control, and the like, but also unemployment, urban reconstruction, population, foreign policy, and many others.

The opinion of some of the national media is expressed in this statement to the court [176]:

> Can one describe the blast at Hiroshima and studies of its victims? Presumably one can and surely many have. But the mere fact that others have published the information in some form is apparently no guarantee that the information has been declassified -- i.e., is no longer "restricted data." How is an individual to receive "fair notice" ...that his conduct will violate the criminal laws?...
>
> See, for example, the account of the apparently calculated decision, made at the highest levels of our federal government, to withhold information concerning adverse effects on the public health of atmospheric nuclear testing conducted during the nineteen-fifties and sixties.... Federal policy with respect to the safety of nuclear power plants has become an issue of the utmost national concern in light of the accident at Three Mile Island, Pennsylvania. Here too questions have been raised about the adequacy of federal disclosure with respect to nuclear issues affecting the public at large.

The Fusion Energy Foundation observed [170]:
> Without access to classified material, the clearest example
> of the impact of classification of scientific research on
> military research and development is that of the so-called
> beam weapon.... There has been a long and acrimonious de-
> bate in the United States over primarily, the feasibility
> of the weapon.... The debate has been based on inadequate
> knowledge of the basic physics of the processes involved in
> accelerating, guiding and propagating such a beam....

A league of writers favoring freedom of expression and availability
of information filed an amici brief evaluating the article's purpose
[173]:
> Morland was making an important public policy statement
> that (1) our whole secrecy system of national security is
> based on a myth and must be defused; (2) it is necessary to
> counteract the mystique of recondite technical knowledge
> justifying decision by experts separated from the people by
> a wall of secrecy; (3) in the long run the only way of
> halting or reversing the arms race and strengthening the
> rule of law is to provide the people with all the informa-
> tion necessary for them to decide important policy
> questions on the nuclear arms race.

Morland in his first affidavit [38A] expressed his own views:
> The point of my article is that the myth of secrecy is used
> to create an atmosphere in which public debate is stifled
> and public criticism of the weapons production system is
> suppressed. I hope to dramatically illustrate that thesis
> by showing that what many people considered to be probably
> the ultimate secret, is not really a secret at all. The
> information is easily available to anyone who wants to
> acquire it; therefore the attempt to keep such things
> secret is bound to fail in that other governments will have
> access to the information anyway. Despite that, however,
> as long as secrecy is employed, the people of the United
> States will have no opportunity to discuss the vital issues
> involved. Thus the people who are being hurt are the
> people of the United States. The accuracy of my descrip-
> tion has no impact on my belief in the validity of my
> thesis. However, the value of the article is directly
> dependent on whether the information is accurate or not.

> J. Robert Oppenheimer, the scientific director of the
> Manhattan Project, said, "No responsible person will hazard
> an opinion in a field where he believes that there is
> somebody else who knows the truth, and where he believes he
> does not know it."... The clear implication of Oppen-
> heimer's remark is that if the government bomb builders can
> maintain even the appearance of an information monopoly by
> comparison with the citizenry, they can also maintain a
> monopoly on "responsible" opinion. If an actual
> information monopoly cannot be maintained, an apparent
> information monopoly will still be effective in suppressing
> public debate. In the course of my research, I have felt
> the force of the intimidation described by Oppenheimer, and
> I have seen it operate in others.

On the basis of its publication experience, the Scientific American filed an amicus brief [175] that made the following supportive statement:

In any event it would appear plain that the sort of information conveyed by the article is essential for public decision-making. Issues pertaining to the number, use, deployment, and limitations of nuclear weapons depend upon such knowledge. So also the current debate over whether to start production of the so-called neutron bomb turns on such factors. The very question of whether there is a "secret" of the hydrogen bomb which other countries have not discovered, and which limits the prospect of other countries possessing the bomb, is a matter of great public import. In addition there are moral, political and economic questions to be answered.

There is another reason why the information contained in the Morland article is vital to public decision-making and has not been delegated to the exclusive use of the military. The article raises crucial qustions with respect to the functioning of a security system in a democratic society.

A brief [152] filed by Morland's lawyers says that his article discusses the important political issues of proliferation of nuclear weapons and the dangers of government secrecy. The article is not a blueprint for the manufacture of a hydrogen bomb. Rather, it is political speech designed to foster and encourage public debate about important public issues.

The defendants quoted [52A] the following passage from the Atomic Energy Act in support of their argument regarding the intent of Congress in passing the Act:

The dissemination of scientific and technical information relating to atomic energy should be permitted and encouraged so as to provide that free interchange of ideas and criticism which is essential to scientific and industrial progress and public understanding and to enlarge the fund of technical information. (Underlined language added in 1954).

In introducing their appeal brief [167], the defendants made effective use of this statement by Albert Einstein on January 22, 1947:

We scientists recognize our inescapable responsibility to carry to our fellow citizens an understanding of the simple facts of atomic energy and its implications for society. In this lies our only security and our only hope -- we believe that an informed citizenry will act for life and not death.

Although the public -- Congress, the media, and other institutions -- need knowledge to make decisions, a boundary must be drawn in a gray, indeterminate area to guard against divulging information harmful to the public interest. That task has to be left to conscientious human beings, armed with guidelines that are as precise, and adjustable, as the circumstances permit.

Halperin and Hoffman [H&H1-77] summarize their observations about government secrecy as follows:

In the aftermath of these episodes [through 1977], many
outside the executive bureaucracy have come to agree on the
need to reexamine the way our government balances the
public's right to know against the requirements of secrecy.
... The executive branch today has the capacity to
conceal, for substantial periods of time, information that
would significantly contribute to legitimate public debate
on major issues.... Secrecy has delayed the correction of
divisive and irrational policies. In some cases, moreover,
the attempt to prevent or punish unwelcome disclosures has
led to significant infringements of our civil liberties.

Contrary Views

One of the few dissenting views about the public need for technical
information was filed by the Justice Department [166] without further
elaboration:

Technical information describing the design, construction
and utilization of nuclear weapons...while useful to
bombmakers, will do nothing to enhance political debate or
commentary on issues before the public, including nuclear
policy or defense.

Ralph S. Hager [47], a physicist at Lawrence Livermore Laboratory,
did "not recommend publishing the Morland article, because it unnecessarily draws attention to an issue which has not been demonstrated to
be in the interest of national security."

A slightly negative note was offered by the Fusion Energy Foundation
[170]: "The editors of The Progressive seem to have gone out of their
way to provoke government censorship." That statement, and a few by
others in a similar vein, appear to be addressed more to tactics than
principle. There was fear, particularly among the news media, that the
delicacy of the subject matter was likely to render this a lost cause
-- that there was too much public, congressional, and judicial sympathy
with the government's side.

That theme was reflected in the view of Jeremy Stone, the director
of the Federation of American Scientists, who said that The Progressive's "socially useful purpose" did not require it to "resist most or
all of the deletions." Stone stated [51] that the FAS knew of "no
plausible reason why supporters of the test ban are hampered by not
knowing technical details of how the bomb is built."

Actually, that statement is inconsistent with the FAS practice of
assembling well-known technical advisors to make statements on various
public issues. Many of these people (George Rathjens, George
Kistiakowsky, and Hans Bethe, for example) have access to classified
information; consequently their statements are made in light of
knowledge of such details or with the implied consent of the few who
have such knowledge. Some supporters of the test ban do, in fact, know
"technical details of how the bomb is built" when they issue their
public pronouncements. (As a matter of fact, Theodore Taylor, in a
publication [Annual Review of Nuclear Science, 25:406 (1975)]
explaining his concern over the adequacy of safeguards over nuclear
reactor fuel, found it necessary to apply specialized weapons-related
technical information in support of his arguments.)

In fairness to Stone, he had not seen the article and perhaps had been taken in by the exaggerated implications, by both The Progressive and the government, that the article was in some sense a blueprint for an H-bomb. As we have already indicated, we agree that the public does not need a blueprint. However, as we shall show, that sort of detail was not to be found in the article.

In any event, concerned about the precedent that might occur if the Supreme Court permitted a permanent order of prior restraint, Stone said that The Progressive had "an obligation to its colleagual organs of the press not to provoke unnecessary and possibly unwinnable fights over the first amendment." [51] Although it turned out that The Progressive did not suffer a permanent injunction, we do not find Stone's concern unreasonable. The theme was also expressed by some of the news media in their initial reactions to the charges.

OVERVIEW

Though we would not have chosen the subject Morland used to dramatize his point, his article contained data and information relevant to: ongoing public debates regarding U.S. government policies and budgets; practices in the areas of national defense, public safety, environmental impact, production and shipment of nuclear weapons, and deployment of weapons of mass destruction; and the use of governmental secrecy to obscure the extent to which nuclear-weapon activities are spread in the industrial, geographical, and work sectors of American society.

Morland's article, moreover, is an attempt to draw attention to the moral issues that surround the continued manufacture and deployment of weapons that can destroy large cities. It points out important non-technical public issues associated with H-bomb development and production. These include the financial cost to the public, the visibility of the nuclear munitions establishment, and the continuing low-profile development, testing, and production of thermonuclear weapons. All of these issues have arms-control and proliferation implications; all of them require sufficient public understanding of design concepts to permit informed discussion.

Arms control and proliferation are two major areas where there is definite need for independent derivation of the underlying concepts. Without government authentication, such independent analysis cannot damage national security; on the contrary, it benefits the nation by making possible intelligent public debate of major governmental policies.

Weapons concepts can reach the public directly or indirectly. Direct exposure to the ideas, at least on a primitive level, is needed to establish the basis for discussion. Indirect information comes through independent scientists, engineers, technical journalists, and knowledgeable persons who can assimilate the weapons information at a more sophisticated level. These knowledgeable specialists have a need and responsibility to be informed well enough to give the public a worthwhile, independent view of technology-related government actions.

Earlier in this chapter, the interdependence of various technical issues related to strategic offensive and defensive weapons systems was discussed in some detail. Failure to adequately account for the long-range impact of offensive and defensive strategic technologies on the security of the country has resulted in a spiraling, self-defeating effort to regain security through the acquisition of more and more exotic and technologically dubious weapons systems. Public interest in policies that more clearly take into account the capabilities and limitations of such technology may be the only hope for bringing these technologies under control.

In the past there have been important decisions that did not have the benefit of public debate. Perhaps the most significant decisions on technological policy were those associated with the Manhattan Project. It is certainly not obvious that public discussion about atomic bombs would have led to a different situation today, and it is also true that there was a period where secrecy about the atomic bomb served a legitimate national security need. But the secrecy was carried too far, and as a result the public was not able to take part in formulating policies that affect us to this day. Furthermore, there has grown up an acceptance, even awe, of secrecy in the most influential areas of American military and industrial development, and concurrently the threat of mass destruction of civilians has, without conscious decision, become an instrument of foreign policy.

Holloway [HOL-79] has commented on the changed nature of things:

> The use of atomic energy for military purposes has provided the most important turning-point in the history of warfare and has had a profound influence on international relations since 1945. Moreover, the creation of nuclear weapons has raised difficult [and troubling] questions about the relationship of science to politics, of truth to power -- questions that are posed and answered differently in different societies. The manner in which the Soviet Union entered the atomic age had a major influence on later Soviet policy and has become part of the experience on which Soviet leaders draw in their dealings with the Western powers and in their pursuit of technological progress.

There are critical questions still facing the country regarding fission weapons. What are the essential technical and diplomatic elements of an effective nonproliferation policy? Safeguards, a ban on testing, and self-control among the superpowers may all be vital ingredients. A thorough knowledge of the underlying technical questions and their relationship to diplomatic strategies has been lacking. Neither the government's nor the public's conception of how to direct the uses of technology has been influenced by attempts to analyze policies with an eye on technical realities. The nuclear-weapon states have failed to agree on a comprehensive ban on nuclear testing or on otherwise limiting their own nuclear armaments. Safeguards procedures for nuclear power are inadequate. The illusion that secrecy will control the spread of nuclear weapons persists, and the lack of creative diplomatic initiatives continues to take its toll.

To be effective, antiproliferation policy must be formulated in the light of reality, as determined from the relevant, accurate facts. A detailed look at fission technology reveals that a ban on nuclear explosive testing would be effective in squelching proliferation, and further that proliferation will be hard to prevent without a test ban. To arrive at that conclusion, one requires extensive information about fission explosives, information of a type that is already available to experts around the world who do not have access to classified information. That individuals can and do derive such conceptual information is a benefit to the public, not a threat.

How about fusion weapon proliferation? We are still at a threshold, beyond which, perhaps, lies unlimited spread of H-bombs. What will hold the line? Again, a ban on testing, self-control -- and the corresponding restraints on the prerequisite fission weapon proliferation. And again, to comprehend these solutions, none of which the superpowers have adopted, it is necessary to have some understanding of the conceptual basis of fission and hydrogen weapons.

There are many other technological questions essential to society's health and well being that must be analyzed publicly: genetic manipulations, computer data privacy, biological and chemical warfare agents, nuclear reactors. Each poses new challenges to civilization, and each must be dealt with realistically and openly if applications are to be a benefit rather than a disaster.

The Bottom Line

There are many reasons why people must be guaranteed adequate access to information. Technology is growing in scope, pervasiveness, and complexity, demonstrating both benign and malignant aspects. Information about it is essential to the health and stability of our society. Three of the most significant decisions in world history were made in closed chambers: to undertake the development of the atom bomb, to use the bomb on Japan, and to develop the hydrogen bomb. Each of these decisions has had a direct impact on our current predicament.

Consider, in particular, the secret decision to proceed with the thermonuclear bomb. Since the consequences for the future security of the U.S. (and the world) were not debated openly, the public had no chance to learn that an immense and visible nuclear explosive testing program was required to develop that weapon -- a program that could have been forestalled by verifiable international agreement. Had it been known that the concepts were independently deducible, that others could eventually devise such weapons (as they did), and that there could be strong assurances against surprise, we would perhaps be far better off.

In view of the national suicide that could be triggered either by first use of any type of nuclear weapon or by retaliation in kind, national security decisions clearly must be based on more than mere short-term military considerations. Questions about the reliability of command, control, and communication networks that govern nuclear weapon systems, especially in a hair-trigger mode that might not be accident-proof, point up the need for the public and Congress to have access to more of the information that should be factored into strategic policy. In fact, because of secrecy within the various departments of government, the executive branch itself perhaps does not know enough about the thinking of competetent military strategists in the various armed services.

Today, as we survey the landscape of nuclear technology's impact on society, we find it covered with issues in which there is significant vested public interest: the prevention of further strategic arms escalation; the safety, command, and oversight of nuclear weapons; the social and political effect of modern weapons; the banning and verification of nuclear explosive testing; the slowing of proliferation by technical measures in the fission fuel cycle and in the development of fusion power. In all those areas there is the need for enough technical understanding to permit the technologies to be kept in constructive channels. Independent scientists must have access to enough information to give accurate, timely advice to the public, the Congress, and the courts in the ongoing effort to keep technology controlled and directed. That is the bottom line.

4 The Opposing Legal Arguments in the Progressive Case

Howard Morland and The Progressive saw decisions about hydrogen weapons as too important to be left to government insiders. The insiders (although not all of them) felt that Morland had information that was too dangerous to be left out in the open. In accordance with the American way of resolving such conflicts, the matter went to court.

As a guide through the legal maze, here is a brief roadmap. The dispute over publication of Morland's composition became a legal issue when in March 1979 the U.S. government moved to prevent publication by bringing a civil suit. The federal court was asked to issue a temporary restraining order (TRO), to be followed by preliminary and permanent injunctions against publication. The government presented its case in a series of briefs and affidavits by officials and by scientists on its behalf, trying to show that the Atomic Energy Act of 1954 would be violated if the article were published, and that the consequences would be harmful to the United States.

Because detailed opposing arguments were not heard before the TRO was issued on March 9, the defendants' first opportunity to present their case was at a March 26 hearing on whether there would be a preliminary injunction. The defense obtained supporting affidavits from a number of scientists throughout the country, and some amici curiae briefs were filed. The injunction was granted, and both sides began preparing for the appeal.

In summarizing its proposal to delete about 20 percent of Morland's article, the government said that the sensitive parts of the article revealed "three secret concepts" that were important in designing thermonuclear weapons. (Those concepts were ultimately revealed to be "separate stages," "radiation coupling," and "compression.")

During the litigation, documents and articles about fusion that included mention of the forbidden concepts were found to be publicly available. Especially damaging to the government's case was the discovery that some of its weapons reports had been declassified by mistake, particularly one designated UCRL-4725. For several years, that report and others, revealing not only general concepts, but also experimental details about thermonuclear weapons, had been available to the public! On the basis of this, a motion to vacate the preliminary injunction was filed by the defendants on June 15 -- but to no avail.

The litigation entered the Circuit Court of Appeals in Chicago. On September 17, before a judicial decision was reached, the government withdrew.

Two types of arguments had been presented, statutory and constitutional. The government primarily argued that publication was forbidden by the Atomic Energy Act, while the defense held that the Act would be unconstitutional unless it also required the Pentagon Papers test of harm to be met before prior restraint could be imposed. Not contested was the right of the government to bring criminal charges after any publication that resulted in unauthorized disclosure of classified data. A unique element of the case was the technical component: Whether the technical concepts contained in Morland's article were already in the public domain was one question, and another was whether the alleged risk of proliferation of nuclear weapons was real.

Throughout the book we make reference to the Pentagon Papers case, a most important legal precedent from 1971. That case is known in legal circles as New York Times Co. v. United States (403 U.S. 713 (1971)), or, for short, as New York Times. Its outcome was that the New York Times and the Washington Post could continue to publish a top-secret history of the Vietnam war that had fallen into their hands.

Mention is made below of documents and proceedings held in camera, which is legal jargon that means the public (and even the defendants) may be excluded. In order not to prejudice the government's claim that the Morland article contained secret information, Judge Warren agreed to place a protective order on affidavits and briefs. Public versions of the documents could be released after deletions. Many of the in-camera documents were made public after the litigation was terminated.

The legal issues in the Progressive case are summarized at the end of this chapter. In subsequent chapters we evaluate the technical issues, leading up to an analysis of the litigation in Chapter X.

FILINGS FOR A TEMPORARY RESTRAINING ORDER

On March 8, 1979, the government filed a civil action complaint [1] for a temporary restraining order (TRO) to prevent the defendants (Morland, The Progressive, Knoll, and Day) from publishing the article. Having jurisdiction was the U.S. District Court, Seventh Circuit, for the Western District of Wisconsin. The claim was that the article contained Secret Restricted Data as defined in the Atomic Energy Act of 1954, which permits the government to seek a court order restraining publication [Note IV-1]. The Act (see Appendix C) defines "Restricted Data" as including, among other things, "all data concerning...design, manufacture, or utilization of atomic weapons."

Officials of the Department of Energy had advised the defendants that the article contained Restricted Data as defined by the Act. Accordingly, the first count of the charge was that such notification gave the defendants reason to believe that publication of the article would injure the United States or secure an advantage to foreign nations. The second count was that publication of the article would result in "grave, direct, immediate and irreparable harm to the national security of the United States and its people." That language was chosen to satisfy the criteria for prior restraint specified by some of the Supreme Court justices in the Pentagon Papers case.

The district court was requested to issue a temporary restraining order and a preliminary injunction, with the intention that both would subsequently be made permanent.

Briefs for the Government

In supporting their application for restraint and injunction, the government lawyers laid out their arguments [4]. First, they contended that the information in the article, "particularly in the form presented," was not available elsewhere, and that the potential for proliferation jeopardized the security of the United States [Note IV-2].

Second, to justify temporary injunctive relief, the government advanced these claims: (1) there was prima facie evidence the defendants were about to violate the law, (2) the United States would suffer irreparable harm in the absence of an injunction, and (3) an injunction would serve the public interest without substantial harm to the defendants.

"Born classified". In trying to establish the merit of its argument, the government suggested that even if some of the "Secret Restricted Data" contained in the article represented "an original work product," its restricted status would not be changed. The argument was that Congress, by not altering the AEC's interpretation of the Restricted Data provisions of the Atomic Energy Act, deemed this "classified at birth" concept to be necessary to "ensure that sensitive information would not be divulged before the United States had an opportunity to assess its importance and take appropriate classification action" [Note IV-3].

Prior restraint. In further arguments, the government noted that "prior restraints have been upheld by the courts where the government has demonstrated the need to preserve the secrecy of classified or sensitive information." Examples cited included secrecy restrictions imposed on former CIA employees, and restraints against a government contractor's communication of details about constructing and operating a torpedo.

In anticipation of counterarguments, the government asserted that the action for restraint was not "barred by the Supreme Court's decision in New York Times v. United States.... The present case is readily distinguishable...in several significant respects.... First, this litigation is brought pursuant to a statute...which specifically authorizes...injunctive relief." The government requested judicial deference to congressional judgment in the matter.

It also argued that "the nature of the material sought to be published by the defendants here is...fundamentally different from that involved in New York Times...." The government suggested (contrary to its position in 1971) that the Pentagon Papers were "newsworthy" because of their "historical importance to the then-ongoing debate over American involvement in the war in Vietnam," whereas in Progressive the article

> will disclose technical information on the design and operation of a hydrogen bomb. This information is of questionable historical significance. Rather, the Secret Restricted Data involved here is of current military

significance to any nation attempting to develop a hydrogen
bomb capability.

The government invoked national-security arguments, citing the
constitutional powers of the President regarding events that are
"kindred to imperiling the safety of a transport already at sea."

Irreparable harm. In support of its contention that harm would
befall the United States if the article were published, the government
alleged:

> The potentially grave consequences to the security of the
> United States and the world itself resulting from the
> threatened disclosure are obvious and frightening....
> Present and potential enemies of the United States will be
> materially assisted in their development of the most
> destructive weapons known to mankind. Nations which are
> not currently seeking to develop such devices due to the
> high cost of years of experimentation may decide to do so
> as a result of the "shortcut" presented in the challenged
> publication.

The consequences of publication were projected by the government to
endanger policies relating to "nuclear nonproliferation and strategic
arms limitation," in which case "modern civilization will be one step
closer to its potential destruction in a nuclear holocaust."

United States obligations under the Non-Proliferation Treaty were
also invoked, by noting that nations are bound "not in any way to
assist, encourage, or induce any nonnuclear-weapon state to manufacture
or otherwise acquire nuclear weapons or other nuclear explosive
devices, or control over such weapons or explosive devices."

The court was assured that the defendants would not suffer unduly,
because the government's "interests in protecting the security of the
United States...clearly outweigh any inconvenience to the defendants,"
and "the alleged 'newsworthiness' of the information sought to be
published will [not] be lost or diminished by a publication delay."

In camera filings. In a memorandum [59] that was originally filed
in camera, but released when the case was dropped, the government
stated that the Morland article contained "a core of data that has
never been publicly disclosed in any fashion." It admitted that, by
bringing suit, it had officially confirmed the contents of the article
[Note IV-4].

> By its nature...this litigation and the circumstances in
> which it was brought confirm that the information which the
> United States has designated as Restricted Data in the
> Morland article is in fact essentially correct and does in
> fact describe the operation of a hydrogen bomb.

The process of confirmation started at the very first hearing.
Presented to the court was an impressive array of affidavits from high
government officials attesting to the accuracy and sensitivity of the
article. Under Note IV-5 we give some pertinent excerpts from
statements sworn to by such dignitaries as the Secretary of Energy, the
acting director of the Arms Control and Disarmament Agency (ACDA), the
head of the ACDA's Nonproliferation Bureau, various other government
officials, and the directors of the two major nuclear weapons
laboratories.

Prominent in this collection is the affidavit [23] of Jack W. Rosengren, a weapons physicist and government consultant. The nub of his testimony (see also Note IV-5) was this part:

> Nowhere is there a correct description of the type of design used in U.S. weapons. This type is far superior in efficiency and practicality to any other known type of design.... The Morland Article goes far beyond any other publication in identifying the nature of the particular design used in the thermonuclear weapons in the U.S. stockpile. [It] describes in a relatively detailed manner the design concepts and certain specific design features of U.S. thermonuclear weapons. This accomplishment would normally take a substantial investment of time and resources which would be obviated by the publication of the article, and it is therefore an extremely important disclosure to a nation seeking a thermonuclear capability.

We say more about this testimony further on.

Hearing on the Temporary Restraining Order

On March 9, United States of America vs. The Progressive, Inc., et al. was called for hearing in Milwaukee on a temporary restraining order, with Judge Warren presiding [31]. Lawyers for the government and The Progressive made their statements, and then Judge Warren, just before announcing his decision, orally expressed some thoughts about the issues, nonlegal and legal:

> I'd like...to think a long hard time before I gave the hydrogen bomb to Idi Amin. It seems to me that's just what we are doing....
>
> There is a difference between spoiling the relationship that I have with another member of the world community and making it possible for them to take me out of existence....
>
> I can't help feeling that somehow or other to put together the recipe for a do-it-yourself hydrogen bomb is somewhat different than revealing that certain members of our military establishment have very poor ideas about how to conduct a national effort in Vietnam....
>
> You can't speak freely when you are dead. And time, which was mentioned here, is one of the factors. There are times in the tableau of human history when time can be important. I think back as a World War II soldier to what would have happened to me and all my colleagues and probably all of us if the V-2 had been developed just a little bit faster that it was, and I question very much whether anybody is entitled to express their freedom of speech at the expense of my liberty or my life.

Regarding the legal issues, Judge Warren said,

> At the outset, I recognize that any prior restraint on publication comes into any Federal Court with a very heavy presumption against its validity....
>
> We have to consider four factors in deciding whether or not to grant a temporary restraining order: One, plaintiff's likelihood of success on the merits; two,

whether plaintiff will suffer irreparable harm if the
temporary restraining order does not issue; three, whether
the issuance of the order would substantially harm the
other party in the proceedings, the so-called balancing of
the harms factor; and then, finally, the interest of the
public....

No one would question but that a government might
prevent actual obstruction to its recruiting service or the
publication of the sailing dates of the transports or the
number and location of troops.

So on similar grounds the primary requirements of
decency may be enforced against obscene publications, the
[security] of the community life may be protected against
incitement of actions of violence and the [overthrow] by
force of orderly government. The constitutional guarantee
of free speech does not protect a man from an injunction
against uttering words that may have all the effect of
force....

Now, when anybody thinks of the First Amendment rights
and any limitations on them, why everbody talks about...
the case where famous Justice Holmes talked about yelling
fire in a crowded theatre. The most stringent protection
of free speech would not protect a man in falsely shouting
fire in a theatre and causing a panic....

I am impressed here by the fact that contrary to the New
York [Times] case, we do have a specific congressional
application of public policy in the forms of prohibited
statute.... [sic]

I am not particularly entranced by the argument that I
seem to be hearing from the respondent: that somehow or
other newspapers occupy a different status in things than
any other person. I think that is a very dangerous
constitutional concept to start adopting....

Even though I recognize that it's very close to a deep
constitutional issue and being unable to find any real harm
that would substantially run to The Progressive in a mere
delay of this article...the Court does find that a
temporary restraining order should issue.

Therefore, the defendants, including Mr. Morland, their
agents, servants, employees and all other person in active
concert or participation and each of them, are hereby
temporarily restrained from publishing or otherwise
communicating, transmitting or disclosing in any manner any
[restricted] data contained in the article, "How a Hydrogen
Bomb Works."

Now, this restraint on publication, since it is a prior
restraint, and, therefore, of...the kind that we must
guarantee against, will be for the shortest possible period
consistent with the opportunity for the government to
substantiate its claim at a hearing on the request for
preliminary injunction.

FILINGS FOR A PRELIMINARY INJUNCTION

Judge Warren ordered the hearings on a preliminary injunction to be held within ten days. The defendants were then just beginning to assemble their witnesses and their legal support.

Brief in Opposition to Preliminary Injunction [52A]

Five primary arguments against the preliminary injunction were advanced by the defendants. They contended (1) that the government had failed "to sustain the heavy burden necessary to overcome the First Amendment's presumption against prior restraint"; (2) that the information in the article was in the public domain, and therefore not subject to the Atomic Energy Act; (3) that dissemination of information that is public cannot be deemed injurious to the country; (4) that the Atomic Energy Act did not really authorize prior restraint; and (5) that if, nevertheless, Congress did intend to authorize prior restraint in the Atomic Energy Act, its overbreadth and vagueness render that authorization unconstitutional. [Note IV-6]

To buttress their third point, the defendants quoted from Judge Learned Hand in United States v. Heine:

> When...information has once been made public, and has thus become available in one way or another to any foreign government, the "advantage" [to a foreign country] intended by the [Espionage Act] cannot reside in facilitating its use by condensing and rearranging it.

Affidavits on Behalf of The Progressive

Affidavits initially filed for The Progressive were either by the defendants or by scientists on their behalf. The nontechnical affidavits dealt with the process of researching and reviewing Morland's article. The technical ones focused mainly on the public domain issue.

Howard Morland. The author of the article submitted a declaration [38A] describing his background and how he obtained his source material [Note IV-7]. His visits as a reporter for The Progressive to government facilities and contractors were arranged through the Department of Energy. He visited a few of the facilities as a member of the public. He documented his official conversations, included copies of diagrams from the open literature, and described his process of eliciting, elucidating, deducing, and adducing the technical information included in the article.

> On the basis of my experience, I conclude that a nuclear scientist would have no trouble picking the correct diagram [of the H-bomb concept]. There is no information in my diagrams which is not present in the attached [encyclopedia] diagrams, logically deducible from information that is present in the attached diagrams, or published material. The whole story can be discovered by reading encyclopedias with a critical eye....

In one portion of his testimony, the answer that a student gave to Morland in response to a question was originally censored, but ultimately released when the case was settled. He described the incident like this [57]:

> I was giving a talk to approximately 30 undergraduate
> students at a dormitory at the Unversity of Alabama...and I
> asked if anyone in the audience knew how thermonuclear
> weapons work... One person in the room said that the U-238
> casing focuses gamma rays from the exploding trigger onto
> the fusion fuel.

Although not quite correct, implicit in that remark were what would
later become known as the forbidden concepts of separate stages and
radiation coupling. Morland in the remainder of his affidavit went on
to recount his conversations with some scientists, including Stanislaw
Ulam, John Gofman, and Sidney Drell, mentioning further clues that he
picked up.

One of the in camera affidavits submitted by government affiants
Rosengren and Grayson charged [68] that Morland must have had "a great
deal of guidance from a person or persons with access to secret design
information," and found great significance in the fact that Morland
cited no public reference for many of his details.

Although such charges had a strong psychological effect on the
court, they could not then be openly discussed, because the government
refused to declassify any part of those affidavits. Without that very
strong but undocumented allegation that Morland had access to secret
information, the government's case would have been substantially
weaker. Our retrospective examination of the government's analysis of
the Morland article indicates no justification for the charge, and we
note the lack of eventual criminal prosecution of anybody.

Although Morland had not seen any in camera filings, he was aware
[76A] of the contention by Rosengren and Grayson

> that I must have obtained government documents showing the
> design of a thermonuclear weapon to write such a detailed
> and accurate article and that I then made it appear I
> fashioned the article from my own research.
>
> It is obvious the government is embarrassed by my
> article and by the public literature which explains the
> very concepts the Department of Energy (DOE) claims are
> "secret."...
>
> In preparing the Morland Affidavits I and II [38, 38A,
> 57], I did not purport to list every individual with whom I
> spoke or every piece of public information which I exam-
> ined.... As I indicated in the article:
>
>> People who make these weapons enjoy their work.
>> Like most of us, they enjoy talking shop. They
>> must also promote their activities in order to
>> raise funds from Congress and to recruit employees.
>> They learn to talk and write without using
>> classified words, but they can't live in a vacuum.
>
> ...It was a process of elimination based on what others
> told me.... I would constantly ask knowledgeable people
> whether the diagrams were accurate.... I read the public
> literature and talked to many people working in the field
> of nuclear weapons. If I have asked penetrating questions,
> any other person who wants to obtain such information for a
> foreign country and who is more qualified than I could ask
> better questions and obtain the answers much faster and
> with more precision than I did.

In answer [86] to the government's complaint alleging intent to cause grave harm to the United States, Morland denied the charges and noted that enforcement of the Atomic Energy Act has been

> non-existent, inconsistent and inequitable, thereby discriminating against this answering defendant in violation of his right to free speech and press, due process of law and equal protection of laws contrary to the First Amendment and Fifth Amendment to the Constitution of the United States.

Erwin Knoll [43].   The editor of The Progressive provided background information on the history of the magazine and its involvement in many societal issues, including the nuclear arms race. Because under the Atomic Energy Act the intent of a person who might divulge classified information is a significant legal factor, Knoll said explicitly:

> This affiant has no reason to believe that any information in the Morland article will be utilized to injure the United States or to secure an advantage to any foreign nation.

Samuel Day, Jr. [44].   The managing editor of The Progressive provided background information on his arrangements with DOE to tour "unclassified portions of some of the key facilities in the nuclear weapons production cycle," and recalled the events leading up to the filing of legal proceedings by the government (see Chapter I).   In addition, Day confirmed the statement of intent sworn to by Knoll.

Theodore A. Postol [45].   Postol's affidavit was introduced to represent the opinions of a physicist who had no weapons research exerience. Postol was one of the original group at Argonne National Laboratory that had technically reviewed the article.   He gave his opinion that it contained no information or ideas that were not already common knowledge among scientists, including those without access to classified information, and supported it by outlining some physical reasoning that could lead to some of Morland's conclusions.

After Postol's affidavit was written, it became clear that the government would not allow it to be filed publicly in its original form; consequently, it was partitioned into two parts, the second one to be submitted in camera. A clue to the origin of its sensitivity is found in this excerpt from the first part:

> It was my judgment at the time of reading the Morland article, and it is my judgment now, that the article contains no ideas or information which could not be readily concluded or obtained by any competent physicist after seeing the diagram prepared by Dr. Edward Teller for his article on the hydrogen bomb in the Encyclopedia Americana (Vol. 14, p. 655), attached hereto. Furthermore, the ideas and information contained in the Morland article would be arrived at not within years, but within hours.
> In my Affidavit No. II filed contemporaneously with this Affidavit, I demonstrate that a careful examination of the Edward Teller article in the Encyclopedia Americana would result in a physicist quickly coming to the same conclusion as did Morland....

Postol cautioned the court about excesses of secrecy, but pointed out that secrecy can have a useful role as an instrument of "technology denial" -- as a method for slowing the spread of potentially dangerous technologies.

His second affidavit [58], released in expurgated form not long after it was filed (and in total after the government dropped its case), was written "to discuss in rudimentary physics terms the analysis which a physicist would use to arrive at the conclusion in the Morland article." Starting with known information about yields of thermonuclear weapons, the established basic thermonuclear reactions, and the properties of possible fusion materials, Postol drew some then-classified conclusions (originally deleted) about the magnitude of the radiation pressure available from the fission trigger. Regarding the mechanism for energy release in nuclear reactions, he referred to estimates of energy density and internal weapons temperatures that are available in a widely available article by Harold L. Brode [BRO-68]. Postol's conclusions were deleted from the expurgated version of his affidavits, along with the specific page references to Brode and two college textbooks, but it would have been a simple matter for another physicist to deduce from the public record the concepts the government sought to suppress. In addition, although the page numbers had been removed from the references in the expurgated release of Postol's second affidavit, they were not removed from the identical set of references appended to his first affidavit --thereby highlighting the sensitive portions.

Postol said that "reference to the Encyclopedia Americana diagram supplied by Edward Teller" helped to "provide the information necessary to qualitatively understand some features of fusion ignition in thermonuclear weapons." Some parts of his discussion of Teller's diagram were also deleted, as well as some material for which, as we mentioned, the references were not deleted. Later we have more to say about the Teller diagram.

Postol concluded:

> The arguments here contained in no way indicate how one would go about...designing, engineering and constructing a successful thermonuclear weapon. Thermonuclear weapons are so complex and subtle in design that no nation-state which had not engaged in a program of extensive testing, in addition to development, can realistically be regarded as a thermonuclear state.

In its memorandum [59] opposing public filing of certain affidavits, the government said that Postol's second affidavit [58] disclosed the essential aspects of thermonuclear weapon design and attempted to quantify mathematically those aspects, resulting in public disclosure that

> would surely result in damage to the security of the United States.... Otherwise innocent references are used in a manner which clearly divulges the classified portion of an article [Morland's] which has already been confirmed as containing an accurate analysis of how the hydrogen bomb functions.

Seven other physicists -- representing a range of experience including work on the Manhattan Project and past or present employment at one of the weapons laboratories -- supported Postol's contentions about the deducibility of Morland's information in a series of depositions that were nearly identical to each other [Note IV-8].

Important testimony in support of the same point also came from Hugh Edgar DeWitt [Note IV-9], a theoretical physicist at Lawrence Livermore Laboratory, and from Ray E. Kidder [Note IV-10], a senior weapons physicist and associate division leader in the Theoretical Division of that same laboratory. Kidder claimed that "statements made in the affidavit of Jack W. Rosengren are misleading and, in part, factually in error."

Briefs by Friends of the Court

The American Civil Liberties Union was granted permission to submit a memorandum as amicus curiae, with emphasis on the constitutional issues. They argued [34] that the First Amendment prohibits prior restraints upon press except perhaps in extraordinarily limited and narrow circumstances; that the court needed independent expert testimony to assist it; and that, to the greatest extent possible, the proceedings should be conducted in public.

Regarding the first argument, the ACLU noted that in the Pentagon Papers dispute (New York Times), "the Supreme Court reaffirmed its strong commitment to the long-standing rule against prior restraints upon the press." However:

> The opinions in the New York Times case...leave open the possibility that the government can restrain the publication of a narrowly defined category of technical information whose publication would in fact "surely result in direct, immediate, and irreparable damage to the Nation or its people."

The ACLU argued that the "grave consequences asserted by the government in this case must be subjected to an exacting standard of proof in order to overcome the heavy presumption against prior restraints." They claimed that the government's affidavits were either "conclusory or speculative, or both," citing passages from the public affidavits of Van Doren, Pickering, Sewell, and Griffin. ("Conclusory" was used to mean "stating unsupported conclusions.")

To be explicit about what was not at issue, the ACLU noted that the case did not involve government employees, the acquiring of restricted data through unlawful means, or the applicability of criminal sanctions after publication. "Rather," they said, "this case raises the quite different question of whether the government can enjoin the press from publishing information it has lawfully acquired."

The ACLU said that the Atomic Energy Act "violates the First and Fifth Amendments, because the definition of prohibited information is dependent on the ad hoc judgment of the Executive Branch." The need for independent expert testimony was supported by the observation that "experience has shown that governmental claims in national security cases are often erroneous or exaggerated." One example cited was the Pentagon Papers, whose publication has failed to result in the "grave and immediate danger to the security of the United States" that the government predicted. Another example (Marchetti) was an injunction against a former CIA employee.

Regarding the need for independent expert witnesses, the ACLU noted that "the allegedly sensitive material in the article is probably unfamiliar to persons trained in the law." Consequently, consistent

with previous precedents involving "special masters," the court should
have obtained independent advice in evaluating the information and its
significance.

Affidavits by Friends of the Court

Kosta Tsipis [55]. Having read the article, Tsipis, an academic
physicist with publications in weapons science and technology, said in
an affidavit that, while the article did not contain "nearly enough to
permit another nation to develop and manufacture such a fusion device,"
the "total time necessary for another nation to arrive at a successful
device could be foreshortened by the information made available by the
article" [Note IV-11]. As mentioned in Hugh DeWitt's "Commentary"
elsewhere in this book, Tsipis also told how he had easily deduced the
secret concept of "radiation implosion" in 1973.

Gerald E. Marsh, George S. Stanford, and Alexander DeVolpi [62].
These three physicists had read and technically reviewed Morland's
article before the injunction was sought. They filed a declaration on
behalf of the ACLU. Although each had a Q-clearance, allowing access
to classified DOE information, none of them at the time had seen
classified data regarding thermonuclear weapons. The affiants had
research experience with fissionable materials and were familiar with
the open literature on atomic weapons and arms control. They made the
following recommendation:

> We support the position of the American Civil Liberties
> Union in urging the Court to appoint an independent panel
> of experts to determine whether publication of the article
> would surely result in direct, immediate, and irreparable
> damage to the nation and its people. Also, we are of the
> opinion that the Government should offer firm,
> substantiated proof by expert testimony that the Morland
> article contains vital information that could not be
> readily deduced by competent scientists or engineers from
> well-established, commonly understood physical principles
> combined with information already in the open literature,
> such as the article by E. Teller in the 1976 edition of the
> Encyclopedia Americana.... We draw attention especially to
> the highly suggestive diagrams appearing in Teller's
> article that have much similarity to those given by
> Morland.

> It is our opinion -- based on a study of the article,
> based on knowledge of related technology, and based on our
> understanding of the technical literature -- that an
> independent panel of technical experts may very well
> conclude that many competent scientists, in the United
> States or in foreign countries -- using public source
> documents, logical and inductive reasoning, and a universal
> base of common understanding of physical principles and
> technology applications --would probably arrive at
> conclusions at least as suggestive of thermonuclear weapon
> design and operation as those described by Morland.

Marsh, Stanford, and DeVolpi expressed support for proper and
authorized protection of information, resources, and facilities that
might be misused "to the detriment of national and international

security." At the same time, they observed, "World peace is best served by a pervasive, abiding, and vigilant public awareness of the operations and implications of institutional activities."

Alexander DeVolpi [63]. Having just made a study that led to a book on nuclear weapons proliferation [DEV-79], DeVolpi was in a good position to challenge government assertions that publication of Morland's article could measurably contribute to the proliferation problem. Addressing what turned out to be a major issue as the case moved through the courts, DeVolpi referred to possible ulterior motives behind the government's actions:

> The significance placed by the Government upon the vague information contained in Morland's article is open to question. Behind the Government's interpretation there is a possibility of political motivations. If the Government is relying primarily upon a shallow structure of secrecy and technological denial to resist proliferation, such a policy will be inadequate because the knowledge and techniques of weapons concepts are publicly available, as Morland has shown. There are more substantive technological and institutional commitments -- such as the reduction of national emphasis on nuclear armaments, the recycling of plutonium under safeguarded conditions, and the discontinuation of the testing of nuclear weapons -- that should be discussed in the public arena. Moreover, intelligent framing and consideration of these questions requires at least the level of conceptual knowledge that the Executive Branch seeks to forbid. To take issue with Government policy in the areas of arms control and proliferation is tantamount to taking issue with the Government's interpretation and selected release of information about underlying technologies.

DeVolpi commented that prevailing official weapons policy was likely to spur proliferation, and that some aspects of national defense policy were inconsistent with public safety [Note IV-12]. He noted that there were certain inconsistencies regarding proliferation potential in the government's case, along with some indiscretions. The point was made that more than enough information already exists in the public domain to satisfy the broad conceptual planning of thermonuclear weapon development. The key to slowing proliferation most effectively, he said, is a total ban on the testing of nuclear weapons.

DeVolpi concluded:

> In my opinion, open inquiry should not be entrained by government fiat simply because data, information, or ideas are not consistent with policies promoted by the Administration in office. The Courts should not allow incremental conscription of concepts that are born outside the pale of federal jurisdiction. There are other, less infringing methods of deterring proliferation than censorship of The Progressive. It is further my judgement, having read the Morland article and the petitions from the Departments of State and Defense, that publication would not directly, immediately, or irreparably jeopardize national efforts to impede proliferation or ensure security.

Reply by the Government

In response to the defendants' contentions, the government submitted several affidavits and a brief. The most renowned person to file a declaration was Nobel laureate Hans Bethe. He is former chairperson of a panel to evaluate foreign nuclear weapons technology, was responsible for theoretical development of fission weapons during the second World War, and is a consultant to the government in many matters dealing with nuclear arms and technology. He said [72] he was

> thoroughly familiar with the theory, design, and operation of thermonuclear weapons and with the state of knowledge in this area as it exists in the United States and numerous foreign nations.

Dr. Bethe went on to confirm for the government, as had so many other distinguished affiants, the article's sensitivity and general accuracy [Note IV-13]:

> Analysis of [Morland's affidavits] does not compel the derivation of all the essential principles of thermonuclear weapons set out in the Morland manuscript. The translation of publicly available information into the concepts and design information set out in the text and illustrated in the diagrams of the Morland manuscript would require extensive analysis and creativity.... It is my belief that public dissemination of the Morland manuscript would substantially hasten the development of thermonuclear weapon capabilities by nations not now having such capabilities.

A supplemental affidavit by Bethe [143], originally classified, said this about the article and The Progressive:

> the Morland Article if published would add a significant increment of knowledge to a country [interested] in pursuing thermonuclear weapon design....
>
> [A] scientist in a Third country will more likely pay attention to an article in a serious magazine like the Progressive, than one in the daily press. Most important, I believe, is that the Progressive is more likely to come to the attention of a group of scientists in a Third country; they are likely to scrutinize periodicals such as the Progressive especially since this periodical has previously written about atomic energy.

Bethe further explained his point of view in some side correspondence with Ray Kidder of Lawrence Livermore Laboratory, much of it still classified. In a letter of May 1, 1979, Kidder had maintained that the

> probability that the public articles to which I have drawn your attention would escape...a systematic literature search is nil.... The probability that an HSX [H-bomb study group in Nation X]...would fail to deduce the H-bomb secret upon carefully analyzing the contents of those articles when placed side by side is also nil.

Responding, Bethe wrote:

> I think you have correctly identified the source of our disagreement, namely whether the published articles accompanying your letter are considered independently, or collected together.

An affidavit by Harold W. Lewis [Note IV-14] claimed that Morland could not have derived his information from the open literature.

The government alleged in its public reply brief [66] that the Morland article posed "serious inescapable injury to the national security," that the requirements for a preliminary injunction under the Atomic Energy Act had been satisfied, that the showing of harm demonstrated by the United States satisfies any constitutional standard sought to be imposed by defendants, and finally that "it would be inconsistent with the appropriate scope of judicial review for the Court to appoint an independent panel to decide the questions raised in this case." Opposing the independent panel proposed by the ACLU, the government contended that the "principal dispute in this litigation is not factual but judgmental."

In reaction to The Progressive's claim that Morland's information came from the public domain, the government [Note IV-15] commented on the qualifications of The Progressive's witnesses:

> Defendants have attempted to counter the above showings [of weapons expert J. Rosengren] by filing with the Court several conclusory affidavits by affiants who are not, and do not profess to be, designers of thermonuclear weapons with a working knowledge of the Restricted Data that is at the core of this suit.... The defendants' efforts...to denigrate personal and careful consideration of four Cabinet-level Secretaries and the Acting Director of the Arms Control and Disarmament Agency are wide of the mark.

The government added in an in camera brief [141] that there was no need for the public to know technical details about thermonuclear weapons. An earlier classified brief [68] had tried to capitalize, somewhat out of context, on the statements by DeWitt and Tsipis that the Morland article could be of minor help to other countries.

Another Amicus Brief

The Fund for Open Information and Accountability, Inc., submitted a memorandum of law [80] as amicus curiae, based on extensive litigation experience "in dealing with problems of classification and secrecy relating to information and documents pertaining to atomic weapons and nuclear development." The Fund took issue with the claim that "scientific concepts and information in the nuclear field or in other fields have been or can be kept secret" [Note IV-16]. They cited the Rosenberg case as "a Tragic but Relevant Lesson." (There is a limited discussion of some aspects of the Rosenberg case in Chapter VI.) The Fund concluded:

> The fragile and unsupportable nature of the government's claims in this case compels it to use and exploit a doctrine of "born classified" as a means of creating "restricted data" where none exists, just as in the past, it invented and invoked all manner of doctrines and justifications to support claims of calamity and then hid and concealed the truth.

Decision of the Court, March 26

Judge Warren denied relief from the injunction [82]. He wrote that a
panel of experts would "merely proliferate the opinions of experts
arrayed on both sides of the issue." He acknowledged that "any prior
restraint on publication comes into court under a heavy presumption
against its constitutional validity," but stated, on the other hand,
that "First Amendment rights are not absolute. They are not
boundless." He indicated also that he was particularly impressed with
the affidavit of Nobel laureate Dr. Hans Bethe.

In his findings of fact [85], the judge, essentially quoting
Rosengren's affidavit, concluded that

> the article in question contains concepts that are not
> found in the public realm, concepts that are vital to the
> operation of the bomb.... Although various information in
> the public realm suggests a number of possible designs for
> a thermonuclear weapon, nowhere in the public domain is
> there a correct description of the type of design used in
> United States thermonuclear weapons.

The judge asked and answered a rhetorical question [82]:

> Does the article provide a "do-it-yourself" guide for the
> hydrogen bomb? Probably not. A number of affidavits make
> quite clear that a sine qua non to thermonuclear
> capability is a large, sophisticated industrial capability
> coupled with a coterie of imaginative, resourceful
> scientists and technicians. One does not build a hydrogen
> bomb in a basement. However, the article could possibly
> provide sufficient information to allow a medium size
> nation to move faster in developing a hydrogen weapon. It
> could provide a ticket to by-pass blind alleys.
>
> The point has also been made that it is only a question
> of time before other countries will have the hydrogen bomb.
> That may be true. However, there are times in the course
> of human history when time itself may be very important.
>
> Defendants have stated that publication of the article
> will alert the people of this country to the false illusion
> of security created by the government's futile efforts at
> secrecy.... However this Court can find no plausible
> reason why the public needs to know the technical details
> about hydrogen bomb construction to carry on an informed
> debate on this issue.
>
> The defendants have also relied on the decision in the
> New York Times case.... This case is different in
> several important respects.

He went on to agree entirely with the government that the Pentagon
Papers contained "historical" data and that their publication might
have caused "embarrassment" to the Government. The "vital difference"
between the two cases is that "a specific statute is involved here."
Regarding constitutionality, he found that "the statute in question is
not vague or overbroad." As for the applicability of the Atomic Energy
Act, he decided that "the defendants had reason to believe that the
data in the article, if published, would injure the United States or
give an advantage to a foreign nation." Finally, he concluded that

publication of the technical information on the hydrogen
bomb contained in the article is analogous to publication
of troop movements or locations in time of war and falls
within the extremely narrow exception to the rule against
prior restraint.
In his findings of fact and conclusions of law of May 15, submitted
to the United States Court of Appeals for the Seventh Circuit by agreement between the various attorneys as Supplemental Record (II) [120],
Judge Warren stated conclusions similar to ones he had reached
earlier:

> The Morland article contains text and schematic diagrams
> that correctly and specifically describe the operation and
> design of a thermonuclear weapon....
>
>   The Morland article contains Restricted Data that is not
> publicly available either in the literature or in
> unclassified conversations.... Although the Restricted
> Data portions of the Morland article also contain some
> information that has been previously disclosed in
> unconfirmed and scattered public sources, the article
> provides a more comprehensive, accurate, and detailed
> analysis of the overall construction and operation of a
> thermonuclear weapon than any publication to date in the
> public literature....
>
>   In view of the showing of harm made by the United
> States, a preliminary injunction would be warranted even in
> the absence of a statute authorizing it because of the
> existence of "direct, immediate, and irreparable injury to
> our nation [and] its people...."
>
>   Issuance of a preliminary injunction does not, and the
> ultimate issuance of a permanent injunction would not, in
> the circumstances presented here, violate defendants' First
> Amendment rights.

MOTION TO VACATE THE INJUNCTION

The government opposed having its in camera submissions available
to the defendants. This made it difficult for the legal staffs and
expert witnesses for The Progressive to prepare a knowledgeable
defense. The government asserted that its submissions were [109]

> substantially more sensitive than defendants' in that they
> provide official confirmation of certain concepts with
> respect to the design and construction of a nuclear weapon
> and discuss these concepts with much greater thoroughness,
> detail and accuracy.

A public affidavit [109A] by Jack Rosengren and William Grayson
discussed the sensitivity of government documents in the case filed at
that time in camera [Note IV-17]:

> The Government material is particularly sensitive because
> it includes authoritative weapon design information which
> can be recognized as such and sensitive intelligence
> information on possible proliferation of nuclear
> weapons....

The affidavit of Thomas R. Pickering of the State
Department contains sensitive information of a different
sort. Rather than weapon design data, he presents U.S.
intelligence information on potential proliferator nations.
This material is Secret, National Security Information.
Most of the errors in the Morland article and in the
defense affidavits are identified and discussed in the [in
camera] Rosengren-Grayson affidavits. This sensitive
discussion was necessary in order to address several
topics, including the difficulty of inferring weapon design
features from unclassified information. These
authoritative corrections make the Government material more
sensitive than that of the defendants. The Government
material contains basically the same concepts as does the
defendants' material but adds further important design
information and corrects significant errors.

In combination, the various classified Government
documents [filed in the case] present an important,
although limited, general description of U.S. thermonuclear
weapon designs....

Moot Because of Public Literature

The discovery of an assortment of relevant public literature, some
emanating from government weapons research, gave rise to revived
arguments that the material in Morland's article had been published
elsewhere [Note IV-18]. Among these documents was the extremely
sensitive weapons progress report UCRL-4725. This document, entitled
"Weapons Testing During June 1956," was discovered in the open shelves
at the Los Alamos library by Dimitri Rotow, a researcher for the ACLU
(see Chapter V).

An in camera motion [123] to reconsider was heavily censored,
although it is clear that the grounds for the motion were the
appearance of "some or all of the concepts...in the following journals,
periodicals and texts...." Aside from the mention of UCRL-4725 and
UCRL-5280 ("Weapons Testing During June 1958"), the names of the other
sources were deleted from the public version of the motion, despite the
fact that the references were to readily available publications. The
motion, which was supported by affidavits, continued with the
statement, "These documents show that the three concepts which the
Government seeks to suppress are already clearly stated in public
literature."

A defendants' memorandum [124] to Judge Warren observed that a
"[Seventh] Circuit Court [of Appeals] panel on May 24, 1979, said the
District Court had jurisdiction to consider the defendants' motion to
vacate" and, taking note of the public disclosures, "encouraged" a
hearing on the motion as quickly as possible [Note IV-19].

Gerald Marsh filed an affidavit [133] saying that he was in general
agreement with the district court's earlier observation that there is
"no plausible reason why the public needs to know the technical details
about hydrogen bomb construction to carry on an informed debate" on issues related to the production and use of nuclear weapons. However, he
believed that the court erred in finding that the Morland article contained such technical details, the conceptual principles being already

revealed in, or readily derivable from, information in the public domain. Supporting documentation for this assertion was censored.

Apart from the three critical concepts, which were then clearly in the public domain, Marsh said, the technical aspects of the Morland article were to a large degree confused; moreover, the article was in part conceptually in error. UCRL-4725, in striking contrast, subsumed everything accurate in the Morland article and accurately (certifiedly so) went far beyond it, both conceptually and technically.

He then listed some of the information found in UCRL-4725 that could be useful in designing or constructing a fusion weapon. The list was (properly) censored from the version released to the public. (The government countered [141] that the Morland article contains several concepts not present or so clearly described in UCRL-4725.)

In a declaration [134] that was largely censored, Alexander DeVolpi restated his conclusion that "the Morland concepts are clearly in the public domain," and contrasted the article with the sensitive data in UCRL-4725 [Note IV-20].

Theodore Taylor, one of the most experienced former designers of nuclear weapons, read a copy of UCRL-4725 and agreed [135] that it was very sensitive [Note IV-21].

On the other hand, Duane Sewell, head of the DOE branch that contains the atomic data classification office, did not let The Progressive's submittals sway him from his opinion [146] that the Morland article contained "Secret Restricted Data" [Note IV-22].

Warren's Decision [154] on Motion to Vacate, June 15

Judge Warren's memorandum and order of June 15 consisted of a one-page order denying the motion to vacate the preliminary injunction, and an in camera appendix that gave the substance behind his decision. The appendix has since been declassified. It appears to have been originally filed in camera in its entirety by the court because it mentions the name of one of the concepts (radiation coupling) still being litigated. Some appropriate passages are quoted here:

The Court is compelled to the conclusion that, from a legal point of view, the government's error in inadvertently declassifying UCRL 4725 and UCRL 5280 did not move these documents into the "public domain" and further, that there is no showing that the injunction became ineffectual.

At the time of the issuance of the preliminary injunction, the Court found that information was [publicly] available on possibly two of the key concepts [separate stages and compression]. However, the Court found that the concept of radiation coupling had not previously been revealed in the public literature and that the maintenance of the secrecy of this concept was so vital to the security of this nation that a preliminary injunction against the defendants was justified. ...the Court finds that the Milwaukee Sentinel articles, the Fusion magazine articles and other publications cited by the defendants are clearly dissimilar from the Morland article.... Only the Morland article contains a comprehensive, accurate and detailed analysis of all three concepts utilized in the construction of a thermonuclear weapon.

ARGUMENTS ON APPEAL

Both the preliminary injunction granted by Judge Warren and his later refusal to vacate it were appealed. The defendants were willing to go to the Supreme Court if necessary.

Briefs for The Progressive

On June 15, 1979, the appellants filed a brief [162] with the seventh District Court of Appeals in Chicago to "expedite consideration of their appeal." The motion was based on developments that occurred after the injunction was issued on March 26, namely the discovery that the government documents UCRL-4725 and -5280 had been publicly available at Los Alamos for long periods of time. The government, in fact, had stipulated that UCRL-5280 "reveals in a thermonuclear weapons context the three concepts which the government has described as the essential secret of the H-bomb."

The government requested of the court that the entire oral argument be conducted in camera. This was opposed by the defendants [163], who cited case law examples, including the Pentagon Papers case, in which the entire oral argument to the Supreme Court was ruled to be public. In camera alternatives of written submissions or "limited" argument were proposed.

Brief of Appellant, The Progressive [164]. In a booklet extensively expurgated by the government, the following case for appeal was made:

I. To determine whether the Government has overcome the heavy constitutional presumption against prior restraint, this Court must conduct an independent review of the record....

II. The information in the Morland article is not secret, it is already in the public domain, and there is no basis for prior restraint under the Atomic Energy Act or under any inherent power of the Executive Branch.

III. Even if true, the Government's affidavits do not meet the substantive standard for prior restraint under the first amendment, the most rigorous standard in the law.

A. The harm must be "virtually certain," "sure" or "inevitable," not "speculative." The Government did not meet this standard.

B. The harm must follow "directly and immediately" upon publication. The Government did not meet this standard.

C. The harm must be "grave" and "irreparable." The Government did not meet this standard.

D. Instead of strictly applying the New York Times standard, the district Court erroneously reached its decision based on what it thought the public "needs to know."

IV. The Government has failed to prove that publication of the Morland article would violate the Atomic Energy Act, a necessary but not a sufficient condition for an injunction.

A. The Government must meet not only the strict constitutional standard of the Pentagon Papers case but also the requirements of the Atomic Energy Act.

B. The Act does not prohibit publication of the Morland article.
    1. The Government has not shown that the article "will be utilized" to injure the United States or to secure an advantage to a foreign country.
    2. The defendants have no "reason to believe" the information in the article will be so used.
    3. The Act also requires a showing of bad faith, and the plaintiff cannot prove that here.
V. The construction of the Atomic Energy Act urged by the Government would render it unconstitutionally vague and overbroad under the first and fifth amendments.
A. Congress must legislate with precision when it attempts to regulate protected speech.
B. The Act's vagueness and overbreadth permit its improper application.
C. The Government's contention that the Act classifies information "at birth" demonstrates the dangers inherent in the Act.

Joint Brief of Appellants Knoll, Day and Morland [152]. This brief consisted of a public filing in which the editors of the Progressive were represented by Bruce Ennis, Mark Lynch, Charles Simms, and George Kannar of the ACLU, and Morland by T.P. Fox and Paul Friedman of the firm of White & Case. Before presenting the arguments, the brief provided a discussion of the statutes involved, a jurisdictional summary, and a statement of the case that described the defendants, the article and its genesis, the government's objections and claims, and the decision of the district court. The defendants took issue with Judge Warren's intercession in the editorial process:

The First Amendment does not permit a court to exercise its judgment as to what the press does or does not "need" to print in order to advance the author's or the publication's political views, or to balance its assessment of such "need" against the government's national security claim.

They argued that the government had not met the required tests of certainty, imminence, and gravity, and that the government had failed to show that the defendants had reason to believe that the article would "be utilized to injure the United States or to secure an advantage to any foreign nation." Also, constitutional questions of vagueness, overbreadth, and heavy burden of proof were raised. The brief contended it was the government's burden to shown that the central concepts described in the article were not in the public domain, and that an independent review was needed to answer that question.

Supplemental Brief of Appellant [165]. In July The Progressive filed a supplemental brief in appealing Judge Warren's June 15 order denying the motion to vacate the preliminary injunction. The salient points were that recent developments, including the UCRL-4725 revelation, had served to confirm that the "three secret concepts" were publicly available, that the government had shifted its legal position and generally been inconsistent, and, very important, that the

Government's refusal to furnish material evidence or to allow live testimony [with cross-examination] has obstructed defendants, led the District Court into

reversible error, and betrays its inability to meet the
extraordinary constitutional standard for prior restraint.

Briefs for the Appellee, the U.S. Government, August 7 [166]

The brief by the government opposing the arguments raised on appeal
commenced with an extensive review of the case, the law, and the facts.
It is here that the government raised for the first time the novel idea
that technical information does not enjoy First Amendment protection.
The contention was that "technical data" are not constitutionally
protected because they are not an "essential part of any exposition of
ideas" and are not of any "social value as a step to truth."
     Five major issues were covered [Note IV-23] : (1) publication of the
"Restricted Data" contained in the Morland article would violate the
Atomic Energy Act and, therefore, should be enjoined; (2) the
"Restricted Data" contained in the Morland article is not in the public
domain; (3) the civil injunctive provisions of the Atomic Energy Act
are constitutional; (4) the United States is entitled to a preliminary
injunction under the inherent power of the executive even in the
absence of statutory authorization; and (5) the district court properly
stayed discovery pending appeals and properly issued the injunction on
the basis of affidavits and argument.
     Under the third point, the government claimed:
     1. Where the asserted interest in speech is outweighed by
     the compelling nature of the Government's interest in its
     regulation, Congress may constitutionally authorize a prior
     restraint.
     2. The compelling public interest in prohibiting
     publication of nuclear weapons design data far exceeds any
     constitutional interest in publication of this dangerous
     technical information.

Reply Brief of the Appellant, August 28 [167]

The reply brief of the appellant, The Progressive, Inc., began with
Albert Einstein's 1947 statement, "We believe that an informed
citizenry will act for life and not death." It went on to comment on
the litigants' emotions:
     Fear is central to this case. And both the government and
     the defendants premise their case on it. The fear of the
     defendants is an historically cultivated concern for the
     excessive power and control of a monolithic, bureaucratic
     government over the thoughts, speech and freedom of
     individual citizens.
          The fear of the government, however, is a panic-filled,
     emotion-charged cry that the worst possible catastrophe in
     history might occur.
Six major claims were made [Note IV-24] :
     I. The Government proposes strange constitutional concepts
     which would emasculate the First Amendment.
     II. The Government cannot avoid its heavy burden of proving
     each of the categorical standards of harm under the New
     York Times case.

III. This is neither a Freedom of Information Act case nor a Government employee disclosure case, and such cases relied on by the Government do not apply.

IV. The Atomic Energy Act suffers from vagueness and overbreadth, which is compounded by the construction urged by the Government.

V. The District Court erred in refusing to permit discovery and live testimony in this critical First Amendment case.

VI. The Government ignores defendants' experts and other evidence as to the public availability of the three concepts.

Joint Reply Brief of Appellants, [169, 168]. In further reply to the government, a joint brief by Knoll, Day and Morland commenced with a summary analysis:

The government's brief represents a retreat from each of the positions it previously has taken in this case. In place of its arguments in the district court, it now urges desperate new theories of constitutional law and statutory construction which are without support and should be rejected by this Court.

The reply went on to argue that technical information was not exempt from First Amendment protection, that the injunction was neither authorized nor required by the Atomic Energy Act, that the government had not met its burden of proving that suppressing the Morland article would be effective in keeping the information in it from the public, and that the court had no discretion to deny a hearing with presentation of evidence and cross-examination [Note IV-25].

Regarding the issue of technical information, the appellants observed that there was a lack of precedent for exempting technical data from First Amendment protection, that technical data are essential to informed political and scientific debate and are not a new unprotected category of speech, and that the technical data in the article were relevant to public debates.

Affidavits for The Progressive

DeVolpi [134] reported on the probability of free access to declassified reports UCRL-4725 and UCRL-5280 at the public library of Los Alamos. From personal experience he was able to say that foreign nationals from advanced nonnuclear-weapons states who attended a meeting in the library building could easily have walked through the open doors of the library downstairs and read or copied those reports (see Chapter V).

Much of an affidavit [133] by Marsh was protected from public disclosure by court order because it contained a comparison of the Morland article with articles published in the Milwaukee Sentinel and other newspapers and magazines, as well as a previously mentioned detailed comparison with UCRL-4725. Marsh addressed the proliferation-risk implications of the Morland article and UCRL-4725 [Note IV-26].

Briefs and Affidavits by Amici Curiae

From the media came several friend-of-the-court briefs that turned out also to be friend-of-The-Progressive. The Chicago Tribune and two groups supporting the First Amendment [172] objected to the lack of an evidentiary hearing and the absence of testimony from the experts for The Progressive, observing that "On the Progressive's behalf, eleven nuclear physicists filed affidavits and in substance concur with Morland's public domain conclusion."

The Committee for Public Justice et al. [173], a group of organizations supporting the rights of authors, said that information about nuclear weapons would

give citizens the sense that they are capable of understanding how nuclear weapon development affects their lives, and they do not have to abdicate responsibility to bureaucrats and technicians who operate behind closed doors.

The Committee for Public Justice brief provided a detailed breakdown of the Pentagon Papers decision, dissecting the application in this case of the qualifiers "surely, direct, immediate, grave, and irreparable." They also took issue with the conduct of the national-security secrecy system and the concept of an original work product being born classified [Note IV-27].

Scientific American magazine, in a supporting brief [175], concentrated on First Amendment issues, emphasizing that the "process [for prior restraint] is itself a system of prior restraint," giving examples from its own publication history.

The New York Times Co., some other newspapers, and their associations submitted legal arguments [176] emphasizing the Pentagon Papers (New York Times) case. They noted that

the willingness of the District Court to accept a less than adequate showing of potential injury is reflected in its misstatement of Justice Stewart's New York Times test. The Court misquoted the test as requiring the "likelihood of direct, immediate, and irreparable injury to our nation...[and] its people."

A variety of magazine interests together (The Nation et al. [174]) asserted that "the independent periodical press do indeed support The Progressive in this case and are deeply distressed by the censorship imposed by the District Court." They were alarmed about the broad sweep of the statutes applying to virtually "all public discussion on the issues of nuclear energy and nuclear weaponry," except what was declassified by the government.

Because of its involvement in promoting thermonuclear research for peaceful applications, the Fusion Energy Foundation [170,171] entered its opinion that further development of atomic energy (both fission and fusion) were "being stifled by an overly restrictive and misguided application of classification procedures." A particular example given was the classification of fusion-target designs that "makes the engineering studies for commercial application of fusion almost impossible." The Foundation's public brief included a discussion of at least two of the concepts, or features of them, that the government sought to suppress. It also contained a history of American censorship of the statements and lectures of a prominent Russian physicist when he visited this country.

SUMMARY OF LEGAL ISSUES

In filing its civil action against The Progressive, the government held that it had the right to restrain publication under the "born classified" interpretation of the Atomic Energy Act. It maintained that it did not have to meet the standards for prior restraint set by the Supreme Court decision in the Pentagon Papers case because litigation was being brought under a statute that specifically authorizes injunctive relief. Nevertheless the government also argued that it could meet those standards anyway, since publication would result in "grave, direct, immediate and irreparable harm to the national security of the United States and its people."

The defendants, on the other hand, argued that the government did indeed have to meet the Pentagon Papers standards. They held, further, that even if the Atomic Energy Act did allow an injunction, it would have to be declared unconstitutional in two respects. First, the Act would authorize an injunction even in circumstances that did not meet the standards set in the Pentagon Papers case. And second, it was impermissibly vague and overbroad, not only with respect to an injunction, but also in terms of due process.

Two additional issues appeared on appeal. The government maintained that technical information does not enjoy constitutional protection, and the defendants argued that the information contained in the Morland article -- in particular, each of the three concepts that appear to be central principles in the design of megaton, multistage H-bombs -- was to be found in the public domain.

5 Technical Discussion

The conflict over Morland's article raised questions relevant to constitutional law, foreign policy, diplomatic strategy, national security, science policy, and freedom of scientific inquiry. There were differences in technical judgment by experienced scientists inside and outside the weapons program. Complicating the situation further, affiants with diverse technical and professional experience were being called upon to make judgements outside their areas of expertise.

Energy and State Department personnel, as well as cabinet-level officials whose main experience was in policy, submitted sworn testimony that made sweeping technical assertions. Some affidavits on both sides were written by people with little or no weapons experience. Those statements were often expanded upon or responded to by experienced weapons physicists (both for and against the injunction) some of whom may have had little familiarity with the open literature, but who were called upon to assess the availability of information from public sources. As is not surprising, there were many erroneous claims, and questionable declarations made by affiants, legal counsels, and, disturbingly, by the court itself.

A number of frightening assertions were made by the government and its affiants (Chapter IV), claiming that the Morland article contained information that would substantially aid national or subnational organizations in constructing thermonuclear weapons. The defendants and their affiants disagreed.

One issue was whether the article would help an organization with the industrial means to construct a thermonuclear weapon. Did such entities already have access to the information? Certain officials in the cabinet or State Department might have been surprised by the contents of the Morland article, but that was not proof that the information had been unavailable to scientists and engineers the world over.

The government's main objections were that the article discussed "essential principles of the operation of the hydrogen bomb" [8] and "basic concepts underlying the design and operation of thermonuclear weapons, as well as the manner in which these concepts are applied" [9]. Early in the case, certain filings [45,52A,56,74A,75A] tried to show that the conceptual and detailed information regarded as sensitive

82

by the government could be deduced by careful scrutiny of the public literature. This chapter reviews some of the considerations underlying that issue. We shall give relevant scientific background, mention some of the unclassified sources of information, and outline the scientific reasoning that was classified by the government.

FISSION VERSUS FUSION

For the nontechnical reader we start with some background information on the difference between fission and fusion, as applied to weapons. Because explosive yield, complexity, and implications differ substantially between A-bombs and H-bombs, it is important for the coming discussion to recognize the underlying principles and terminology. (A glossary at the back of the book defines some of the technical terms.)

Fission

When an atom undergoes fission, its major constituent, the nucleus, is broken into two smaller nuclei called fission fragments. Fission is often triggered when a neutron enters the nucleus of certain susceptible atoms. Only the "heavy" elements, such as uranium or plutonium, are useful for this purpose, and some species (isotopes) of those elements are more prone than others to having fission induced. Along with the fission fragments, other radiation is given off, including gamma rays and additional neutrons. The most fission-prone isotopes are said to be "fissile."

In the process of breaking up, considerable energy is released -- "nuclear" energy -- in several forms. The very high temperatures result mainly from the kinetic energy of the fission fragments, associated with their speed: The energy they lose as they are slowed down from high velocity shows up as heat. The rest of the fission energy is in the other forms of nuclear radiation that are liberated when the atom splits.

More neutrons are released than are needed to cause the fission event, which means that a chain reaction can be started. With the right arrangement, the extra neutrons expelled will cause fissions in nearby fissile atoms, and the rate of fissioning grows exponentially. This process, under favorable conditions, will continue until the adjacent fissile material is exhausted or until other limitations take effect.

As early as the 1930s, scientists anticipated that this chain reaction process could be applied to produce a large amount of nuclear energy from uranium under the right conditions. The self-sustaining nuclear reaction might be used either for a controlled release of energy that would produce heat to create steam, or for an uncontrolled burst that would constitute a destructive explosion. Both of these prospects were confirmed in the early 1940s.

The isotopes that have turned out to be of most interest are uranium-233, uranium-235, and plutonium-239. (The isotope is identified by the numerical suffix, which is the number of "nucleons" -- protons plus neutrons -- in the nucleus.) Uranium-235 occurs in nature, but only as a small fraction (0.7 percent) of natural uranium.

The other two isotopes are manufactured as by-products in fission reactors. Unless there is a sufficient combination of these isotopes (or appropriate substitute materials), the chain reaction will die off before producing much energy. Thus a minimum amount of material is required: this is called the "critical mass." A "subcritical" mass will not support a self-sustaining chain reaction; a "supercritical" mass is more than sufficient.

An unrestricted chain reaction releases a great deal of energy in a very short time -- which is to say that there is a nuclear explosion. It is the task of the weapons designer to develop a configuration of fissile material that will be safe while stored but will explode when desired (in contrast to a nuclear power reactor, whose core is incapable of exploding).

Fusion

Fusion is another process that produces energy. In this case, two light nuclei, isotopes of hydrogen, are caused to collide with each other. The hydrogen isotopes most suitable for this process are deuterium and tritium. When these two isotopes "fuse" together, the result is a release of energy and radiation. Some of the radiation consists of fast neutrons, whose role is discussed below.

Because all nuclei have a positive electrical charge, they repel each other. In order for fusion to occur, the nuclei must approach each other at speeds great enough to overcome the repulsive electrical forces, and this will happen only at very high temperatures. That is why the fusion process is called "thermonuclear."

Fusion is a more difficult process than fission to start and propagate, because of the high temperatures required -- temperatures comparable to those in stars (or in nuclear fission explosions). Also, deuterium and tritium can only be produced in highly specialized facilities.

To recapitulate, a controlled fission reaction can be generated with natural materials, starting at room temperature. A fission explosion requires special isotopes carefully arranged in a weapons configuration. A fusion explosive must have special isotopes of a different kind, and is much more complex to design and build. The materials and the processes for H-bombs are not at all like those for A-bombs.

TYPES OF NUCLEAR WEAPONS

There are at least three basic types of nuclear weapons: those that derive their explosive power from fission alone (called fission weapons or A-bombs), those that mainly use fission but have their efficiency enhanced by fusion reactions (fusion-boosted fission), and those that fully exploit a combination of fusion and fission, deriving large amounts of explosive power from both processes (multistage thermonuclear weapons, or H-bombs). In general, the pure fission weapons are the least powerful, fusion-boosted come next, and the H-bombs have the largest yields of all. Conceptual diagrams of the three different types of weapons are in Figure 1.

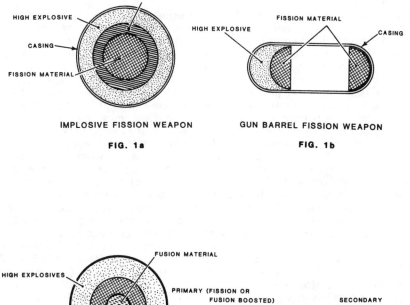

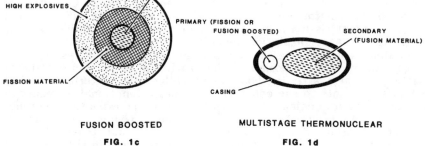

Fig. 1. Design configurations of four types of nuclear weapons:
(a) implosion A-bomb; (b) gun-barrel A-bomb;
(c) fusion-boosted A-bomb; (d) multistage H-bomb.

The explosive energy (yield) of a nuclear weapon is usually expressed in kilotons or megatons. A kiloton is the amount of energy liberated in the explosion of 1,000 tons of TNT (4 terajoules), and a megaton is a thousand times as large. The fission bombs that destroyed Hiroshima and Nagasaki had estimated explosive yields of 13 kilotons (0.013 megatons) and 22 kilotons, respectively. Together those two weapons killed more than 150,000 people. Typical fusion-boosted weapons yield hundreds of kilotons (tenths of megatons), and typical multistage weapons yield megatons.

Fission Weapons

Because fission reactions do not require unusually high temperatures or densities, all that is necessary for an explosion is to "assemble" a critical mass of fissionable material rapidly enough to allow an uncontrolled chain reaction to develop. This is done with chemical explosives that either implode a spherical subcritical mass of fission material (as depicted in Fig. 1a) or else drive two subcritical sections together in a gun-barrel type of arrangement (Fig. 1b).

An important technical detail about A-bombs is that once the mass is critical or supercritical, the chain reaction may be started by injecting some neutrons -- and for optimum yield the injection must be done at just the right time as the fissile material approaches its critical configuration. In particular, if there are too many neutrons around too soon the bomb may be triggered prematurely (predetonate) and "fizzle" (yield only a fraction of its potential). The implosion technique was developed to counter the predetonation tendency of plutonium bombs, which inherently have a high neutron background. The poorer the quality of the plutonium, the worse the predetonation problem, and the more painstaking the bomb design becomes.

According to a former director of the Livermore weapons laboratory [YORK-76], fission weapons have been tested up to approximately 500 kT (the King shot of Operation IVY in November 1952). Calculations promoted by and performed by Theodore Taylor apparently indicated that "very efficient fission bombs in the megaton class could be made by adopting the latest implosion techniques."

Fission weapons were the outcome of the United States' massive three-year Manhattan Project during World War II. It is not a simple matter to design a fission bomb or to collect the materials, despite public statements to the contrary. The basic functional elements of the technology of nuclear weapons may be broken down into five groups [DEV-79] [M&M-80]: (1) casing -- electronics, arming, and fusing; (2) detonating system; (3) high-explosive system; (4) nuclear assembly; and (5) initiator. The first three groups are largely within the bounds of conventional arms technology. These categories apply specifically to fission devices, which also serve as triggers for fusion weapons. Similar categorization may be applied to fusion weapons, if one views the fission trigger as the "initiator" of the thermonuclear explosion.

Part of the nuclear assembly is the tamper. In explosives technology, a tamper is a common means of confining an energy buildup until it reaches explosive proportions. The reflector (which may also be the tamper) in nuclear bombs helps to trap radiation within the casing.

The initiator is employed to start a fission chain reaction at a precise moment after the critical mass is compacted by the detonation of a chemical high explosive. The timing of initiation must be correct to within a thousandth of a second or less, depending on the type of weapon and its fissile material; otherwise, as was mentioned, the explosive yield will be less than expected -- perhaps much less.

The interested reader may obtain considerably more information on the subject of fission weapons by consulting Proliferation, Plutonium and Policy [DEV-79] and the references cited therein. The information on fusion weapons that follows is gleaned from various publications cited during the Progressive case.

Fusion Weapons

Fusion devices (fusion-boosted and multistage) comprise one component of the superpowers' strategic arsenals. It was the prospect of higher yields and efficiencies that drove Edward Teller, "father of the H-bomb," to push for development of large thermonuclear weapons [B&O-76].

Fusion boosting. York [YORK-76] describes the early investigation of how to work fusion energy into atomic weapons:

In the spring of 1946, a group...at Los Alamos...again took up the study of how thermonuclear reactions might be produced on the earth. This study soon branched along two quite distinct lines with very different objectives. One such line of research had the comparatively easy objective of igniting a relatively small mass of thermonuclear fuel by means of the energy produced in a relatively large fission explosion.... The United States successfully accomplished this objective in 1951, and the Soviet Union did so in 1953. This particular objective later became important in connection with a process known as "boosting" or the "booster principle." These terms "refer to the notion of using a fission bomb to initiate a small thermonuclear reaction with the possibility that...the neutrons from this reaction might increase the efficiency of the fissile material." This meant that in certain circumstances there can be a synergistic interaction between fission and fusion reactions that can substantially increase the efficiency of the fission reaction.

In a fusion-boosted warhead, when the sphere is compressed (imploded) by the chemical explosion, an uncontrolled chain reaction begins. The fissionable material rapidly (in tenths of a millionth of a second) gets as hot as the center of the sun. If there is fusionable material inside the device (see Fig. 1c), fusion will occur.

Because fission reactions need neutrons and because neutrons are an incidental by-product of fusion reactions, it is possible to use the neutrons from a fusion burn to enhance a fission rate. Very high temperatures occur in the fission process, and, because a fission chain reaction can be started without unusual temperatures, it can be used to ignite a fusion reaction. The neutrons from fusion have much more energy than those from fission. When fusion neutrons are used to cause fission in heavy nuclei, it happens that those nuclei give off more neutrons when they split than they would if struck by the slower neutrons from other fissioning nuclei, and thus the chain multiplies more rapidly. This leads to even higher temperatures, causing fusion reactions to occur still more rapidly, which in turn introduces fusion neutrons into the fissioning material at a faster rate. A bomb that uses this synergistic process is more efficient than a pure fission device, because more of the fissionable nuclei will split before the device comes apart ("disassembles") in the nuclear or thermonuclear explosion.

This type of weapon is called "fusion-boosted" because the fusion reactions do not contribute very much to the explosive energy, but instead enhance the fission rate, as York has pointed out. Fusion-boosted weapons are militarily more desirable than pure fission weapons because they are generally lighter, more efficient, and more powerful.

H-bombs. Multistage thermonuclear weapons are conceptually quite different from fission and fusion-boosted bombs. They contain three essential components, which are physically separated from each other (Fig. 1d). One of the components is a small fission or fusion-boosted weapon called a "primary" or "trigger." Separated from the primary is an assembly of lithium deuteride fusion material called the "secondary." Surrounding the primary and secondary is the third major component, a massive casing. Before thermonuclear ignition, neutrons from the exploding primary convert the lithium deuteride in the secondary to a mixture of deuterium and tritium. The following passage describing the fusion process is from a declassified letter from Ray E. Kidder to Congressman Paul N. McCloskey (September 26, 1980):

> In thermonuclear weapons, radiation from a fission explosive can be contained and used to transfer energy to compress and ignite a physically separate component containing thermonuclear fuel.

The fission triggers are themselves highly sophisticated, efficient nuclear explosive devices. As for materials, the type, chemical form, isotopic content, density, and geometrical arrangement are important. Precision is needed in fabricating the fissile core, tamper, reflector, high explosive, and casing. Clearly, complicated technologies are involved, substantial resources must be invested, and -- most important -- extensive testing of nuclear explosives must be undertaken for optimization. Once a country's weapons program had taken those steps, it would have a device capable of triggering a thermonuclear reaction in an H-bomb's secondary system.

When detonation of an H-bomb is initiated, the exploding trigger -- which could be a fusion-boosted fission device -- emits a great deal of energy as photons, in what physicists call "black-body radiation." At the temperatures present (about 50 million degrees Centigrade), much of that energy is in the "soft x-ray" region (wavelength shorter than that of light). In a fraction of a millionth of a second, the photons fill the inside of the casing like microwaves in a microwave oven. They travel hundreds of times faster than the material portions of the exploding primary and other parts of the bomb. The casing behaves at first like a bottle, for a time keeping the energy confined. There is so much energy that very large compressive forces are exerted on the secondary, balanced by expansive forces on the casing, while the primary disassembles. Because the casing is massive relative to the fusion package, it moves slowly compared with the rate of compression of the fusion materials. Soon those materials reach densities and temperatures where thermonuclear ignition occurs, liberating many times more energy than came originally from the trigger.

Neutrons from the thermonuclear reactions escape in large numbers from the fusing materials and strike the nuclei in the casing. If the massive casing is made of natural uranium, the fusion neutrons will cause uranium nuclei to undergo fission, giving off still more energy. A device of this sort can be regarded as a three-stage "fission-fusion-fission" bomb.

The preceding discussion does not necessarily include every step in the process an H-bomb goes through when it explodes. It is our intention to provide enough conceptual information to permit the rest of this book's material to be understood, not to give a complete, correct description of the H-bomb.

The chemical explosives that are used to implode fission weapons do not have the power to compress very large amounts of fissionable material quickly enough that a substantial number of fission reactions can take place before the bomb blows itself apart. Hence fission or fusion-boosted weapons cannot be made indefinitely large. But the multistage fusion weapons are another story -- the largest to be exploded so far was a 58-megaton bomb set off by the Soviet Union over Siberia in the days when atmospheric testing was still going on. It would reportedly have produced a 100-megaton blast had not the element lead been substituted for uranium-238 in the casing, to reduce the fallout.

Thus the main feature of H-bombs, those weapons of mass destruction, is their immense explosive yield. At the same time they are far more complex than the fission weapon or the booster type of fusion weapon, which makes them far less likely to proliferate -- an important point, considering the fears that Morland's article would lead other nations or even subnational terrorists to assemble their own.

THE IDEAS IN MORLAND'S ARTICLE

Morland's "The H-Bomb Secret" deals mainly with the big, multistage bombs. In moving to suppress the article, the government was trying to keep under wraps three concepts that are basic to that type of weapon. The joint reply brief [169] of Knoll, Day, and Morland, which was originally filed in camera and has since been declassified, lists those concepts as "separate stages," "radiation coupling," and "compression." The government alleged that revelation of those ideas would substantially enhance the possibilities that multistage thermonuclear weapons would proliferate.

Separate stages has already been explained. The government asserted that the idea of spatial separation of trigger and fusion material within a casing was a critical and valuable piece of information that was not available from open sources. This turned out to be untrue, since diagrams showing similar configurations can be found in encyclopedia articles over the names of Hans Bethe and Edward Teller, two of the United States' most prominent physicists with extensive weapons experience. (The government required that reference to the Teller encyclopedia article be deleted from the public version of Morland's affidavit [38].)

We have also discussed radiation coupling. According to claims made in the legal proceedings, the radiation-coupling concept was revealed by any statement that electromagnetic radiation from the fission trigger was the means by which energy was transferred from the trigger to the fusion package. Of particular sensitivity was the recognition that soft x-rays, specifically, were the transporting medium.

The third idea the government wanted to suppress had to do with the fact that compression is necessary for the fusion reactions to proceed as vigorously as is needed in a thermonuclear weapon -- that it is not enough just to heat the fusion material. It appears unlikely that compression itself was the sensitive concept, as any student of chemistry knows that reactions in dense media proceed more rapidly than when the reactants are dilute. What probably concerned the government more was how the compression could be accomplished by radiation from the primary -- the means of coupling.

The ideas that we have been discussing were formulated as "three concepts" for legal convenience in the Progressive case. A competent physicist attempting to explain how a multistage thermonuclear configuration works (knowing that it does work) would be unlikely to think of compression and radiation coupling as distinct or separable phenomena. Thermal radiation and compression, which play a central role in the process of detonation, are phenomena that are natural consequences of the extreme environment within a nuclear explosion. Those "concepts" would be no more separable than several others that could result from analyzing the operation of such weapons.

The specific parts of Morland's article that were objectionable to the government could not all be identified publicly during the case without use of classified information, but they could be determined with a high probability by comparing the article with statements in affidavits and briefs. Some of Morland's assertions (Appendix A) that appear to contain technical information related to the three concepts are summarized below. Note, by the way, that not all of these statements are necessarily correct [95].

> The secret is in the coupling mechanism that enables an ordinary fission bomb.... The physical pressure and heat generated by x- and gamma radiation, moving outward from the trigger at the speed of light, bounces against the weapon's inner wall and is reflected with enormous force into the sides of a carrot-shaped "pencil" which contains the fusion fuel....

> The diagrams that accompany this article are a close approximation [to] the progression of events that occur during the detonation of a hydrogen weapon. The energy of an exploding fission bomb, the circular object near the top of each drawing, is transferred by means of radiation pressure to the hydrogen part of the weapon. Radiation pressure -- a term never mentioned in the open literature -- is the essence of what remains of the H-bomb secret....

Morland identifies the physical separation of the weapon stages as an additional central concept, noting the position of the primary system "inside one end of a three- or four-foot-long hollow cylinder casing," with the fusion fuel "located inside the other end." He adds that the cylinder is "normally eighteen inches in diameter, large enough to contain the soccer-ball-sized primary system inside one end and leave a few inches to spare around the sides." Morland describes the fusion component as a "charge of lithium-6 deuteride" that "makes a [tapered] column one or two feet high and several inches in diameter."

Morland proceeds to consider the role of the cylindrical casing as a "radiation reflector," and throughout his paper there are interpretations of the functional elements shown in his diagrams (also in Appendix A).

Further elaboration on the use of radiation pressure as a means of coupling the primary energy to generate the fusion burn are found in phrases or sentences such as these: "source of the radiation pressure," "x- and gamma radiation...is the only thing fast enough and manageable enough to be harnessed [for causing fusion in time]," "the radiant energy of the primary system will have time to race ahead of the expanding nuclear debris and reach the fusion fuel first," and "Its radiant energy can exert enormous force on an object only inches away."

His recognition of compression as a principle element in the process is amplified in the following quotations: "A fission bomb is the only force on Earth powerful enough to provide the compression and heat needed to detonate a fusion bomb," "Without tremendous compression, the fusion fuel would not fuse fast enough," and "fuel in a weapon must...be compressed before it reaches ignition temperature."

In addition to the three basic concepts in the article, numerous unrelated pieces of information were considered sensitive by the government. Such information was frequently excised by the government from public versions of affidavits.

DEDUCIBILITY OF MORLAND'S IDEAS

As we have said, the government's main arguments against publication of the Morland article were that it contained three sensitive concepts -- ideas that were classified "Secret Restricted Data" by DOE under provisions of the Atomic Energy Act of 1954. Of great concern were the diagrams in the article. The illustrated sequence not only had the weapons components separated within a casing, but also showed that radiation from the trigger was responsible for the initial compression of the fusion material in the secondary. Much was made of the fact that the diagrams, although obviously conceptual, contained many detailed speculations that the government considered sensitive.

One of the first affidavits to be filed on behalf of The Progressive by a scientist [45] claimed that all the relevant information contained in the Morland article was derivable, if one assumed that high-yield thermonuclear weapons contained a separated primary and secondary within a casing. That claim became the focus of arguments and counterarguments among opposing expert witnesses.

The discussion in that affidavit was built heavily on a diagram of a multistage weapon published in the 1974 edition (and later ones) of the Encyclopedia Americana [TEL-74] (see diagrams in Fig. 2). The author of the article, Edward Teller, is famous for his leading role in the American H-bomb project. Morland's diagrams, although conceptual, appear to contain considerably more information than the less detailed Teller diagrams. But do they? We shall show that the information in the Morland article is scarcely more significant than the Teller diagram, in the sense that everything in Morland's work can be deduced from the Teller diagram or is incorrect or irrelevent, or speculative in the sense that a large experimental program would be needed for verification.

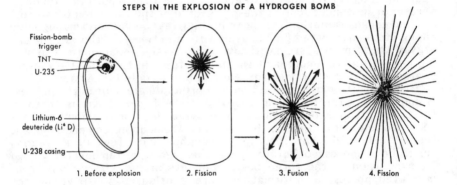

STEPS IN THE EXPLOSION OF A HYDROGEN BOMB

Fission-bomb trigger
TNT
U-235

Lithium-6 deuteride (Li⁶ D)

U-238 casing

1. Before explosion   2. Fission   3. Fusion   4. Fission

1. A fission bomb is used to ignite the thermonuclear explosion. 2. Detonation of TNT compresses the U-235, and causes it to undergo fission; neutrons are released and the temperature rises to millions of degrees Celsius. 3. The neutrons hit lithium nuclei, transforming them to helium and tritium, and the tritium fuses with the deuterium in the Li^6D, producing more neutrons. 4. Some neutrons strike the casing, causing it to undergo fission.

Fig. 2.   Encyclopedia Americana version of H-bomb conceptual design. © Encyclopedia Americana. Caption and figure published with permission.

Implications of the Teller Diagram

In order to support such a seemingly far-fetched assertion, we need to go into the scientific background somewhat. Although there were arguments between various weapons physicists over supposed inaccuracies or oversights in the original affidavit [45], there is little doubt, at this point, that the claim was scientifically defensible in most, if not all, essential points -- that is to say, the Teller diagram alone, combined with elementary scientific knowledge, could be used to produce one possible design of a multistage thermonuclear weapon at least as accurate as Morland's. The amount of scientifically useful information that could be derived from either the Teller or Morland diagrams was comparable.

The detail, correct or not, in the Morland diagrams was the subject of much discussion in both classified and public affidavits. The issue that the court had to decide was whether the article really contained information that was not in the public domain and would materially help an H-bomb design project, as the government asserted, or whether the information was basically straightforward deduction and unconfirmed speculation based on publicly available information. Morland, for instance, showed a primary that contained a core of fusion material surrounded by concentric spheres of two different types of fission materials -- a plutonium-239 inner shell surrounded by an outer shell of uranium-235. These shells were, in turn, surrounded by another pair of concentric shells of uranium-238 and beryllium. The primary in the Teller diagram on the other hand, was merely a sphere of fission material sitting nonconcentrically in a slightly distorted shell of high-explosive material. To the uninformed layman, the detail in the Morland diagram would therefore appear to be far more revelatory than that contained in the Teller diagram. Not so!

The primary. As was explained in the preceding section on types of nuclear weapons, fusion-boosted weapons derive most of their energy from fission but are made more efficient by introducing fusion material into the fission weapon. Morland's speculative depiction of fusion material surrounded by fission material is therefore his conception of the well-known fusion-boosted arrangement. Since fusion boosting was no secret, it is immaterial that the Teller primary is not presented in enough detail to indicate whether it is fusion boosted.

Morland depicts the fission material as concentric spheres of uranium-235 and plutonium-239. An arrangement of two types of fission material is plausible, but there is no reason to think that it is essential for the operation of any nuclear device, be it fission, fusion-boosted, or multistage fusion. Such an approach is of no conceptual value to a would-be weapon maker.

Surrounding Morland's shell of fissionable materials is an empty space, followed by a shell of uranium-238 and then one of beryllium. The composite uranium-beryllium shell, according to Morland, is explosively driven inward toward the fissionable materials. The purpose of the space, he said, is to allow the massive shell to gain momentum before it hits the fission materials it surrounds. His explanation as to why such an arrangement might be chosen is correct, but is it a new or surprising idea that could be expected to aid weapons designers? The technique of explosively accelerating a block of material until it hits another piece of material in order to multiply (by factors of thousands) the intensity of a compressive shock is a standard technique in the study of the physics of materials at high pressures. Theodore Taylor made the concept intuitively obvious in John McPhee's The Curve of Binding Energy [MCP-75]:

> [Taylor] said there was something about the structure of implosion bombs that he had not gone into, and that he could not go into, which contributed greatly to their yield... "All I can say is this: They had known all along that the way to get more energy into the middle was to hit the core harder. When you hammer on a nail, what do you do? Do you put the hammer on the nail and push?"

Morland's insight that a more effective implosion can be achieved by separating the shells of material is scientifically sound. This speculation, however, could not provide any would-be bomb builders with insights they would not otherwise have.

Some of the detail in Morland's conception of a primary in a multistage fusion weapon might correspond to what is actually done in U.S. weapons, and some might not. In any event, there are no useful ideas that were not already available elsewhere. This is of course also true of the Teller representation of a primary.

The secondary. The fusion secondaries contained in both the Morland and Teller diagrams also differ from each other. Teller's diagram has only a prolate spheroid of lithium-6 deuteride, while Morland's shows more detail. An analysis of these differences will first require a few more comments on the nature of fusion.

The densities of fusion materials like lithium-6 deuteride, lithium-6 tritide, tritium, and deuterium in their normal state (that is, as they would exist at room temperature and pressure) are well known. It can be shown, using elementary nuclear physics and statistical mechanics, that fusion reactions in these materials cannot proceed rapidly enough to give a thermonuclear explosion unless two important conditions are satisfied: The materials must be compressed, and they must be heated to millions of degrees.

The high temperature means that the atoms will be traveling at great speed. Thermonuclear "ignition" and "burn" will occur only if the energy released by the thermonuclear reactions exceeds what will simultaneously be pouring out of the system in the form of light and heat. If the nuclei are traveling fast enough when they encounter each other, they will come very close in spite of the electrical forces that normally keep them separated, and nuclear reactions can take place. The density must be high so that the atoms will be crowded and no nucleus will have to move very far before there is a collision.

The H-bomb secret was not that high temperatures and pressures are needed; the secret was how to create those conditions.

The role of radiation. The idea that radiation plays a coupling role is contained in both the Teller and Morland diagrams. It follows from the spatial arrangement of fission (or fusion-boosted) trigger, fusion secondary, and casing. The spatial separation is clearly shown in the Teller (and Morland) diagrams and is, by deduction from government affidavits, part of the Teller-Ulam idea (see below). We emphasize that this configuration is by no means a demonstration of how to build an H-bomb. But it is a key idea, independently arrived at by the United States and Soviet Union, that contributed to the success of the Soviet and American H-bombs. Once this configuration is unambiguously identified as workable, the remaining details follow from elementary physical reasoning and the detailed calculations that would be a natural part of the design process.

To a physicist, the details in the Morland diagram that are not in Teller's can be divided into four categories: (1) obviously correct; (2) obviously incorrect; (3) could be shown to be correct or incorrect in the course of more detailed design calculations; or (4) speculative ideas that could only be checked out and usefully quantified in a comprehensive experimental program.

As an example, consider one of the obvious details contained in the Morland diagram but not in the Teller diagram. Morland's fusion package is covered by a thin sheet of uranium-238, while Teller's does not indicate any covering. How would a trained physicist, using the Teller diagram only, arrive at the conclusion that the fusion material should be covered with a heavy-metal (such as lead or uranium) jacket?

The physicist would start at the fission trigger, noting that the trigger would, upon detonation, reach a temperature of tens of million degrees centigrade in a small fraction of a millionth of a second. Impressed by the magnitude of the temperature and the shortness of the time interval, the physicist would estimate the expansion speed of the exploding trigger materials, and would note that the violently expanding debris moves relatively slowly over the entire period of the energy release. A computation would show that, because of the high temperatures, a large fraction of the energy is not in the expanding debris, but is in the form of thermal radiation, much of it in the soft x-ray region. Because the radiation travels at the speed of light, hundreds of times faster than the expanding debris of the trigger, the fact that a great deal of radiant energy is trapped in the cavity created by the walls of the massive casing would immediately be recognized. The casing, of course, will eventually be vaporized as the explosion evolves, but for a long time (relative to the time it takes the radiation to permeate the cavity) the casing will hardly move. All this would be quickly deduced by a physicist presented with only the Teller diagram.

The physicist would also conclude that the x-rays should and could be kept out of the fusion material by covering it with a heavy metal like lead or uranium (just as lead shields are used to protect radiologists and their patients from exposure to stray x-rays). That is how, starting from a knowledge of elementary nuclear and statistical physics, and given the knowledge that the Teller conceptual diagrams refer to a workable fusion weapon, the physicist would conclude that a thin foil of heavy metal should surround the fusion package.

This shows how information that does not appear explicitly in a diagram might implicitly be there for those with the relevant scientific background. The details in the Morland diagrams do not constitute key information required by those who would wish to build a bomb. The critical insights are the spatial arrangement of separated components, and the knowledge that such an arrangement can be made to function. Further, Morland, not being a weapons physicist, was not in a position to establish his details as credible. Confirmation and elaboration by the government, of course, would cause seriously interested experts to give them more weight.

The Teller-Ulam Configuration

The "Teller-Ulam idea" is famous for making deliverable H-bombs possible -- yet exactly what that idea was has not yet been made public. Some clues are in the open, however, especially since the Progressive case got so many people thinking about it. Part of the Teller-Ulam idea, judging from the court record, is the spatial separation of the fission trigger and the fusion secondary within a massive casing. Could it be that this was deducible from previously published data?

Before it was demonstrated that high-yield thermonuclear weapons were possible, individuals working from public literature would have been unlikely to duplicate the idea of separate staging. That concept was originally conceived (for the U.S. weapons program) by Stanislaw Ulam and Edward Teller [Note V-1]. Their flash of insight occurred late in the H-bomb project, while Ulam was trying to calculate the evolution of thermonuclear ignition. His calculations indicated that the configuration of fission and fusion material he was studying would disperse before any significant thermonuclear burning could occur. During his work he must have noted the large amounts of x-radiation emanating from the fissioning primary, and the very slow motion of the expanding mass of the fission material relative to the flow of radiation. He also must have noted the recoil forces generated by the x-rays as they deposited their energy in the surrounding materials. His observations led him and Teller to propose a multistage configuration such as the Teller diagram depicts.

But now things are different. The world knows that large thermonuclear weapons can be built. They are known to derive about half of their energy from fission and the remainder from fusion. In addition, the dimensions of the cylindrical weapons casings are known, a most revealing item being that they are considerably greater in length than in diameter (they have a large aspect ratio). Any physicist pondering the implications of the known diameter and aspect ratio of H-bombs would be forced to conclude that the stages were almost certainly separate.

Aspect ratios and Teller and Morland diagrams aside, there is another route to the same conclusion. If a physicist were to set out to calculate how to get the thermonuclear yields that had been achieved, the following reasoning would be duplicated, in one way or another. Relative densities are such that a given volume of uranium or plutonium is about twenty-five times heavier than the same volume of the fusion material, known to be lithium-6 deuteride. Also, it is elementary to calculate that the complete burn of fusion material will yield about three times as much energy as the complete consumption of an equal weight of fission material. Hence, any weapon that derives equal amounts of explosive yield from fission and fusion has used up a volume of fusion material that is perhaps ten times larger than the volume of fission material used. Combining this with the known yields of the larger thermonuclear weapons (such as the Soviet Union's 58-megaton weapon), the physicist would find that garbage-can-sized volumes of fusion materials can be ignited by small volumes of fission materials. This casts serious doubt on the notion that the megaton H-bombs are concentric shells of fission and fusion material.

The known diameters and aspect ratios, the ratio of fission-to-fusion volumes, the sheer volume of fusion materials: These factors all point to the probability that H-bombs consist of spatially separated components.

Admittedly, we have constructed that chain of reasoning after the fact, and therefore, no matter how logical it is, it does not prove beyond doubt that the separate-stages concept would inevitably occur to any physicist who set out to work on the problem. Still, the line of thought is so elementary that it would be surprising indeed if it would not occur to at least the more inventive investigators. In fact, at the 1980 meeting of the American Physical Society in Washington, D.C., the audience at a session discussing the Progressive case was asked how many had figured out "the secret" on their own. Several people raised their hands. Since most physicists would not even bother to try, that any at all responded affirmatively is significant.

THE ARTICLE SHOULD HAVE BEEN IGNORED

If the government could have argued convincingly that the Morland article contained detailed information (exact dimensions, weights of materials, or other quantitative information based on weapons tests) that could not be derived from public data by application of well-known scientific principles, then in our opinion there would have been a case for restraining publication. But that argument could not be made.

The article should have been ignored, not confirmed. What initially appears to be an obvious technical solution to a problem -- any problem -- may not work because of some unforeseen complication. If it is known that a solution exists (for instance, if someone has demonstrated that H-bombs are possible by detonating one), then interested and able workers will explore promising technical approaches until something works. There is no way to stop an adequately trained and equipped group from eventually repeating a demonstrated technological achievement of some other group. However, if it is deemed desirable to create as much delay, expense, and effort as possible for those who might wish to mimic the achievement, it makes no sense to confirm (or deny) the speculations of people who have not been privy to information from the developmental work. Had the government ignored the Morland article, it would have been of no significant value to a foreign nation. Even as it is, the only value to a would-be proliferator (although perhaps a very significant value) is the revelation that U.S. weapons are actually made along such lines. (That, of course, was revealed by the government through its own affidavits.) But the implied detail that has not been confirmed, such as the dimensional proportions of Morland's sketches, is quite possibly wrong. Therefore it would be useless to a bomb designer -- no help, in other words, in shortening the development and testing program that would be necessary.

The reasoning that we have gone through here, showing some of the things that follow from open information, is elementary to a physicist. By making the arguments a little more sophisticated, we could deduce much more in the way of plausible detail about how an H-bomb might be built -- deductions that could be made by physicists anywhere in the world. But that would serve no purpose, and we will not do it.

The idea that Morland's information is deducible is further supported by an assessment of the article by an Australian physicist, Sir Philip Baxter. Dr. Baxter, showing indiscretion comparable with that of some U.S. government affiants, stated that the Morland report "does contain correct instructions on building an H-bomb." Granting that "instructions" is not an appropriate word, how would he have known whether Morland was close to the mark if he or his government had not already given the matter thought? (We assume that he was not privy to American classified information.)

Inaccuracies

A number of affidavits and briefs refer to inaccuracies in some of Morland's description. For example, an appellant (defendant) brief [169], originally filed in camera but released with some deletions, states:

As for accuracy, plaintiff repeatedly acknowledges that
portions of the Morland article are inaccurate...and the
only concept the district court believed was not already in
the public domain is so inaccurately described by Morland
as to be both useless to, and quickly rejected by, any
competent scientist....

Essentially, the X-rays produce a plasma of energized
matter which pushes on the fusion fuel tamper in much the
same way that boiling water produces steam which pushes on
the blades of a turbine. But Morland's discussion of the
role of radiation coupling in the compression of fusion
fuel is as inaccurate as if he said that boiling water
turns the blades of a turbine -- he leaves out the
steam....

[Part of footnote DELETED.] The Teller article correctly describes the critical role played by neutrons; it
simply leaves out the role played by X-rays before the
neutrons reach the fusion fuel. Morland correctly
concluded that neutrons do not cause the compression, but
he then incorrectly concluded that neutrons have no role at
all in the fusion process.

Since Morland's discussion of the role of radiation
pressure is entirely incorrect, publication of that discussion could not harm the national security. Any country
applying Morland's concept of radiation pressure would
waste enormous time and resources and would produce an
unworkable bomb. [DELETED]

The government asserts that the inaccuracies in Morland's article "would not mislead any interested weapons
scientist" and that "analysis by competent physicists"
would identify "the deficiencies" in Morland's article and
would result in "appropriate corrections" so that even
Morland's inaccuracies would still disclose sensitive
information.

After the government's case collapsed, The Progressive printed a
one-page "Errata" by Morland. In it he made some changes and
additions, modifying some things that he concluded were inaccurate in
his original article. For completeness we include it in Appendix A,
but as it was not an issue in the case we will not analyze it.

PUBLIC INFORMATION SOURCES

Although it can be argued from a scientific point of view, as we have
done, that the information in the Morland article was deducible, this
is not necessarily demonstration enough for a court of law. Not only
because of limited expertise, but also because of legal tradition and
precedents, courts require evidence of a different type than would a
panel of scientists. A court might not accept the claim that certain
information is in the public domain unless to a nonexpert the source
and its context are unambiguously similar to the material under
litigation.

During the court proceedings many published documents were exhibited
which defendants and their affiants said contained information that

duplicated what the government wanted to suppress in the Morland article. There were pertinent articles in encyclopedias, technical journals, newspapers, periodicals, and government documents. Many of the articles and documents were from highly authoritative sources. During the course of the suit, three other types of information appeared: publicly filed government briefs and affidavits, data in the responding briefs and affidavits of the defendants, and published letters and articles stimulated by the publicity. The court acknowledged some of these items as relevant, while rejecting others as too far removed from the issue being decided.

Encyclopedias

A strange place to find information similar to what the goverment is asserting to be sensitive is an encyclopedia. Not long after the Progressive case began, two encyclopedia articles on fusion and thermonuclear weapons were found that contained diagrams showing the spatially separated, multistage configuration. Since the claim was that this information was not in the public domain, the discoveries were embarrassing to the government. Adding to the government's difficulties, the articles were written by highly regarded authorities on thermonuclear weapons, Hans Bethe (a Nobel laureate) and Edward Teller. We referred earlier to Teller's article in the Americana, which was accompanied by the frequently mentoned "Teller diagram." Bethe's was in the Merit Students Encyclopedia. It was difficult for the Government to argue that those sources were obscure or unavailable.

The Bethe-Teller diagrams. An interesting sidelight to the encyclopedia story is that Dr. Teller disclaims responsibility for the diagram that appeared with his article. In a letter to Congressman Paul N. McCloskey (May 29, 1979), he wrote:

> The illustration...accompanying the article...was not provided by me to the Encyclopedia Americana, nor did I see it before publication. I have no idea from what source it was derived. Shortly after the time of publication, there was communication between me and the staff of the Americana, which failed to resolve the question.

There is no reason to doubt Dr. Teller. We have received permission from the Americana to reproduce the Teller diagram, and from the Merit Students Encyclopedia to print the Bethe diagram. They are in Figs. 2 and 3. While they appeared at least as early as 1974 and 1967, respectively, we do not know the original publication dates, nor which was published first.

Note that there exists a remarkable similarity between the two figures. For example: four sketches, the first a cut-away drawing, the rest not; similar labels; arrows pointing to the second and third stages, but not to the fourth; an elliptical fusion package; downward arrow in the "fission" stage; outward arrows in the "fusion" stage; captions containing virtually identical information.

The mystery is not, however, resolved by these similarities, even though they suggest that the two sets of diagrams had a common origin. In a letter to Charles Hansen dated June 11, 1979, Hans Bethe, responding to a question regarding the origin of his diagram, says, "I do not recognize the diagram.... I am pretty sure that I did not prepare it, and I believe that I was not involved in its preparation."

The Bethe diagram put the concept of separate stages into the public domain in 1967, if it was not there before. (All but one of the current H-bomb powers had tested their first multistage weapons by then, and France did so the following year.) Whoever originated the Bethe-Teller diagram presumably considered the idea to be in the open by then. We note, however, careful wording in the caption that avoids any hint at the other two of the three concepts -- radiation coupling and compression.

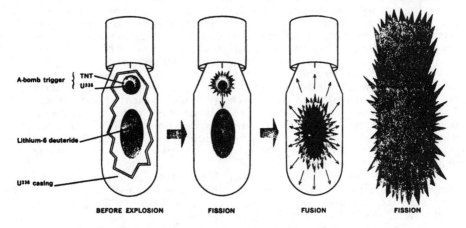

In the explosion of a hydrogen bomb the detonator in the A-bomb trigger explodes first, compressing the U^{235} and causing it to undergo fission. Neutrons are released and the temperature rises to 50 million degrees centigrade. In the following fusion reaction, lithium-6 deuteride is transformed into tritium and helium. The tritium fuses with deuterium, releasing more energy and neutrons. Finally, the high-energy neutrons strike the U^{238} casing, causing it to undergo fission. The sequence occurs in a few millionths of a second.

Fig. 3. Merit Students Encyclopedia version of H-bomb conceptual design. © Merit Students Encyclopedia. Caption and figure used with permission.

Technical Literature

Further information came directly from articles concerning nuclear weapons, while other relevant data could demonstrably be derived from elementary physics texts and various articles in the Scientific

American. (The list of references in Postol's affidavits [45] is representative.) A feature of the assembled articles that the government had quite obviously failed to appreciate was the amount of information that could be straightforwardly sifted from them without recourse even to declassified government documents.

Several technical studies of fusion processes for power and weapon applications have been placed in the technical literature, particularly in Germany, by Dr. Frederick Winterberg, based on work he has done largely without government support [Note V-2]. An interesting sidelight is that DOE contended [151] that an article on laser fusion published in Russian in the USSR by a Soviet physicist was Restricted Data in the United States.

Government Documents

Government reports are a prime source of information on weapons concepts -- and sometimes weapons detail. This is as it should be, as long as the details are properly screened before release. Among the highly technical, declassified documents with useful information about fission and fusion weapons, there is a rather important one that has not received much attention: DNA-4501F, on the "Physics of High-Altitude Nuclear Burst Effects." Dated December 1977, it was prepared for the Defense Nuclear Agency and "approved for public release; distribution unlimited." Chapter 3, entitled "Nuclear Physics and Nuclear Weapons," has sections on "Conceptual Design of Nuclear Weapons," with subsections on "Fission Weapons" and "Fusion Weapons." Another section deals with "Weapon Outputs."

In that report there is much information on the thermal radiation yield, x-rays, debris kinetic energy, and various energy-loss and energy-transfer mechanisms. Although radiation coupling was a concept that was considered by DOE to be still under lock and key, DNA-4501F, under "Fusion Weapons," refers to "the possibility of igniting a thermonuclear device with a fission device." In the description of what happens after an explosion, thermal x-rays receive specific attention:

> The energy is released and deposited in a very short time, say a few shakes [ten-billionths of a second]. During this interval some of the energy is transferred to the electromagnetic field in the form of thermal radiation.... At this stage the radiation is trapped in the interior by the opaque surrounding debris.
>
> After a few shakes the configuration resembles an enclosure filled with a very hot gas in or near equilibrium with the radiation field. The radiation field diffuses through the outer layers of the enclosing material, the radiation front eventually reaching the surface, at which time a sizable fraction of the total yield is radiated away as a pulse of thermal x rays...
>
> During the time the radiation field remains trapped by the debris the whole mass of debris experiences an outward acceleration as a result of the pressure being exerted on it, an important component of which is radiation pressure.

The x-ray yield is subsequently given as 45 percent of the total yield of the weapon.

The reaction of the government [142] when the above paragraphs were pointed out [134] was: "In excerpts [of DNA-4501F] cited by DeVolpi, there is no suggestion of any relation to thermonuclear weapon design," and when the excerpts were filed with the court in association with the case, the director of DOE classification required [146] that the excerpts from the public document be filed in camera as Restricted Data. While at first that might seem illogical, it was a straightforward application of the classification principle that mentioning public information in a sensitive context can in effect release nondeducible information.

Nevertheless, almost any physicist who came upon that information, being aware of the separate stages involved in a multistage weapon because of the Teller diagrams, and being aware of the need to produce compression, is very likely to realize that thermal x-rays, properly coupled to the fusion material, are a good candidate to be the main agent for inducing the requisite pressure. Because DNA-4501F is an official and comprehensive weapons document, there would be a high degree of confidence in its statements about radiation release, which could be checked against other public information.

Newspapers and Magazines

After the suit was brought, articles were published in Fusion magazine and in the Milwaukee Sentinel dealing with the idea that soft x-rays were the energy-coupling mechanism in a thermonuclear weapon. In addition, the Washington Post published an article on Postol's unclassified affidavit [45], in which he had observed that the concept of separate stages was contained in Teller's diagrams. The Post reproduced the diagrams from the Encyclopedia Americana, along with excerpts fom the affidavit. A similar though less comprehensive article appeared in the New York Times, which also reproduced the Teller diagrams. Thus the concepts that high-yield weapons are multistage and that x-rays play a role in the process of thermonuclear ignition appeared in a number of major newspapers and at least one magazine. At about the same time, the Washington Post printed (on March 18, 1979) the affidavit of Jack Rosengren, which contained assertions that, in conjunction with the Postol excerpts, flagged the Teller diagram as a relevant weapon configuration.

The Secretary of Energy, James Schlesinger, commented:

> With regard to the articles in the Milwaukee Sentinel and the particular Fusion magazine source, it is my judgment that, absent any confirmation by authoritative persons as to the technical validity of some of the material therein, it is unlikely that intelligence services of non-thermonuclear weapon states would have discussed their significance.

A classified affidavit [141] of Rosengren and Grayson contained the remark that "the referenced statement [in Fusion magazine] is actually somewhat ambiguous and there is no reason to accept it as authoritative."

An astute reader of the Washington Post alone would have learned that the court case being fought had something to do with the fact that H-bombs consist of separated stages within a weapon casing. This would have been learned from the article about the Postol affidavit. From the same newspaper, the person would also have found out from Rosengren (a bona fide government weapons physicist) that the Teller multistage configuration worked.

Rosengren's public affidavit volunteered new information that was not even at issue in the case. It said that the Teller-Morland multistage arrangement, relative to others known by the United States, is the easiest to implement, that when properly refined such a configuration would ultimately result in a weapon giving the highest yield-to-weight ratio known, and that this configuration is the one on which U.S. thermonuclear weapons are based. One can safely assume that any attentive foreign expert reading the Washington Post would have alerted his government to this information.

More disconcerting yet, none of these points (except possibly the last) had been speculated on by Howard Morland. He had focused on what he believed to be general design features of thermonuclear bombs and never discussed questions of ease of development or performance details of different weapons. An indication that a multistage weapon such as Morland depicted might work was all that was in the public domain before the government provided confirmation and made additional information available through the major newspapers.

MISTAKENLY DECLASSIFIED DOCUMENTS

While the litigation was in progress, Dimitri Rotow, then a student with an interest in nuclear weapons, agreed to travel to Los Alamos on behalf of the ACLU. His purpose was to try to collect publicly available documents from the open shelves of the Los Alamos Scientific Laboratory library that might be relevant to the court proceedings. Rotow had visited that library the year before and had found some mistakenly declassified documents, including plans for a nuclear-warhead trigger called the TX-7.

Shortly after entering the library this time, Rotow located, through the card catalog, a report designated UCRL-4725, "University of California Radiation Laboratory, Weapon Development During June 1956." The document had been declassified in error in July 1975 and had been freely available to the public since April 1977.

The Chicago Sun Times of May 18, 1979, told something about the contents of UCRL-4725:

> The report...contains such information as the yield, weight and configuration of various nuclear devices.... There are descriptions of the Swan and Swallow, two atomic "trigger bombs" that are used to set off the thermonuclear reaction. Charts give the destructive power, or yield, and the yield-to-weight ratios of many devices. Tests mentioned... include the Bassoon Shot and four detonations at Eniwetok Atoll in the Pacific: Zuni, Yuma, Kickapoo and Inca. [The report discusses the] amount of fusionable material in the bombs, and the types and properties of materials used in bombs.... [It also mentions] various computer codes used to make design calculations.

The value of that sort of information to those with the scientific and industrial capacity to use it would be immeasurable. On this point there appears to be virtually unanimous agreement among all the scientists who have seen the document. Having filed affidavits contesting government assertions about the sensitivity of the Morland article, they submitted supplemental affidavits after being shown UCRL-4725. The public affidavits of Gerald Marsh [133] and Alexander DeVolpi [134] [Notes V-3 and -4] both contrasted the inaccuracies and inadequacies of the Morland article with the authentic, government-supplied data of UCRL-4725. They noted that each of the three central concepts was at least implicitly to be found in UCRL-4725.

UCRL-4725 is possibly not the most sensitive document containing thermonuclear test data that has been mistakenly declassified and put onto public shelves at Los Alamos. Another one, UCRL-5280, "Weapon Development in June 1958," had been discovered a year earlier in a check of the library by the Senate Subcommittee on Energy, Nuclear Proliferation and Federal Services, headed by Senator John Glenn. There is no detailed public report of the contents of this document, but its title is similar to that of UCRL-4725. The latter presumably distills the insights developed from the seventy-five-odd weapons tests that preceded it. If UCRL-5280 is similarly inclusive of experience gained from 1945 to 1958, it contains insights from an additional seventy-nine tests. Those would almost certainly have been for developing and refining already very sophisticated thermonuclear devices. That report was declassified when UCRL-4725 was, and was freely available to the public between April 1977 and May 1978.

Relevance to the Progressive Case

Because indirect but scientifically reasoned evidence that a panel of scientists might accept would not necessarily be considered admissible in a court proceeding, any evidence that could, on its face and without relying on deducibility arguments, establish that the information in the Morland article was in the public domain would strongly help the defendants in Progressive to challenge the restraining order. UCRL-4725 and UCRL-5280 were almost made to order.

The complication was that it could not be proved beyond doubt that the documents had been seen by anybody who might use them to the detriment of national security. Government affidavits submitted by the then Secretary of Energy, James Schlesinger, and the head librarian at Los Alamos claimed that they were unlikely to have been compromised. (In Chapter IX that conclusion, which seems questionable, is discussed in greater detail.)

Other considerations added to the court's confusion about how to deal with UCRL-4725. As was mentioned, the scientists who opposed the government's attempts to restrain publication of the Morland article completely agreed that UCRL-4725 should never have been publicly available. These scientists also said that, in spite of their opinion that it had almost certainly been compromised, further dissemination of the document should not be allowed. Of similar mind was Theodore Taylor when he testified before Senator Glenn's subcommittee while UCRL-4725 was still being discussed in court. Taylor stated that UCRL-4725 would allow a physicist to "infer the basic design principles used in thermonuclear weapons" if that scientist had read "encyclopedia articles and other publicly available literature which describes nuclear weapon behavior."

The affiants for The Progressive pointed out that UCRL-4725 and (apparently) UCRL-5280 contained the results of a large and expensive series of weapons calculations and tests. Such information, in their opinion, could materially aid other countries in their efforts to construct weapons of mass destruction. It was specific to the weapons program, and only available to the public because it had been accidentally put there by DOE. In contrast, the scientists noted, the Morland article contained no information that could materially aid a foreign power, because that information was already available.

Because of its obvious relevance to the case, the second accidentally declassified weapons document, UCRL-5280, also became an issue in the court proceedings. Since it too had sat on the public shelves at Los Alamos for over a year, the defense wanted to establish the nature of its contents for the court record. DOE was unwilling to surrender copies of the document for the inspection of the expert witnesses for the defense. So sensitive was this document in the eyes of DOE, that in spite of its obvious interest in winning the case the Department agreed to submit the following stipulation to the court in order to avoid exposing the document to additional readers [140]:

1. UCRL 5280 reveals in a thermonuclear weapons context the three concepts which the government has described as the essential secret of the H-bomb.

2. If a competent scientist read UCRL 5280, he or she would derive no significant additional information or benefit from reading the Morland article and diagrams.

3. A notice of declassification for UCRL 5280 was issued in December, 1973. The declassification marking on the Los Alamos copy of UCRL 5280 is dated July 30, 1975. In May, 1978, the document was removed from the public stacks at the Los Alamos scientific library and placed in the area reserved for classified documents. On May 16, 1979, the document was again marked "classified."

THE GLENN LETTER

It was apparent to those of us who filed statements on behalf of The Progressive that the government was revealing information in its affidavits that it had previously claimed to be secret. More important, the information being released was authoritative, since it was coming from cabinet-level officials and trained weapons physicists with inside knowledge. The government affiants not only confirmed information in the Morland article that could otherwise only have been regarded as speculation, but they volunteered a lot that that was not at issue in the litigation. Because the officials had been unresponsive to direct queries and the court showed no comprehension of the seriousness of the situation, we decided the responsible thing to do was to contact Congress.

Accordingly, on April 25, 1979, we sent to Senator John Glenn, chairman of the Senate Subcommittee on Energy, Nuclear Proliferation and Federal Services, a communication that we shall call "the Glenn letter" (Appendix B). We pointed out that the government was selectively releasing weapons-sensitive information that should be classified "Secret Restricted Data" under the Atomic Energy Act. We

outlined the nature of the released information and the way it was put
into the public domain. After some delay, the subcommittee passed the
letter on to DOE for comment. About five weeks after the letter was
mailed, we were informed by DOE that it letter was classified because
it incorporated Restricted Data. We assume that the Restricted Data
consisted of our outline of how any interested party could use the
Teller diagram, along with information that the government had made
public, to make deductions about the principles underlying U.S. H-
bombs. Promptly after it was classified it was published in toto by
the Daily Californian, a student newspaper that had gotten the letter
through a route that we discuss elsewhere in the book.

As the case progressed, there were constant and varied attempts to
establish that the information in the Morland article could be found in
public literature. On August 31, 1979, defendants Knoll, Day, and
Morland, filed an in camera brief [168] arguing that the Glenn
letter, its classification, and its subsequent publication in the
press, mooted the case. Portions of that brief were declassified on
September 24 when the government filed a public reply, and the
expurgated version was made public on September 26 [169]. Because the
arguments in the defendants' brief accurately assess the contents of
the Glenn letter and its relation to other information mishandled by
the government, sections of the brief are worth quoting directly, which
is done in Note V-5. The defendants show, incidentally, the reasoning
that DOE might have followed in deciding to classify the Glenn letter.
The fact remains, however, that the letter introduced nothing new into
the public domain, but merely spelled out what was already there -- the
reasoning that would be obvious to any agent of a foreign power who
read the court record.

THE HANSEN LETTER

The straw that finally broke the camel's back was what became known as
the Hansen letter. Chuck Hansen, as we mentioned earlier, was a
computer programmer by profession and an enthusiastic self-styled
"amateur weapon designer." He had been following the Progressive
case carefully. Although not trained as a physicist, he had read
popular accounts of nuclear weaponry and had developed an extensive
knowledge of the open literature. In a letter to Senator Charles
Percy, with a copy to DOE, Hansen maintained that a double standard was
used in the classification system. He outlined his conception of how a
hydrogen bomb works. Although claiming that his description was
gleaned only from the open literature, Hansen predicted that the
government would classify it. He was right.

Hansen's letter is quite long; some of it is obviously correct, some
obviously not, and some is of unknown validity. In one part that was
probably considered classifiable, Hansen speculates on just what the
Teller-Ulam idea was -- the idea that reputedly made the H-bomb
practical:

> The Teller-Ulam configuration was a geometric design and
> arrangement of bomb components that allowed heat and
> pressure to be generated within the fuel mass by means of
> "soft" (low energy) X-rays. About 70 to 80% of the initial
> energy of an exploding atom bomb is manifested as these

"soft" X-rays, and Teller and Ulam hit upon a scheme to use them to compress the fusion fuel.

Hansen apparently had not seen the Morland article, and did not say how he arrived at his conclusion. By then, however, that same supposition had been placed in the public domain through a different route: Underground copies of the Morland drafts were in circulation, and public affidavits by the directors of the two weapons laboratories, Robert Thorn (Los Alamos) and Roger Batzel (Lawrence Livermore) volunteered that the Morland article contained the Teller-Ulam idea.

AUTHORITATIVENESS

The public, the news media, and even the courts are often inclined to give heavy credence to official pronouncements. Judge Warren made it clear that he was highly impressed by the credentials of the government affiants.

The Justice Department stressed [109], correctly, that government submissions provided official confirmation of technical information. Within bounds, official government sources must be taken as authoritative on nuclear weapons because, by virtue of the government's effective monopoly on weapons research, they have a corner on the technical information. However, although offical documents have the sanction of authority, they are not necessarily authoritative in the sense of being entirely correct or expressing the consensus of other experts.

Somewhat inconsistently, in a brief to the appeals court [166] the government said, "Nothing that has been published approaches the comprehensiveness, authoritativeness, and accuracy of the Morland article." And earlier the government had pressed the suggestion [21] that because Morland was not "uneducated and unsophisticated," having written an article on nuclear weapons secrecy, his work had some credibility. Morland, of course, had no official status, and certainly would not be considered a nuclear weapons authority by experts in the field. The government was trying to establish that Morland knew enough to be able to report correctly technical information that he got from authoritative sources. While that was possibly true, it a diversion from the main point that anything that could be put together by someone who had taken only a few scientific courses would be well within the grasp of interested parties with more technical training.

In any event, the unique technical knowledge of the government in matters dealing with nuclear weapons is not transferrable to a similar competence in judgments about the risk of proliferation. Already public is enough information about nuclear weapons and the nuclear fuel cycle to permit nonproliferation policies to be evaluated. Further, the policies have much more political content than technical. Thus the government's authoritative status in nuclear weapons data should not be confused with an unchallengeable position in estimates of proliferation potential.

CONCLUSIONS: DEDUCIBILITY OF THE THREE CONCEPTS

In deciding to prosecute The Progressive and confirm the general validity of the Morland article, the government placed unrealistic reliance on being able to prevent underground dissemination if it won the suit, to say nothing of the wide distribution if they lost. The difficulties the government faced in attempting to squelch the letter to Senator Glenn illustrates the futility of such efforts in a matter so tainted with political overtones. At least a half-dozen college newspapers published the Glenn letter, despite or perhaps because of the fact that publication was forbidden.

Further, it was probable and foreseeable that some or all of the three concepts would be independently derived, as was partially done by Hansen. Finally, the U.S. government lacks control over publication in other countries. The mobility of Morland's drafts is evidenced by the fact that one turned up in Australia [Note V-6].

The deducibility picture is clearer now, with the open sources of information spotlighted as a result of the lawsuit -- but it should have been comprehensible in March 1979. The key to understanding how high-yield thermonuclear weapons work is realization that the stages must be separate. A competent physicist who is told that idea, either verbally or by means of the Bethe-Teller diagrams, would quickly develop many of the subsidiary ideas in Morland's article, including the other two concepts. With separate stages explicit in two encyclopedias, the other two critical concepts were already at least latently in the public domain at the time Morland attempted publication. Regardless of whether radiation coupling and compression had been explicitly linked to H-bomb design officially, the connection (to a physicist) was only logical. Clearly, some had, in fact, made that connection, but wisely chose not to broadcast their deductions.

Further, a well-trained and astute physicist would be likely to deduce the concept of separate stages itself from open knowledge, even without reading the relevant encyclopedia articles. This is not to say that the insights of Ulam and Teller were not clever. But since the time of their breakthrough the base of scientific evidence has become substantially broader, providing many more indicators than were available to them before the first successful H-bomb. Clues and verification are available in many authoritative places -- in the scientific knowledge that has grown since the early days of the H-bomb effort and in formerly classified materials and other government documents, as well as in the articles published over the names of Edward Teller, Hans Bethe, and others.

The government questioned that all of Morland's information came from unclassified sources. Rosengren and Grayson [68] said, "He nowhere presents a flow of logic...." "The fragmentary nature... suggest a great deal of guidance from a person or persons with access to secret design information, i.e., classified information." The allegation does not appear to have been justified, however, in view of the traceability of the Morland material and the lack of criminal prosecution.

Under any circumstances, to call the Morland article a blueprint for the construction of an H-bomb was an outright absurdity. Anyone with practical experience in technology would recognize that a few conceptual phrases and undimensioned diagrams do not constitute a blueprint. Judge Warren must be faulted for falling victim to that misconception -- for failing to recognize that he needed the technical help that a panel of experts could have given him. He became lost in the technical smokescreen, confused by the barrage of specialized jargon and conflicting affidavits that he could not evaluate.

There was no quantitative information in Morland's article or diagrams. As a source of ideas on how a bomb might be put together, without authentication by the U.S. government anything that looked like a design detail would have to be regarded as based on rumor, if not outright speculation -- possibly right, possibly nonoptimal, possibly wrong, almost certainly incomplete. Perhaps vital features were lacking, without which the bomb would not work at all, no matter how carefully designed. The article had no self-standing credibility. Had it been ignored, its information would have been worth nothing to a foreign nation. Even now, the implied detail, such as the dimensional proportions of Morland's sketches or the general shapes or relative placement of the various parts, have (wisely) not been confirmed or denied and so remain of unknown validity. What the government has done is announce to the world that Morland was barking up the right tree.

6 Proliferation Risk

As a military man who has given half a century of active service I say in all sincerity that the nuclear arms race has no military purpose. Wars cannot be fought with nuclear weapons. Their existence only adds to our perils because of the illusions which they have generated.
— Lord Mountbatten

Defense is not the primary purpose of nuclear weapons; for the superpowers their value lies in deterrence, and for Third World countries in prestige as well as deterrence. Most nations recognize the self-defeating nature of nuclear warfare (the superpowers' rhetoric notwithstanding). Among nonnuclear-weapons countries, of which there are about 150, there is concern that nuclear weapons will be fabricated and deployed among new states, and they worry over the growing arsenals of the five known weapons states. Despite good intentions, the multiplication of nuclear weapons and the growing dependence on them may result in nuclear warfare -- perhaps devastating the planet.

In the United States the executive branch is charged with ensuring the common defense and national security, and it has realistically decided that the propagation of nuclear weapons to other countries would be detrimental. It was ostensibly in accord with that policy that the injunctive process of the Atomic Energy Act was invoked against The Progressive. In so doing, the government had to establish in court the probability and type of harm that might result if the Morland article were published.

PROLIFERATION RISK FROM MORLAND'S ARTICLE

To meet legal criteria, the government's case against The Progressive required a showing of consequential harm to the nation. In particular, to satisfy the Pentagon Papers standard (which the government tried to do, even though claiming it did not have to) the nature and imminence of the danger had to be proven. Consequently an array of affidavits from officials of the executive branch and from some government

110

consultants were submitted to the court expressing concern over an enhanced risk of proliferation of nuclear weapons if Morland's article were published.

In general, the concerns expressed fell into three categories: the danger of nuclear war, the danger that proliferation would contribute to nuclear war, and the risk that Morland's article would or could either induce more proliferation or shorten the time before other nations would make nuclear weapons. The government's position is reflected in the words of three Cabinet members:

Secretary of Defense Harold Brown: "Any increase in the availability of thermonuclear weapons increases the potential for use or threat of use of such weapons against the United States."

Secretary of State Cyrus Vance: "[The Morland article] would substantially contribute to the ability of foreign nations to develop thermonuclear weapons."

Secretary of Energy James Schlesinger: "Such information would materially aid foreign nations by enabling them to develop such weapons in a shorter period of time than otherwise would be possible. This result would be contrary to the non-proliferation policy of the United States, including that adopted in the Treaty on Nonproliferation of Nuclear Weapons, and would increase the risks of thermonuclear war."

Additional statements were supplied by officials within the Department of State and the Arms Control and Disarmament Agency. The argument tendered by the government was that the Morland article would "facilitate and accelerate" national efforts to develop high-yield thermonuclear weapons [Note VI-1]. Although it was frequently emphasized that the time required to achieve thermonuclear capability would be shortened, few of the officials offered an estimate of how much time -- whether days or years. Some of the statements, without providing specifics, suggested that the Morland information would reduce the resources required by another nation intent on making hydrogen bombs.

In an affidavit [7A] classified "Secret--National Security Information," Assistant Secretary of State Thomas Pickering apparently gave the only specifics of the administration's argument that proliferation would result from Morland's article. This affidavit is still classified "Secret--NSI." Later on in this chapter we provide some quotations from an erroneously declassified CIA memorandum that gives some insight into probable State Department views regarding countries that have threshold capabilities.

On the side of the government was one of the more respected members of the scientific community, Hans Bethe [72]. He stated:

It is my belief that public dissemination of the Morland manuscript would substantially hasten the development of thermonuclear weapon capabilities by nations not now having such capabilities.

In the course of a profile of Bethe printed in the New Yorker (December 10, 1979), but probably written before the government folded its case, Bethe was asked if there was still reason to keep secret the Teller-Ulam idea. He responded:

Yes. It is not an obvious idea. It took the French ten years to find it, and their scientists are not stupid. Somehow, the Chinese got it awfully fast. We don't understand how. But if it took the French ten years, then it will take a new country with fewer and less competent scientists much longer than that, so it seems to me that keeping the secret is very much worthwhile.

We are inclined to disagree with Bethe's assessment of the reason for delay, despite his probable access to intelligence information regarding French weapons development. In view of established French competence in nuclear physics and engineering, it is unlikely that any lack of understanding of the underlying principles caused the few extra years in their case; it might simply have been the lack of political or financial resolve to undertake thermonuclear weapons development at the time. Measured from the time of first detonation of a fission device, it required the French eight years to test a fusion explosive, compared to seven for the United States. For China it was three years; Russia, four years; and England, five years.

The government presented the risk as follows [4]:

The potentially grave consequences to the security of the United States and the world itself resulting from the threatened disclosure are obvious and frightening. As plaintiff's affidavits show, present and potential enemies of the United States will be materially assisted in their development of the most destructive weapons known to mankind. Nations which are not currently seeking to develop such devices due to the high cost of years of experimentation may decide to do so as a result of the "shortcut" presented in the challenged publication.

In support of that point, the various government affiants [Note IV-5] made the claims we discussed in Chapter IV that publishing the article would spur proliferation and thereby increase the risk of nuclear war. No balancing of possible counterproliferative value of publication was given by the government, nor was mention made of the relative impact of alternative policies to prevent proliferation and nuclear war. Further on, we point out that past policies of the United States may, in fact, already be contributing to additional proliferation risk and the possibility of atomic war.

Amici and affiants for the defense contradicted the government assertions [Note VI-2]. Although agreeing that proliferation is a serious problem, the remedies were disputed. Secrecy and technology, it was pointed out, are only two facets of a comprehensive antiproliferation program. The executive branch was accused of trying to divert attention from the failures of American antiproliferation policy.

In addition, it was observed [Note VI-3] that to acquire thermonuclear capability, the five nations that have developed such weapons have shown that a country must have the technological capability as well as the political will, and moreover must engage in a self-revealing program of nuclear explosive testing. The fact that more nations have not undertaken fission and fusion weapon development is rooted more in the self-defeating nature of such armaments than in the non-availability of technical information.

An amici memorandum by the Fund for Open Information and Accountability [80] reminded the court that

The threat of nuclear peril and world holocaust, the possibility of massive destruction of people and property exists now, world-wide, through the existence and availability of atomic bombs and weaponry. The massive

destruction possible through existing and potential atomic
fission bombs makes a mockery of the government's claims
herein that the threat of thermonuclear holocaust will be
increased by publication of the Morland article.

Giving the Bomb Away?

Federal District Judge Warren said [31] that he would like time to
think "before I'd give the hydrogen bomb to Idi Amin." And so would we
all -- but this is far from the issue raised by the government's
attempt to censor the article in The Progressive magazine.
The New York Times had this to say in a March 29, 1979, editorial:
The judge concedes that the result is probably not a do-
it-yourself guide to hydrogen bomb construction. Indeed,
he allows that such a bomb can be built only by those with
"a large, sophisticated industrial capability coupled with
a coterie of imaginative, resourceful scientists and technicians." And as he was told, that coterie would already
need to know how to build an atomic explosive to trigger
the hydrogen weapon. So where is the grave and certain
threat[?]... As any honest official would have to
testify...this fear of harm is conjectural and contingent,
clearly not direct and immediate, far from certain and no
threat to the nation's safety. [Emphasis in the
original.]
The overwhelming viewpoint of knowledgeable technical persons is that
it would be extremely unlikely for unsanctioned, nongovernmental
groups to achieve fusion weapon capability, even if they knew how.
Moreover, the destructive power of the simpler fission weapons -- in
fact and in public perception -- is so great that there would be little
potential gain to balance the various risks a subnational group would
have to take if it tried to build a thermonuclear weapon. Thus it is
hard to understand Brown's allegation [37] that "a subnational
element...would gain technical assistance in determining the
appropriate direction to pursue in developing high yield thermonuclear
explosives."
Fortunately for us all, that statement appears to be incorrect. To
make an H-bomb, subnational elements (terrorists) would first have to
attain a sophisticated understanding of fission explosives to use as
the trigger for the fusion reaction -- as would any nation that wanted
to build H-bombs. They would have to design in detail and fabricate
with extreme care a device made of materials that are rare and highly
safeguarded. They are likely to need several of these fission devices
in order to conduct an explosive test program, which would be readily
detectable because of the special effects of nuclear detonations.
Moreover, if successful to that stage, they would have to carry through
what appears to be a highly complex series of calculations using major
computer facilities before being able to engineer the fusion weapon.
Although the concepts of radiation-induced compression and
thermonuclear ignition appear to be simple, the practical calculations
and implementation are not.
There are many difficulties associated with developing a crude fission explosive, especially with low-quality fissile material [DEV-79].
Even with good quality materials, Hans Bethe thinks that it is "totally

unlikely that a terrorist group could make a [fission] bomb" [New York, December 10, 1979]. Bethe was asked, "Suppose one had available all the open literature on making a bomb...and one had all the enriched uranium or plutonium that one needed -- where would one be in the construction of an atomic bomb?" "Nowhere," he is quoted as responding. Bethe explained that, though the general principles involved in making such a device are "well known" and "are available in the open literature," the details "which are extremely intricate, are not."

Once they had their fission trigger, the terrorists would then have to acquire the fusion source material: special, isotopically separated lithium deuteride, available only in certain government weapons channels. If the fission and fusion materials were accumulated, the entire thermonuclear system would have to be tested at least once in order to have anything but minimal credibility, because of the extreme complexity of the undertaking.

Success in even one of these steps is improbable; it is extremely unlikely that any nongovernmental group could carry through all of them and develop hydrogen weapons. Realistically, public disclosure of the Morland article could not help terrorists get an H-bomb.

Time Needed to Develop H-Bombs

One of the issues in the Progressive case was the time that it would take a country to design and build thermonuclear weapons. At the first hearing [31], Judge Warren commented:
> What we are talking about, to some extent, is time....
> Time in which to make agreements, time in which to
> establish lines of communication, time in which to deal
> with this problem in a peaceful fashion. That time is
> crucial and important, as the affidavits of all those who
> have the responsibility in this government to deal with
> that problem indicate.

Emphasis on the time factor was heightened by the following question to defense counsel by Judge Warren, at the hearing [95] for a preliminary injunction:
> What would your attitude be towards his [Tsipis's]
> statement [see Note IV-11] that time itself could be
> shortened? The question I would have for you is whether
> that time factor can constitute itself a direct irreparable
> harm.

In the only government affidavit [see Note IV-5] that was specific about the time factor, Pickering [7] claimed that if publication of the article were allowed,
> Both the time to make this progression and the uncertainty
> in achieving a succesful progression would be reduced. In
> my opinion, the decade it might take some countries to de-
> velop thermonuclear weapons could be reduced to a few
> years.

Opposing views were presented in affidavits by defendants and friends of the court. For example, Hugh Dewitt said [56] that it would shorten the progression by "only a few days." Others [62] said it "might be of negligible or at most minor consequence to the speed with which additional nations could succeed in developing thermonuclear weapons."

One point not addressed by the government was this: If time is needed now to "deal with the problem," what has the government been doing for the past third of a century to curtail proliferation effectively? As pointed out in defense affidavits, a three-decade time delay has already been bought, paid for, and expired. It is time to start using more than secrecy to retard proliferation.

Comments

The government relied on the "authority" of its officials, and did not feel any need to substantiate its arguments about proliferation. It explicitly expected the court to grant "judicial deference" [4] to the official viewpoint.

Despite the lack of supporting evidence, the official government pronouncements clearly impressed Judge Warren [82], who believed that "a mistake in ruling against the United States could pave the way for thermonuclear annihilation for us all." He found [85] that

publication of the Restricted Data contained in the Morland article would be extremely important to a nation seeking a thermonuclear capability, for it would provide vital information on key concepts involved in the construction of a practical thermonuclear weapon.

In his memorandum and order [82] for the temporary restraining order, Judge Warren decided that

the article could possibly provide sufficient information to allow a medium size nation to move faster in developing a hydrogen weapon. It could provide a ticket to by-pass blind alleys.

Government assertions that the article would aggravate proliferation have to be taken in a political context. Paragraph 4 of the declaration by Cyrus R. Vance [36] mentions the "importance to the United States that as few nations as possible develop thermonuclear weapons." We agree. But open to question is whether past actions of the United States have been consistent with that importance. Five nations have already tested such weapons: To what extent is that proliferation a reaction to steps taken, or not taken, by this country? What policies have led to the nuclear-armed world we already live in? Should these policies be modified?

We examine these questions below, cognizant that the nuclear weapons that provide a national security blanket, if used in anger or by miscalculation, could cause self-initiated national devastation. One of the objectives of the Morland paper was to demonstrate how government attitudes and policies perpetuate the false impression that the United States is safe -- that secrecy will protect America from the spread of nuclear weapons.

FIVE NUCLEAR-WEAPONS STATES

The five established nuclear-weapons states are the United States, the Soviet Union, Great Britain, France, and China. Each of them has tested both fission and fusion weapons. One reasonable definition of a nuclear-weapons state is a country that has both tested and deployed deliverable nuclear warheads. Thus India -- which has categorized its testing of a nuclear device as a "peaceful nuclear explosion" -- is a marginal nuclear-weapons state that has neither announced that it has atomic bombs nor been observed to deploy them. Other marginal states might be Israel and South Africa, who are reputed without confirmation to have fission weapons. In any event, extending nuclear weapon capability from fission explosives to multistage fusion explosives is a major step -- a leap comparable to developing fission weapons in the first place.

Proliferation occurs in two geopolitical directions, horizontal and vertical. Horizontal proliferation refers to the spread of nuclear weapons to more countries, whereas vertical proliferation occurs when more weapons are stockpiled by those nations that already have some.

In addition to numerical escalation, any improvements in the quality of guidance systems, weapons explosive yield, countermeasures, decoys, defenses, and delivery systems must be recognized as vertical proliferation. Unrestrained development and testing of cruise missiles would be an example. Both the United States and the Soviet Union have been engaged in vertical proliferation for a long time. Currently the United States plans to increase its destructive capability and accuracy with the Trident submarine and missile, the MARV (maneuverable reentry vehicle), rapid firing of ICBMs, remote and rapid retargeting of Minuteman III, the MX (mobile ICBM), the ABRS (advanced ballistic reentry system), and NAVSTAR global positioning for SLBMs (submarine-launched ballistic missiles). The USSR has developed very large ICBMs, high megatonnage thermonuclear warheads, some antiballistic defenses, and possibly destroyers for orbiting satellites.

France, following the lead of the United States, has begun developing a neutron warhead. The president of France said, according to the Chicago Tribune of June 27, 1980, that research began in 1976, and that his country will be ready in about 1982 or 1983 to "decide about putting it into production." A few days before this announcement some underground nuclear explosive tests took place on the French testing grounds of the South Pacific.

The growth of horizontal and vertical proliferation is illustrated in the following table [DEV-79 and SIPRI, Yearbook of World Armament and Disarmament (1980)]:

TABLE I

Summary of Nuclear Weapons Tests Through 1979

Nation	Year of First Fission Test	Year of First Fusion Test	Number of Nuclear Explosions
USA	1945	1952 "wet", 1954 "dry"	653
USSR	1949	1953 ("dry")	426
UK	1952	1957	30
France	1960	1968	86
China	1964	1967	25
India	1974		1

INDUSTRIAL STATES

For admission to the thermonuclear club, a certain level of technology is needed. Secretary of Defense Harold Brown [37] saw that level as rather low:

> If the Morland paper were disseminated, there is a substantial increase in the risk that the availability of thermonuclear weapons would be increased. A country or a subnational element within a country that had the mechanical capability to develop and produce an unsophisticated fission-type nuclear explosive would gain technical assistance in determining the appropriate direction to pursue in developing high yield thermonuclear explosives.

To understand the credibility of such a proposition, one must look to see what actions are needed to produce nuclear weapons and what countries are in a position to achieve success -- which we did in Chapter V. The required steps entail the development and fabrication of both fission and fusion components so complex that massive resources are a prerequisite. Nations not members of the communisit bloc that might be in a position to carry out such development (but do not necessarily have the means for covert testing) are India, Israel, Canada, Sweden, Japan, Italy, Germany, Australia, and some others. They have an established, general technical capability and adequate technical personnel; they do not now have all the resources that would be needed, nor the national commitment. Less is known about the indigenous capabilities of communist bloc countries.

While Pickering's affidavit [7A], mentioned earlier, remains classified NSI, we can gain some insight into administration thinking about the capabilities of other countries from a mistakenly declassified document, "Prospects for Further Proliferation of Nuclear Weapons." It was originated by the CIA in September 1974 after the nuclear explosion by India ("the Budda is smiling," as the coded dispatch put it in May of that year). The CIA assessment is that "in the 1980s, the production of nuclear [fission] weapons will be within the technological and economic capabilities of many countries." The agency believes from circumstantial evidence that "Israel has already produced nuclear weapons." Countries that "could have fabricated nuclear devices more easily" than India and Israel from a "technological and financial point of view," are listed by the CIA as West Germany, Sweden, Canada, Italy, Japan, the Republic of China (Taiwan), Argentina, and South Africa. Although a nuclear weapons test is "not absolutely necessary," the agency believed that indications of a covert development program are "virtually certain to reach the outside world."

Israel has expressed its special concern that Iraq may be working toward a fission weapon capability. Pakistan is also being watched for such signs.

The CIA added the following to the main technological and economic conclusions of its "Special National Intelligence Estimate":

> The principal determinant of the extent of nuclear weapons proliferation in coming years will, however, be political considerations -- including the policies of the superpowers with regard to proliferation, the policies of suppliers of

nuclear materials and technology, and regional ambitions
and tensions.

If a nation has committed itself to develop nuclear weapons, it must
first acquire the difficult technology and the necessary precious
materials to make fission-type explosives, a prerequisite for
thermonuclear weapons. If it suceeds in developing fission weapons, a
nation will have the means to devastate any population center in the
world. If it goes beyond that point -- developing thermonuclear
weapons -- it can destroy any metropolitan area.

In short, without alerting its potential enemies and without
diversion of power reactor fuel, advanced nations could gain a credible
city-destroying arsenal of fission explosives within a few years. They
would not need to develop thermonuclear weapons. To reach the type of
strategic nation-destroying capability that the major powers have
acquired, and that China is approaching, requires additional years of
massive, overt, and expensive development. Moreover, a significant
political commitment, usually supported by successive government
administrations, and most likely in secret, must be made to undertake
the conversion to strategic thermonuclear systems. Final, and most
important, is the need for prototype and proof testing of the
thermonuclear weapon in its entirety; this will be discussed later on
in more detail.

ESPIONAGE

U.S. government policy depends heavily on control of information that
might contribute to proliferation. However, the effectiveness of
secrecy is limited by the reality of espionage. Valuable information
of a nondeducible nature is likely to be a prime target for spies. For
example, in late January 1950 Dr. Klaus Fuchs admitted that from 1942
to 1949 he had passed information on top-secret American research to
the Soviets. As a scientist, he understood and had access to detailed
information on implosion techniques and many other aspects of fission
weapon development at Los Alamos. In addition, as a member of a
British-American liason committee he was aware of U.S. interest in and
technical concepts regarding development of all types of thermonuclear
weapons.

The first public indication that the United States was working on
thermonuclear weapons was when columnist Drew Pearson let word of it
slip in 1949. Official acknowledgement came early in 1950, from
President Truman, after Fuchs confessed. In 1952 the United States,
and in 1953 the Soviet Union, exploded hydrogen devices -- large,
multistage, megaton H-bombs -- apparently using their respective
versions of the Teller-Ulam principles. "Mike," the 1952 United States
shot, utilized liquid deuterium and tritium in a physically very large
device that was called a "wet" bomb, whereas the August 1953 Soviet
shot, "Joe 4," was reportedly an air-deliverable "dry" (lithium-
deuteride) bomb [B&O-76]. Joe 4 apparently was somewhat cruder than
the American "Bravo" test of early 1954, the first U.S. explosion of a
lithium-deuteride superbomb.

These events suggest that trying to maintain secrecy over concepts
and deducible details is of limited value. First, they can be derived
independently. Second, they are prime targets for espionage. Third,

they have proven to be of little value in forestalling H-bomb development. The American and Soviet development programs proceeded in parallel. At this point there seems to be no evidence that even espionage had a pronounced influence on the way things went. It is unlikely that any information about the Soviet work would have speeded up the American program, or vice versa. The main determinant for progress in such matters is the technological inertia inherent in a massive undertaking such as the Manhattan Project. (Of course, we have no way of knowing just how much the United States and the Soviet Union knew about each other's progress.)

At any rate, U.S. secrecy policy has done little to deny America's competitors access to technology and related data. Instead, secrecy has disguised from the public and Congress implications of the nuclear weapons program, and created in the judiciary an aura of reverence, a deference, a presumption of legitimacy for anything classified.

NUCLEAR WEAPONS TESTING

To evaluate the various claims and counterclaims about what secrecy can and cannot do, classified information is not needed. To illustrate, here is a brief discussion of the testing of nuclear weapons and the limitations on what secrecy can accomplish in that area.

If a nation decides to advance from simple A-bombs to megaton (that is, thermonuclear) weapons, it must first master the technology of fission-explosive triggers, which are more complex than run-of-the-mill A-bombs. In so doing, that nation probably will find it necessary to amplify the explosive power of the fission trigger through known principles of "fusion enhancement" -- incorporating some fusion material in the trigger itself. To succeed will require explosive testing that can be readily detected. To achieve efficient burn of the thermonuclear fuel in a megaton-size weapon, all five of the thermonuclear powers have felt compelled to do open-air testing, in the face of worldwide disapproval. Sophisticated nuclear weapons will proliferate only to the extent that testing is permitted.

The United States and the Soviet Union have already conducted over a thousand nuclear weapons tests to develop their strategic and tactical arsenals. Hence the two superpowers have carried out about ten tests for each test by all other weapons states combined, and the United States has performed more tests than the USSR, Great Britain, France, China, and India together. As a result of their many dozens of tests of nuclear devices, France and Great Britain have reached an intermediate magnitude of nuclear-weapon strategic capability. China is known, on the basis of its nuclear testing program, to have reached a deterrence level vis-a-vis the superpowers, having recently tested long-range ballistic missiles.

Military Rationale for Testing Nuclear Explosives

Why is nuclear explosive testing so important? To answer that, consider how the information from testing impinges on several different aspects of nuclear weapons: nuclear criticality, explosive yield, reliability, and strategic and tactical uses. Much of the material below is adapted from DeVolpi's book on proliferation [DEV-79].

Criticality. For an atomic bomb to be accurately designed, it is vital to determine the "critical mass" of the fissile explosive in its weapons configuration -- that is, the precise amount that will explode when desired, but remain subcritical during manufacture and storage. Explosive testing is not needed at this stage, but "criticality approach" tests with a small, "zero power" experimental reactor (whose core is a simulation of the desired bomb configuration) are needed for each new design. Even the U.S. Atomic Energy Commission, with more than two decades of design and development experience with nuclear weapons, found it necessary to test a "simple" fission weapon made with what was termed reactor-grade plutonium, to be sure that it could be made into a fission explosive. The team that did the design had the benefit of the most sophisticated experimental and computed weapons data in the world.

Explosive yield. Military planners want to know how big a bang their A-bombs will give them. Usually this means explosive testing, especially if relatively low-grade plutonium is used. The type of bomb dropped on Hiroshima had not been exploded -- an indication of confidence in the uranium gun-barrel method -- whereas the plutonium implosion design that was used at Nagasaki had been tested first at Alamogordo. Some nations might now be able to stockpile untested weapons based on uranium-235, uranium-233, or high-isotopic-purity plutonium-239 with reasonable confidence that they would work.

It has become clear that thermonuclear burn in multistage fusion or single-stage fusion-boosted weapons depends on the relative placement of high explosives, reflectors, tampers, radiation-coupling materials, special (fissile, fertile, and fusion) materials, and structural members. There are many possibilities for placing such components, for choosing chemical and physical compositions, for optimizing quantities of materials. Extremely complicated hydrodynamic codes are required to model the behavior of each design. The codes must contain accurate physical data about the properties of all the different materials over the entire range of temperatures and pressures encompassed during the detonation process -- hundreds of millions of degrees of temperature and hundreds of millions of atmospheres of pressure. Detailed and correct radiation- and materials-transport, density, and compressibility data must be input.

In such complicated codes there are always significant uncertainties from unresolved questions about the accuracy of numerical procedures, the correctness of the physical data, and the faithfulness of the different mathematical models that describe the varied physical interactions that dominate the dynamics at different temperatures and densities -- to say nothing of outright mistakes. As U.S. weapon experts Rosengren and Grayson [68] admitted, "Even elaborate computer analysis [of thermonuclear-weapon design] does not necessarily lead to definitive conclusions." Testing is the only way to resolve these questions. (Theodore Taylor, the famous weapons designer, was once asked about the fact that the Castle-Bravo shot yielded fifteen megatons rather than the design value of eight megatons; he appeared to have been unaware of this fact, but expressed surprise that the test results had only been a factor of two away from calculated prediction) [MCP-75].

Despite the possibility of foreign dissemination of mistakenly declassified documents (such as UCRL-4725 and UCRL-5280) containing detailed nuclear test results, government weapons experts [142] testified in rebuttal to a defendant's witness [134] that "the test data in UCRL-4725 would not allow another nation to avoid nuclear tests. The description of the devices tested is much too fragmentary."

Testing is the sine-qua-non of offensive nuclear weapons proliferation.

Strategic and tactical uses. Much of the nuclear testing by the superpowers is of warheads for tactical (mininuke) and multiheaded weapons systems, or of triggers for thermonuclear warheads. Recently tests have also been directed at so-called neutron bombs: warheads with enhanced radiation for reduced "collateral effects."

Nuclear explosive tests have brought U.S. weapons to a level of performance that is very close to what is theoretically achievable. The Mk12A warhead, for instance, weighs no more than 220 pounds (110 kg) (including a heat shield, which is unrelated to weapon performance), and yields approximately 350 kilotons. (The weapon that destroyed Hiroshima had one-twentieth the yield and was forty-five times as heavy.)

For H-bomb triggers of unproven design, tests are mandatory to give confidence that the weapon will work at all. This is revealed by the series of nuclear explosive experiments that have been conducted by each of the four nations that developed fusion weapons, after knowing that the United States had succeeded.

Reliability. Although testing for reliability has often been cited as an important factor in nuclear weapons upkeep, the case seems clear -- as we showed in Chapter III -- that reliability tests are overrated.

A devious reason for pushing the reliability argument would be to provide a cover for qualitative improvements -- that is, for more vertical proliferation. Each new weapons system has special mass, yield, geometry, and performance requirements, which may differ substantially from system to system. For instance, an ICBM warhead, in addition to having a unique mass and geometry, must resist unusual accelerations as well as bursts of fast neutrons from possible interceptor missiles. Warheads for artillery shells will have other requirements, as will warheads used in air-launched cruise and attack missiles, surface-to-air missiles used in ship-based air defense, nuclear depth-charges and torpedoes. Both superpowers are constantly developing and diversifying their nuclear forces. The new weapons must be designed, developed, and, most important, tested if their performance is to be known to the high degree of certainty that military planners demand. No competent military officer is willing to base tactical or strategic planning on a weapons system that has never been tested.

Once a warhead configuration has been tested in detail, the situation is very different. There is no need (see Chapter III) to exercise the entire weapon explosively to determine its reliability. In fact, explosive testing is not the surest way to check the reliability of proven designs. The kind of checking necessary is readily deducible from the available conceptual information now in the public domain. Because the nuclear explosive dynamics of the weapon are determined solely by the placement of materials relative to each other, there are only limited possibilities for changes in the weapon that could result in degraded performance: changes in the tritium or deuterium concentrations in the various components, radioactive decay processes that introduce "poisons" into trigger materials (affecting criticality), malfunctions of various electronic devices or components, and chemical aging of high-explosive materials.

The radioactive isotopes, precursors, and daughters of plutonium all have well-defined and easily measured radiation signatures. The concentrations of these materials in either fissile or fertile weapons components can routinely be measured to better than one part in 10,000. Chemical explosives are readily analyzed with standard analytical and physical procedures, and are easily remanufactured and replaced when necessary. Electronic components are also easy to test and replace. Nonnuclear mockups of the electronic and chemical detonation of entire weapons assemblies, with fissile substances replaced by dummy materials, are also not hard to do. All these tests are convenient, routine, and inexpensive standard procedures of a "laboratory benchtop" nature (unlike even the smallest underground nuclear test), and they can be performed with such certainty and in such quantity that nuclear testing would not only be unnecessary, but it would in fact be an incomplete means of determining the state of the stockpile.

Once a nuclear warhead has been developed, nondestructive testing becomes a cost-effective and sufficient method for assuring reliability.

NUCLEAR TEST BANS

Since World War II three arms control issues have impinged directly on people's lives and thereby attracted broad public attention: civil defense, atmospheric testing of nuclear weapons, and proposals for antiballistic missile (ABM) systems.

Civil defense was an issue in the early sixties. It would have required people to pay out money for shelters, and to get used to the idea of using them. The effects of nuclear weapons were on people's minds. For a variety of reasons, civil defense was rejected.

Atmospheric testing caused radioactive fallout. People paid attention long enough to realize that the national-security benefit of open-air testing was not worth the risk. Atmospheric testing by the major powers was discontinued when the partial test ban treaty was signed in 1963. Underground testing, which did not irradiate people, proceeded and still continues.

The ABMs were to be deployed near major cities -- "H-bombs in the back yard." Again, the realities of nuclear war were brought closer to people's consciousness, for a time. Those working for arms control were able to get the attention of citizens long enough to explain some of the implications and deficiencies of policies that included ABMs. The ABM was rejected as a city defense in 1969.

In each case, public interest in nuclear strategy disappeared once the problem was taken from the back yard and put behind a fence. No fundamental solutions were achieved.

Although all of those topics are currently dormant in the public mind, they are by no means dead. Particularly relevant here is the matter of testing nuclear weapons. The limited test-ban treaty is still in effect. It prohibits signatories (France and China are notable nonsigners) from testing in the atmosphere. Testing underground with a maximum yield of 150 kT (TNT) is allowed, as long as no radioactivity crosses international boundaries. A comprehensive test ban treaty (CTBT) that would ban all testing has been under consideration in various quarters for twenty years. Hans Bethe, according to a profile of him in the December 10, 1979 New Yorker, advocated one as early as 1957, and he has continued vigorously to support prohibitions on testing.

The Comprehensive Test Ban Treaty

The CTBT is the neglected Cinderella of arms control treaties. It would benefit the Nuclear Non-Proliferation Treaty, the Strategic Arms Limitation Treaty, the ABM Treaty, and any other covenant intended to limit the deployment or use of nuclear weapons. It is the cornerstone on which further political accords that aim at controlling the proliferation of nuclear weapons will have to rest.

Negotiated by the United States, the Soviet Union, and the United Kingdom, the CTBT would bind the signatories to test no more nuclear weapons in an explosive mode. The worldwide political effects of a treaty that is only trilateral could be appreciable. For one thing, Article VI of the Non-Proliferation Treaty (NPT) clearly assigns to the weapons-state signatories an obligation "to pursue negotiations in good faith on effective measures relating to the cessation of the nuclear arms race at an early date and to nuclear disarmament." The nonnuclear-weapons states who signed the NPT have bitterly criticized the superpowers for failing to stop underground testing or to show any other significant progress toward meaningful arms control as called for in Article VI. It is explicitly for that reason that India has refused to sign the NPT.

Verification would be vital, of course, since no treaty is either acceptable or useful if the parties cannot be sure that its terms are not being importantly violated. A test ban could be verified by a wide assortment of techniques: overt and covert unilateral intelligence information, sporadic or periodic on-site inspection, electronic monitoring, satellite surveillance, aerial flights, ship-based observation, data-sharing, observer exchanges, rewards for informers. Extensive discussions of such methods have been published.

A worldwide ban of all nuclear explosions, even small ones, by all countries is desperately needed. Very small explosions, well underground, might be hard to detect. However, because some tests that yield less than 1 kt(TNT) can be detected, the superpowers would probably have little interest in jeopardizing the treaty for the small gains in weapons knowledge that a few very low-yield tests could provide. A threshold state, under certain circumstances, might undertake the risk. Even so, by eliminating aboveground tests, excluding peaceful nuclear explosions, and imposing a total ban on all nuclear weapons testing, entry into the nuclear club could be made financially expensive and politically risky. All would realize that there could be no assurance that any weapon that needed a new type of nuclear warhead would perform as desired, whether it was designed by an advanced nuclear state or by a nonnuclear one.

Because only countries that have engaged in testing can be certain that they truly have a nuclear-weapons capability, a worldwide comprehensive test ban would inhibit political leaders who might otherwise be inclined to develop nuclear weapons.

A trilateral CTBT would perhaps be a necessary first step toward a universal ban. The nonnuclear-weapons states, long antagonized by the competition between the superpowers, would see in such a step evidence that the big powers were starting to show some genuine desire to move toward nuclear restraint. Even lacking a formal treaty, if the nuclear powers were to renounce -- unilaterally or collectively -- all nuclear weapon testing, there would be considerable counterproliferation impetus. All would benefit from a temporary ban, pending conclusion of a treaty. As it is, however, although opposing proliferation rhetorically, the nuclear-weapons states continue to augment their own arsenals.

Further complicating the situation, the United States has consistently and energetically opposed all attempts to amend the NPT with provisions that would prohibit the superpowers from using, or threatening to use, nuclear weapons against signatories who did not have nuclear weapons (provided these states are not hosting nuclear weapons of a weapons state). The additional resentment created by this policy is predictable.

A CTBT could have extensive impact in limiting improvements in U.S. and Soviet weapons that are based on nuclear explosives. Unfortunately it would not turn the clock back on current weapons systems, but at least it would seriously reduce the flexibility to develop new ones. It would, in effect, constrain new systems to be designed around existing ones, in place of the arms-escalating practice of designing new systems around new warheads.

Cessation of nuclear weapons testing by the United States and the USSR could be expected have a number of effects that would promote political and technical stability:

* It would make it impossible to determine the performance capabilities and reliability of all untested nuclear explosive configurations, thereby freezing signatories into a fixed level of warhead technology.

* It would remove the political liability of a testing program that is viewed with concern by nonnuclear-weapons states. This could increase Soviet and American influence for nonproliferation among some states contemplating weapons programs, and in general help set the stage for a worldwide comprehensive test ban.

* It would be a significant step toward meeting the arms control provisions set down in Article VI of the Nuclear Non-Proliferation Treaty.

The main arguments that have been used against the complete cessation of weapons testing are:

* Confidence in our existing stockpile of nuclear weapons will be eroded because, when questions of reliability of existing stockpiled weapons arise, testing will not be possible.

* Clandestine testing of very small nuclear weapons will be hard to monitor, even if some form of on-site inspection can be negotiated. Other ways of cheating, like testing in deep space, may also be possible.

* The risks of losing an edge in weapons capabilities, as a result of undetected cheating, are too great compared with any of the possible benefits.

The arguments against the CTBT can be evaluated by examining both the goals of the treaty and the correctness of the various technical points. The treaty is intended to take advantage of the fact that all new designs of nuclear warheads must be tested if performance is to be certified, regardless of who designs the weapon or the level of experience with weapons design. Therefore, any limitation in weapons development that is imposed on one signatory is, by definition, imposed on the others. On that basis, any and all signatories to such a treaty can justifiably claim a demonstrated commitment toward bringing this technology under control. This clearly beneficial and stabilizing gain must be balanced against possible losses in security stemming from inability to test.

Since under the treaty the United States could lose its existing edge in nuclear weapons sophistication only if there were significant cheating, perceptions of how hard it would be to cheat become important. The actual difficulty is illustrated by the ways that have been thought of. In 1962, for instance, an argument used against a test ban was that Soviet clandestine testing on the far side of the moon could be carried out undetected by the United States. Now the United States can go to the moon (and presumably monitor it), so the argument has been changed to Mars.

Further, a secret testing program would have to be extensive in order to be significant -- a few shots on the other side of Mars would not be worth much. Soviet weapons technology, acknowledged to be considerably less sophisticated than American, has only come within a factor of 2.5 of the American yield-to-weight ratio. Therefore, assuming that their weapons program is at best no more efficient than ours, they would have to successfully hide about two hundred high-yield detonations in order to achieve our level of weapons efficiency. A test program that large would be, practically speaking, impossible to hide. But even if successfully carried out, the result would only be a lessening of the weight their already portable, very destructive weaponry by a factor of two or three. This risk must be balanced against the proliferation potential that exists without the CTBT.

On September 22, 1979, while in orbit in the Southern Hemisphere, the optical sensors of a U.S. Vela satellite registered an event reported to have the double-flash characteristic of a nuclear test. Whether it actually was a nuclear explosion is, at this writing, under dispute. Although an independent presidential panel of prominent scientists concluded in April 1980 that it was unlikely that the signal came from a nuclear explosion, the Naval Research Laboratory has sent to the White House a classified report that disagrees. [See Science 207, p.504 (1980) and 209, p.996 (1980).] If a nuclear test did take place, Israel and South Africa would be suspected, though both have vigorously denied involvement. The White House has been charged with playing down the evidence, because if the explosion were real it would indicate further failure of American nonproliferation policy.

Although there remains uncertainty about the interpretation of the Vela satellite data in this incident, it is more indicative of inadequate coverage than of deficiencies in national verification technology. Observation satellites now in orbit are directed primarily towards verification of the limited test ban between the superpowers. Worldwide monitoring, both by satellite and other means, can improve and undoubtedly will.

PROLIFERATION CONCERNS

Concern has been growing over the possibility that nuclear weapons could fall into the hands of terrorists, maverick governments, or, simply, nations not now part of the nuclear-weapons club. The U.S. government has dealt with the problem by assuming that it can do little more than rely on denying or controlling access of nonnuclear countries to information, technology, and materials. Some professionals believe that official emphasis has been misplaced. Ted Taylor, who was once an expert designer of nuclear warheads, "came in from the cold" and wrote about proliferation. His concerns are characterized by Cox [COX-75] in the following way:

> Taylor believes that the only way to control nuclear proliferation and clandestine bomb building is not through secrecy, but rather by carefully developed safeguards to control the special nuclear materials required to make nuclear weapons.... Taylor, like [Edward] Teller, considers most nuclear weapons secrecy an obstacle to sound policy and essential public awareness.

Reactor Technology

In an effort to limit proliferation, reactor technology has recently been singled out by some as a target for unilateral or international restriction. While this particular example does not illustrate current secrecy problems (because the technology is no longer secret), it is a vivid example of the need for public understanding of certain technical issues. At a time when adequate energy is vital for world peace, any potential for conflict between the need for energy and the risk of proliferation needs to be well analyzed.

To the extent that the nuclear fuel cycle contributes to that risk, reactor technology and the fissile materials derived from reactors must be subject to technological and institutional controls. Implicitly assuming that adequate controls are not possible, the Carter administration held up U.S. progress toward reprocessing, which will recover the plutonium from spent fuel and separate components such as the "actinide" isotopes. Ironically, any time so bought was not used, so far as we can tell, to develop the control methods that will increasingly be needed. We see that as not in the national interest, for several reasons. First, because the plutonium cycle exploits one of the two known inexhaustible energy resources (the other is solar power), its use will inevitably grow in other parts of the world as well as in the United States; the U.S. should take a leading role in helping the technology to develop safely. Second, removing the long-lived actinides from spent fuel alleviates waste-disposal concerns. And third, to the extent that the United States meets its energy needs by depleting increasingly scarce reserves of oil, gas, and uranium-235, world prices for those commodities will be driven up, making them increasingly unavailable to Third World countries for whom large, central-station electric plants might not soon be practical. The results are likely to be alienation of energy-poor countries, increasing anarchy and lack of safeguards in the reprocessing of reactor fuel, and, generally, greater international turmoil.

We have already mentioned that the fissile materials ordinarily associated with reactors are of poor quality for use in weapons. If the option of nuclear power were miraculously to vanish, the potential for nuclear weapons propagation would not be reduced; in fact, proliferation could well be accelerated because of conflicts over increasingly scarce energy supplies. Power reactors have not been attractive to any of the current nuclear-weapons states as a route to fissile material. All the needed weapons technology and materials are available in better quality and quantity, and with less fanfare and cost, from other, clandestine routes. Moreover there is much more to a bomb than the fissile component: The technology that accompanies the nuclear power fuel cycle can provide a stepping-stone to weapons technology, but it is neither necessary nor sufficient.

A further consideration is that the main driving force for proliferation has little or nothing to do with reactors: It comes from international instability and the vertical-proliferation policies of the nuclear-weapons states, who arrogantly continue to develop, test, and deploy weapons of mass destruction.

DISINCENTIVES TO PROLIFERATION

To become a nuclear-weapons power, a nation must first of all make the decision that, in spite of various drawbacks, there is a political advantage to be gained: It must expect increased net security. One risk is that of being discovered, especially through the effects of testing. If neighboring states do find out, they will become less secure and might even be moved to preemptive military action. There are inherent technical difficulties as well -- obstacles that could be enhanced by technical and institutional steps, such as technology denial and secrecy, that weapons states can implement or strengthen.

Technology Denial

Technology denial, the simple refusal to export blueprints, machinery, materials, and hardware to a candidate nuclear-weapon state, can be effective. Control of fissile materials, for instance, is essential. Inasmuch as a fission trigger is needed for a fusion weapon, safeguarding weapons-grade fissile materials creates an important hurdle against proliferation of thermonuclear weapons (H-bombs) as well as pure fission weapons (A-bombs). In addition, there are some materials, such as tritium and lithium-6 deuteride, that are needed in large ("strategic") quantities for fusion weapons but not, in such amounts, for anything else. Effective international monitoring and safeguarding of strategic quantities of these materials would be a useful antiproliferation measure.

Secrecy

Although we have seen that other nations can independently develop fusion weapons, restrictions on access to nuclear weapons data are still important. Secrecy, however, should be limited to the nondeducible details of weapons design and fabrication. The general concepts are available to anybody with the ability to understand them, making secrecy in that area nearly valueless. As Edward Teller, coinventor of the hydrogen bomb, has said [B&O-76], "the real 'secrets' are exactly those production procedures which one cannot communicate readily but which must be learned by experience." Dr. James Beckerly, former director of classification for the Atomic Energy Commission, said as early as 1954 [M&M-80], "atom bombs and hydrogen bombs are not matters that can be stolen and transmitted in the form of information."

As examples of protectible information in the nuclear weapons business, one might mention chemical and metallurgical materials processing, optimum materials, fabrication methods, detonation techniques, precise arrangement of components, and general know-how in technological methods. Also amenable to protection are blueprints, results of engineering calculations, and -- most important -- experimental data resulting from nuclear weapons testing.

From time to time there will be outside speculation about sensitive details, sometimes correct and sometimes not. An important element in safeguarding critical information is a strict official policy never to comment on the accuracy of such deductions. This principle, "never confirm or deny," is normally well appreciated in working-level classification circles, but seems to have been consciously violated by government officials in the Progressive case. We have reason to believe that the decision to do so was not unanimously supported in the government, particularly by the office of the Assistant Secretary of Energy for Defense Affairs, the office directly responsible for DOE classification policy.

Institutional Actions

Institutional and multinational steps to deter proliferation should not be confined to safeguarding fissile or fusionable materials. It is important also to foster an international climate that both removes the incentives to proliferate and provides active disincentives.

Some needed antiproliferation actions do not seem to be consistent with current official policy. This is highlighted in the recent report of the International Fuel Cycle Evaluation, especially in remarks by participants from other countries, who charged that the commercial interests of the United States have been placed above nonproliferation considerations. In the Progressive case, another example, the U.S. government's outmoded reliance on secrecy as the mainstay of antiproliferation policy clashed with the reality that the information was already out.

Antiproliferation Strategy

Effective prevention of further spread of nuclear weapons would require a variety of complementary measures. No one of them could do the job by itself, but each one is worthwhile. Secrecy is no more than a minor, temporary part of the picture. At least one comprehensive antiproliferation strategy, combining technology denial, secrecy, and other institutional actions, has been proposed [DEV-79].

Most important is the need to remove the incentives for proliferation, because a country that wants A-bombs badly enough will be able to get them. To reduce international tension, multilateral measures -- such as accepted nonnuclear mechanisms for resolving conflicts, and assurance of adequate energy -- would be helpful, if not essential. At the same time, to feel secure each country would need to have confidence that its neighbors were not getting nuclear bombs. Further help could come from the superpowers: If they showed progress toward reversing the nuclear arms race, they would dim the prestige of being nuclear-armed.

On the technical side, barriers to proliferation could be heightened by banning testing, maintaining tight security over existing nuclear weapons, effectively safeguarding nondeducible information from programs of weapons development, and exerting adequate international control of sensitive parts of the nuclear-power fuel cycle.

An urgent element in a strategy to minimize proliferation is recognition of the importance to other nations of being militarily secure and having a secure energy supply. Military security can be aided by alliances; energy security requires of energy sources that are independent of political vagaries. Nuclear power represents one such stable, assured source of baseline energy -- an option that has been developed vigorously by France, to the envy of many nations that lack indigenous sources of exploitable energy. Consequently, policies that cause the United States to appear unreliable, especially in the transfer of technology and fuel for peaceful application of nuclear energy, create instability and stimulate nations to provide their own independent capabilities.

CONCLUSIONS REGARDING PROLIFERATION RISK

The gap between concept and execution in nuclear weapons design is much greater than the U.S. government acknowledged in its affidavits in the Progressive case. Its assertions exaggerated the proliferation potential of Morland's article without supporting evidence, and in essence were political in that they tried to rationalize the administration's antiproliferation policy -- a policy that has not been demonstrably successful.

Policies that will effectively impede proliferation must be devised with an understanding of the needs of other countries. As an example, for the United States to attempt to discourage India from developing nuclear weapons it is not enough to embargo fuel for her reactors or ask her to accept full-scope safeguards. Those measures would be useful only as part of a broader policy. What do we in the United States propose to forego on our side? Would we be prepared to stop testing nuclear explosives or take other measures that India asks as a quid pro quo?

Trade-offs can be made among measures to resist proliferation. Greater emphasis could be placed on institutional rather than technological measures. For promoting suitable nonproliferation, some technological measures are suitable, but concessions may have to be made in commercial or national advantage. Current approaches should not be frozen without full consideration of alternatives and their national security implications. By way of example, we see the continuing production and testing of nuclear weapons as inconsistent with conducting SALT negotiations. The Carter Administration has evidently set in motion the budgetary and planning process for the manufacture of perhaps 10,000 new nuclear warheads, and the Reagan administration has indicated it will continue that program. The United States and the Soviet Union cannot forever disregard the proliferative influence of their arms race upon other nations.

We cannot overlook the fact that thermonuclear weapons have so far been tested by four nations that followed the U.S. technical and political lead. Whereas the government argued in Progressive that valuable time would be lost if the Morland article were published, there was no indication that any grace period would be used constructively -- no sign that past U.S. policies were likely to change for the better. The administration described its policy as one of antiproliferation; in fact, America's role -- as an unreliable supplier of nuclear fuel and technology and as an undeterred producer and tester of nuclear weapons -- has been viewed by other nations as a hypocritical one that stimulates further proliferation.

Nations that have developed fission weapons are in a position, if they so choose, to carry out the development of multistage, high-yield fusion weapons -- but only if they can openly test such devices. That is why a moratorium on nuclear weapons testing would be such a substantial help in retarding the spread of hydrogen bombs

American policy has been affected by political compromises unrelated to the danger of proliferation. Greater emphasis is needed on control of special materials and on developing an international consensus on how to stem proliferation. It was self-deluding to believe that Morland's article would have accelerated proliferation, or that technology denial and secrecy are sufficient to prevent the propagation of thermonuclear weapons.

7 Government Secrecy

Secrecy has always had a role in operation of all branches of the government. Courts sometimes find it necessary to preserve privacy of sensitive information, as in the Progressive case, by having at least part of the proceedings in camera. Congress occasionally must keep information privileged in order to conduct its business. The executive branch has permitted secrecy not only in military activities but also in civilian agencies. Even in the private sector -- banks and industry, for example -- secrecy has been commonplace, but generally without government involvement.

"Legal authority for the operation of the security classification system...stems in part from the constitutional authority of the President in Article II" [F&W-74]. United States government secrecy currently is authorized by a combination of congressional acts, implemented through executive orders. The primary structure for secrecy is established by federal codes applying to espionage and censorship [H&H2-77], by the Atomic Energy Act of 1954, and by the National Security Information Executive Order 12065, with implementing directives issued by the National Security Council. There also are regulations governing invention secrecy.

For our purposes, the relevant statutes are the Atomic Energy Act and Executive Order 12065. Each of those instruments specifies criteria for classifying information. Material classified under the former is termed Restricted Data (RD); if classified under the executive order, it is called National Security Information (NSI). More detail follows shortly.

Analyses of secrecy trends may be found in works by Cox [COX-75], Halperin and Hoffman [H&H1-77], and Franck and Weisband [F&W-74], among others. We are mainly interested here in secrecy as it pertains to inhibiting the spread of nuclear explosive devices, where some secrecy is helpful, even though its potential is limited.

Secrecy has both benefits and drawbacks. Some of the former are pointed out by Franck and Weisband:

> Chief among the benefits of secrecy is the maintenance of the minimal defense security that is still essential in a world of national rivalry. A second and almost equally important benefit is that secrecy preserves a certain

131

flexibility among advisers and members of the Government
negotiating with each other prior to reaching an official
policy decision.... A third related benefit is that
secrecy makes it easier for opponents of a policy to oppose
it from inside the government without having their loyalty
questioned. The fourth benefit is that secrecy makes
possible a higher level of candor in the routine exchange
of confidences among governments....

An evaluation by Arthur Macy Cox [COX-75] suggests that the
following four areas deserve to be within the "legitimate boundaries"
of secret information: war plans and contingencies, secret diplomacy,
secret intelligence, and secret military weapons systems, especially in
early stages of development. This is consistent with Morton Halperin
and Daniel Hoffman [H&H1-77], who set aside categories of sensitive
information that should be "presumptively secret" because of "their
limited use to the public": weapons systems (details of advanced
weapons systems design and operational characteristics), details of
plans for military operations, ongoing diplomatic negotiations, and
intelligence methods (codes, technology, and spies).

With respect to weapons-system data, Halperin and Hoffman comment
that

one category of such information is already required to be
kept secret by the Atomic Energy Act, which specifies that
information useful in the manufacture of atomic weapons and
other atomic explosive devices should be classified as
"restricted data."

Technical characteristics of many nonnuclear weapons
systems are quite sensibly kept secret. Secrecy makes it
harder for other countries to manufacture these weapons, to
counteract them, or to exploit their vulnerabilities....

After analyzing existing classification systems in the United
States, they observe:

Two specialized systems, relating to cryptography and
atomic energy, are authorized by law and protected by
criminal penalties for unauthorized disclosure. Other such
systems protect satellite reconnaissance programs, the
military plans for general nuclear war (known as the SIOP),
and covert operations of the CIA. It is, of course,
impossible to know what others may now exist.

In addition to the classification features of congressional laws and
excecutive orders, there are more subtle restrictive classification
systems in use:

By creating special designators and special dissemination
channels, the bureaucracy generating the information
determines what classification levels should be used and
who shall have access to the information.

THE ATOMIC ENERGY ACT OF 1954

Congress has deemed that government control of development, operation,
and regulation of nuclear energy, nuclear weapons, and special nuclear
materials is warranted under constitutional provisions of interstate
and foreign commerce, common defense and security, health and safety,

and general welfare. The original Atomic Energy Act was passed in 1947. The changes made in 1954 were primarily to improve the control and dissemination of information about peaceful atomic energy [170]. Analyses of the history of the Act may be found in several of the references given above, as well as by Cheh [CHEH-80] and in reference HR-80. Appendix C contains selected passages from the 1954 Act.

Sensitive information is controlled under the Act in two ways: Restricted Data is accessible only to people with security clearance, and "espionage-like activities are prohibited" [CHEH-80].

Restricted Data

As defined under §2014(y), "Restricted Data" broadly includes "all data concerning (1) design, manufacture, or utilization of atomic weapons; (2) the production of special nuclear material; or (3) the use of special nuclear material in the production of energy." Data may be declassified -- removed from the Restricted Data category.

The definition is sweeping. Note the phrase, "all data concerning." It conveys a vastness that appears to exclude nothing related to nuclear matters. Under a literal interpretation, "Restricted Data" would presumably include the proposed SALT II treaty and matters related to nuclear reactor safety -- two of the major public issues of our time. The only exceptions allowed are pieces of information affirmatively declassified by the government.

The term "design" as used in the Act [§2014(i)] means "(1) specifications, plans, drawings, blueprints, and other items of like nature; (2) the information contained therein; or (3) the research and development data pertinent to the information contained therein." The term "concept" does not appear explicitly in the Act. Research and development includes, besides theoretical analysis and experimentation, the application of scientific theories and investigative findings.

Different degrees of classification are designated by the labels "Top Secret," "Secret," and "Confidential," derived from the Executive Order on National Security Information (see below). As a former DOE Director of Classification explained [24]:

> Top Secret is applied only to information the unauthorized
> disclosure of which could reasonably be expected to cause
> exceptionally grave damage to national secrecy. Likewise,
> Secret is applied for "serious damage" and Confidential for
> "identifiable damage."

Interestingly, the Atomic Energy Act does not give the government any power to classify (or reclassify) information. It specifies categories of information that is by definition Restricted Data, conferring upon DOE and NRC the duty to regulate and protect material so classified. Those agencies may declassify such information, however, if it can be done safely [CHEH-80].

> This procedure is exactly the opposite of that which
> governs the classification of all other government
> documents. [The power to classify affirmatively] is based
> principally on executive orders that apply only [almost] to
> information owned, produced or controlled by the
> government.

Control of Dissemination

The Atomic Energy Commission (now divided into the Department of Energy and the Nuclear Regulatory Commission) was required by Congress (§2161) "to control the dissemination and declassification of Restricted Data in such a manner as to assure the common defense and security." The Commission was to be guided by principles of permitting and encouraging "the free interchange of ideas and criticism."

In 1979 the director of DOE classification indicated [24] that

With regard to protection of Restricted Data, personnel may be authorized access to Secret Restricted Data in the nuclear weapons area only if:

a. They have...a "Q" access authorization....

b. They "need to know."

The basic provisions that control the dissemination of Restricted Data are contained in §§2274-2277, the main teeth of the Act being in §2274, which defines criminal and civil violations and provides penalties for unauthorized transmission of restricted data. Under §2274(a), if communication took place "with intent to injure the United States or with intent to secure an advantage to any foreign nation," on conviction the punishment could be imprisonment for life. Lesser penalties are prescribed for conviction under §2274(b), which requires proof of "reason to believe such data will be utilized to injure the United States or to secure an advantage to any foreign nation."

Both unauthorized receipt of and tampering with restricted data are forbidden under §§2275 and 2276, with conviction subject to the same proof of intent as in §2274(a). These provisions apply to any form of data, including documents, writings, sketches, photographs, plans, models, instruments, appliances, or notes. Penalties up to life imprisonment may be imposed.

Disclosure of Restricted Data by government employees is enjoined under §2277 -- which covers not only present government employees, but also essentially anyone with present or past connection with the government, even if never exposed to classified documents or other information from secret government programs.

Enforcement Actions Under the Act

The Act forbids unauthorized communication, transmission, or disclosure of Restricted Data in any form (§2274). This has been interpreted (reasonably) by Judge Warren [82] to include "publishing." It was under §2274(b) that the Act was invoked in the Progressive case. In the view of the government [166], "reason to believe" can be created simply by official notification that the disclosure of the data classified as Restricted "would...injure the United States or...secure an advantage to a foreign nation," and The Progressive had been so notified. No supporting evidence, according to the government, no proof of injury or advantage, should be required.

Injunctive proceedings are authorized by §2280. To our knowledge, before the Progressive case an injunction action had never been obtained under the Atomic Energy Act, although publications have been stalled or censored by the threat of legal action. Morland [86] claimed in his defense that enforcement has been "non-existent, inconsistent, and inequitable." Charles Hansen, in his letter to

Senator Percy, raised the same point about discriminatory application of the law (Chapter VI).

Other Cases of Prior Suppression

Although restraint of publication may be requested under the Act, the Progressive affair was the first occasion during peacetime in American history [174] that the government successfully caused publication of an article to be held up by court order granted under the Act. Before the Pentagon Papers case, the government had never even sought an injunction against publication under either the Act or the Executive Order.

Several impositions of prior censorship have been incurred by Ralph Lapp, who has published many articles and books on radiation effects, nuclear weapons, and strategic arms policies. One of the events took place in 1955. Lapp later wrote [LAPP-79]:

> In the early 1950's I considered that it was vitally important to provide the American public with essential information about thermonuclear weapons because the nature of the fission-fusion-fission weapon dramatically altered the very dimension of warfare, introducing as it did the potential for radioactive fallout lethality. I was also concerned about the health effects of nuclear testing.

In 1955 the New York Times was interested in an article "on the H-bomb. What it is, how it works, what it means." Lapp mailed a copy to the AEC for clearance; he was advised that the article contained classified data. After revising the article he got a letter of clearance from the AEC. However, the Times resubmitted the article for review to the AEC, which decided it still contained classified information. Despite Lapp's paragraph-by-paragraph documentation of the public source material he had used for the article, the AEC refused clearance. In 1960 Lapp wrote to the Times requesting clarification of the article's status, and in answer to the Times's renewed inquiry the government again refused to change the article's classification level. In 1979 Lapp again wrote to the Times reminding the newspaper of the censorship that had continued for twenty-five years. Lapp and the Times still have copies of the "classified" article in their files, including a copy returned by the AEC to Lapp.

One of the amici briefs [175] summarizes a similar experience of Hans Bethe's:

> In 1950 Scientific American was about to publish an article by Professor Hans A. Bethe, the distinguished physicist, regarding the newly projected hydrogen bomb. After the issue had gone to press the Atomic Energy Commission requested Scientific American to withhold publication of the technical portion of the article. Scientific American asked the AEC to specify its objections. At first it refused, insisting that to do so would betray the secrets it was trying to keep. Later it agreed to indicate the objectionable portions. Scientific American decided to comply and stopped the presses. The AEC then asked that all copies of the original article be destroyed. A security officer visited the printing plant and supervised the destruction of the type, the melting down of

the plates, and the burning of 3000 copies of the magazine which had already been printed.

The original, uncensored article was declassified in 1962. Gerard Piel, publisher of Scientific American, in a recent letter to the New York Times, describes some of the material that the AEC claimed would have endangered the national security: "The first three cuts involved information already published by others in the open litera- ture, already printed before in Scientific American and already published elsewhere by Bethe himself."

There is a bit of irony in the situation. It has been said that the fourth item was a piece of misinformation deliberately planted by Bethe, presumably to put other nations off the track. This too suffered the censor's cut.

Born Classified: Doctrine and Implications

The DOE Classification Office has declared, "All information falling within this definition [Restricted Data, §2014(y)] comes into existence as classified." One of the issues at hand is whether ideas, information, and data that are considered sensitive by the government are legitimately "born classified." Such a doctrine is fraught with danger to a free society. The government justified the doctrine as follows [4]:

> This concept, known as "classified at birth," was deemed necessary by Congress to ensure that sensitive information would not be divulged before the United States had the opportunity to assess its importance and take appropriate classification action.... In hearings...Congress was advised that the Restricted Data definition "has been interpreted...by the [Atomic Energy] Commission to mean that all information in these fields at birth, that is, when there is a new discovery, development, or article, is instantly classified." Despite some objection by scholars and scientists to this interpretation, Congress declined to modify it, thus giving occasion for application [of the] venerable principle that the construction of a statute by those charged with its execution should be followed... especially when Congress has refused to alter the administrative construction.

> One of the concerns expressed [52A] by the defendants was that a journalist's "original work product," a private scientist's independent research, a university professor's deductive reasoning can all be "classified at birth" -- instantly characterized as "Restricted Data," their communication banned subject to the criminal sanctions of the Act without the individual's knowledge.

Like plankton in the sea, technical concepts and ideas float around in the public domain. Some of these concepts coincide with classified information; they may have been derived within the classified laboratories, but they are also subject to independent deduction. Government attempts to capture these concepts for its exclusive use are not only unrealistic, but likely to be counterproductive: They call attention to military implications that might otherwise go unrecognized and certainly would go unconfirmed.

DECLASSIFICATION

The Atomic Energy Act provides for declassification of information "upcn an administrative determination that the data may be published 'without undue risk to the common defense and national security'" [166]. According to DOE [24],

Classification reviews may be prompted for various reasons, including program changes, Freedom of Information Act requests, unauthorized releases of classified information and requests by individuals or publishers who may wish to publish materials possibly containing Restricted Data.

Whereas the Freedom of Information Act (FOIA) might trigger classification review of certain information, that law expressly does not permit public access to classified material.

With regard specifically to the "basic principles of thermonuclear weapon design and operation," the director of DOE classification stated [9]:

My office has periodically examined these thermonuclear weapons concepts to determine if they should be declassified and in each reexamination have concluded that the information should remain classified in the interest of the national defense and security.

Potentially there is a serious difficulty in trying to divine just what information is classified and what is not. In a legal analysis, attorneys for the periodical press [174] observed that no compilation exists of data that has been declassified or removed from the Restricted Data category. Because data may not be published without inviting serious criminal consequences until affirmatively declassified, the citizen has no sure guide as to which thoughts or deductions might be classified.

EXECUTIVE ORDER ON NATIONAL SECURITY INFORMATION

On June 29, 1978, President Carter issued Executive Order 12065, providing for classification of certain data as "National Security Information" (NSI); extracts from the order are in Appendix D, and parts of a statement he made on that occasion are in Note VII-1. He gave as the objective "an increased openness in Government by limiting classification and accelerating declassification." The President said the standards for classification had been "tightened." An interagency office for overall supervision was created.

According to one policy analyst, David Wise [WIS-78], Carter's order is an improvement over the preceding (Nixon) order in several respects:

Carter promised..."most" documents...are to be declassified in six years.... Secrecy labels may now be applied only to documents which, if released, "could reasonably be expected" to cause some stated degree of damage to national securty...and, for the first time, information must be declassified if the need for secrecy is "outweighed by the public interest in disclosure of the information."

One of the unquestioned virtues of the Carter secrets order is that for the first time, classifiers are required

to mark which paragraphs or portions of a document are
secret, and which are not.

On the other hand, there remain exceptions -- such as undefined
"other categories" that may be classified, and a sufficiently vague
provision "for review in twenty years" that could allow government
officials to classify a document indefinitely. As Wise points out,
"secrecy is one of the tools of power."

National Security Information (NSI)

The only basis other than the Atomic Energy Act of 1954 for classifying
information is established in that executive order. Like Secret
Restricted Data, SRD, information classified NSI falls into one of
three categories, depending on the degree of harm that unauthorized
disclosure "reasonably could be expected to cause": (1) Top Secret
("exceptionally grave damage"), (2) Secret ("serious damage"), or (3)
Confidential ("identifiable damage"). Even though a given piece of
information might fit in one or more of those categories, it may not be
classified "unless an original classification authority also determines
that its unauthorized disclosure reasonably could be expected to cause
at least identifiable damage to national security." Thus information
is not automatically "born secret" under the executive order. Only
government data can be designated NSI.

To be subject to classification, data must concern one or more of
the following: military plans, weapons or operations; foreign
government information; intelligence activities, sources, or methods;
foreign relations or foreign activities; scientific, technological, or
economic matters relating to national security; programs for
safeguarding of nuclear materials or facilities; "other categories of
information which are related to national security." Some observers
(including us) feel that the area that could be construed to be within
those limits is excessive.

"The order specifically prohibits classification of privately
developed information" [CHEH-80]. Unlike SRD, private citizens cannot
inadvertently generate NSI, which is defined as

Information or material...that is owned by, produced for or
by, or under the control of, the United States Government,
and that has been determined pursuant to this Order or
prior Orders to require protection against unauthorized
disclosure, and that is so designated.

Although the duration of classification is nominally given as six
years, the exceptions and the lack of means for enforcement may make
automatic declassification almost meaningless in practice.

Definition of National Security Information. NSI is essentially
boundless in scope because a logical -- if sometimes loose --
connection can be found to nearly any subject. As defined by the
order, "national security means the national defense and foreign
relations of the United States." By virtue of their military nature,
most items of possible application to national defense, but not
including conceptual information, have been subject to classification.
Although the order covers "military plans, weapons, or operations," it
also states, "Nothing in this Order shall supersede any requirement
made by or under the Atomic Energy Act of 1954, as amended." Inasmuch
as they are not necessarily confined to military matters, foreign

policy and related activities allow a wide expanse for classification, including the subject matter of treaties to which the United States might become bound. International proliferation readily falls under the category of foreign relations.

It should be noted that "unauthorized disclosure of foreign government information or the identity of a confidential foreign source is presumed to cause at least identifiable damage to national security." This automatically subjects government officials and employees to the administrative sanctions applying to the unauthorized release of "Confidential" information, without the government having to bring forth supporting evidence of such damage.

The pervasiveness of secrecy in foreign affairs is amazing. A taxonomy by Frank and Weisband [F&W-74] of principal foreign affairs secrets contains the following categories: defense plans (strategy, operations, deployment); weapons research and development; diplomatic negotiations; treaties, agreements; information about other nations (defense plans, secret diplomatic negotiations, secret treaties and agreements); executive process (cabinet minutes, intradepartmental memoranda, expert advisory briefs, reports from diplomats); monetary negotiations; executive preparations for tariff negotiations or new regulations; tariff or import agreements; intelligence reports from own agents; and intelligence reports from allies. With this umbrella of secrecy, it is not surprising that official American overseas involvement can be hidden from public scrutiny.

Prohibitions. Certain classification practices are explicitly forbidden by the order: concealment of violations of the law, inefficiency, or administrative error; prevention of embarrassment to a person, organization, or agency; and restraint of competition. Basic scientific research information that is not "clearly related to national security" may not be classified. Nongovernment research and development products that do not incorporate or reveal classified information "to which the producer or developer was given prior access" may not be classified under the executive order (unless the government "acquires a proprietary interest in the product," as by buying a patent).

References to classified documents in ways "that do not disclose classified information" are not classifiable, nor can they be used as a basis for classification. Classification may not be used "to limit dissemination of information that is not classifiable under the provisions of this Order or to prevent or delay the public release of such information."

DOE guidelines on proliferation. As guidance to those involved in government-sponsored nonproliferation studies, the director of DOE's classification office has distributed "rationales" [see Note VII-2] to be used in determining whether such studies might be classified as NSI. In general, some evaluations of clandestine ways to treat and conceal nuclear materials may be considered SRD or classifiable as NSI.

Declassification and reclassification. Declassification policy under the executive order is primarily embodied in two subsections, one of which says declassification should occur if the "public interest in disclosure" outweighs the need for protection of the information. The other subsection calls for mandatory review procedures "to handle requests by a member of the public, by a government employee, or by an agency, to declassify and release information." Declassification requests under this provision are supposed to be "acted upon" within sixty days.

The executive order expressly forbids restoration of classification to documents "already declassified and released to the public," and no authority to reclassify is granted by the Atomic Energy Act. However the government has used "erroneous" or "mistaken" declassification as the basis for recalling certain sensitive documents.

The courtroom conflicts over two of those reports, UCRL-4725 and UCRL-5280, raise some serious legal questions with respect to the government's ability to protect legitimately classified materials that have been mistakenly declassified. In view of the highly sensitive nature of those official reports, it is hard not to be sympathetic with the government in its predicament. Even though there is a reasonable likelihood that their contents have been divulged to one or more nonnuclear nations, it is unlikely that a country that had the information would share it with others. There is a clear benefit to the national security to continue protection. Furthermore, Congress left the definition of declassification and its procedures up to the executive branch.

At the same time, reclassification by claiming mistaken declassification is potentially subject to abuse, as well as probably being contrary to the executive order. The example of the two UCRL progress reports points to the need for formal, legal means of accommodating legitimate mistakes, which would protect the public interest against disclosure of the contents of sensitive documents that may have gotten into the possession of private parties (for instance, the Xerox copies of UCRL-4725 originally made and disseminated by ACLU researcher Dimitri Rotow). Such a process is proposed in Chapter XI.

WHAT THE GOVERNMENT HAS BEEN CLASSIFYING

The actual scope of government classification is difficult to visualize. Besides the Atomic Energy Act and the Executive Order on National Security Information, other statues and executive orders specify classifiable subjects. For example, the Espionage and Censorship statutes [18 U.S.C. 792-799], define "defense information," "defense intallations," "communications intelligence," and classified information relating to codes, ciphers, and cryptographic systems.

Halperin and Hoffman [H&H1-77] point out:

> In practice the apparent simplicity of the executive order's three-tiered system is totally undone by the myriad of special procedures and classifications that have grown up with or without proper legal sanction. For example, the categories of "restricted data"...and "communications intelligence" are authorized by separate congressional legislation. Also in use are several special clearances and a vast number of restrictive distribution designators....
>
> Moreover, under the procedure known as derivative classification, any document that contains information from a document already classified must itself be classified....

An example of derivative classification is the set of "Cannikin Papers," (see Chapter VIII) which dealt with the large underground nuclear explosion in Amchitka, Alaska [F&W-74]: "By attaching one classified page to a volume or series of volumes of innocuous materials, the entire mass of material [was made] immune from disclosure."

As Howard Morland concluded [38A] after visiting various government facilities, "it is impossible for a person on the outside of the system to figure out what is classified and what is not classified information."

Examples of misuse of the classification system -- that is, applications in ways not intended by the framers of the laws or executive orders -- are reserved for the next chapter.

Patents

Secrecy for reasons of national security extends to the granting of patents. As background information for March 20, 1980, hearings of the House Government Information and Individual Rights Subcommittee, the subcommittee staff issued a summary [Note VII-3] of the Invention Secrecy Act. They point out that an invention may be kept secret as long as the "national interest requires." Secrecy requests can come from the military services, NASA, NSA, DOE, or the Department of Justice. In 1979 there were 3,300 active secrecy orders, some as much as thirty years old [HR-80].

E.J. Fygi, a DOE counsel, in testimony before the subcommittee, gave the following statistical summary:

We have sponsored 1,117 secrecy order renewals in the last year. Of these, 924 were issued on OSRD/AEC/ERDA/DOE generated inventions under Government ownership. Of the remaining 193, 117 were issued at the request of foreign governments under mutual security agreements. The other 76 renewals were on privately owned patent applications.

Of those patent applications not owned by DOE on which renewals have been issued, the average age is eight years for those secrecy orders requested by foreign governments, and 11 years for the secrecy orders on privately owned applications.

Through patent and Restricted Data control, the government can prohibit commercial development. For example, four companies suffered economic loss when they were deprived of their right to use information developed by their own research in gas centrifuge enrichment technology [CHEH-80].

Cryptography

In a remarkable paper, "New Directions in Cryptography" [Institute of Electrical and Electronic Engineers, Transactions on Information Theory (November, 1976)], Whitfield Diffie and Martin E. Hellman, electrical engineers at Stanford University, showed how it is possible to create unbreakable ciphers that do not require concealment of the method of encoding or advance sending of a key. Such systems are known as "public-key cryptosystems." Their novel property is that publicly revealing the encryption key does not reveal the decryption key.

The information explosion in cryptology greatly worries the National Security Agency as a result of such developments. Public discussion and development of cryptology may induce other nations to change their codes, with a consequential loss of intelligence information to the United States. The U.S. government has been attempting to stem the spread of cryptographic information through secrecy orders -- some of which were lifted as a result of public pressure [HR-80]. Such vacillation suggests that the issue of security versus First Amendment rights has not yet been resolved within the agency itself.

As David Kahn put it in the Fall 1979 issue of Foreign Affairs:

Cryptology, in 1945 a nation's most closely held secret, has gone public...and the problems are almost impossible to predict. Will the experts in the National Security Agency (who are reported to have invented their own type of public key cryptography some years ago), be able to stay a step ahead of the inventors, or will their closed work system eventually be matched (as it may have been in that case) and even surpassed by the open interactive community of bright scientists who refuse the restrictions and nonrecognitions of work in a clandestine agency? Will the study of cryptology become an epidemic that even all the government's resources will be unable to stem?

The availability of public-key cryptosystems does not compromise United States government secrets, of course; rather, it limits the ability of any third party -- including governments -- to intercept and decode encrypted national or industrial information.

VOLUME AND COSTS OF CLASSIFICATION

The amount of classified material is impressive. One estimate [F&W-74] was that in 1971 there existed 20 million classified Department of Defense documents -- perhaps one million cubic feet of documents in DOD files. The State Department was believed to have about 50 million classified documents. In 1971 some 55,000 government officials were authorized to classify documents. A General Accounting Office study in 1972 estimated a cost of $126 million annually for maintaining the security classification system. And Wise [WIS-78] reported that a House subcommittee found that 4.5 million new documents were classified in 1976.

The defendants in Progressive [52A] quote Senator William Proxmire as saying that a General Accounting Office study of government classification reveals "massive overclassification of national security documents and flagrant noncompliance by the Pentagon and other agencies with procedures set up to prevent abuses of the classification system."

During a hearing on May 23, 1979, before the Senate Subcommittee on Energy, Nuclear Proliferation and Federal Services, a representative of DOE estimated that the department generated a total of "approximately 20,000 [classified] documents per year." A subsequent insertion in the record indicated that the correct number was almost 130,000 classified documents for 1977 and as many again in 1978. At Los Alamos, one of several large DOE laboratories, there are stored "at least one-half million classified documents."

According to a report by the General Accounting Office, "Improved Executive Branch Oversight Needed for the Government's National Security Information Classification Program" [LCD-78-125, March 9, 1979], the Interagency Classification Review Committee in its 1977 annual report showed for all U.S. Government agencies,

> 4.5 million classification actions, but the total number for any year is not really known. GAO believes the total number is at least 70 million, but it could be over 100 million. ...most were exempt from the general declassification schedule, meaning that the information would not be automatically downgraded and declassified within the prescribed 10-year period.

The GAO report noted that many agencies that produce large quantities of classified documents, such as the CIA, FBI, and NSA, significantly understated the number of their classification actions. These agencies also failed to report infractions of Executive Order 12065 as required. The order calls for reporting on unnecessary classification, overclassification, repeated abuse, classification without authority, unnecessary exemption from general declassification schedule, exemption without authority, failure to apply downgrading and declassification assignments, failure to show classification authority, failure to apply internal classification markings, and incorrect computation of general declassification dates.

Another GAO report, "Continuing Problems in DOD's Classification of National Security Information" [LCD 80-16, October 26, 1979], found "improper use of classification authority, improper classification of information, and deficiencies in the marking of classified information." In a sampling of documents, 24 percent "contained information that had been improperly classified": They were unrelated to national security, referenced classified documents but did not reveal classified information, were classified at too restrictive a level, had been inconsistently classified, or were not downgraded when no longer containing sensitive information.

Secrecy also has costs not measurable in dollars. Franck and Weisband observe [F&W-74]:

> There is first the threat to the internal balance of power.... Information is power....
>
> A second cost of secrecy is the loss of public support for government policy, such as occurs when there is a real or imagined "credibility gap" based on evidence of frequent non-disclosure by a government. Closely related is...the loss of public interest in foreign affairs which sets in when a government refuses to let legislators and the public in on their deliberations....
>
> Still another disadvantage of secrecy -- the obverse of one of its benefits -- is that it obscures from the public the divisions and dissensions comprising the administrative history of most important Executive decisions....
>
> Finally, to be counted among the costs of secrecy is the procedure known as "leaking." The cost of excessive secrecy is excessive leaking of confidential information -- with its possible threat to national security.

And, we might add, secrecy can be misused for personal benefit.

SECRECY AND TECHNOLOGY DENIAL

Technology is not a secret -- it is a system.
- Henry Kissinger

Technology is a complex system, with interrelationships between information, materials, and processes. And technology is not completely unfettered: It is bounded by economic, political, legal, and social restraints.

Broadly, there are two classes of secrets. One kind, internal policy decisions, military or diplomatic plans, and the like, can be effectively protected if nobody in the know reveals them. The secrets, however, that have to do with methods or processes for manufacturing or utilizing products of advanced technology are a different matter: They are susceptible to independent discovery. Secrets of military technology are in that category. Because there are very few aspects of military technology that have no civilian applications, the key to the military use is almost always to be found in civilian knowledge. All advanced nations have land and air vehicles, computers, energy sources, and other technologies. Thus, although they can sometimes be bottled up for a time, the secrets of military technology are transient.

Technical information circulates in a variety of ways. Scientists continually share what they know, through meetings and publications. There are trade journals and other industrial and commercial methods of exchanging data. And let us not forget espionage, which has an impact now and then. Two of the most notable cases were those of the Rosenbergs and of Dr. Klaus Fuchs. Although the Rosenbergs were executed, the information they passed seems, in retrospect, to have been of marginal significance (Chapter VIII). Fuchs's information was more important. He had been assigned to atomic weapons research at Los Alamos. According to historian David Holloway [HOL-79], from 1941 to 1943 Fuchs would have been able to inform the Soviet Union that "Britain considered the uranium bomb a definite possibility"; he "provided the results of his own calculations on the theory of gaseous diffusion process for separating the isotopes of uranium, and told the Soviet Union that U-235 produced in this way might be used in an atomic bomb."

Fuchs continued to pass information to the Soviet Union in 1944 and 1945, but "it does not appear to have stimulated the expansion of effort that might have been expected." Evidently some of his information reached appropriate Soviet physicists, because in one of his confessions Fuchs noted that "questions had come back to him from the Soviet Union" about the derivation of a certain formula (Bethe-Feynman) for estimating bomb efficiency.

Knowing the "secret" is not the same thing as being able to use it. Implementation very often depends both on industrial capacity and on accumulated experience -- the many, often unverbalized, tricks of the trade called know-how. Without the appropriate foundries, knowledge of metallurgical processes to make titanium alloys for combat aircraft would be of no use. Even given the foundries, learning how to operate them properly is a slow process. For a current example, when foreign oil wells or refineries are expropriated, the new owners sometimes have trouble getting them back into production.

Effective technology denial will make use not only of secrecy about processes, but -- more important -- of a careful policy of limiting access to the pertinent expertise. Two methods are used -- secrecy (attempting to prevent the transfer of knowledge about nuclear weapons), and export controls (safeguarding fissile materials and restricting the transfer of hardware needed to manufacture fissile substances).

A policy of technology denial, to be useful, must be admininstered by realists. One of the considerations was brought out in a Scientifc American amicus brief [175]:

> The reality of prior restraint proceedings is that the challenged information will in fact become public, not only in spite of the effort of suppression, but because of it.... It would not be surprising in the slightest to find that there are now, throughout the country, numerous individuals energetically trying to learn just what it is that The Progressive knows. Nor would it be surprising to find that some of these efforts proved fruitful or that the information was soon published.

This indeed happened, as the government acknowledged when it withdrew from the case, ostensibly on account of Hansen's letter. As Thomas I. Emerson summarized the point in his brief for the Scientific American [175], "The government here is engaged in the highly dubious and improbable task of attempting to stop the march of time." Postol, in his first affidavit to the court [45], argued that

> Reducing the availability of information in technical areas where military or industrial applications could threaten our national security may sometimes be an effective means of technology denial and I support such measures when they are necessary. However, capricious or arbitrary suppression of information which is already generally available has an adverse effect on national security....

Information of the sort gathered by Howard Morland is clearly subject to independent discovery either by compilation from public sources or by inductive reasoning by scientists in technologically advanced nations. Of such nations, those that choose not to proceed with developing fission or fusion weapons do so mainly because of the self-defeating nature of such armaments: The perceived benefits do not outweigh the perceived risks. Other countries, less technologically advanced, are deterred by such safeguards and technical obstacles as currently exist. The primary barriers to nuclear weapons production are not informational.

Nevertheless, secrecy about how to make and use weapons, most would agree, is usually justified. Noncontroversial examples are the detailed design of nuclear weapons, detailed methods of isotopic enrichment of fissile materials, and the ways that weapons and reactors are physically protected. These are the primary areas governed by existing secrecy regulations.

We do not accept the argument that abolishing all secrecy would hasten the coming of international arms security and peace -- that the nuclear-weapons states, realizing that they are mutually endangered by horizontal proliferation, would finally undertake meaningful arms control. The idea, however, has some currency. It is not unlike the suggestion that the nuclear devastation of another populated city is

needed to bring the world to its senses. The obvious problem with
these proposals is the irreversible dangers they involve. The
"redemonstration" of the catastrophic qualities of nuclear explosions
is not likely to be any more effective in bringing about nuclear
disarmament than the bombing of Hiroshima and Nagasaki was. The day
when all the secrets of operable nuclear weapons are out in the open is
coming quickly enough; there is no need to hasten its arrival. As it
is, gradual proliferation is making it progressively harder to reverse
the situation and prevent accidental or malicious use of nuclear
weapons. Frustration with national arms control policies is scarcely a
valid reason for making things worse.

Weapons Technology

There are some who think that information-secrecy programs were
effective in delaying the Soviet Union's development of its first fission weapon. The study [HOL-79] by Holloway of the Soviet decision to
build nuclear weapons suggests otherwise. First, the Soviets recognized early the weapons potential in the fission process. In 1939 a
leading Russian physicist, Igor Tamm, remarked to a group of students:
> Do you know what this new discovery [of nuclear fission in
> uranium] means? It means a bomb can be built that will
> destroy a city out to a radius of maybe ten kilometers.

Secret research can even stimulate investigation. In 1942, the
Russian physicist Flyorov found that "nothing was being published on
nuclear fission in American or British journals." He correctly deduced
from the "dogs that did not bark" that nuclear research in the United
States had been made secret. In April 1940 scientists in the United
States had voluntarily stopped publishing papers that "might help
Germany to develop the atomic bomb. They thus unwittingly alerted
Soviet scientists to American work on the bomb."

As Holloway has pointed out, because the Russian government already
had information about German interest in the military uses of atomic
energy, "the key factor in the [Soviet] atomic decision of 1942 [to
initiate a small atomic bomb project] was Soviet knowledge of German
and American work on the bomb." In addition, Klaus Fuchs had already
begun to pass information to the Soviet Union by the summer of 1942,
and two other scientists were discovered to have passed on technical
data during World War II.

Another factor that limits the effectiveness of technology denial is
the single piece of information conveyed by a demonstration of
workability. According to Holloway, use of the atomic bomb on Japan
sent two messages to the USSR:
> The final Soviet decision to develop the bomb was taken
> after the Alamogordo test of 16 July and the dropping of
> the bombs on Hiroshima and Nagasaki on 6 and 9 August
> [1945] had made it clear that the atomic bomb was
> feasible.

> The significance was not merely that the bomb was power-
> ful, or that it was possessed by the United States alone,
> but also that the United States was willing to use it in
> circumstances that did not seem absolutely to require it.

Consequently, we see that secrecy and technology denial had little
or no influence in preventing or diminishing Soviet development of the

atomic bomb. "The decisive factor," concludes Holloway, "was the knowledge that Germany and the United States were conducting research in secret." The decision ultimately was based on "the world-view of the Soviet leadership that made the American possession and use of the atomic bomb evoke an automatic Soviet response."

In trying to deny nuclear weapons technology to foreign states, the items to concentrate on are those that are unique to nuclear weapons. Unfortunately, many features of nuclear devices are also found in conventional military weapons, and prohibiting the export of conventional arms technology would run counter to government policy of supplying such arms overseas. To some extent, design, material, and fabrication details of these items can be protected, but only from nongovernmental groups.

Weapons materials. Some of the materials needed to make a fission explosive are not always easy to come by: beryllium or uranium for the tamper, weapons-grade fissile uranium or plutonium for the core, and beryllium with polonium (or other types of neutron generators) for the initiator. For fusion, more special separated isotopes are needed: tritium and lithium-6 deuteride.

Proper quality of fissionable materials -- weapons-grade -- is crucial to would-be bomb makers. If a low grade of fissile uranium or plutonium is all that is available, the design of the weapon and its critical dimensions will be severely affected [DEV-79]. However, some serious destruction (not necessarily of military value) could be accomplished with a fission explosive device fashioned with poor quality (reactor-grade) plutonium.

For fusion weapons, high-quality fissile material is even more important. An establishment sophisticated enough to engage in the development of thermonuclear weapons would insist on good material for its fission triggers. Limiting the manufacture, exchange, and stockpiling of weapons-grade fissile materials has been the most effective technical impediment to proliferation of both fission and fusion weapons.

Technological processes. The manufacturing processes required to shape the radioactive fuel pieces (precisely spherical for an implosion weapon) and to fabricate the explosive lenses are by no means common knowledge. Furthermore, it is apparent from available descriptions of various types of thermonuclear weapons that their fabrication requires high-level skills, machinery, technology, and quality control. Obviously the processes specific to such applications should not be divulged or confirmed.

Computations and testing. Other technological capabilities that are needed to develop the fission trigger include ability to draft detailed designs of the explosive assembly and to execute critical experiments to determine exactly the needed amount of whatever fissionable material is available. This is true for fusion-boosted weapons as well as multiple stage. Moreover, for the fusion portion of the weapon, extensive calculations and experiments are necessary to verify certain important parameters. It is known [YORK-76] that some trials even by an experienced nation have been duds. To achieve dependable weapons, the same computation-and-experiment route must undoubtedly be followed by any would-be entrant to the H-bomb club. Because of diffusion of knowledge and the improvement of computers, the calculations may not be as difficult, expensive, and time-consuming as they once were -- but they still have to be done, and done correctly, and validated by experiment.

The value of nonexplosive experiments is limited. There is just so much that can be done in a laboratory before a nuclear explosion must be undertaken. For good reason, military management has always insisted upon demonstrated reliability of weapons in its arsenal (the "general's test"). Unless a convincing scale of testing takes place, the credibility to the military of both fission and (especially) fusion explosive weapons would be undermined or even nonexistent. As we have said, a universal ban on nuclear explosive testing is critical. A comprehensive moratorium on all forms and locales of nuclear-weapon testing is nearly, if not entirely, the sine qua non of proliferation control.

Defense Department Recommendations

Cogent and credible comments [Note VII-4] on the efficacy, durability, and timeliness of technology denial were made in 1970 by the Defense Science Board Task Force on Secrecy, in a report [DSB-70] to the Secretary of Defense. In essence, the report suggested that when a weapons system is deployed, it is no longer practicable to maintain the same level of classification that applied during development. The task force guessed that five years is about the longest one can keep control over information -- with secrecy of vital information even more transient. They clearly recognized that secrecy failed to prevent other nations from learning how to make nuclear or thermonuclear explosives.

The Court's Understanding of Technology Denial

In his stated opinions [82, 85] and comments in court [31, 95], Judge Warren revealed several of the technological misunderstandings that are sometimes found among nonspecialists.

The German rockets argument. Judge Warren wrote, "Once basic concepts are learned, the remainder of the process may easily follow." As we hope this book makes clear, that is the opposite of what is really the case. Once it becomes known that a certain technology (for example, an H-bomb) is possible, the concepts come rather readily; it is the nondeducible details that take the time.

The judge went on say that delay could sometimes be important, mentioning that the outcome of World War II might have been different if Hitler had had more time to get the V-1 and V-2 rockets operational. Though possibly true, the illustration does not support the judge's position. The Germans (and the rest of the world) had the basic rocket concepts, as well as some rather detailed designs by von Braun in Germany and Goddard in the United States, before the war. That rockets were not available sooner (in either Germany or the United States) resulted from development problems, defense perceptions, political options, and available resources. The concepts were known, but the nondeducible details required time and effort, once work began, to discover and implement.

Nuclear chain-reaction theory. Another instance of confusion over technical matters was the court's failure to grasp the significance of the parallel international development of the theory of the nuclear chain reaction. The judge was impressed [82] by the fact that, in early studies, a French team overlooked the concept of neutron multiplication and "[did not realize their] oversight for about a year." Apparently he felt that a year was a long time, an opinion not shared by other commentators. An article in the American Journal of Physics [45, 1049 (1977)] states that the chain-reaction formula "offers a striking example of independent discovery," and adds, moreover, that the formula "was discovered independently at least six times in four countries (France, Germany, the Soviet Union, and the United States)." A key point is that, at the time, none of the investigators knew that a self-sustaining chain reaction was truly achievable. The character of the problem changed entirely, once the outcome became known (first established by Fermi's experiments in Chicago). With that question out of the way, all the important terms could be and were confirmed.

As with the controlled chain reaction, the explosion of the first fission bomb and subsequent testing of the first hydrogen bomb were enlightening. As soon as the outcome became known, the theoretical basis could be derived. In early research where even the possibility of an eventual solution is in question, as in prewar studies of neutron chain reactions, it is quite possible for secrecy and compartmentalization to make for slow progress to the correct conclusion. Remove the uncertainty about whether, and it is much easier to figure out how.

Rate of proliferation. Judge Warren eventually realized that the article did not provide a do-it-yourself guide to the H-bomb. But he was apparently still impressed with the argument that "the article could possibly provide sufficient information to a medium-size nation to move faster in developing a hydrogen weapon." Let us examine that proposition in more detail.

Five nations (the USA, the USSR, Great Britain, France, and China) have already developed their own thermonuclear weapons. Other high-technology nations, including most European and some South American and Asian states, could make thermonuclear weapons if they so chose. Low-technology nations, such as Uganda, are not in a technical position to make them, even if they knew how. So that leaves only the medium-technology nations -- such as Mexico, Iran, and Cuba -- as the sort of candidate weapons states that, the judge felt, could move faster in developing a hydrogen bomb thanks to the Morland article. We submit that if these medium-sized nations wanted to make thermonuclear weapons they could do so -- with or without the conceptual information contained in Morland's article -- though it would take years and a program that swallowed up a good fraction of their gross national product. Furthermore, nuclear explosive testing would be essential. The large technical component in that assessment is the reason that Judge Warren would have been able to issue more realistic rulings if he had appointed a qualified panel to evaluate whether Morland's article would contribute to proliferation.

DEDUCIBILITY AND CLASSIFICATION POLICY

Early in this chapter we referred in passing to the idea that deducibility is an important criterion in any rational classification policy. That thought is worth considering at greater length. What sort of information can be protected by secrecy, and what sort cannot?

While there are borderline cases, the common-sense test for information that can be protected through a policy of secrecy is whether it is deducible from known physical principles, careful reasoning, and the large body of information that is already in the public domain. For example, nondeducible engineering details can be protected, under certain circumstances and for limited periods of time, but facts that follow logically from known principles can be deduced by competent workers familiar with the field regardless of secrecy provisions.

Because it is completely senseless to try to protect information that is deducible (it is essentially already known), the only type of data that is susceptible to protection is what is nondeducible. Nondeducible information can be divided into two broad and quite independent categories, which could be described as "operational details" and "research discoveries."

Operational Details

The first of these categories contains details that are logically disconnected and are not deducible from physical principles, known technological capabilities, or other public data. Examples of such details are planned troop movements, secret codes, positions of submarines, precise (but not general) surveillance capabilities, military contingency plans, and ICBM targeting strategy. Such information is completely protected as long as nobody leaks it.

Research Discoveries

In the second of the protectible categories, the information is nondeducible not in an absolute sense, but in the relative sense that it can be generated only with major research effort. There are two somewhat overlapping subcategories here, which we will refer to as "concepts" and "details." Examples of nondeducible details would be optimum frequencies for laser separation of isotopes, best composition of ablation shields for reentry vehicles, and most efficient configuration for a fusion weapon.

By "nondeducible concepts" we mean (a) military applications of publicly known principles in ways that would probably not be thought of without access to, and stimulus from, the results of secret research, as well as (b) totally new physical principles that might theoretically be discovered in the course of secret research (although we know of no such case). An example of a military concept that was (perhaps) nondeducible when originated (1950) within a military program is the Teller-Ulam idea on thermonuclear weapons, which is central to the Progressive case. Although the classification system prevented public dissemination of that idea for perhaps two decades, the extent to which the concept was effectively protected is debatable. We have no evidence that any nation has been held back from developing thermonuclear weapons by lack of access to the Teller-Ulam idea.

What can retard foreign military exploitation of some publicly known principles is lack of the resources needed to validate the effectiveness of the military application. This is where secrecy is especially important, and where official acts that confirm or deny the accuracy of public speculation can be especially damaging. In the Teller-Ulam example, the applicability of the concept, and the optimum way to use it, could only be determined (in the absence of access to Restricted Data and of revealing pronouncements by the government) by extensive calculations and testing, on a scale beyond the capabilities of all but a few technologically advanced nations.

Information of the "research discoveries" type is available to anybody with the time, resources, and motivation. It is ultimately in the public domain. Classification can delay the spread of such information, but only to the extent that other interested parties have to expend time and effort to determine it on their own.

Since the protectibility of information in this category depends on the research effort needed to uncover it, and since the magnitude of such effort can vary from negligible to immense, depending on the problem, there is a no clear-cut division between information that is worth major effort to protect and information whose safeguarding is hopeless. The gray area is where the disputes over classification guidelines tend to arise.

Responsibility for Protection

Protection of classified information must be the responsibility of those entrusted with it. Only someone involved in the classified effort has an accurate basis for determining what is sensitive information and what is not. Is it realistic to expect a reporter, for instance, to make such a decision? We think not. If a reporter asks a question of someone with classified information, and that question is answered, the reporter has every right to assume that the answer is not sensitive to national security. To prosecute a person for someone else's failure to protect sensitive data would scarcely be consistent with American justice.

Application to the Progressive case is clear. One of two situations must exist: Either (a) The Progressive's reporter was given information that he should not have been given, in which case (since he is not accused of espionage) the fault is not his, or (b) he was given information that is legitimately in the public domain, in which case his deductions, to the extent that they were accurate, were eminently deducible, and thus hopelessly beyond protection by classification. The only actions the classification authorities should have taken (in camera) was against those believed responsible for disclosure to the reporter.

The situation is not changed if the data are originated by a professional scientist instead of a reporter. Any country that could conceivably exploit such data has scientists who could deduce it. (The United States, in fact, actively trains scientists from other countries.) Any scientist who independently synthesizes something new from public information must assume that others interested in the same problem will arrive at the same conclusions. It would be preposterous to ask that such work be submitted for classification, to say nothing of prosecuting the person after the fact for failing to read the mind of some anonymous classification officer.

METASTABLE NATURE OF SECRETS

The general, worldwide diffusion of technology is making secrets harder to keep. Consider the abundance of computers and copying machines. The new, faster, cheaper computers permit rapid calculations that once took years. The exchange of systems- and applications-software makes the computers almost immediately useful for any purpose. Copying machines everywhere (including the public section of the library at Los Alamos Scientific Laboratory) make it feasible for unattributed duplicates of almost any document to be scattered about without limit. Short of catastrophe, technology is an unstoppable train on the track to an unlimited future. We need to recognize the rapidly changing conditions it is bringing about, so as to be able to develop appropriate ways for coping with their impact on our society. Nuclear weapons proliferation, for instance, will not be controlled by playing ostrich with outmoded policies.

The remarkable growth of worldwide telecommunications and airline travel has also helped to erode the effectiveness of secrecy. At one time it was no simple matter for secret information to be transmitted, as is illustrated by the many stages it took to forward to the Soviet Union the atomic information collected by Klaus Fuchs during the highly secret Manhattan Project. But now ideas and data, clandestine or public, may be readily transmitted, especially in peacetime, with much less prospect of being noticed.

An incident of a type likely to occur more frequently was reported by the Chicago Tribune on November 29, 1980. The Australian government had recently banned a new book containing unpublished diplomatic papers concerning weaknesses of its foreign policy. In spite of Australia's efforts to prevent further distribution, copies of the book have appeared overseas. An interesting question is whether the book can or will be banned in the United States by classifying it NSI.

Niels Bohr is said [DSB-70] to have expressed the opinion after World War II that, while secrecy is an effective instrument in a closed society, it is much less effective in an open one in the long run; open societies should recognize that openness is one of their strongest weapons, for it accelerates mutual understanding and reduces barriers to rapid development.

In a House of Representatives' debate [79th Cong., 2d sess. (1946)], one of the sponsors of the original Atomic Energy act of 1946 cited the testimony of Major General Leslie Groves:

> The big secret was really something that we could not keep quiet, and that was the fact that the thing [the A-bomb] went off.
>
> The secrets, as they are loosely termed in the public discussion, are divided properly, I think, into about three classes. One class of these secrets consists of established scientific facts which were not secret at all.... They had been published in odd places, but were easily collectible. Anyone who wanted to could find those secrets.
>
> The second classification of secrets is the scientific developments which went beyond this, and most of those developments were not basic.... [They] could undoubtedly be achieved by other nations if they spend the money, the

labor, and the time and have the scientific organization with which to do it. In time, they can, of course, do it. It is merely a case of relative speed.

The other class of secret, which is the biggest field, is the ingenuity and the skill of the American worker and the American management...and that is a secret I do not think any other nation has, and I do not think anyone is going to have it in a hurry.

The general test for information that can be protected, and through such protection perhaps yield an advantage, is whether it is deducible from knowledge in the public domain. In any event, the Defense Science Board Task Force on Secrecy noted that the advantage gained cannot be expected to persist for longer than a few years. They also pointed out that it would be difficult to obtain acceptance of changes in classification procedures because of "understandable conservatism and deeply ingrained attitudes." A useful concrete example of this last point comes from official actions in the Progressive case.

One of the three concepts related to thermonuclear weapons that the government sought to suppress was that of "separate stages," the idea that the fission trigger and the fusion package are physically separated. However, the fact that the Soviet Union had exploded a device yielding some sixty megatons is more than enough to permit a physicist to deduce the separate-stages concept. This claim was used by Bruce J. Ennis, of the ACLU, in his oral pleadings before Judge Warren. The court did not understand Ennis's argument, however, and so it had little impact. The chain of reasoning that was missing is as follows:

More than 50 percent of the energy released by the Soviet test was known to derive from the fusion process (the casing material apparently was not fissionable), and the energy released by the fusion of a deuterium atom and a tritium atom is known; that permits a minimum value for the total number of deuterium-tritium pairs which must have existed before the explosion to be determined. As the fusion fuel is known to be lithium-6 deuteride (the lithium is converted to tritium in the explosion), the number of deuterium-tritium pairs is also the minimum number of lithium deuteride molecules. Once this is known, the minimum volume of the fusion fuel can be determined if the physical constants of lithium deuteride are estimated from those of lithium hydride. This volume is much too large to be contained, in any way, in the fission trigger. Thus the fusion fuel and fission trigger must be separated.

That much may be done on the back of an envelope. However, to go further in deducing a workable geometrical arrangement requires access to the public literature on thermonuclear fusion and some knowledge, also in the public domain, of energy release in fission explosions. Such an exercise yields, incidentally, the two other concepts -- radiation coupling and compression -- that the government sought to suppress (Chapter V).

Secrecy in our society has become an institution that, like all institutions, reflects the attitudes of many individuals. As the world view of an institution becomes less consistent with the world around it, it increasingly fails to fulfil its mission. Although perhaps originally useful, such institutions tend to become detrimental.

In 1950 the Teller-Ulam concept for initiating and maintaining
fusion in a thermonuclear weapon was truly a significant breakthrough:
it permitted a deliverable warhead to be developed. The same approach
was contemporaneously devised in the Soviet Union, which exploded the
first "dry" bomb -- one that used lithium deuteride as a fusion fuel
instead of a mixture of deuterium and tritium. That Soviet test was
soon followed by successful American ones using the Teller-Ulam idea.
In 1950 the concept (or set of concepts) was a legitimate secret; by
1979 it had become deducible by anyone who developed an interest in the
subject and explored the open literature.
    As Edward Teller and other scientists have observed, there are no
secrets in science.

RESTRICTIVE EFFECTS OF SECRECY

The secrecy provisions of the Atomic Energy Act of 1954 are broader
than is necessary for protecting sensitive information. There are
drawbacks to relying on secrecy without a clear understanding of what
secrecy can and cannot achieve, an error that is at the heart of the
"born secret" interpretations of the 1954 Act, but is unfortunately not
unique to it.
    Those most likely to be able to use deducible information are those
who can and will deduce it most easily. Suppressing communications by
citizens who glean information from the public record, therefore, has
no appreciable effect on the accessibility of the information to
interested, motivated experts. It is, however, very effective with
respect to the nonexpert. The lay public, which must rely on
assessments by various experts, can easily be denied that information
in spite of the fact that it may be very relevant to different policy
choices, and may already be well known to people with the relevant
training, as well as to insiders. A conclusion drawn by Cheh [CHEH-80]
is that the Atomic Energy Act "necessarily inhibits politically
relevant discussion about whether the government is adequately
protecting against nuclear proliferation."
    That information related to weapons would not long stay secret was
noted in a still heavily censored letter [89] written on November 2,
1977, by Arthur D. Thomas, a classification officer at Lawrence
Livermore Laboratory. He predicted that forbidden thermonuclear
concepts would be "widely recognized and discussed publicly in a few
years."
    Failure of the Atomic Energy Act to define narrowly the purpose of
restricting information has brought no clear benefit to the American
people. Because "Restricted Data" broadly includes "all data
concerning... design, manufacture, or utilization of atomic
weapons...[except] data declassified [by the government]," and because
there seems to be precedent for considering general concepts to be
"data," the opportunity for abuse is virtually guaranteed. Under that
sweeping definition, for instance, it was legal, perhaps obligatory,
for officials of the old Atomic Energy Commission to withhold fallout
levels after nuclear weapons tests in the 1950's and 60's, even though
the readings indicated a health hazard that threatened the general
public and had no bearing on national security. There are some people
in the western United States who may suffer from the consequences of

this distorted, though legal, use of the 1954 Act. Quite simply, citizens have been purposefully confused and perhaps unnecessarily injured by their government in the name of their own security.

Before the Progressive incident, Howard Morland was involved in litigation dealing with nuclear-weapons safety, when he supported local citizens in a suit to require the U.S. Navy to file an Environmental Impact Statement on its plan to store 1200 nuclear weapons two miles west of the Honolulu International Airport. Various public groups had brought the Navy to court, asking for an impact statement on the weapons storage plan. Testifying in federal court, a DOE specialist in information classification said [HEN-80] that

the Navy could not even discuss the environmental impact of nuclear-weapons storage. The release of such information, he explained, would be a violation of the Atomic Energy Act's secrecy provisions because, by necessity, the disclosures would include restricted data about how those nuclear weapons are designed.

Could he at least say whether an airplance crash near the "igloos" (housing the H-bombs) might lead to a scattering of radioactive material? No, under the Atomic Energy Act, the public is not allowed access to that information.

In other words, even if the government officials wanted to disclose pertinent information that presumably had no adverse impact on national security, their hands were tied by the Atomic Energy Act.

The Atomic Energy Act of 1954 has created the lawful means for an unmonitored agency, with its own vested interests, to deny citizens access to information they needed to intelligently chart their own futures.

Thermonuclear Power Research

Rumblings may be heard in the research community about the impact of DOE's classification practices with respect to studies of nonmilitary applications of thermonuclear energy. Research in this area is being conducted at the weapons laboratories and at academic institutions. One particular, characteristic problem is that many underlying concepts were once secret in the context of weapons, but are now being rediscovered in open laboratories all over the world.

In an article in the Federation of American Scientists' (FAS) Public Interest Report [33, April 1980], Ray E. Kidder, who launched and for ten years ran the laser fusion project at Lawrence Livermore Laboratory, addressed the question of classification in one of the several thermonuclear projects, the inertially confined fusion (ICF) program:

The basis for the classification of the ICF Program is that some of the concepts employed in ICF target design are also needed in the design of nuclear weapons. If these concepts were indeed secret, it could reasonably be argued that ICF targets employing these concepts should be classified. However, these concepts can be considered to be secret no longer.... It is...possible to maintain the necessary classification of nuclear weapons, while at the same time declassifying ICF.

Implementation Problems

The operation of the security classification system appears to be
getting unmanageable. The General Accounting Office concluded [LCD
78-125, March 9, 1979] that Executive Order 12065 "does not provide
solutions to the oversight and monitoring problems discussed in this
report."
    A secrecy system has inherent problems to contend with -- problems
that are minimized if the quantity of material to be classified is kept
as small as possible:
    1. It is difficult to decide who will determine what is secret, why
it is secret, whether it is useful to keep it secret, or whether to
promote or ignore dissemination. The process of trying to deal with
these issues creates ponderous bureaucratic institutions. For proper
functioning, the people with security responsibilities have to be able
to make sound technical decisions, and be dedicated enough to resist
the temptation to use the system for their own personal and political
purposes. Even in bureaus that are open to public scrutiny, not all
the public servants have those qualities. To assume that similar
problems do not arise within large security-oriented bureaucracies
would be unrealistic.
    2. Serious problems arise from the absence of external review.
(Even in agencies where there is congressional overview, abuses of
power can be expected.) Often the organization's own management has
trouble getting information, so that internal misuse of power is
difficult to control.
    3. Wrong directions in classified engineering and science programs
are hard to catch. Programs that are ill-advised and unlikely to
succeed can drag on indefinitely because of lack of review by experts
external to the effort, coupled with the tendency of most projects to
be self-perpetuating. Some charges to this effect have been made
regarding thermonuclear power research: It may be that classified laser
fusion programs are receiving an inappropriate share of nonmilitary
research funds vis-a-vis other types of inertial confinement.
    4. Internally, secrecy leads to compartmentalization that inhibits
adequate peer review, a process involving competent people with diverse
scientific and engineering experience that is important to the
successful, efficient functioning of any research or development
program. It helps prevent diversion into dead-end paths and permits
"cross fertilization" -- infusion of ideas that can lead to novel,
cost-effective solutions.
    5. It impossible for Congress and the public to determine whether
money is being effectively administered and spent.

SUMMARY: SECRECY AND GOVERNMENT INSTITUTIONS

The first legislation to control the spread of nuclear information was
the Atomic Energy Act of 1946, revised in 1954. Classification today
is regulated by that act and the current relevant executive order,
#12065. With the passage of time the system has become unwieldy, and
some of the controls over information are no longer appropriate. Of
special concern is the interpretation that the Atomic Energy Act calls
for restrictions on information already in the public domain or

deducible therefrom. A blanket "born classified" criterion for atomic weapons matters may dilute the effectiveness of the law in the long run because of its unenforceability.

In practice, secrecy covers far more than just weapons information. Many government and public institutions have secrets as a matter of course for personal, commercial, diplomatic, and political reasons. Therein lies a potential for abuse, which is addressed in more detail in the next chapter.

The potential benefits of widespread secrecy seem greater than they actually are, and the drawbacks are far more serious than is at first apparent. A system that is forced to work under a heavy burden of secrecy is isolated from the rest of society, and therefore only indirectly benefits from the knowledge of many of the most able and informed experts. Because information within a classified program is limited to those who have a "need to know," the classified projects do not fully benefit from the varied expertise even of the cleared personnel -- a necessary penalty if the information being developed is truly sensitive and the potential for security breaches must be minimized.

The difficulties cost time and money, and tie up unique national resources. They lead to severe management, engineering, and scientific problems. Private industrial and commercial progress is impeded. And democracy is eroded when the government implements technological developments without the informed consent of the citizen.

These are some of the tolls that secrecy exacts. There is a place for secrecy, but it does not come free. If we do not keep it to the minimum necessary, we shall lose more than we gain.

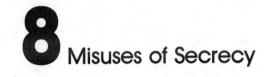

8 Misuses of Secrecy

When everything is classified, then nothing is classified, and the system becomes one to be disregarded by the cynical or the careless, and to be manipulated by those intent on self-protection or self-promotion.

- Justice Potter Stewart

National security is well served by safeguarding certain weapons data, but restrictions that are not important to national security are contrary to the public interest. For one thing, injudicious attempts to prevent the spread of information considered sensitive might in fact -- as happened in the Progressive case -- lead to the leakage of still more classified data. There are other cases where government policy in interpreting and applying the laws dealing with classified information has had untoward effects.

MISUSE FOR POLITICAL PURPOSES

The secrecy used by the executive branch "to fend off inquiries from the Legislature produces one of democracy's major headaches" [F&W-74]. The common reasons for denying information -- national security, internal management, and constitutional privilege -- are sometimes invoked when the real reason is less laudable. Even inquiry about past events that are too stale to pertain to national security is often frustrated.

Franck and Weisband observe that civil servants have more power if they have exclusive access to information, which tempts them to limit others' access. Unfortunately, "the bureaucrat's advice, protected from challenge by secrecy, tends to be conformist rather than innovative." In general, the

principle purpose of secrecy is to retain power -- especially freedom of initiation -- unfettered in the hands of the Executive. To share secrets [with the legislature, press, or public] is to share competence both to make decisions and to criticize them....

158

During the Vietnam crisis, the Government constantly intimidated opponents with the warning that they did not know the whole story and should therefore suspend arguments based on nothing more than common sense. The Pentagon Papers have shown, however, that the secret intelligence reports hidden from the Congress usually did no more than confirm the common-sense view and information readily available in The New York Times and Le Monde.

Anybody with authority to classify information might sooner or later be tempted to use that authority for political purposes -- that is, for personal or partisan advantage, or to avoid embarrassment or revelation of wrongdoing. Political use of classification might be rationalized under the guise of "judgment" or "best interests of the public" or "national security" or under a variety of other code words. In any case, there is enough potential ambiguity in purpose -- legitimate governmental function versus questionable political indulgence -- to warrant close public scrutiny of any classification system. We do not claim that every action or policy cloaked in the code words is political in intent or nature, but only point out that the potential exists and the public is entitled to know enough about what is going on to be assured that the political components are kept to a minimum.

Political use of secrecy is possible on several levels of consciousness. First, there are acts of overt individual self-interest. These are perhaps relatively rare compared with the next level, political actions that conform to a collective standard. Suppose that all members of an administration are expected, for better or worse, to support current policies, to "pull together." This can give rise to stretching the rules. The Progressive case may be an example, in that the collective actions of several executive branch Departments -- Energy, Defense, Justice, and State -- appear to have been harnessed to support an ill-conceived course of action.

Secrecy laws might be invoked to protect secrecy itself as an institution. If this were a motive, one would expect the regulations to be applied in a capricious, opportunistic manner. We see the action against The Progressive somewhat in that light: The suit might have been brought partly because it seemed a good chance to bolster the legal basis of the secrecy provisions of the Atomic Energy Act, in a misguided attempt to make the Act a more effective antiproliferation tool. Unfortunately, the consequences were not well analyzed in advance, to say nothing of the failure to undertake national policy changes that could really be meaningful in slowing the propagation of nuclear weapons.

Every U.S. administration finds itself establishing policies that should be publicly discussed. Current controversial topics include a reduction in national emphasis on nuclear armaments, the recycling of plutonium under safeguarded conditions, and the discontinuation of the testing of nuclear weapons. The executive branch, however, traditionally tries to deny to the public some of the conceptual knowledge that is needed for intelligent consideration of those questions, an attitude that is incompatible with democratic functioning. The result is that taking issue with government policy in the areas of arms control and proliferation requires one to take issue with, or expand upon, the information that is selectively released by the government about the underlying technologies.

Drawing from recent American history, we now look at some specific examples of politically motivated secrecy.

The Pentagon Papers Case

In 1967 there was considerable division both inside and outside the government regarding the U.S. intervention in Vietnam. In order to assess the decision-making process and possibly to keep from repeating mistakes, Secretary of Defense Robert S. McNamara commissioned a history of American involvement in Southeast Asia. Over a period of one-and-a-half years, a forty-seven-volume study was produced, entitled United States-Vietnam Relations, 1945-1967 -- popularly known as the Pentagon Papers. It was classified Top Secret, with distribution outside the government limited to a number of former officials and the Rand Corporation.

Dr. Daniel Ellsberg, who had worked on the study, decided that the U.S. government duplicity evidenced in the volumes should become public knowledge. After Ellsberg was unsuccessful in arousing congressional interest, the New York Times and other newspapers received copies. The Times started publishing daily installments on June 13, 1971, but three days later was ordered by a federal judge to halt publication on grounds of "grave and immediate danger to the security of the United States" -- the "first time in American history that the press had been restrained from publishing foreign-policy material which the government claimed was a threat to national security" [COX-75].

During appeals, President Nixon's director of communication told the press that "whether the Times had endangered the nation's security was of less concern to the administration than permitting a precedent that would encourage future leaks" [COX-75]. The Supreme Court ruled that the government, in light of the First Amendment, had not justified prior restraint.

As Halperin and Hoffman [H&H1-77] explained:

> The Pentagon Papers showed how successive administrations kept Congress and the public in the dark about vital foreign policy decisions. Later the disclosure of the secret bombing of Cambodia dramatized the ease with which even major and protracted operations can be concealed. Congress and members of the public came to feel that they had been systematically excluded from decisions of the utmost importance, decisions in which they had a consti-tutional right to participate....

> The Pentagon Papers reveal a consistent pattern of deception by the administration, centered on withholding from Congress and the public vital information that raised devastating questions about the effectiveness and propriety of administration policies and the credibility of responsible officials. It is not hard to understand why, given the policies and rationales to which the government was committed, the Pentagon Papers had to be kept secret.

Two important aspects of the Pentagon Papers case that pertain to U.S. statutes are: (1) the information was not passed on by Ellsberg directly to foreign nations, and (2) its publication turned out to have no adverse effect upon national security. Moreover, judging by statements by some of the justices and various parties in opposition to the injunction, publication of the Pentagon Papers had been predictably unlikely to injure the United States. Suppression was clearly not in the interests of an informed public, nor would it have helped future administrations in conducting foreign or national affairs.

The Case of Ethel and Julius Rosenberg

There are some striking parallels between the Progressive litigation and the travail of the Rosenbergs and Morton Sobell in the early 1950s. According to a memorandum [80] filed by The Fund for Open Information and Accountability, Inc. in the Progressive case,
> The government claimed that the Rosenbergs and their alleged cohorts had stolen and given to the Soviet Union the "secret" of the atomic bomb, as a result of which the Soviet Union was able to develop and detonate such a bomb in 1949. The actual facts concerning the alleged theft of the secret of the bomb were withheld from the public until long after the execution of the Rosenbergs. The truth was finally elicited over the strenuous opposition of the government.... A suit brought under the FOIA...has served to reveal further facts.

One of those facts was the weak foundation underlying the statements of AEC "scientists" who "testified as to the accuracy, importance, and significance of the information allegedly transmitted," and "verified that the information constituted the 'secret' of the bomb." Twenty-five years after the trial, the secret sketches and description were released under the Freedom of Information Act. According to the Fund:
> Leading atomic scientists, chemists and physicists examined these documents and found that this material was totally inaccurate, incomplete, a child's caricature of a misconception of the atomic bomb. The scientists knew that there was no "secret" of the atomic bomb, that the construction of such a weapon involved thousands upon thousands of technological devices, techniques, experiments and inventions, pragmatic testing and other technological problems of such magnitude that it was well nigh impossible to set forth.

At a new hearing on behalf of Morton Sobell, the Rosenberg's codefendant, held on August 3, 1966, the government announced, in the words of the Fund [80] "that it was withdrawing its claims of secrecy; it further acknowledged that the material upon which the Rosenbergs were convicted, sentenced to death and executed was essentially worthless, of no value or significance." In 1979, as a result of a request made under the Freedom of Information Act, an interesting statement came to light. It was made during the Oppenheimer hearings of 1954 by General Leslie Groves, who was in charge of the atomic bomb project:
> I think the data that went out in the case of the Rosenbergs was of minor value. I would never say that publicly. Again that is something while it is not secret I think should be kept very quiet, because irrespective of the value of that in the overall picture, the Rosenbergs deserved to hang, and I would not like to see anything that would make people say General Groves thinks they didn't do much damage after all.

The Rosenbergs were charged with violating the Espionage Act [18 U.S.C. §794, "Gathering or delivering defense information to aid foreign governments"], allegedly having transmitted to the Soviets diagrams of an implosion-type atomic weapon design received from David Greenglass. Greenglass, brother-in-law of Ethel Rosenberg, admitted drawing the diagrams from information he learned at his job as a machinist at Los Alamos. He testified that an initial sketch and some information were turned over to the Rosenbergs for transmittal to the Soviet Union.

The question of whether they actually did transmit such information is outside the scope of this book. Harry Gold, the courier who picked up the technical data from Fuchs, also obtained an envelope with diagrams made by Greenglass. Although the Rosenbergs may have had no direct part in its transmittal, a diagram (Fig. 4) that Gold himself passed to the Soviets was used as evidence against the Rosenbergs. Our interest is confined here to examining relevant actions and statements of the government, particularly with regard to the technical significance of the diagram and accompanying instructions used in the trial.

The Espionage Statutes (18 U.S.C. §793) provide that "whoever, with intent or reason to believe that it is to be used to the injury of the United States or to the advantage of a foreign nation, communicates, delivers or transmits...information relating to the national defense, shall be punished by death or by imprisonment for any term of years or for life." Although it is not readily apparent in the statement above, the national-defense significance of the information was an important element in convicting and sentencing the Rosenbergs.

In addition to doubts as to the technical significance of the Rosenberg data, Gerald E. Markowitz and Michael Meeropol [M&M-80] have raised questions about the correctness of the judicial process in that case.

It is important to keep in mind that Klaus Fuchs, a former member of the British scientific team at Los Alamos, confessed [YORK-76] on January 27, 1950, that "he had engaged in espionage on behalf of the U.S.S.R. between 1942 and 1949." This was not revealed during any of the Rosenberg trial proceedings. During that period, as mentioned in Chapter IV, Fuchs had access to most of the truly sensitive fission weapon data, as well as to the most important postwar U.S. thinking about thermonuclear weapon devices. Moreover, in May 1950 he had drawn for the FBI a conceptual diagram of the implosion bomb that coinventor Philip Morrison called "the real thing" [New Republic, June 23, 1979, p. 24].

Despite its awareness that much of the requisite design knowledge had already been authoritatively conveyed to the Soviets by Fuchs, the government charged that the Rosenbergs imparted "information, sketches, and material vital to the national defense" (emphasis added) [NIZ-74]. It was also known that two other scientists, Allen Nunn May and Bruno Pontecorvo, punctured the secrecy curtain of the joint American, Canadian, and British Manhatten Engineering District project that was formed to make the atomic bomb in secret. The two scientists, May and Fuchs, who were eventually caught in Canada and England, were sentenced to prison terms of 10 and 14 years respectively for violation of their espionage laws.

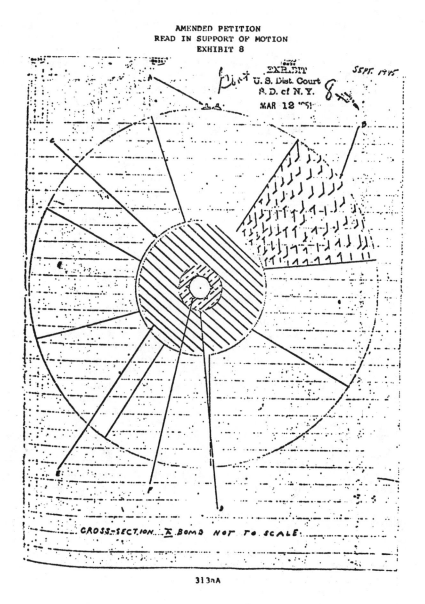

Fig. 4. The most significant "Greenglass Diagram"
used as evidence in the Rosenberg case.

The Rosenbergs were the first and only people ever sentenced to death under the U.S. espionage statutes by a nonmilitary tribunal. The death penalty was put into those statutes in the aftermath of World War I (it is still there), and even in 1950 might have been considered anachronistic. (The Atomic Energy Act contains no death penalty.)

In seeking death for the Rosenbergs, the government was exploiting prevalent fears. The war between North and South Korea was underway in 1951, with American participation; the McCarthy binge of anti-communist paranoia was in full swing; and there was fear of atomic war because the Soviets had detonated a fission explosive two years before, depriving the United States of its monopoly in nuclear weapons. That was the environment in which the court issued this statement to justify the death sentence:

> I consider your crime worse than murder.... In your case, I believe your conduct in putting into the hands of the Russians the A-bomb years before our best scientists predicted Russia would perfect the bomb has already caused, in my opinion, the Communist aggression in Korea, with the resultant casualties exceeding 50,000 and who knows but that millions...more of innocent people may pay the price of your treason. Indeed, by your betrayal you have undoubtedly altered the course of history to the disadvantage of our country. No one can say that we do not live in a constant state of tension. We have evidence of your treachery all around us every day -- for the civilian defense activities throughout the nation are aimed at preparing us for an atom bomb attack.... [You] passed what [you] knew was this nation's most deadly and closely guarded secret weapon to Soviet agents.

As that reveals, the judge was impressed by the government's portrayal of the significance of the data for whose transmittal the Rosenbergs were convicted and executed. Although the government presented its case by innuendo and argument, rather than by direct testimony, the judge accepted those representations at face value.

While the death penalty was not a consideration in Progressive, a number of the government's actions in that case are reminiscent of Rosenberg: (1) exaggeration of the importance of the "secret" at issue; (2) the conceptual rather than detailed nature of the weapons diagrams; (3) the inadequacies and lack of dimensional scale of the drawings; (4) the errors contained in the diagrams and descriptive prose; (5) the existence of alternative open routes to more useful and more authoritative information of the same sort; (7) the testimony heralding great danger to national security; (8) scientific testimony (kept from the jury in the Rosenberg case and not revealed until fifteen years later) contradicting the technical claims of the government; (9) efforts to keep the record indefinitely sealed; (10) government reluctance to agree to live testimony; and (11) eventual withdrawal by the government (but not until 1966, in Rosenberg) from its efforts to maintain total secrecy.

Perhaps most ominous is an unethical undercurrent that may be common to both cases. The apparent puffing up of the national security significance of Morland's work has its counterpart in what Markowitz and Meeropol claim was a government conspiracy to put on "a big case" by "presenting evidence that Greenglass had stolen vital atomic secrets."

The Cannikin Papers Case

The Cannikin incident was described by Cox [COX-75] as follows:
> In 1971, Congresswoman Patsy Mink (D-Hawaii) and 32 other
> members of Congress requested documents from the
> Environmental Protection Agency dealing with the planned
> underground nuclear test explosion on Amchitka Island,
> Alaska. The U.S. District Court refused to compel disclo-
> sure, but the U.S. Court of Appeals reversed that decision.
> However, Supreme Court overruled, deciding that the
> documents were properly classified under the Executive
> Order and involved "highly sensitive matter vital to our
> national defense and foreign policy." The court turned
> down the proposition that exemption in the Act authorizes
> or permits, in camera, inspection of a contested document
> bearing a single classification so that the Court might
> separate the secret from the supposedly nonsecret
> components. Mink et al. had contended that some of the
> components were not classified for national defense
> purposes....

According to Representative Mink [F&W-75], this was the first time
that the Freedom of Information Act was tested at the Supreme Court
level.

The Alaska site had been selected for the shot, to be named
"Cannikin," after the government decided that the Nevada test range was
not well suited for the large (5 MT) underground nuclear explosions
that were planned for antiballistic missile development. Although a
one megaton "calibraton shot" 4,000 feet underground at Amchitka had
indicated that adverse environmental effects were unlikely, extensive
public opposition developed, based on environmental and arms control
issues. The environmental concern was over wildlife, radioactive
venting, earthquakes, and tsunamis; the arms control concerns related
to the lack of ultimate utility of the ABM system. Both Japan and
Canada were relatively close to the detonation site, and they objected
to the explosion near them of a weapon 250 times the size of the
Hiroshima bomb.

Congressional cancellation of appropriations for the test was
stalled by actions of the executive branch, until a leak to the press
occurred suggesting that various government agencies were in
disagreement on the test. In fact, five agencies (the State Deparment,
Office of Science and Technology, United States Information Agency,
Environmental Protection Agency, and Council on Environmental Quality)
advised the President that the test be postponed or canceled and only
two (the Department of Defense and the Atomic Energy Commission)
favored going ahead. The executive branch refused to release this
information, claiming it was Top Secret or derivately "classified"
because it was attached to Top Secret material. It was at this point
that members of Congress brought suit under the FOIA for release,
charging that the administration was refusing to provide information
needed by Congress to deal with pending legislation.

The Office of Science and Technology was reported to have said that
the nuclear warhead to be tested was already obsolete. Many opponents
of the test objected to the escalation of the arms race represented by
a heavy investment in the ABM system. In addition, the notion of

conducting ultimate warfare by exploding nuclear weapons (our ABMs) over the American homeland was repugnant to many.

There was a suggestion that an earthquake might be triggered, since the site was near a geologic fault.   Released documents were in conflict. The Atomic Energy Commission stated in its introduction to a report, "Underground Nuclear Testing" [TID 25180, September 1969]:

> On the basis of its various studies of this and other safety related matters, the AEC is convinced that the experiments can be conducted with complete safety. This evaluation is supported by the findings of the many scientific experts whose efforts have been involved.

Compare that with the following statement by the presidential advisory committee, the Pitzer Panel ["Report on the Ad Hoc Panel on the Safety of Underground Testing," November 1968], which is buried in an appendix to the AEC report:

> The Panel is seriously concerned with the problem of earthquakes resulting from large yield nuclear tests. Although the possibility that underground nuclear tests might initiate one or more earthquakes has been suggested in the past, new and significant evidence demonstrates that small earthquakes do actually occur both immediately after a large-yield test explosion and in the following week.... There does not now appear to be a basis for eliminating the possibility that a large test explosion might induce...a severe earthquake of sufficiently large magnitude to cause serious damage well beyond the limits of the test site. This possibility is more serious for tests of greater than a megaton....

The test was performed on November 6, 1971. It has been reported that the explosive yield was only two megatons instead of four, and there has been no evident adverse environmental effect.   The ABM program was subsequently phased out as part of the SALT I treaty.

For Congress, according to Representative Patsy Mink [F&W-74], at stake was "whether the courts have the right to hold the Government accountable for actions taken under the FOIA to withold data," or whether the "Executive Branch is adjudged to have an absolute power to determine what may be concealed."

> The case symbolizes what is fast becoming an information crisis in the country. More than ever before, information is power. Those who have the most direct access to, and control over, the information needed to make decisions in our complex society are the ones who are truly in command....
>
> Unless we are to abandon our concept of the separation of powers, the Congress must have equal access to the information necessary to make wise and informed decisions on governmental policy.

CIA Censorship

Episodes such as the censorship of books about CIA operations by Phillip Agee [Inside the Company: CIA Diary, Bantam (1976)], Victor Marchetti and John D. Marks [The C.I.A. & the Cult of Intelligence, Knopf (1974)] indicate that the government is unduly interested in suppressing arguments that could call into question its political decisions. Marchetti, a former CIA employee, had written about the agency in a book that he did not want to submit for prepublication review.

> In the Marchetti case, the Court of Appeals has upheld a permanent injunction, requiring Marchetti to submit all his writings to the CIA so that classified information can be deleted. The court justified this wholly unprecedented order by invoking secrecy agreements Marchetti signed during his tenure as a CIA official. Congress has not authorized such agreements, much less the sweeping waiver of First Amendment rights they are now said to entail. [H&H-77]

Marchetti thus differs from the Progressive case in that enforcement of a two-party agreement, rather than federal legislation, was involved.

After Marchetti (joined by Marks) submitted his manuscript, the CIA "demanded deletions of 339 items" [34]. Here are some of the passages that the government wanted to delete:

> ¶ The Chilean election was scheduled for the following September, and Allende, a declared Marxist, was one of the principal candidates.
>
> ¶ Henry Kissinger, the single most powerful man at the 40 Committee meeting on Chile.
>
> ¶ On occasion, the agency will sponsor the training of foreign officials at the facilities of another government agency.
>
> ¶ As incredible as it may seem in retrospect, some of the CIA's economic analysts (and many other officials in Washington) were in the early 1960's still inclined to accept much of Peking's propaganda as to the success of Mao's economic experiment.

Anthony Lewis, writing for the New York Times ["The Mind of the Censor," April 7, 1980], analyzed other passages that the CIA had cut out but were recently cleared after "years of administrative appeals under the Freedom of Information Act":

> The restored lines are innocuous. To the extent that they point anywhere, it is toward a discussion of policy.... The agency cut many passages of no security relevance whatever.... Reviewing courts did not restore the cuts; judges were shy of tangling with the C.I.A.
>
> When C.I.A. officials talk about the need for censorship of books about the agency, they always point to the danger of disclosing agents' names or secret foreign sources or intelligence methods. What is striking about these passages is that they contain no such material.

Other Examples

An episode of censorship occurred during the very limited public discussion in 1950 on whether the United States should develop the H-bomb. Despite the meagre information available publicly, it appeared at one point that opponents of the H-bomb "were building up opposition to the project and were probably hampering recruitment [of scientists]"

[B&O-76]. Thus "the criticism had to be stifled, or so the AEC believed," resulting in a dispatch advising that "all AEC and contract employees working on AEC contracts are instructed to refrain from publicly stating facts or giving comment on...the commission's program of thermonuclear weapons development."

Further instances [H&H1-79] of unjustified protection of information are the secret intervention in Angola, the bombing of Cambodia, and the Watergate events. The bombing of Cambodia remained secret (in America) for more than three years, an example of the concealability of "a major and protracted operation." The story of the 1969-70 Cambodian raids was "covered up, denied, and lied about by the Executive" [F&W-74] to the Congress, the press, and the public, and even to the Senate Armed Services Committee, but "disclosed privately to a few trusted Congressional hawks for purposes of co-option."

Other American military commitments or actions hidden from the public [H&H-79] were the American war in Laos, American commitments to Spain, and American support for Kurds in Iraq. Halperin and Hoffman consider the secrecy abuses surrounding the Watergate affair to have been "a substantial infringement on civil liberties."

SELECTIVE CLASSIFICATION

Selective classification and declassification are time-honored tools for people in government to use in furthering their various objectives -- goals not always dictated by national security or even national interest. At the same time, some classification actions that at first look dubious might really have a valid rationale -- at least in the classifiers' frame of reference.

An incident of that questionable sort arose in connection with an affidavit [62] we filed early on in the Progressive case. It included the sentence, "We draw attention especially to the highly suggestive diagrams appearing in Teller's Encyclopedia Americana article that have much similarity to those given by Morland." The government at first objected to that statement, but reversed itself and permitted it to be included in the affidavit as publicly released. Ironically, the sentence, and its equivalent in one of Postol's affidavits, became a key link in the chain that led to the classification of the Glenn letter.

Why did the government object, and why did it withdraw its objection? We can only draw some inferences from incomplete information, but doing so is interesting because it illustrates the variety of factors that can influence classification decisions.

One of the unknowns is the frame of reference that the government was operating in. The government, of course, is not a discrete entity, but a collection of individuals who do not always act or even think in concert, and who have many demands on their attention. Motivations vary from person to person and from time to time, so that to try to deduce a coherent master plan is not always realistic. The explanation for actions that seem confused, self-contradictory, or counterproductive is often that they were formulated with insufficient forethought.

As we have amply documented, public affidavits from government witnesses affirmed the general validity of Morland's speculations on H-bomb construction, saying that he was describing U.S. weapons. Why was the government confirmation made public? If the government behind the scenes actually did not regard the article to be of national security significance, then the information in the affidavits would not matter much -- but in that case the government indulged in deliberate exaggeration, and bringing suit involved classification for ulterior purposes. In the post-Watergate era officials would probably not toy with the public and the courts through ouright misinformation or deceit, but some hyperbole in what is seen to be a good cause is conceivable. We agree, of course, that the security risk was small, having found that Morland's information was implicitly, if not explicitly, in the public domain. Still, it is possible that the government officials did not appreciate that fact. They should have, but we have no reason to think that they did.

Let us assume, therefore, that the article was perceived to be really sensitive. Why confirm it? The decision to do that must have been based on two assumptions. The first (verging on the incredible, since underground copies were already circulating) would have been that the article could be effectively suppressed if the government's case were upheld in the courts. The second must have been that there was an excellent chance of winning, since otherwise the cat would really be out of the bag. Under those assumptions, the more explicitly the government confirmed the article, the more vital it became to suppress it, and the closer (the hope might have been) the case came to being clinched.

In that hypothetical but possible frame of reference, it was perfectly logical to object to our mention of the Teller encylopedia diagrams. Inasmuch as an encyclopedia is hardly a classified document, it would at first appear that little would be revealed by drawing the comparison that we did -- but when we did it we were unaware that the government was going to be so explicit in confirming the validity of the Morland article. For that matter, we did not know then (not having seen the government's affidavits) whether Morland's ideas were close to the mark or not. But we had inadvertently provided one of the two links in the chain connecting the Teller diagram to actual U.S. weapons; the other essential link was the government's own affidavits.

A contributing reason for the government's objection might possibly have been that it did not want its case to be made publicly questionable by having it known that the main information was in an encyclopedia.

A possible explanation of why the government withdrew its objections to our mention of the Teller diagram is harder to come by, especially in view of the seemingly inconsistent subsequent classification of the Glenn letter. We suppose they classified that letter because in it we pointed out the chain of reasoning just mentioned. Also, the letter called attention to what seemed to us to be official mishandling of classified information -- perhaps thereby providing additional incentive to classify it.

To an outsider, the technical reason for classifying the Glenn letter would not be at all obvious. Further, in order to avoid compounding what the government apparently regarded as a breach of security, a classification officer would not be able publicly to spell out that reason. Thus both the act of classifying and the failure to explain it could lead an observer to conclude that the motive was entirely political (which is not to say that there was no such component). The reaction of nationally syndicated columnist Mary McGrory, as expressed in her column of August 29, 1979, in the Chicago Tribune, is illustrative:

> And [the government] is still trying to stifle dissent on the question. The Department of Energy, which administers the Atomic Energy Act, sought to censor a letter from four Argonne National Laboratories scientists, who contend that the government has breached its own security regulations in its clumsy handling of the case.
>
> One paragraph reads: "The government's confirmation of the general accuracy of the Morland article might be a conscious attempt to influence the outcome of the case, by increasing the apparent sensitivity of Morland's information in hopes of establishing a legal precedent for prior restraint. Such use of the classification process for political purposes is not in the national interest."
>
> A copy fell into the hands of the student paper at Berkeley, the Daily Californian. Energy Department security chief Martin Dowd promptly called on the editors and demanded to have it back.
>
> When asked why the letter, which had been sent to several senators and congressmen, was being classified, Dowd replied with the standard, circular logic: "It is classified, secret, restricted data, and I can't tell you why, because you are not cleared to know."
>
> The Daily Californian published it anyway, and so far, everyone involved is still walking around loose.
>
> If the Progressive had been allowed to publish the Morland article in the first place, it might never have reached more than its regular readership of 40,000. Now the whole world wants to know why the government is going to such lengths to keep it a secret -- and how much farther it will go in its assault on the First Amendment.

We certainly concur with the thought in that last paragraph. Whether by blunder or more subtle miscalculation, the government's selective release of classified information through its affidavits did not help to safeguard sensitive information. The public and the press sensed that something was wrong, even if they did not always understand just what.

ACQUIESCENCE TO CLASSIFICATION ABUSE

When official hypocrisy is perceived in the application of rules, public support for those rules tends to be eroded. The selective release and leaking of information by federal officials in order to further their aims is not without its price in public cooperation. Acquiescence by one branch of the government (either by action or inaction) to such practices by another branch further tends to diminish credence in the need for secrecy, including cases where enforcement is really needed to safeguard truly sensitive materials and information.

Failure of Congress, the public, and the media to protest misuse of classification powers by the executive branch is tantamount to acceptance. This implicitly promotes further abridgment. One example involving Congress given by Halperin and Hoffman [H&H1-79] is what they saw happening to Senate investigators of CIA activities:

The permanent Senate committee on intelligence shows signs of being co-opted into the system. Its members, becoming acclimated to secret briefings, have adopted stringent secrecy rules and begun to talk of the burden of knowing secret information.

For a time we wondered whether this had happened to Congressman Paul N. McCloskey, who introduced a bill ("in order to provide a focus for [upcoming] hearings, but without final endorsement") that would expand the scope of the criminal sanctions of the Atomic Energy Act to cover "all persons" (see Chapter XI) -- this despite earlier comments he had made about the unmanageability of existing secrecy laws. McCloskey had been given high-level security clearance and briefed by the Department of Energy just before he formulated his bill. Since then he has withdrawn that proposal, and has submitted instead a bill, House Resolution 1406, for reforming the restricted-data portions of the Atomic Energy Act.

Hansen's Charges

In his letter to Senator Charles Percy, Charles Hansen charged that the government had failed to prosecute security violations by three DOE consultants: Drs. Edward Teller, Theodore Taylor, and George Rathjens.

In Teller's case, Hansen alleged that the article written for the Encyclopedia Americana [TEL-74] was never cleared. The most sensitive element of the article appeared to be the diagrams (which we discuss in Chapter V). Hansen, understandably but apparently in error, attributed the diagrams to Dr. Teller. The fact that the DOE sought to classify any affidavit or letter making reference to the Teller article or diagrams, Hansen said, would lead one to conclude that DOE still considers them to contain restricted information -- or at least did so up until publication of the Morland article.

Hansen's allegations regarding Dr. Taylor concern the biography done by McPhee [MCP-75]. Hansen felt that Taylor furnished "80% of the technical information a person would need to build a crude atomic bomb." We disagree with the magnitude in that assessment, but agree that the book is useful in assessing fission explosive principles and design. Taylor has acknowledged that he was reprimanded for not clearing the interview with the AEC in advance of publication.

According to Hansen, some of the information that Morland deduced from public sources might have been indirectly and inadvertently confirmed by Dr. Rathjens in conversations with Morland. Rathjens, in reponse, is reported to have written to Hansen threatening a libel suit.

Hansen's primary concern about lack of prosecution was his belief that

the government, acting through the DOE, seems to use a double standard when it comes to the classification and release of sensitive technical and political information. On the one hand, prominent government scientists are apparently free to break the law with impunity, while more junior scientists and members of the general public are threatened with all sorts of legal ramifications for repeating or republishing information that is already in the public domain.... It seems that the classification policies and authority of the DOE need a major overhaul and redefinition.

SELECTIVE DECLASSIFICATION IN THE <u>PROGRESSIVE</u> CASE

There might have been some deliberate, selective release of information calculated to further the government's side in the trial and to foster public sympathy outside of the courtroom. In making public its affidavits and briefs, the government released some of the most sensitive information disclosed in the case. That is not to say that it was truly damaging to national security, but to the extent that it was released to furter the parochial goal of trying to win the suit, there was some compromise of duty to protect classified information.

The Brown and Rosengren Public Affidavits

Secretary of Defense Brown made the suggestion [37] that as a result of publication of Morland's article, "a subnational element within a country that had the technical capability to develop and produce an unsophisticated fission-type nuclear explosive would gain technical assistance in determining the appropriate direction to pursue in developing high yield thermonuclear explosives." We explain in Chapters IV and VI why we see that assertion as, fortunately, a gross exaggeration -- a form of gamesmanship. Treated as a justifiable evaluation, it must be taken as an example of selective declassification. In releasing Brown's assessment, it appears the government tried to take advantage of public and congressional tendencies to uncritically accept official pronouncements based on classified information.

There was another uncalled-for elevation of sensitivity in Brown's affidavit: "The information that has been identified as Secret Restricted Data contained in the Morland paper describes correctly, in general, the basic principles of the functioning of a thermonuclear weapon." Because he was the Secretary of Defense, and because he identified himself as having a "direct and thorough knowledge with respect to nuclear weapons design" (Ph.D. in physics, former director of Lawrence Livermore Laboratories, etc.), Brown's statement has the highest level of credibility. Can it be that Brown, who is, as he said, "responsible to the President for the...development and acquisition of nuclear weapon delivery systems," did not recognize the unnecessary confirmatory nature of his affidavit? We doubt it. At the same time, we do not know at what level the decision was made to make such affidavits public. Again we wonder whether this and other overstatements about the correctness of the "basic principles" were deliberately released to clinch the case against the article.

Here are some specific passages [also see Notes IV-5 and IV-17] from the public affidavit of Jack Rosengren [23], a government nuclear weapons expert, providing new information about U.S. hydrogen bombs:

The Morland Article goes far beyond any other publication
in identifying the nature of the particular design used in
the thermonuclear weapons in the U.S. stockpile.

It provides a more comprehensive, accurate, and detailed summary of the overall construction and operation of a thermonuclear weapon than any publication to date in the public literature.

The Morland Article describes in a relatively detailed manner the basic design concepts and certain specific design features of U.S. thermonuclear weapons.

Any interested foreign scientist would immediately go on the alert. The affidavit, although superficially innocuous, offers enough confirmatory information if carefully read to make it a veritable Rosetta stone. Even without access to Morland's article, notice is served that it is possible to deduce the concepts from the same sources used by Morland. With Morland's article -- copies of which had been distributed in draft form prior to the injunction proceedings -- the Rosengren affidavit provides a direct channel to validated concepts. Release of that affidavit violated the standard practice of avoiding specific comment on classified material in the public domain. Sensitive specifics and opinions could have been limited to Rosengren's in camera affidavits, and his public statement could have been noncommittal.

Information Released for Tactical Reasons

When the government brought suit against The Progressive, it apparently felt that a good tactic would be to turn public opinion against the magazine. The government lawyers were no doubt concerned about the heavy burden of proof that any prior restraint action would carry, and presumably felt that an effective public barrage would not only bring considerable external pressure on the magazine but would frighten off potential witnesses for the magazine. They were very nearly correct, but they placed themselves in a potentially untenable position at the beginning of the case.

Initially, The Progressive had a hard time getting any expert witnesses to read the article and testify on its contents -- for various reasons. First of all, there is the prevalent disinclination to "get involved," a malady that afflicts scientists as well as others. Then there were those who, once the article had been classified, felt that their ability to speak freely would be compromised if they obtained clearance to read it. And of the small number who had actually read a draft of the article, some considered it genuinely sensitive.

Complicating the situation, there were premature outcries from many liberal members of the scientific community. For example, Henry Kendall of the Union of Concerned Scientists and Jeremy Stone of the Federation of American Scientists took the government's allegations at face value and sharply criticized The Progressive. When offered the opportunity to read the article and testify for or against The Progressive, they declined. The government campaign had succeeded in misleading these and other influential figures in the scientific community.

In desperation, The Progressive contacted Ted Postol, a scientist at Argonne National Laboratory who had seen and reviewed an early version of the Morland article. He agreed to write an affidavit on behalf of the magazine. After arriving the next day at Madison, Wisconsin, where The Progressive is published, he wrote a detailed statement explaining why he regarded the contents of the Morland article as already in the public domain. He and The Progressive's lawyer, Earl Munson, worked closely to incorporate the different scientific and legal perspectives into the final statement.

Upon returning to Munson's law offices the next day, Postol was surprised to find that what had originally been a single statement had been broken into two affidavits marked "Postol I" and "Postol II." Munson's edited version of Postol II contained almost all the technical discussion relevant to the Morland article. Postol I contained only an oblique reference to the Teller diagram and the list of references used in Postol II to construct the technical discussion (the set of references was marked "Exhibit A"). Munson explained that he expected the government might try to classify Postol II and possibly even parts of Postol I.

The references used in Postol II had been carefully put together so that the court could identify the specific portions of the publicly available books and articles in which concepts relevant to the technical discussion were used. The articles and books referenced were elementary. However, they did include the Teller encyclopedia article, as well as references showing how to calculate certain properties of thermal radiation fields. An interested reader of the affidavit could have learned from the references two of the three concepts (multiple staging and radiation coupling) that were relevant to the case. Although classifying such material appeared useless to him, Postol indicated to Munson that if the government classified Postol II, then it would also have to classify the references in Postol I. They thereupon decided that if Postol II were classified, Munson was to point out to the government that at least the page numbers in the Postol I list of references should also be classified.

The government did classify Postol II, but, for reasons unknown, left the reference list in Postol's Exhibit A intact and unclassified, in spite of the fact that Munson did call attention to the anomaly. This should have alerted the court to the possibility that the government was not as serious about the alleged sensitivity of Morland's article as was being claimed. However, the court appeared to be preoccupied with the question of who was saying what, rather than determining whether what was being said made sense.

(Somewhat later, the government compounded their error by releasing an expurgated version of Postol II with only the page numbers deleted from the references -- thus pinpointing the ideas even more precisely, for anyone who bothered to compare the two reference lists.)

According to the government, Postol's second affidavit, now released, was originally classified because it

> discloses the essential aspects in thermonuclear weapon design, and attempts to quantify mathematically these aspects. This identification and discussion, along with other selective references to concepts alleged to be in the public domain, divulge substantial information properly classified as Restricted Data, the public disclosure of which would surely result in damage to the security of the United States.

On the plane returning from Madison, Postol had his first opportunity to read carefully the affidavits submitted by the government. They were disturbing in both tone and content, the most worrisome aspect being the level of indiscretion exhibited at least by DOE classification personnel, if not by the government's affiants as well. If the government's claims had any basis in truth, considerably more information was being put into the public domain than appeared to be in the Morland article. For instance, it was not clear why, if they really wanted to protect weapons concepts, the directors of both weapons laboratories would volunteer in public affidavits [26A,26B] that the Ulam-Teller idea was contained in the article, especially since Morland had made no such claim. It was even more mystifying that those affidavits could survive a classification review before being filed publicly. The most troublesome of all the affidavits was the one by Jack Rosengren [23], discussed previously.

This worried Postol. If the affidavits were to be taken seriously, releasing them was inconsistent with the government's desire to preserve H-bomb secrecy. But if the affidavits were not correct when they said that the article revealed the design of U.S. weapons, then high-level government officials were stretching the truth in a federal court. Neither possibility was comforting. (A third possibility -- that the statements were correct and were released in a deliberate attempt to influence the outcome of the case by sensitizing the article -- was not considered until later.)

In pondering the situation, Postol recalled that Postol I referred to the Teller diagram. This meant that a scientifically trained reader of his affidavit and the government affidavits would learn critical information that might truly be sensitive. He phoned Munson and alerted him to the contents of the combined affidavits. Munson immediately contacted the United States attorney and indicated the nature of the problem. He said that both he and Postol would cooperate with the government, if necessary and possible, to protect the information in the documents. Repeated attempts by both Munson and Postol to alert the government to the problem were ignored. The United States attorney made no positive response, and the DOE Director of Classification John Griffin expressed no interest in trying to retrieve the documents. They remained public, and shortly thereafter were published in the Washington Post. (We trust that, in private, the government witnesses shared our view that the information was not, in fact, protectible in any event.) Possible official violations of important rules are discussed in more detail in the next chapter.

If suit were to be brought at all, a less revealing (and also, paradoxically, more accurate) statement could have gone something like this: "The article describes some principles, in part correct and in part incorrect, of the functioning of a thermonuclear weapon." This would have confirmed nothing and volunteered nothing specific, in sharp contrast to the authoritative, almost categorical verification volunteered by the Secretary of Defense, who also happens to be a qualified weapons physicist.

Either by virtue of overconfidence or in recognition that the consequences would not be horrendous, the government set out on a one-way path when it called attention to the otherwise obscure article and confirmed its contents.

OVERCLASSIFICATION OF RESEARCH DATA

The classification process has adverse effects on some scientific research for nonmilitary purposes. Cox mentions [COX-75] the 1957 findings of the Wright Commission on Government Security, which after two years of work recommended that the "Confidential" classification be abolished "because too much information was being classified." Other studies [Note VIII-1] indicate that overclassification continues.

The Fusion Energy Foundation, a group interested in promoting the development of thermonuclear energy, pointed out some anomalies [170]:

The classification practices of the United States government in recent years have in effect reversed these priorities [to improve dissemination of atomic energy information] as established by Congress in 1954. The possibilities for further development of peaceful applications of atomic energy (including both fission and fusion processes within the express meaning of the Act) are being stifled by an overly restrictive and misguided application of classification procedures...with the bizarre consequences that even when the Soviet Union has declassified the results of its research on fusion processes, the United States government has promptly re-classified the Soviet findings.

A sequence of affidavits [39] by scientists supporting The Progressive (see Chapter IV) agreed that "government policy designed to preserve secrecy with respect to such matters not only is unsuccessful, but tends to inhibit scientific research by erecting barriers between people in closely related fields."

An official agency can increase its power by overclassifying. This is pointed out by Cox [COX-75], who observes that the Pentagon "controls the defense industries by controlling who gets the contracts," by "unplanned but very real assimilation of military men into the ranks of defense-industry management," and through the secrecy system: "unless an industry or research center has security clearance it cannot have a defense contract." Moreover, "very often, the weapons or information sold by private industry abroad are classified."

A 1971 congressional subcommittee [F&W-74] showed that

existing administrative penalties against overclassification were ignored by Executive departments and agencies. Over a four-year period these agencies carried out 2,433 investigations of violations of regulations governing the security classification system.... But only two of the investigations involved cases of overclassification, and not a single administrative penalty was imposed against overclassification.

Cox agrees that there are no penalties for overclassification: The "views of an individual can be protected merely by marking his opinions Official Use Only." Excessive classification of information is the primary reason for leaks and the casual attitude about the secrecy system.

IMPLICATIONS

In the specific instances cited -- the Pentagon Papers, the Rosenberg case, the Cannikin Papers, and now the Progressive case -- misuses of the classification system have been identified. There is great power and inertia behind overclassification, contributing to manipulation of Congress, the media, and the public by the executive branch. It also contributes to selective adherence to the law, and ultimately to disdain for the law.

We fear, superimposed on legitimate application of the Atomic Energy Act, a self-serving political component in the government's efforts to enjoin publication of Morland's article. The government perhaps wanted to show its determination to enforce the literal terms of the Atomic Energy Act, in order to gain public support for its policies of information denial.

Furthermore, the Progressive case has signs of disregard for established rights of scientific and technological inquiry. Open inquiry should not be squelched by government fiat without valid national-security reason, simply because the information or ideas are not consistent with policies promoted by the administration that happens to be in office. The courts, in turn, should not allow the impounding of concepts that are born in the private sector.

Despite the representations of the Departments of State and Defense, it was unlikely (and is proving more so) that publication would have surely, directly, immediately, or irreparably -- or at all -- jeopardized national efforts to impede proliferation or ensure security. Although all of those criteria must be simultaneously satisfied for the Pentagon Papers test, none of them was met in this case.

Perhaps it will take judicial action to change a de facto classification policy that keeps from the American people, not sensitive information, but things that potential foreign adversaries are well aware of. Informed judgment about important issues tends to be limited to a small group of people -- to persons on government payrolls with access to classified information, a group inherently inclined to support the national policies of the moment.

We must keep in mind, as Cox has said so succinctly, that "control of information is control of power." He notes that Edward Teller and Theodore Taylor are scientists who have opposed excessive secrecy. Teller says [COX-75]:

> Our policy of secrecy in science and technology has created the illusion that we are in possession of valuable information which is not available to other nations, and in particular, not available to our chief competitor, the Soviet Union. In the field of nuclear explosives where we used to have a great advantage, secrecy did not perpetuate this advantage. In the field of electronics and the art of high-speed computers a great national advantage was brought about without the aid of secrecy. That technological secrecy amounts to security is, in my opinion, indeed an illusion....

> The recent era of secrecy had its origin in the Second World War and...was greatly strengthened by the assumption that dangerous knowledge such as the knowledge of atomic

weapons must be kept secret. But every country which managed to produce the materials needed for nuclear explosives also managed within a very short time to carry out a nuclear explosion; lack of knowledge did not prove to be an effective impediment.

Actually secrecy of nuclear weapons has not worked very well. [Six] nations are members of the Nuclear Club [counting India] and the number of people to whom the main lines of relevant information about nuclear weapons is available is probably between one hundred thousand and one million. Under these conditons one must accept the conclusion that nuclear secrets, as a general rule, are secrets in name only.... Today secrecy does give a false feeling of safety. This false feeling permits people to avoid hard decisons which would have to be faced if all the facts were out in the open. On the other hand, secrecy in the nuclear field has also the opposite result of raising fears of the unknown. Ideas which belong in science fiction rather than in military planning, could be more easily eliminated from the discussions if secrecy barriers were broken down.

Control of sensitive information is placed in government hands as a public trust, and that trust is violated whenever the power to classify and declassify is used for reasons unrelated to national security.

9 Offical Infractions of Security Guidelines

In pursuing the Progressive case, the government confirmed the basic ideas in Howard Morland's article, and incidentally released further nondeducible information about a component of the American nuclear arsenal -- with indeterminate harm to national security. The article should have been ignored. Admittedly this is Monday-morning quarterbacking, but is the criticism justified nonetheless? To see whether the consequences were predictable from the outset, consider the character of the information and the way it was divulged.

LEGAL ACTION

Filing the injunction risked calling attention to the sensitivity of the subject matter. The government argued that the injunction would be effective, but it was not, because a few things had been overlooked. The government did not assure itself in advance that no underground copies of the article or its drafts were already out of reach. One copy did soon surface in Australia, and -- in a near-comic episode -- DOE got the Australian government to confiscate that copy. Furthermore, Howard Morland has indicated that if the government had succeeded in preventing publication in The Progressive the underground press would probably have published the article from copies acquired before the restraining order was issued.

Second, what would prevent others from independently deriving equivalent material from similar sources? The publicity could be expected to stimulate such independent activities, as in fact it did.

Assume for the moment that the classified information the government said it wanted to protect was believed to be truly sensitive and dangerous to have in the open. If that was so, the government's strategists apparently put all their eggs in one basket, gambling that they would win the case with little release of information and thereby strengthen their power to enforce secrecy under the Atomic Energy Act. Little planning appears to have been done for the contingency that the case might be lost. Perhaps, however, the administration did take some of these factors into consideration, but miscalculated. There must always be a balancing of risks and benefits; in this case the risk of disclosing more than was originally accessible should have been given greater weight. The way in which the law is enforced can be important in preserving secret data, and alternative tactics with less risk of added disclosure of sensitive information could have been used.

Despite its apparent anxiety over possible publication of Morland's piece in The Progressive, the government did little or nothing to restrict dissemination of drafts of the article. We were personally aware of over a dozen people who reputedly had seen copies of the early draft.

There was an earlier parallel. The Pentagon Papers case had also led to the release of more information than was originally contested. Four "negotiating" volumes of the Pentagon Papers study, unpublished prior to the trial, had to be made public because of that case: The government was obliged to use as evidence the critical information whose release, it claimed, would meet the statutory test of harm to the nation. The volumes were "available to the public for copying in the office of the clerk [of the court]" [H&H1-77]. After the trial, "the Government still refused to make these volumes available to Senator Fulbright or to publish them." As a result of civil suits and FOIA actions, most of the volumes have now been released. Those "negotiating" volumes had not been part of the Pentagon Papers reproduced by Ellsberg, and would not have been made publicly accessible except for the seeking of an injunction by the government.

AFFIDAVITS THAT SPILLED SECRETS

In Chapter VIII we noted that the general validity of Morland's H-bomb arrangement was confirmed by some government affidavits, thereby bringing to mind the possibility of selective declassification to fulfill political objectives. We suggested alternative, less revealing wording that could have been used in affidavits to be made public. Confirmation of many features of Morland's deductions violated official guidelines for protecting secrets. Because of the signicance of this aspect of the case, we reexamine here the more sensitive elements of the affidavits.

Secretary of Defense Harold Brown verified in his affidavit [37] that information independently derived by Morland described "the basic principles of the functioning of a thermonuclear weapon." That specific confirmatory declaration in Brown's statement adds (classified) information not originally in the article.

Another possible prima facie breach of national security would be the allegation by Brown that the article would help subnational (terrorist) element make thermonuclear weapons. If Brown's interpretation of subnational capability were true, it would be an act of national-security indiscretion just to admit it.

The original public affidavit [23] [see Chapter VIII] by Jack W. Rosengren, a government weapons consultant, added another level of damaging specificity when he openly admitted that Morland had identified the nature of the "particular design" used in United States thermonuclear weapons. With the elaboration that follows in his affidavit, and the public portions of his subsequent jointly authored affidavits, Rosengren lent credibility to Morland's deductions. The unwarranted degree of detail divulged by the Rosengren affidavits constitutes perhaps the most flagrant violation of security guidelines.

The Secretary of Defense also claimed that dissemination of the Morland article would cause "a substantial increase in the risk that the availability of thermonuclear weapons would be increased." Assuming that assessment to be correct, care should have been taken not to enhance that dissemination.

The government's selective and authoritative words and deeds appear to result in the compromise of secret information. First, bringing suit to prevent public access had the effect of spotlighting the information; then the government's public elaborations of the article's high degree of sensitivity must have created an incentive for foreign governments to seek out this newly authenticated data.

We do not disagree with the right of the top government defense official to offer opinions and interpretations on a subject that has political overtones, such as the proliferative nature of the Morland material. However, Brown's authentication and augmentation of the factual content of The Progressive article reinforced the validity of the technical assessments offered by Rosengren. The combined effect of these affirmations on the original technical content of Morland's article was significant and unprecedented. If we accepted at face value the pleadings of the Secretary of Defense and other government officials as to the significance of the original unconfirmed article, we would have to conclude that the net effect of government action in this case has been to diminish national security.

As the government itself (the plaintiff) put it [109]:

> Plaintiff's [in camera] submissions are substantially more sensitive than defendants' in that they provide official confirmation of certain concepts with respect to the design and construction of nuclear weapons, and discuss these concepts with much greater thoroughness, detail and accuracy....
>
> It is inescapable that with each additional disclosure there is the risk of compromise, regardless of the best intentions of the parties, their counsel and the Court.

CLASSIFICATION OF THE GLENN LETTER

In our letter to Senator John Glenn (Chapter V and Appendix B), we showed how the government had, in effect, published some of the information it said it wanted to suppress, in violation of one of the primary, well-established precepts of security: never, ever confirm or deny the accuracy of public statements about sensitive subjects.

The Glenn letter was mailed approximately six weeks after the initial filing of government and defense affidavits (which occurred mainly in the period March 12 to March 20, 1979). Copies went to some associates connected with the case, including Hugh DeWitt, a scientist at Livermore Laboratory who also had filed affidavits on behalf of The Progressive. We sent copies to reporters at several major newspapers, with the statement that it was for background information, not for publication. After a delay of about four weeks, the Glenn committee sent the letter to DOE, requesting a response.

In the meantime, DeWitt, finding the letter on his desk upon his
return from an overseas trip, sent a copy to Charles Hansen (who was
later to write the "Hansen letter"). Unknown to DeWitt, DOE had
decided to classify the letter Secret Restricted Data under the Atomic
Energy Act. DeWitt received notification of classification only hours
after he had mailed the letter to Hansen. Before he could retrieve it,
Hansen had copies made and took one to his congressman, Paul N.
McCloskey, who was in Palo Alto. Hansen also sent copies to newspapers
around the country. All this made DOE's situation difficult: Now there
was the problem of trying to get back from newspapers a letter that
raised the possibility that the government had violated its own
security regulations.

The Glenn letter pointed to a set of events that suggested
negligence, incompetence, or deliberate misuse of the classification
system. Further, it seemed to contain no information except some that
had been public domain for a considerable time, plus some more that the
government had made public with DOE's blessing. Some of the newspaper
people already knew that attempts had been made by the signatories to
alert the government to the nature of the information some of its
people were releasing. They also knew that the government had rebuffed
the attempts. The news media regarded DOE's action as motivated mainly
by desire to avoid embarrassment, using an all-too-convenient excuse to
avoid responding in public to a congressional inquiry.

Excerpts from our letter were published on June 11 in the Daily
Californian, a student newspaper at the Berkeley campus of the
University of California. Thus alerted, the government quickly
obtained and served a court order under the Atomic Energy Act to
prevent publication of any more of it. The paper defiantly published
the entire letter on its front page on June 13 -- a clear challenge of
the Atomic Energy Act. The paper's editors had decided to publish the
letter "because we feel that the Department of Energy is abusing its
power of classification for politically motivated reasons. That's all
this letter says and that's all the classification of it shows." (As
explained in Chapter VIII and Note V-4, there actually was more to it
than that, from the government's viewpoint.) Along with their initial
synopsis of the letter, they had published a comment from Congressman
McCloskey, a former member of the House Subcommittee on Government
Information and Individual Rights, who said, "absolutely nothing in the
letter is confidential and there is no imaginable justification for
classifying it.... Under no conditions would there be anything
illegal, criminal or negligent in printing the letter.... If I were
you, I'd run it on the front page." That's what they did.

Although the government had notified the Daily Californian that
publication might violate the Atomic Energy Act, no action was taken
when it was published. Other student newspapers began printing the
letter. Needless to say, the attempt to stop the Glenn letter from
being published simply succeeded in arousing curiosity and attention --
which was not likely to have been the intent.

The treatment of the Glenn letter became one of the examples of "the
government's stamp of authenticity" cited by The Progressive in support
of its public domain argument. The defendants' statement on this point
[169] [Note IX-1] was originally classified by the government.

We wrote that letter to call attention to certain inconsistencies in
the government's actions. By classifying it the government spotlighted

and authenticated otherwise obscure information -- although, to repeat, any foreign scientist who wanted help in designing an H-bomb, attracted by the publicity about the Progressive case, could have read the court records and would independently have followed the reasoning outlined in the Glenn letter.

CHALLENGES TO THE ATOMIC ENERGY ACT

The letter that H-bomb hobbyist Charles Hansen wrote to Senator Percy (Chapter V) drew the government action predicted by its author: the classification stamp.   The technical contents of the letter were conceptually similar to the Morland article, if somewhat less coherent. In the end, the government might not have been disappointed when Hansen's letter was published; it gave them a convenient excuse to drop its suit at a time when the case was embattled and collapsing anyway.

Hansen had sent copies of his letter to newspapers across the country. In spite of the threat of prosecution under the Atomic Energy Act, several newspapers were on the verge of publishing it.   The government got a court order forbidding the Daily Californian to print it, but a now-defunct paper, the Madison [Wisc.] Press Connection did publish it, on September 17, 1979.   Another California bay-area newspaper, The Peninsula Times Tribune, also reprinted one of its diagrams on August 30, 1979.

Although declaring something classified is not the same as confirming it, the act of classifying Hansen's letter was another bureaucratic action that effectively called attention to the few tidbits of correct information that were to be found in a compilation by a hobbyist. That some or much of what was in Hansen's letter may have been incorrect would not deter competent scientists from abstracting the useful components. At the same time, we cannot regard this particular incident as a serious breach of security, since any nuclear physicist could do a far better job than Hansen did of synthesizing an H-bomb concept from publicly available information.

In his letter, Hansen named three people who, he said, should have been prosecuted for "violating terms of their security clearances," but were not. Ironically, in offering an explanation of why nothing was done, he attributes to the Justice Department the remark, "Action by the United States would highlight the sensitivity of the material involved in these cases."   Without taking a position on Hansen's charges, we can agree that there has been rather abitrary enforcement of the Atomic Energy Act.

Although the temporary restraining order prevented publication by the Daily Californian, the Madison Press Connection had not been officially warned that the Hansen letter was classified, since the government did not know they had a copy. The Chicago Tribune published most of the letter on September 18, by then knowing that it had been classified.   Technically each additional publication is also prosecutable because, unless the information is declassified by the DOE, any transmittal to unauthorized individuals might be a violation, regardless of whether the information is in the open.

The collective, deliberate challenges to the Atomic Energy Act, confronted the government with another difficult situation. If it chose to prosecute, still more newspapers would probably be moved to publish one or both of the documents -- the New York Times, for one, was threatening to publish Hansen's letter. Thus a move against any of the newspapers that had published either the Glenn or Hansen letter would quite possibly result in a Supreme Court confrontation between the government and some of the major newspapers in the country. There was reason to think that the secrecy provisions of the Atomic Energy Act might not survive the test of a constitutional review (see Chapter X). Having already been stung by the Progressive case, the government seems -- wisely -- to have chosen to avoid another confrontation. It immediately took the opportunity to withdraw its case against The Progressive, claiming that publication of the Hansen letter had mooted it, the Justice Department filed a motion rescinding its objection to publication of the Morland article, and there was, eventually, an announcement that there would be no prosecutions.

In the last analysis, the most serious violations of the Atomic Energy Act were the government's. At the time, some of the official actions seemed to be low-level blunders, which is why Postol attempted to alert the DOE classification office about the unprecedented confirmatory nature of government affidavits (Chapter VIII). We do not know the details of the review procedure that the government's own affidavits went through before they were released, but we now suppose that the final decisions were made at a rather high level.

GOVERNMENT WEAPONS DOCUMENTS

Probably the most serious declassification threat to national security was the inadvertent release of certain government documents containing extremely sensitive thermonuclear weapons data. We have already had occasion to mention the two outstanding examples, UCRL-4725 and UCRL-5280, both routine (classified) progress reports of weapons programs conducted by Lawrence Livermore Laboratory in the mid-1950s.

As is detailed in Chapter V, physicists said that UCRL-4725 contains the "Teller-Ulam concepts" [135], would be "useful in designing or constructing a fusion weapon" [133], and has "valuable technical details" and "the three central concepts" [134]. The document stood "in sharp contrast to the Morland article." There is no substitute for an official report classified at the highest levels (Secret Restricted Data) for reliable weapons data. In fact, according to the cover page of UCRL-4725 printed in the Chicago Sun-Times on May 18, 1979, it was designated "Sigma-1," which we understand to be the very highest DOE "need to know" classification.

In the words of Dr. Theodore Taylor, who worked at Los Alamos on nuclear weapons design at the time the report was originally issued:

I was thoroughly shocked by the classified content of the document.... It contains design and performance data related to several past and planned tests of fission and thermonuclear explosives. It presents key numbers and tables of numbers representing the results of highly detailed calculations of times, dimensions and densities, and explosive yields of the test explosives. It contains masses of various types of nuclear fission and fusion materials used in the explosives. Although the report contains no diagrams, it describes or directly infers the

basic design principles used in H-bombs and fission
weapons....

The erroneous declassification of UCRL-4725 and the
provision of unrestricted public access to it for nearly 4
years, until quite recently, is the most serious breach of
security I am aware of in this country's post-World War II
nuclear weapon development programs....

In response to Senator Glenn's question whether the document gave
away "the Teller-Ulam concept which has been characterized earlier as
the secret of the H-bomb," Taylor replied, "This is hard because I know
the Teller-Ulam secret. To me it goes way beyond that. It describes
the results of situations in which the Teller-Ulam is being used."

Public Access

The degree of public access to the documents was important in
Progressive. The head librarian at Los Alamos affirmed [147] that
the Los Alamos Scientific Laboratory Library is the only
such facility associated with a DOE weapons laboratory
which permits certain limited physical access to the
public.

From July of 1975 to May, 1978 and May, 1979,
respectively, UCRL 5280 and UCRL 4725 were not treated as
classified.

From July, 1975 until April, 1977, UCRL 4725 and UCRL
5280 were available to the public only if specifically
requested.... Therefore, prior to April, 1977, a member of
the general public would have had to know independently of
the specific existence of these documents in order to gain
access to them. There was no direct method by which a
member of the public could have discovered the existence of
UCRL 4725 and UCRL 5280 through research of the catalogs,
collections, or other information available at the Los
Alamos Scientific Laboratory Library....

The public entries in the card catalog, or file points,
under which UCRL 4725 could be found as of May, 1979,
included:
UCRL-4725
California. Univ., Livermore. Radiation Lab.
...
Nuclear Rocket Propulsion
Redwing [public name for a nuclear-weapons test]
Sparrow ["   ]
Swallow ["   ]
Swan   ["   ]
...
Weapon 38 -- Atlas (referenced from "XW-38 Atlas
              Warhead Installation")

While doing research for academic purposes on nuclear weapons design
at the Los Alamos library in May 1978, Dimitri Rotow [137] "became
aware of the hundreds of declassified reports describing nuclear
weapons and science useful in weapons design publicly available there."
A year later, after researching the literature for the defendants, he
described his experience as follows:

My ideas concerning H-bomb design were immediately
confirmed by my reading of UCRL-4725, which I located in
the first half hour of my research at the Library using the
card-catalogue under "W" for weapons.

It came out at hearings before Senator Glenn's subcommittee on October 2, 1979, that 590 foreign visitors from fifty-two countries were
known to have been at Los Alamos from April 1977 to May 1979. Morland
apparently visited the public section of the Library in 1978 [136].

In a statement prepared in the course of the case, Alexander DeVolpi
discussed the probability of public access to the declassified reports
at the public library of the Los Alamos laboratory [Note IX-2]. He
noted that the library is readily accessible to the public, with no
identification required. In fact, in the same building he attended a
meeting that included many foreign nationals. For a period of years,
anyone could have gone the the Los Alamos library and, without leaving
a trace, made a copy of one of the two documents. On the basis of his
research experience, he concluded that, because it had been so
accessible, UCRL-4725 "must be considered to have been compromised."

The government rebuttal [141] (in camera) was this:

[The DeVolpi] statement falls far short of evidence that
even one such individual [from a potential thermonuclear
weapons state] (1) used the library and (2) located UCRLs
4725 or 5280 and (3) understood the significance of the
information in them and (4) transmitted that information to
even one country.

Copies of UCRL-4725 made by Rotow during his library research at Los
Alamos were sent to a number of individuals and newspapers. At the May
23, 1979, hearing before the Senate Subcommittee on Energy, Nuclear
Nonproliferation and Federal Services, Rotow said that "several dozen"
copies had been made and that he had mailed out at least six. As of
that date the government had not asked him for the names and addresses
of the recipients. At least two newspapers received copies. In the
opinion of the Comptroller General [GAO Report EMD-79-109], DOE "failed
to act decisively, thus permitting a highly sensitive weapons report to
be distributed."

Bordering on irrelevancy (no foreign party acquiring UCRL-4725 is
likely to notify DOE), Secretary of Energy John Schlesinger said in
camera (now released):

Although I am aware of the abstract possibility that "UCRL
4725" and "UCRL 5280" could have been compromised to
foreign intelligence services, I have no evidence that any
nations have in fact obtained access to these documents.
Moreover... it is my judgment that it is highly unlikely
that many of these nations have in fact acquired the
Restricted Data in "UCRL 4725" or "UCRL 5280."

We hope that the government has traced all copies and retrieved them
or ensured their security, but we fear that is not the case. We
received our copy, as others did, via the regular first class mail.
Our copy is in a properly secured DOE facility, but possibly other
copies have not been so well guarded. The government argued [141] that
the "possibility of some compromise [of UCRL 4725] as to some countries
can hardly be said to place the secret of the H-bomb in the public
domain," referring, presumably, to the likelihood that no country that
got a copy would be inclined to share it.

Legal Point of View

Because Executive Order 12065 specifically prohibits reclassification, the government finds itself in a difficult situation vis-a-vis UCRL-4725. Here is a very sensitive document, with an unknown number of copies not necessarily in secure facilities. Official action to retrieve them might well do more harm than good by causing more widespread dissemination. Further, even if the copies were located, there would be no legal means for confiscating them. The situation highlights the need for a means of protecting truly sensitive information that is erroneously declassified. This is discussed in Chapter XI.

In denying the motion to vacate the injunction, Judge Warren took notice of a prior court ruling (Knopf v. Colby) that "classified information was 'not in the public domain unless there has been official disclosure of it.'" He was further "unable to conclude one way or another whether the vital data [in UCRL-4725 or UCRL-5280] was obtained by scientists or intelligence agents from other nations." He also cited Aspin v. Department of Defense and Halperin v. Central Intelligence Agency with the remark, "Prior release of classified information should not be binding on the government if, at a later time, it is determined that further release would jeopardize national security." Therefore,

the Court is compelled to the conclusion that, from a legal point of view, the government's error in inadvertently declassifying UCRL 4725 and UCRL 5280 did not move these documents in the "public domain" and further, that there is no showing that the injunction became ineffectual.

Legalities aside, there is a real need to minimize dissemination of such documents as UCRL-4725, a pragmatic viewpoint shared by the scientific experts and the lawyers who supported The Progressive in its legal battle. Thus, while much postappeal activity has been directed at achieving release of documents detailing government arguments and dealing with the Morland concepts, there is substantial agreement that UCRL-4725 should continue to be protected.

We sympathize with government officials who, because of pending litigation or (belated) fears of making matters worse, must deal cautiously with such sensitive matters as attempting to recover or protect outstanding copies of UCRL-4725. They have been caught in a bind. But the situation did arise because of their ill-conceived suit against The Progressive.

10 Legal Considerations

Congress shall make no law...abridging the freedom
of speech, or of the press.
                                    - the First Amendment

We ask indulgence while we address some legal issues, even though we
are physicists. The book would be deficient if we kept our remarks
entirely technical, as the case was fought primarily on the
battleground of law, with the facts of proliferation risk a secondary
consideration. We do not try to give a complete legal analysis [Note
X-1]; it would be just as hard for us to do that as it would be for
lawyers to dissect the technical components.

THE TEMPORARY RESTRAINING ORDER

Not many temporary restraining orders (TROs) affecting the press in
America have been issued. The Supreme Court has consistently and
unanimously agreed that there is a "heavy presumption" against any
"prior restraint" of speech. One such order was issued against the New
York Times, and another against the Washington Post, to suppress
publication of the Pentagon Papers pending a hearing for an injunction.
However the TRO lasted only for four days in the case of the Times, and
not at all for the Post, because of the expedited appeal to, and
decision by, the Supreme Court [Note X-2]. Thus Progressive is the
first case in which an injunction has been issued in the name of
national security and "it marks the first time the government has
sought and obtained judicial imprimatur to extend security controls to
private, nongovernmental, industrial, scientific, university, or
journalistic activities" [CHEH-80].
     In filing to prevent publication of the Morland article, the U.S.
government made two allegations. The first was that publication would
violate the Atomic Energy Act by injuring the United States or giving
an advantage to a foreign nation, and that The Progressive had been
given "reason to believe" there would be such consequences. The
second, broader count was that publication would "result in grave,

188

direct, immediate and irreparable harm to the national security of the United States and its people." Though the first charge was brought pursuant to a statute, the second appears to have been intended as a hedge in case the statute were declared unconstitutional; the phrasing came from certain judicial opinions articulated in the Pentagon Papers case.

Under a literal interpretation of the Atomic Energy Act (Appendix C), the government may seek an injunction upon learning of impending publication of anything ("all data") concerning nuclear weapons, unless declassified. Interpretation is unclear. "All data" could subsume almost any subject with a remote weapons connection; it could cover everything pertaining to atomic weapons that is derived or deduced in the public domain, including privately developed data.

"Declassification" in a strict formalistic sense covers only documents specifically removed from a list of classified papers; interpreted somewhat more freely, the term could apply to general ideas and specific facts released in the course of classification review. However, the Department of Energy has held that whether a publication is classified is determined by the context in which the weapons information is used. In that case nothing is truly declassified, because declassified information might be inadvertently reassembled into a classified configuration.

The government contended that notifying the defendants, either by phone or letter, gave them sufficient "reason to believe" that publication would cause harm, so that additional proof was not necessary. It claimed that neither the defendants nor the court could challenge that official determination.

An attempt was made, rather successfully in terms of Judge Warren's reaction, to equate the information in the article with the sailing date of a troopship in wartime. Although all the criteria of the Pentagon Papers decision readily apply to the troopship situation, they fail miserably to apply to Morland's article -- as we have seen -- with the exception of the potential gravity of the alleged consequences.

JUDGE WARREN'S DECISION ON THE PRELIMINARY INJUNCTION

Turning to the constitutional points, Judge Warren [82] wrote, "As applied to this case, the Court finds that the statute...is not vague or overbroad." We wonder about that finding, if only because of the many possible interpretations of "classified data."

In his "Conclusions of Law" [85], Warren ruled that a preliminary injunction "would be warranted even in the absence of statutory authorization" and that it would not violate the defendants' First Amendment rights. He accepted the government's contention (Chapter IV) that the case differed from the Pentagon Papers case in "several important respects" [82]:

> The study involved in the New York Times case contained historical data relating to events some three to twenty years previously.... The Supreme Court agreed with the lower court that no cogent reasons were advanced by the government as to why the article affected national security except that publication might cause some embarrassment to the United States.

A second and most vital difference between these two
cases is the fact that a specific statute is involved
here....

Apparently the judge thought that all authority to determine the
potential for "injury" was vested in the government, for he ignored
assessments submitted on behalf of the defendants. Despite his
admission [95] that a showing of "irreparable harm is a requirement for
any preliminary injunction," he accepted as adequate a government
complaint based on nothing more than one-sided affidavits that offered
no concrete evidence. He appeared to accept without proof any
assertion by members of the cabinet.

In granting the preliminary injunction, Warren found [95] that the
United States had a "reasonable likelihood of success on the merits"
and would "suffer irreparable harm if the injunction does not issue."
His oral and written opinions betray failure to give the issues a
logical, independent examination.

In large part, the legalities in the Progressive case revolved
around a conflict between First Amendment rights and the specific
statutory authority of the Atomic Energy Act. As the ACLU pointed out
[34], in the New York Times (Pentagon Papers) case Supreme Court
justices White and Stewart gave the Constitution high priority, and
concurred in denying a preliminary injunction even though they were
convinced that publication was not in the national interest and would
do substantial damage. The ACLU contended that "the statutory
authority embodied in [the Atomic Energy Act] does not suffice to
[authorize] prior restraint free from the careful scrutiny required by
the First Amendment." They said that unless the act is "limited by the
constitutional standard specified in New York Times, [it] is
unconstitutionally vague and over-broad." Later in the chapter we
discuss the Pentagon Papers standards.

FACTUAL DISPUTES

In his findings of fact [85], Judge Warren took the government's
arguments at face value [Note X-3]. He accepted the claim that
publication "could materially reduce the time" for other nations to
make thermonuclear weapons. Applying a balancing test, he surmised
that "the United States and citizens will suffer irreparable harm" if
the article were to be published, while "the defendants will not be
substantially harmed" by not publishing. The constitutional fallacy of
that kind of test is summarized by Mary M. Cheh [CHEH-80]:

The perceived public interest...will almost always outweigh
a single instance of censorship. When the question is, "in
light of the possible harm, do we need to know that
particular information, that specific data?," the answer
will invariably be "no."

Taking most of his language from the government briefs, Judge Warren
concluded that publication "will result in direct, immmediate, and
irreparable damage." And he agreed with the government's contention
that the defendants had "reason to believe" that their actions would
lead to the consequences asserted, thereby affirming that the Atomic
Energy Act did, in fact, apply.

Burden of Proof

One of the major bones of contention, one that was pursued into the
appeal level, was the denial of an evidentiary hearing. The government
argued that the court should be satisfied with affidavits; the defense
insisted that it needed to cross-examine the witnesses and to have the
right of discovery, calling [169] the denial of an evidentiary hearing
"the most serious constitutional deprivation." Vigorous concern about
the validity of the government's affidavits was expressed [164] by the
defense because of the "extremely rigorous standards for prior
restraints imposed by the First Amendment."
    The ACLU [34] put the constitutional argument like this:
        The government must meet its heavy burden of persuasion
        with concrete proof, not conclusory predictions. "[T]he
        First Amendment tolerates absolutely no prior judicial
        restraints of the press predicated upon surmise or
        conjecture that untoward consequences may result.... In no
        event may mere conclusions be sufficient..." [New York
        Times Brennan, J. concurring]... Not one of these...affi-
        davits asserts the publication of the article "will surely"
        cause anything. And not one asserts that any "damage to
        our nation or its people" would be a "direct" result of
        publication of the article.
    Defendants' counsel [52A] said that the "government's affidavits are
replete with conclusions, conjecture, and speculative language," and
gave examples -- such as the claim that publication "could"
significantly contribute to nuclear proliferation risk. Words like
"if" and "could" conditioned the assertions of Vance, Brown, and
Sewell. Van Doren used the term "highly likely" in place of "surely,"
and the government's briefs were models of evasion, with a salting of
terms such as "if" and "may." The Secretary of State admitted his lack
of technical competence, but anyway expressed conclusions, based on
affidavits submitted by other offficials.   In the view of the
defendants, the Secretary of Energy gave an affidavit filled with
hearsay and inadequate qualification.

In Camera Proceedings

Another issue was the legality and prudence of holding in camera
proceedings. The ACLU agreed [34] that "the courts have created an
extremely narrow exception to permit the government to present evidence
to district courts for national security and state secrets
information." The explanation for the exception is that it "should not
be necessary to destroy the very secrecy that may ultimately be found
justified in order to resolve the claim of privilege."   Even when
holding in camera hearings, courts have required public affidavits
"explaining in as much detail as possible the basis for [the] claim."
The court, according to the ACLU, had to "strictly limit the in
camera proceedings in this case.... An appropriate summary of the
information considered in camera should be released to the public."
In an essay in the March 1980 Harper's, the situation was incisively
dissected by M.M. Mooney:
        Whatever was secret became secret as soon as [the
        Department of] Justice said it was secret; whether secrets

were actually secret was secret; and arguments over what
was secret were secret not only from the community at
large, but also from the editors of The Progressive and
from Mr. Morland....

In connection with these bizarre arguments, Justice
asserted after Morland's article was published in The
Progressive that anyone who communicates the same secret
secrets, either Morland's or those in the eighth-grade
encyclopedia [the article written by Hans Bethe], by speech
or by writing, would be "acting in concert" with Mr.
Morland and The Progressive, and thereby violating the
in camera "protective orders" of the Federal Court,
subjecting the violators to criminal prosecution. Since
the affidavits are secret, and the judge's decision is
secret too, there is no way to know which secrets are
secret, or what secrets make up a criminal violation of
secrecy.

Public Domain

One of the "factual weaknesses" of the government's case was that it
failed to prove that the alleged harm did not previously exist -- that
the information was not already in the public domain. This point is
discussed in detail in Chapter V. The public domain argument was used
as part of the defense, and it was expanded as revelations occurred
concurrently with the litigation (see below).

STATUTORY CONFLICTS

Setting aside for the moment the factual and constitutional conflicts,
how did the Atomic Energy Act of 1954 apply? In the view of one legal
analyst [CHEH-80], "the constitutional questions need not be reached"
if the Act does not apply to "privately developed information."

The Act prohibits anyone from communicating, transmitting or
disclosing any restricted data to any person "with reason to believe
such data will be utilized to injure the United States or to secure an
advantage to any foreign nation." To support the judge's conclusion
that the test of intent was met, as stated in his memorandum and order
of the court [82], one has to assume a very superficial criterion for
determining "reason to believe" -- namely, simple administrative
notice.

Requirements for an Injunction

Consistent with the drift of his other findings, Judge Warren, in his
conclusions of law [85], asserted that there was proper jurisdiction;
that publication would likely be subject to penalties under the Atomic
Energy Act; that the United States was entitled to a preliminary injunction under the Act; that a preliminary injunction was warranted
even in the absence of statutory authorization; that the facts and circumstances fell within an extremely narrow area, involving national security, in which prior restraint is appropriate; and that all prerequi-
sites for the injunction had been met by the government [Note X-4].

What the government had to prove, and the problems in so doing, have been succinctly summarized by ACLU attorney Bruce J. Ennis [ENN-80]:

It is important to understand...that except for persons...who...learn restricted data directly from the government, it is not a crime for non-government employees to publish restricted data, even if they <u>know</u> that it is restricted data.

[For it to be a crime, the government must] prove the defendant knew the information was restricted data and prove, in addition, that the defendant published the data with "reason to believe" the information will be utilized to injure the United States or to secure an advantage to a foreign nation. The government acknowledged in the district court that in order to make out a criminal violation of the Atomic Energy Act, it would have to prove that "reason to believe." And since the government cannot civilly restrain speech under the Atomic Energy Act without proving a prospective criminal violation of the Act, the government could not get an injunction without proving that the <u>Progressive</u> Magazine had reason to believe publication would injure the nation.

The editors of the <u>Progressive</u> Magazine had a very strong defense to that claim. First, they subjectively believed (and no one disputed the honesty or integrity of that belief) that publication would actually help the United States by alerting the public to the dangerous and ill-founded myth that the basic principles of the operation of hydrogen weapons are truly secret and cannot be acquired by foreign countries, and they submitted affidavits to that effect. Second, the editors submitted to the court a great many books, magazine articles, and newspaper articles which publicly disclosed and discussed the same three concepts the <u>Progressive</u> Magazine intended to publish. Thus, given those documents and the government documents on the shelves of the Los Alamos Library, it was clear that if publication of that information would injure the nation, that injury had already occurred. Finally, the editors submitted affidavits from distinguished expert witnesses who reviewed the <u>Progressive</u> article and concluded that its publication would not injure the United States. In those circumstances, it would have been almost impossible for the government to establish the subjective "reason to believe" requirement of the Atomic Energy Act, and therefore impossible to obtain an injunction under that Act.

Regarding the matter of what constitutes an "advantage" to another country, the defendants in <u>Progressive</u> emphasized the Heine case. After the Supreme Court reversed the espionage conviction in <u>Heine,</u> indicating that "it is obviously lawful to transmit any information about weapons and munitions of war which the [military] services had themselves made public," Judge Learned Hand said:

Obviously, this could not mean that it may not be to the advantage of a foreign government to have possession of such information; it can only mean that, when information has once been made public, and has thus become available in one way or another to any foreign government, the "advantage" intended by the section [of the Espionage Act] cannot reside in facilitating its use by condensing and arranging it.

Classified at Birth

The declaration that data considered sensitive are classified at birth, whether derived by the government or produced in the public domain, is based on an interpretion of the Atomic Energy Act that needs clarification by Congress. The proposition is incompatible with a free press because its applications are unbounded. As professor Floyd Abrams [ABR-80] noted, because "the crime is not limited to information about nuclear weaponry," a "journalist's idle musings about...the operation and development of nuclear power facilities...thus fits the category.... And so, if I learn Restricted Data, however and from whomever, I run the risk of criminal penalties." (This point is treated in more detail in Chapter XI).

In a review of the pertinent legislative history, Cheh concluded that born classified is not a valid consequence of the Atomic Energy Act:

DOE and the NRC...now have no statutory authority to control the use, handling, or dissemination of Restricted Data generated by persons unassociated with the government. If this information is governed by the Atomic Energy Act at all, it is governed only by the law's espionage controls.

The government said that it did not have to rely on a born-classified interpretation -- that "Morland's endeavors do not illustrate the 'classified at birth' principle.... He ascertained the secret design features of thermonuclear weapons by asking people with access to this Restricted Data" [166]. No evidence was offered in support of this claim. Nevertheless, the government contended that even if the article was Morland's "original work product, [it] would not change its status as secret Restricted Data" [4]. Judge Warren did not expressly rule on the born-classified doctrine, although his opinion amounts to tacit acceptance at the District Court level.

In any case, the Justice Department decided not to follow through with criminal prosecutions. In September 1980 it announced that nobody would be charged with unauthorized disclosure to Morland or to anybody else.

Another claim by Justice was that even if the information could be found in the public domain, it remained classified. To support this argument, the government relied on several Freedom of Information Act suits. For example, in Lesar, following attempts to gain access to names deleted from investigative reports, the court ruled, "The fact that an expert can piece together identifying data does not make the identifications in question automatically part of the public domain."

Ronhovde [RON-80] seems to feel that legal precedent supports the government's contention:

The few cases specifically on point suggest that while official publication will likely place the information in the public domain, anything short of that will not unless public knowledge is so pervasive as to render classification meaningless.

CONSTITUTIONAL ARGUMENTS

The constitutionality of the requested injunction was vigorously challenged by the defendants, who claimed that it was forbidden by the First Amendment and inconsistent with the Fifth Amendment.

Overbroad and Vague

There is recurring fear among writers that speech now protected by the First Amendment might be made criminal by extending a statute that is not tightly worded. A joint affidavit by some twenty-eight national periodicals and distributors [174] charged that the Atomic Energy Act is unconstitutional on its face because of its broad sweep. We think they are probably right. If all information "concerning" the subject may be corralled as restricted data, coverage could extend endlessly to encompass virtually all public discussion on nuclear energy and nuclear weaponry, unless affirmatively declassified by the government. Not clearly defined in the Act, besides the word "concerning," are "Restricted Data" and "declassified or removed from Restricted Data." The information control provisions are "fraught with imprecision" [CHEH-80], and the criminal provisions are vague regarding "reason to believe." Overbreadth is the "chief vice" of the information controls of the Act if they are read to apply to privately generated data, says Cheh.

Due Process

According to at least one legal brief [174], the absence from the Atomic Energy Act of any ascertainable standard for identifying either classified or declassified data offends the due process clause of the Fifth Amendment.

A related objection is that a process of "fair notice" [52A] is not accorded an individual regarding what data are classified and what are not. Because there are no clear guidelines and nobody can predict what would be considered classified, any policy of restricting privately generated information would inevitably lead to arbitrary and capricious application of the law [Note X-5].

Thoughts about Fifth Amendment property rights ("taken for public use, without just compensation") arise in connection with the Progressive case. A permanent injunction "would have effectively eliminated all monetary value in [Morland's] article" [RON-80]. This type of situation has been partially remedied for invention secrecy, but there is no comparable statutory provision for compensation under the Atomic Energy Act. That could lead to future confrontation on the eminent-domain issue.

Legal Tests of Official Secrecy

The imprecise definition of Restricted Data is the primary ground for challenging the constitutionality of the Atomic Energy Act. The lack of fair warning about proscribed conduct and the absence of clear official guidelines -- both failings that can lead to arbitrary and discriminatory enforcement -- are grounds for concern to persons inside and outside the government.

Although largely untested, not having reached even the appellate decision stage in the Progressive case because the government withdrew, the born-classified aspects are widely considered the Achilles' heel of the Act. Abrams [ABR-80], for example, finds "constitutionally unacceptable" the notion that "the government need not meet Pentagon Papers standards at all and that it need only claim that material -- by its nature -- is restricted and hence subject to restraint and criminal punishment." Cheh invokes the Greene argument that "in the absence of a clear, unequivocal, and express statement, a congressional act may not be read to authorize governmental action of doubtful constitutionality."

According to the study by Halperin and Hoffman [H&H1-77], there have been "four cases [in which] the Supreme Court drew back from ordering disclosure of national security information; these were the Totten, Waterman, Reynolds, and Mink cases." (Totten involved Union spying in the Civil War; Waterman was connected with U.S. air carriers in 1948; Reynolds was a case associated with secret equipment in an airplane crash; and Mink was connected with nuclear-weapons testing -- the Cannikin shot.)

A separate issue, which rarely, if ever, has been litigated on constitutional grounds (there have been various actions under the Freedom of Information Act), is the public's right of access to certain government internal information, such as secret patents and cryptographic data.

The First Amendment

The courts have long agreed that the central purpose of the First Amendment is to prevent the types of prior restraint that had been practiced by other governments. This tradition goes far into common law origins, as reflected in Blackstone's Commentaries on the Laws of England:

> The liberty of the press is indeed essential to the nature of a free state; but this consists in laying no previous restraints upon publications, and not in freedom from censure for criminal matter when published [RON-80].

For all practical purposes, the First Amendment has been bypassed for communications that are forbidden by law to foreign nations. Statutory provisions, similar to the Atomic Energy Act's with regard to communication of data that might "secure an advantage to any foreign nation," have been upheld by the Supreme Court. In Gorin, the Supreme Cout upheld conviction for turning over to a foreign government, then an ally, Naval Intelligence files that were considered information "connected with the national defense." On the other hand, the court noted in Heine that the issue of "advantage to a foreign nation" cannot be stretched to include "repression of free exchange," such as a "work upon modern physics."

An infrequently invoked, but viable, First Amendment tool is the doctrine that an unprotected speech must present "a clear and present danger of producing a substantive harm" [CHEH-80]. Under Schenck and other court decisions, criteria including intent, likelihood, imminence, and seriousness must be met.

Perhaps the most significant and chilling impact of the Progressive case upon First Amendment rights is the personal cost to individuals and organizations not supported by tax money. The Progressive magazine has had to raise close to a quarter of a million dollars in defense funds. The ACLU devoted substantial legal talent, time, and money. Various individuals donated considerable time for the purpose of providing supporting affidavits and giving technical advice. Many organizations contributed amici briefs. None of these had resources comparable with the tax-supplied funds of the Departments of Energy, State, Defense, and Justice.

We know of some (Ralph Lapp, Scientific American, Hans Bethe, and the New York Times) who in the past have capitulated without litigating. How many others have diluted their work by self-censoring compromise, in order to assure trouble-free publication?

Prior Restraint

In a case that did not involve national security (Nebraska), the Supreme Court affirmed that "the guarantees of freedom of expression are not an absolute prohibition under all circumstances, but the barriers to prior restraint remain high and the presumption against its use continues intact." Justice Brennan added that "the decision of what, when, and how to publish is for editors, not judges."

Of course, the most relevant case concerned the Pentagon Papers, where national security considerations were central. The government argued [4] that its Progressive action was not barred by the decision in New York Times. Progressive was different, it said, in that the injunction was sought under a specific statute and the material is fundamentally different, being of current military significance rather than of mere historical interest.

To the New York Times, in its amici position for Progressive [176], matters looked otherwise. The Supreme Court had reaffirmed in the Pentagon Papers case its strong commitment to the long-standing rule against prior restraints of the press. Not once in the past seventy years has that court found it necessary to make an exception. However, the Times admitted that the Pentagon Papers case left open the possibility for a narrowly defined category of technical information that might be subject to regulation.

After the Progressive injunction was issued, a Washington Post editorial [reprinted in the International Herald Tribune, March 29,1979] maintained that Judge Warren's decision was "unconstitutional. The proper procedure would have been for the government to permit The Progressive to print the article, if it chose to do so, and to face the consequences of violating the Atomic Energy Act."

The latent threat of criminal prosecution is a legitimate deterrent to publishing truly sensitive material. But it also serves as a deterrent to publishing material that is incorrectly labeled sensitive by the government. In New York Times there was an admonition by four judges that the espionage statutes might apply if the Pentagon Papers were to be published [F&W-74], and during the Progressive case the government let it be known, as we have mentioned, that individuals were being investigated for possible criminal violation of the Atomic Energy Act. In neither case were charges brought.

From the viewpoint of the press [176], any "national security" exception to the ban on prior restraints must be extremely narrow, based on the Pentagon Papers case only. As cited by the defendants

[52A], Justice Brennan in New York Times asserted that the First
Amendment does not tolerate prior restraint "predicated upon surmise or
conjecture": the undocumented forebodings of the government are
insufficient. In Cheh's view, the district court "misapplied the New
York Times rule," failing to explain whether or why a departure was
justified in Progressive.

Two other major defenses were that the material in dispute was
available to the public from other sources, and that the public had an
inherent need to know about the content of the article. As we show in
Chapters III and V, there are strong arguments supporting both of those
propositions.

The defendants in the Pentagon Papers case also had argued that the
information in many of the documents was already in the public domain.
Such a defense had been approved by the courts in Gorin and reasser-
ted in Heine. If the defendant Gorin had been turning over reports
openly published, the court said, there could be "in all likelihood...
no reasonable intent to give an advantage to a foreign government." In
Heine, the Gorin decision was interpreted to mean that "it is
obviously lawful to transmit any information about weapons and
munitions of war which the services had themselves made public."

The Justice Department [21] labeled as "baseless" the defense
argument that the injunction was unconstitutional because of the
defendants' "special status as members of the press," asserting that
"such a proposition has been uniformly rejected by the courts."
Claiming that a compelling public interest outweighed the defendant's
avowed "interest" in speech, the government argued that its actions
were constitutionally authorized by the inherent power of the
excecutive branch [166].

The government contended that the newsworthiness of the Morland
article would not be diminished by the proposed deletions, which
argument the defense called blatant governmental intrusion into
editorial judgment.

Each side recognized early that this was not a FOIA or government-
employee disclosure case [167], both of which deal with data obtained
and owned by the government. The distinctive feature of the Progressive case is that the government tried to suppress publication of an
article without attempting to prove access to classified information
(although such access was alleged without proof in the government's in
camera affidavits).

THE PENTAGON PAPERS TEST OF HARM

> I cannot say that disclosure [of the Pentagon Papers] will
> surely result in direct, immediate and irreparable
> damage to our Nation or its people.
>   - Justice Potter Stewart [emphasis added]

The precedent set by the Pentagon Papers case figured prominently in
the legal arguments in Progressive. Justice Stewart, concurring in
that case and joined by Justice White, expressed the opinion just
quoted. Although not a majority opinion on behalf of the Supreme
Court, it has provided an important, specific, succinct, and often-
referenced yardstick for evaluating this controversial issue. A

working majority of the Supreme Court in New York Times appeared
ready to support criteria close to those expressed by Justice Stewart
even if there were a declared national emergency. Based on his
analysis of Near v. Minnesota, Justice Brennan strongly indicated
that publication "must" result in the specific effects and that "proof"
has to be given:

> Thus, only governmental allegation and proof that publi-
> cation must inevitably, directly, and immediately cause the
> occurrence of an event kindred to imperiling the safety of
> a transport already at sea can support even the issuance of
> an interim restraining order.... Unless the Government has
> clearly made out its case, the First Amendment commands
> that no injunction may issue.

There were indications in Progressive that the government did not
want to be subjected to constraints on its power that were as severe as
those expressed by Stewart (joined by White) and Brennan in New York
Times. The government objected [66] that the test was "based solely
on the language of two Justices in a concurring opinion." In any
event, both the government and Judge Warren paraphrased the Pentagon
Papers criteria in language that differed from that of Justices Stewart
and Brennan.

For instance, Count II of the government's complaint [1] charged
that publication "will result in grave, direct, immediate and
irreparable harm to the national security of the United States and its
people." There is an omission and a modification to note: the absence
of the adverb "surely" and the change from "damage to our Nation" to
"harm to the national security." Though superficially subtle, these
are actually profound alterations. That sort of rephrasing could have
come from a feeling (realistic, we think) that the strict Pentagon
Papers criteria could not be met in Progressive.

Judge Warren seemed to waver in his opinion on how stringent the
criteria for prior restraint should be. Consider the following two
quotes (with emphasis added) from his decision [85]. The first is an
unqualified forecast, but the second is hedged:

> [Publication] would irreparably harm the national security
> of the United States,...will result in direct, immediate,
> and irreparable damage to the United States....

> [A] preliminary injunction would be warranted even in
> the absence of statutory authorization because of the
> existence of "likelihood of direct, immediate, and
> irreparable injury to our nation...[and] its people."

The portion within the quotation marks (ellipsis in original) is stated
to be from Stewart's concurring New York Times opinion. It seems to
be a misquote, however, since the accurate one is as we give it above.
The substitution of "likelihood" for "surely" not only dilutes
Stewart's criteria, but is inconsistent with the unqualified prediction
in the first excerpt. It is not clear that Judge Warren appreciated
the semantic care with which Justice Stewart chose his words, or fully
understood the government's recharacterization of the criteria.

The government claimed [4] that Morland's material was "so
fundamentally different from that involved in New York Times that the
Supreme Court's decision there simply does not govern the instant
action." In effect, the argument went that the Pentagon Papers were
newsworthy and had historical importance but no weapons significance,

whereas Morland's article was "of questionable historical [but] current military significance." Deprecating the national-security importance of the Vietnam study would be consistent with the goal of keeping enforcement of the Atomic Energy Act unrestricted by opinions from New York Times.

In order further to detract from the legal impact of the Pentagon Papers decision -- to bolster the contention that the Atomic Energy Act was the last word -- the government claimed [31] that the lack of a specific law made New York Times a "fundamentally different" case:

> In New York Times, three of the justices of the six member majority indicated that the absence of exactly the kind of specific statutory authorization that we have here was a determinative factor in refusing to sustain the prior restraint in that case. Indeed, it was the absence of any standard articulated by Congress that caused the justices to articulate the rigorous standard of direct, immediate and irreparable harm before prior restraint could be sustained.

However, because the Act had not been tested for constitutionality, it was not possible to avoid coming to grips in Progressive with the broader standards -- the heavy presumption against prior restraint. The Justice Department took no chances, advancing both statutory and constitutional arguments. And Judge Warren concluded that the government had satisfied the legal requirements of both the Act and the Constitution.

Government officials directly responded to the Stewart-Brennan criteria in four affidavits -- although, according to the defendants, not specifically enough. For example, Sewell [8] stated that disclosure would pose a "danger to the security interests of the United States" that would be "immediate, clear, and irreparable." We note the use of rather vague "danger to the security interests" in place of "damage." Schlesinger [26], similarly, used the words "irreparably impair the national security," with little elaboration and no direct reference to the other criteria.

If the government had not backed out, would application of the Stewart-Brennan criteria have led to a permanent injunction that would have been upheld on appeal? Almost certainly not, on the merits. The legal question in Progressive would have reduced to how "surely" damage to the nation would be done. That, of course, is one of the central topics of this book -- and the evidence is very strong that there surely was to be and will be no national harm resulting from Morland's article. Let us systematically analyze the standards in terms of application to the case at hand.

We note, first, that all of the criteria would have had to be met, individually and collectively. The conjunction "and" in Justice Stewart's concurring opinion is explicit and presumably was carefully chosen.

"Damage to Our Nation"

What constitutes "damage to our Nation or its people" serious enough to warrant abridgment of the First Amendment by prior restraint of publication? Some might argue that the "damage" is meant to be a form of physical destruction; others would hold that any possibility of reduction in national security, however slight, would do. The history of past cases is confused.

Opinions of Supreme Court Justices, even confining ourselves to those who concurred in opinions that upheld the First Amendment, differ. On the one hand, Justices Black and Douglas, in New York Times, were emphatic that there was nothing that would justify prior restraint, maintaining that the constitutional prohibition was absolute; it was a minority view on their court. On the the other hand, the mere obstruction of recruiting services has been considered sufficiently grave. In Near v. Minnesota, Chief Justice Hughes said that, in time of war, "no one would question that a government might prevent actual obstruction to its recruiting service or the publication of the sailing dates of transports or the number and location of troops" [HEN-80]. Justice Brennan, quoted earlier, stressed that nothing less than "an event kindred to imperiling the safety of a transport already at sea" would suffice. It must, moreover, be proven by "clear and convincing evidence" [CHEH-80]. Whether the Stewart-Brennan New York Times criteria would be considered more stringent than Hughes's suggested test is unclear. Stewart and Brennan obviously felt that the Pentagon Papers would not be dangerous enough to warrant suppression, but they gave no guidance for weighing in the gravity of the alleged harm.

The paucity of established criteria for severity of damage is illustrated by the fact that one legal analyst (Cheh) addressing the problem was reduced to quoting from Justice Jackson that freedom of speech and press "are susceptible to restriction only to prevent grave and immediate danger." This opinion was given in a case that was a fore-runner of the Pentagon Papers criteria, and it was given without elaboration -- therefore offering no help in evaluating whether predicted danger is acceptable.

The majority of the justices in New York Times agreed that the government has a "heavy burden" in justifying prior restraint -- that the government was not to be the sole arbiter of what constitutes unacceptable damage. According to Justice White [H&H2-77],

> [The government claimed that] the President was entitled to an injunction whenever he can convince a court that the information to be revealed threatens "grave and irreparable" injury to the public interest.

While White emphasized that the government's judgment should not be decisive, he was noncommittal as to whether he felt the court should apply any such test. On the other hand, there seemed to be general agreement by the justices that imperiling a troopship at sea, the example so often quoted from Near, would justify an injunction. Further, as pointed out in one of the government's Progressive briefs,

> [No] member of the Court [in New York Times] suggests that the United States would also have to demonstrate beyond doubt that an enemy, upon receipt of that information, would, in fact, attack and destroy the ships or soldiers.

Of course, what it takes to convince a judge or jury that danger is imminent depends on the political climate. Under the Near standard, the United States would have to be at war, but the Rosenbergs and Sobel were convicted [NIZ-74] when the country was not engaged in armed hostilities. It was, however, at the height of the cold war, when perception of danger was exaggerated (as evidenced by the McCarthy paranoia). The appeals courts at the time upheld what we now know to have been weak, unsupportable claims that the Rosenbergs had harmed the United States (Chapter VIII).

"Damage to national security," a phrase used by the government, is not necessarily synonymous with "damage to our Nation." For one thing, the former might be only potential, perhaps never to be felt. For another, national security is subjective: Damage to it might be more imagined that real, especially when the prevalent view of what constitutes national security might be out of touch with conditions for true security. Justice Black, in his opinion regarding the Pentagon Papers, concluded that the "guarding of military and diplomatic secrets at the expense of informed representative government provides no real security for our Republic." In other words, an apparent loss in national security might not be real, because of compensating gains.

In the government's Progressive affidavits and briefs there were some assertions that it was United States "policy" to prevent proliferation [2,7,26], and that the article would be "likely to damage U.S. interests in preventing the spread of nuclear weapons capabilities" [6] (emphasis added). Although they made various assertions that publishing the article would be inconsistent with the country's "interests" or "national security," the government affiants made no effort to substantiate those claims with documented evidence or even reasoned argument. The Secretary of Energy, for instance, said [26] that "publication...would irreparably impair the national security of the United States," (emphasis added) but then he went on to say that the "result would be contrary to the non-proliferation policy of the United States." Does the failure to support their implications that damage would occur indicate a bureaucratic tendency to consider damage to policy as equivalent to damage to the nation? This might bring to mind the question (which was not, however, an important factor in Progressive) as to whether substantial judicial weight should be given to preserving a policy, such as excessive reliance on secrecy, in lieu of explicit proof of damage to the nation. That would be seriously at odds with such legal precedents as exist, and citizens should be alert for any tendency in that direction.

Because the net change in national security is often hard to assess without careful examination, the potential for physical damage to the nation or its people, and also the potential for compensating public benefit, must both be put in evidence if any subsequent court decision is to be soundly based.

Direct. Judge Warren, in effect, associated publication with a direct threat to national security on the basis of the government affiants' unsubstantiated opinions.

Would the damage, if any, have been direct? If publication would cause some countries (Cuba or some other Latin American country, for example) to get an H-bomb that they would not otherwise have gotten, the threat to the United States could be considered "direct," and this particular Pentagon Papers test would have been met. Actually, however, only vague, unsupported assertions hinted at a possible direct connection between publication of Morland's article and damage to the nation. We note a legal opinion that, to be considered direct, "the communication must be so facilitative of harm that it is equivalent to it." [CHEH-80]

Immediate. There is a good, practical reason for including a test of immediacy: If the predicted harm were not immediate, there would be time to head it off. In time of war, the publication of current troop locations could have immediate effect, but if troop movements planned for some time ahead were made public, the plans could be changed. There still is some protection, however, against dissemination that would cause damage, even if that damage were not immediate: After-the-fact prosecution on criminal or civil charges (such as libel, contract violation, or revealing classified data) is not ruled out [Note X-6].

Publication in The Progressive would certainly not pose a threat that was immediate in the sense that it could trigger an H-bomb attack within a few days. The government could not, of course, claim immediacy in that sense, for it would take years to develop an H-bomb from scratch. The most the government alleged was that some nations would be aided in achieving thermonuclear weaponry in fewer years, and that was disputed by experts for the defendants. We must remember that Morland's article had little to do with "garden variety" nuclear-fission weapons, or even fusion-boosted fission weapons -- all of which can be developed in a relatively straightforward fashion. His forbidden discourse was on the concepts behind multistage, multimegaton weapons, which cannot be produced until a nation has developed and tested the prerequisite nuclear triggers -- a longer process and many steps removed from the conceptual stage.

The most the government could have claimed, had it addressed the point, would have been that publication would immediately set some nation to work on the project. While to nonlawyers that might seem immediate enough, there is no way to tell what the courts at various levels would conclude.

Another good reason for a test of literal immediacy is that publication might even be in the long-term national interest, even if not to the liking of the presiding administration. Consider in retrospect the possible national benefits if there had been accurate public knowledge of events in the Tonkin Gulf, or of government intent before the Cambodia or Bay of Pigs invasions. With Morland's article, as we have shown, the net result of publication might well be an improvement in American national security.

Irreparable. Would the effect of publication be irreparable? If Morland's article had contained unpublished, valid detailed weapons data, then indeed the effect upon antiproliferation secrecy policy would have been irreparable in the sense that the information could never again be made secret. Yet if that were the extent of it, the scope of damage would be limited -- reparable, in effect -- because policy could be changed accordingly. However, if publication resulted in an eventual H-bombing of the United States, the damage would of course be truly irreparable, and this element of the Pentagon Papers test would be met. How realistic is that risk of nuclear attack?

Suppose someone were to publish an article with valuable details on how to design and build an H-bomb, causing some nation to gain insight it would otherwise not have. Would that be irreparable? Yes. But would it surely be irreparable damage to the U.S.? No! If that other country undertook to develop thermonuclear weapons, it would sooner or later have to do some overt testing of nuclear explosives, thereby revealing its program before it had a deliverable bomb. International measures could then be taken to keep the situation under control.

Consider what happened in the case of India. Over six years have now passed since India's detonation of a nuclear explosive. Perhaps it is international pressure that has caused India to desist from further overt acts toward development of an arsenal of nuclear weapons. (In any event, that situation might change soon because India views as discriminatory the antiproliferation policies of the weapons states.) Partial or even total release of all classified information could only cause an irreparable effect if the time it would take to translate the knowledge into weapons could be and were effectively used.

To help place irreparability in context, we note that the sincere suggestion is sometimes made that all technical secrets of nuclear devices should be made public. The underlying idea is that all nations would then have to abandon secrecy as the main line of defense against proliferation, and thus would be motivated to enter into strict international commitments. The proponents see eventual nonproliferation gains rather than losses, despite the irreversible nature of information release. Although publication of weapons details is not reversible, its effects can perhaps be partly headed off. We do not subscribe to the proposition, however, because the publication of all nuclear-weapon design details would have at least one result that would tend to promote proliferation: Governments would fear that their neighbors would then be able to develop the weapons in secret, without having to test them.

Further light on the magnitude of the damage that could come from publishing Morland's article comes from comparing his material with other common technical currency. A Scientific American brief [175] pointed out that "many of the ideas exchanged by scientists -- in physics, chemistry, biology, perhaps even in psychology or sociology -- could be alleged to be of a character that might result in 'direct, immediate and irreparable damage.'" There is continual discourse and speculation among technical people on the challenging concepts of the day. Weapons of mass destruction are not excluded from the discussions.

In contrast to Morland's article, consider the effect of the Department of Energy's mistaken declassification of technical data on nuclear weapons, which did happen. The public dissemination of UCRL-4725, an official weapons report, in our opinion would surely cause direct injury to the "interests" of the United States, but the effects would not be immediate: there would not necessarily be danger or damage to our nation (see government testimony in Chapter VI). In a technical sense, its widespread disclosure would cause irreparable harm because of the release of specialized experimental data; in a political sense, its disclosure could be counteracted by effective arms control.

Surely

"Surely" means "without doubt"; to be sure is to be certain beyond question; the result anticipated is bound inevitably to occur. That is the literal meaning. In practice, however, it is rare indeed that anything can be predicted with complete certainty. We suppose, therefore, that an impartial court of law would accept as sufficient overwhelming technical evidence that damage would occur -- evidence that would create a very strong consensus among experts. In any event, those persons who are "sure" should supply their supporting arguments and data and be subject to cross-examination. In the Progressive case that did not happen.

Justice Brennan, in New York Times, noted:

The entire thrust of the Government's claim throughout these cases has been that publication of the material sought to be enjoined "could," or "might," or "may" prejudice the national interest in various ways. But the First Amendment tolerates absolutely no prior judicial restraints of the press predicated upon surmise or conjecture that untoward consequences may result.

While in Progressive the government did claim [66] that "the nation and its citizens will be inescapably injured if the injunction is not granted," no attempt was made to prove it. Consistent with the Justice Department's contention [66] that "the principal dispute in this litigation is not factual but judgmental" (emphasis added), the government bolstered its charge by merely offering the statements of various officials who gave their opinion that publication would not be in the national interest. We quoted several such statements in Chapter IV. No government affidavit offered proof that publication would "surely" cause any of the frightening effects foretold -- despite the Department of Justice's claim [166] that "in the course of litigation, the government submitted substantial...evidence... demonstrating the threat of grave and irreparable injury to the United States." (We note that the "threat" of injury is one step removed from the injury itself.)

Nevertheless, the court decided that "publication of the technical information on the hydrogen bomb contained in the article is analogous to publication of troop movements or locations in time of war and falls within the extremely narrow exception to the rule against prior restraint." This is a finding that does not hold up under analysis. While publication would "immediately" have placed on record any dangerous information that might have been in the article, it cannot be said that damage to the nation was "surely immediate." In fact, there was never any true prospect of danger.

Judge Warren linked publication of the article to "nuclear annihilation." Let us look at the chain of cause and effect that must be invoked to support that linkage. First, the article would have to receive attention and credence from nations interested in developing thermonuclear weapons. Second, because there are no quantitative details in the article, the previously unexposed ideas (if any, considering what was already available) would have to be checked out quantitatively to see if any of them made sense. Next, one or more of those nations would have to be nudged by what they learned in following the leads they got from the article into proceeding to develop a thermonuclear weapon. All materials, designs, and techniques would have to be acquired indigenously or by other means; for that, Morland's article would be no help. And then there would have to be development (and testing) of fission triggers and fusion weapons.

At that point, if all those events had taken place without counter-actions by other states, proliferation would indeed have occurred. To get to nuclear annihilation, of course, more steps would be required. Either the new member of the nuclear weapons club would have to go on

to develop sophisticated delivery systems and a large arsenal of
multimegaton H-bombs and then use them on the United States, or else,
by virtue of the existence of the bomb or bombs that would not
otherwise have been created, a nuclear war between the major nuclear
powers would somehow have to be triggered. All of that would have to
occur in spite of whatever countering influences were brought to bear
by other countries.

Clearly, many difficult and unlikely events must take place if there
is to be damage to the nation, and there are many turns of events that
could avert the damage. On examining these pathways, one quickly
senses once more that Morland's article poses essentially no potential
for harm, and that to say that harm would "surely" follow would be
completely unrealistic.

Historical perspective was supplied by Scientific American [175]:

It is not to be ignored that the country has survived again
and again in the face of the most serious predictions of
doom, without having to resort to the method of prior
restraints as a means of assuring national security.

The Criteria and National Security

The government succeeded in getting from Judge Warren a temporary
injunction. Was the judge correct in issuing it? We think not.
Though he perceived a threat that anyone would consider grave --
nuclear annihilation (never explicitly predicted by the government) --
he failed to appoint the qualified committee he needed to help
determine whether such a threat might follow, and he failed to heed the
opposing testimony he did get. He was remiss, further, in not giving
sufficient weight to a possibility we explore in this book -- that
suppression of a publication could, by prolonging excessive secrecy,
pose a far greater threat of nuclear annihilation than the article ever
would.

We hope that this book helps dispel any notion that the nuclear age
has brought the U.S. Constitution into question -- any suspicion that
the Bill of Rights is no longer compatible with national security. We
cannot think of an example, hypothetical or real, wherein stringent
application of the Stewart-Brennan criteria would sacrifice national
security on the altar of the First Amendment.

This was put even more strongly by Justice Black (joined by Douglas)
in his concurring New York Times opinion:

To find that the President has "inherent power" to halt the
publication of news by resort to the courts would wipe out
the First Amendment and destroy the fundamental liberty and
security of the very people the Government hopes to make
"secure."

Events continue to demonstrate that, regardless of doubts from time
to time, the Constitution is a potent source of national strength.

ADVISORY PROCEDURES

In order to help Judge Warren cope with the Progressive case's
complex technological issues, two types of advisory procedures were
recommended to the court by amici briefs. Although the court

accepted one of the suggestions (by the Federation of American Scientists -- FAS), the government initially opposed it and the defendants ultimately turned it down.

FAS Panel

Prior to Judge Warren's decision on a preliminary injunction, Jeremy J. Stone, director of the FAS, advised [51] that the court "consider extending the temporary restraining order and urging the parties to try to resolve the dispute with the aid of mediators acceptable to each side." The suggestion was that

> one or two senior weapons scientists be joined by one or two senior representatives of the U.S. media, and the two to four person mediating committee be chaired by some respected lawyer or retired judge or justice. The resulting committee of three to five would then work together with the two parties and report to the judge on their progress, or lack of it, in dealing with specific deletions at issue. At the least, this could facilitate subsequent litigation by narrowing the issues. The members could be chosen to be acceptable to the two sides.

The Justice Department [66] opposed the FAS proposal as "inconsistent with appropriate scope of judicial review." Significantly, the government's position was, as we have noted, that the issues were "not factual but judgmental" -- that the court should accept the judgment of the government's affiants, without requiring hard evidence -- a position consistent with its opposition to live testimony and discovery.

Judge Warren, remarking [82] that he was "greatly impressed" by the FAS proposal, posed a final choice to the parties: "Each party is to consider whether it would be willing to meet with a panel of five mediators appointed by the Court to attempt to resolve the parties' differences." If that was agreed to, Warren was to set up a mediating panel according to the FAS suggestions. The panel would receive "appropriate clearance" and report back in ten days. Then "the Court will then either dismiss the case by stipulation of the parties or, in the event of inability to agree, issue a preliminary injunction" (emphasis added).

By announcing in advance that he would issue the injunction if no agreement were reached, Warren gave no incentive to the government to compromise. The Justice Deparment could stonewall on any single deletion in Morland's article, and automatically win a preliminary injunction. The panel would have been able to produce an agreement only if The Progressive agreed to be censored or the government abandoned its case -- two unlikely outcomes, in view of the positions already taken. Predictably, The Progressive did not find that acceptable. In addition, some people objected to the bargaining away of First Amendment rights that was inherent in the judge's offer, and questioned the inclusion of media personnel on the panel.

ACLU Panel

In the initial judicial hearing, the ACLU had proposed (and we had supported) a different sort of panel -- one that would clarify the potential for damage to national security. It would have been an independent panel of scientific experts, appointed by the court. Such a panel is needed in cases like this because few, if any, judges have enough technological expertise to evaluate conflicting claims made by expert witnesses for the two sides. Nuclear weapons technology is esoteric enough for the nonscientist; the additional implications of proliferation compound the problem.

The charge to the panel would have been to determine whether the article contained truly sensitive information not already in the public domain and to advise on whether the dangers of publication were as grave as the government asserted. In contrast to the FAS proposal, this panel would have had no editorial role regarding the proposed deletions, and it would have consisted only of technical specialists who would also be sophisticated in nuclear-age international relations. The panel's status would have been purely advisory to the court on this limited, mixed technical-political issue. Judge Warren turned down the proposal [82]; we think that was a mistake. In commenting that it would "merely proliferate the opinions of experts," he accepted the government's contention [66] that facts were not germane to the issue.

A Later Suggestion

After Warren's decision, the FAS countered with another suggestion: that the court convene scientists who had been involved in the case, to take into account the unresolved nature of the testimony. The reasonable underlying concept was that scientists have a way of thrashing out disputes on their own. While that may be true, the proposal was in vain -- perhaps because the technology underlying the case basically had little to do with its clashing political and legal pressures. Certainly there were many people to whom the facts were irrelevant: Some, who had neither read Morland's article nor understood nuclear proliferation problems, were willing to accede to censorship, while others, putting constitutional principles foremost, were supporting The Progressive's unbridled right to print anything it had learned from public sources.

THE APPEALS

Warren's preliminary injunction and his order denying the motion to vacate that injunction were promptly appealed by The Progressive to the Seventh Circuit Court in Chicago. The grounds fall into two categories, procedural and constitutional.

Objections to court procedure centered for the most part on the judge's refusal to have an evidentiary hearing. Various affidavits presented by the Government were "conclusory" (presenting unsupported conclusions), and the defendants wanted to exercise rights of discovery and cross-examination. The constitutional objections were based on the conflict of prior restraint with the First Amendment and the "over-broadness" and "vagueness" of the definitions in the Atomic Energy Act. There were also suggestions that the Fifth Amendment right to due process was also being violated, but it never became a point of contention.

As expressed in the appeal brief by the defendants [164], the factual issues on appeal could be partitioned into three elements:
    1. Whether the information in The Progressive article is [already] in the public domain....
    2. Whether the government's affidavits...overcome the "almost insuperable presumption" against the constitutionality of prior restraint.
    3. Whether the government has shown that publication of the article would violate the Atomic Energy Act and whether the construction of the Act urged by the government, especially the contention that all "Restricted Data" is classified at birth, violates constitutional guarantees of due process, free speech, and free press.

New or Revised Arguments

There were two arguments that received additional stress at the appeal stage: the impact of declassified official documents upon the issue of what was in the public domain, and the government's contentions regarding the relevance of technical information.

    Public domain. In addition to a plethora of open publications, improperly declassified documents such as UCRL-4725 had been publicly available and disseminated to some unknown extent. That placed a strain on the government's contention that the concepts contained in Morland's article were still secret. In particular, published examples of exact wording of the forbidden concepts, like "radiation pressure," could be cited. The government was reduced to arguing that the relationship of the wording to the contextual material determined whether such concepts were already published. Even if such officially declassified documents such as DNA-4501F applied "radiation pressure" in a nuclear-weapons context, it was still not public information (insisted the government) unless placed in the same context as that used by Morland. Although that sort of argument could sometimes have merit, in Progressive it was tenuous.

    Decisions in the Aspin and Halperin cases recognize that some disclosures might be limited to only a small audience, in which case further disclosure could still cause serious harm to national security. While that might be enough legal precedent to deter further exposure of UCRL-4725, it would not seem to apply to information already unequivocally public.

    Technical information. A significant part of the government's effort to protect its legal position was the blanket claim that technical information did not deserve constitutional protection. That was a dramatic shift in position on the constitutional issues. In the District Court, the government had maintained that it could have met each of the constitutional tests established by the Pentagon Papers case, but that it did not have to. On appeal the government repeated that it did not have to meet any of those standards, this time on the basis that the Morland article was not speech at all. Technical data, the government argued, are like obscenity, in that they are not an "essential part of any exposition of ideas" and are not of any "social value as a step to truth" [166].

    Also ignored in the official position was something that should be obvious by now to readers of this book: Secrecy is not a significant

and abiding technological barrier by itself, but often only a way for
the holders of secrets to delude themselves and their constituencies
about their ability to keep their secrets bottled up.

The government described sensitive technical data vaguely [166] as
"technical information disclosing the essential secrets of the most
destructive weapon known to man" [Note X-7]. This somewhat circular
definition is heavily loaded with the government's argument that the
article presented the "essential" secrets -- a point not conceded by
the defense (the title of the article notwithstanding). It is also
impregnated with an emotional element, appealing to worries about "the
most destructive weapon known to man." That reference is reminiscent
of that accepted and applied by Judge Kaufman in sentencing the
Rosenbergs to death (Chapter VIII).

The Nuclear Non-Proliferation Act of 1978 says that "the
proliferation of nuclear explosive devices or of the direct capability
to manufacture or otherwise acquire such devices poses a grave threat
to the security interests of the United States and the continued
international progress toward world peace and development." That
provides an appropriate congressional rationale for restrictions on
uninhibited disclosure of truly sensitive information; it does not
provide for arbitrary government authority over privately generated
information that is considered sensitive.

In Rosenberg, the appeals court ruled that "the communication to a
foreign government of secret material connected with the national
defense can by no far-fetched reasoning be included within the area of
First Amendment protected free speech." As long as one appropriately
interprets "secret material connected with the national defense," it is
difficult to quarrel with that conclusion. Therein, however, lies the
essence of a continuing dispute. In Progressive the government
offered no explicit definition of technical information or data,
apparently expecting the court to overlook the imprecision. Such
vagueness leaves open wide avenues for misuse. Unless restrained by
court interpretation, the legislatively undefined range of restrictable
data could be as broad as the government chose at any time. The First
Amendment could be circumvented, inhibiting constructive public
discussion to the detriment of the national interest. Nuclear weapons
are clearly intended by Congress to be a special case, yet application
of the government ground rule that communication of technical data is
unprotected speech could touch all military systems, regardless of
connection wih nuclear devices. If the court had accepted the
government's view, it would have authorized broad prohibitions of
public discourse about national defense.

DISMISSAL OF THE SUIT

Rather unexpectedly, the Justice Department announced on September 17,
1979, that it was requesting leave of the court to withdraw its civil
suit. In the words of Duane Sewell, testifying later before the House
Subcommittee on Government Information and Individual Rights,

> The Executive Branch was then forced [after publication of
> Hansen's letter in the Madison Press Connection] to seek
> dismissal of the temporary injunction against publication
> of the Morland article and the restraining order against

publication of the Hansen letter, since the Restricted
Data, which had been verified by the Government, now had
been published and was widely available. At the same time,
the Deparment of Justice announced that it would undertake
criminal inquiry into possible violations of the Atomic
Energy Act and of the Court order in the two cases.
[Emphasis added]
There are other suspected reasons for the government's withdrawal,
not the least of which is that the case was fast becoming hopeless, at
least in the view of the Justice Department. A court decision that the
untested Atomic Energy Act was unconstitutional could wreak havoc with
the system for protecting nuclear data. And continuation of the
litigation might have led to more disclosures of information that
either should be protected or would embarrass the government.

LEGAL PRECEDENTS

Whether legal precedents unfavorable to the First Amendment were
created by the Progressive case remains untested. The fact that a
prior restraint was in effect for six months against a national
publication, by far the longest time in American history, is probably
not without consequence. Moreover, a preliminary injunction was issued
and a decision in support of that issuance on the merits of the case
was made by the federal district court. One of Ronhovde's observations
on behalf of the Congressional Research Service is that "the clash
between national security interests and First Amendment freedoms
present in Progressive is not new to the courts. However, it has
been litigated rarely and with less than clear results." On the other
hand, no permanent injunction ensued, and The Progressive did get to
publish the Morland article without any deletions, despite the ominous
charges brought by the government.
    Ronhovde went on to say:
        New York Times is instructive regarding the issues posed
        by Progressive in that it elucidates what little case law
        exists to be relied on, it demonstrates the diversity of
        opinion which exists even among those arriving at similar
        results, and it suggests that such result in any given case
        will in large measure depend on delicate shadings of
        factual circumstances giving rise to the controversy.
        Many of the controversies which raged as The
        Progressive battled for the right to publish subsided soon
        after dismissal of the Government's legal actions. But the
        factors which gave rise to that dispute remain largely
        unaltered today. The outcome is subject to a variety of
        interpretations, to include: (1) a noble effort at
        protecting national security through enforcement of
        information security was thwarted by a journalistic
        unwillingness to have the issue resolved in the courts and
        be bound by the results; (2) an effort to infringe on
        fundamental precepts of free speech and press failed as a
        result of determined citizen resistance to heavy-handed
        governmental regulation; or (3) all in all, the "system"
        functioned much as it was designed to, with enforcement

powers upheld but overruled by the weight of First
Amendment pressures in this particular instance....
    At the heart of the controversy lie the secrecy
provisions of the Atomic Energy Act. That Act has been
subjected to criticism during this period both for being
impotent to deal with national security leaks and for
having become outmoded in its approach to atomic energy
information, data which is generated in a field that has
undergone great change since passage of the Act....
    Where...the specific intent to hand over government
secrets to a foreign power need not be shown, the First
Amendment boundaries are less clear, and the culpability
standards of "reason to believe", "will be utilized", and
"advantage to any foreign nation" have never been
adequately defined.
Some gratuitous remarks by the Supreme Court in the Snepp case
might be straws in the wind. Snepp was found in violation of his
employee contract, which called for prior review and approval before
publication, even after he left the CIA. Some of the justices added
their opinion that even in the absence of a contract, there was a
"fiduciary obligation" to submit material for prior review. That
causes concern over the extent to which the judiciary is permeated with
thoughtless deference to government secrecy, or, in the words of
Anthony Lewis, "contempt for the rule of law." Whether the fiduciary-
obligation concept will become embedded in case law remains to be
seen.

SEQUEL

Morland's article was published in The Progressive in the November 1979
issue; an erratum was carried in December 1979. In addition, his
diagrams of the explosion stages have appeared in the March 1980
Harper's and in overseas magazines (and also in Appendix A of this
book). His work has obviously received much more attention than if
there had been official silence.
    Most legal activities after the suit ended centered about removal of
the protective order from the in camera materials and an investigation for possible criminal violations of the Atomic Energy Act.
    There have been several published analyses on the case, and Congress
has taken notice of the secrecy dilemma.

Alleged Criminal Violations

The government said that, for Morland to have gathered the material he
published and for Hansen to have written his letter, scientists with
security clearances must have divulged classified information. At the
request of the Justice Department, a former CIA legal counsel undertook
a preliminary inquiry to ascertain whether there were any indications
of criminal violations. We do not know what he reported, but the
government eventually announced that there would be no prosecutions.
That was on September 4, 1980, in conjunction with formalizing the
agreement between the government and The Progressive regarding the
disposition of the in camera material. (The Progressive and

associated parties had said that they would not sign the agreement until the government decided whether there would be any prosecutions.)

The questions the Glenn letter (Appendix B) raised about possible goverment misuse of the classification system have not yet been resolved. During the second part of hearings conducted by the Senate Subcommittee on Energy, Nuclear Proliferation and Federal Services, the following interchange took place on October 2, 1979 between Senator Glenn and Duane Sewell, Assistant Secretary for Defense Programs:

> Senator Glenn: On May 25 of this year I received a letter from four Argonne National Laboratory scientists which asserted that DOE, in public affidavits it filed in the Progressive Case, was giving away the very information the case was trying to keep secret. I forwarded this letter to you for comment. We received what we considered a somewhat cursory reply. Given that that case is now over, I would like to have your views on what those scientists were claiming. Have you changed your views on that at all?
>
> Mr. Sewell: With respect to one statement you made; I do not believe from where I sit that the case is over in view of the fact that the Justice Department still has this investigation going on. Therefore I don't believe it is appropriate for me to comment on that.

Although that investigation has been over for some months, Senator Glenn's question is, to our knowledge, still unanswered.

One Progressive participant who encountered problems is Hugh DeWitt, an outspoken physicist at Lawrence Livermore Laboratory. His research requires an active security clearance.   After an investigation, he was charged with minor violations of security procedures. The alleged infractions (which, in any event, did not compromise sensitive material) occurred under the pressure of a time limit for filing affidavits. A reprimand was placed in his file. In addition, Roger Batzel, the director of Lawrence Livermore, requested that the matter (including DeWitt's forwarding of the Glenn letter to Chuck Hansen) be "referred to the Federal Bureau of Investigation for consideration of investigation into probable illegal activities of Hugh DeWitt," according to FBI documents released to DeWitt under a FOIA request. The FBI concluded that there was no basis for action.

DeWitt filed a formal grievance, which was to be heard by an outside arbitrator. The matter was brought to the attention of the scientific community and certain congressmen, who expressed concern and began their own investigations. On October 17, 1980, DeWitt and the Lawrence Livermore administration came to an agreement, part of which was that the reprimand was withdrawn without need for the arbitration hearing.

Removal of Protective Order from In Camera Material

Subsequent to the government motion to vacate the preliminary injunction, most activity centered on attempts to settle the disposition of the in camera materials.   Although the DOE has realized the impossibility of protecting information already released, the Department of State and the Arms Control and Disarmament Agency have been sensitive to not only the nature of the materials released, but also to the manner of release. Conscious of U.S. obligations under the Non-Proliferation Treaty, these organizations would not like to see certain types of weapons-related information released from the in camera materials in a form directly attributable to the U.S. government.

The settlement finally reached divided the in camera documents into three categories, listed in Appendices A, B, and C of the agreement: those to be released without change (A); those to have Secret Restricted Data or National Security Information components deleted (B); and those that, though not designated SRD nor classifiable under Executive Order 12065, nevertheless require special treatment (C). The State Department and ACDA requested that selected portions of the "Appendix C documents" be protected by court order "because they were sensitive for foreign relations reasons" [Note X-8]. Although not classified, the government may not be named as the source of any of the information in those protected portions. This special arrangement, which is to be effect for five or more years, was agreed upon by all parties in order to settle the case. In this book's list of Progressive case legal references, the category for each document is indicated.

CONGRESSIONAL HEARINGS

Hearings concerning the Progressive case have been held not only by Senator Glenn's subcommittee, but also by the House Subcommittee on Government Information and Individual Rights, chaired by Richardson Preyer. An account of the Senate subcommittee hearings has been issued in two parts under the title "Erroneous Declassification of Nuclear Weapons Information." The House subcommittee's report, "The Government's Classification of Private Ideas," has also come out [HR-80].

Senator Glenn's subcommittee has been mainly concerned with the secret government documents that were made publicly available through a combination of inadvertence, corner-cutting, and ambiguous instructions [Note X-9]. The senator commented in his opening statement (Part 1 of the subcommittee's hearings record):

For more than 4 years a document [UCRL-4725] containing critically important details of U.S. nuclear weapons programs, including thermonuclear weapons, sat on the public shelves of the library at the Los Alamos Laboratory available to anyone who cared to take the time to go to Los Alamos and spend a few minutes looking up "nuclear weapons" in the card catalog.

During the hearing, ACLU researcher Dimitri Rotow described how he had located UCRL-4725 in less than half an hour. In response to a question, Rotow said that DOE had never asked him for his distribution list. Although DOE might appear negligent in this respect, one must remember that Rotow's research was in connection with litigation in Progressive, and DOE's actions had to be coordinated with the Department of Justice. The inhibiting effect of the court case was summarized by Senator Glenn in Part II of the hearings:

We had testimony last May as to why the Department did not move. It turned out, I believe, that someone was so concerned about prejudicing the court case pending at that time that they did not attempt to recover the copies that

Mr. Rotow may or may not have distributed to various people here or abroad.

The subcommittee report sums up the nonproliferation policy implications of the Progressive case as follows:

Thus, while secrecy can buy time that may help to increase chances of reaching international agreements to rid the earth of nuclear weapons, a viable nonproliferation policy must proceed from the realistic assumption that scientific or technological information cannot be narrowly contained for any significantly long period of time. The controversy surrounding the Progressive Magazine case, the Hansen letter, and the erroneous release of sensitive information by the Government serve to underscore this point....

Faced with the realization that information on the design and fabrication of nuclear weapons may now be available to those who avidly seek it, it is apparent that only limitations on access to the materials needed to fabricate nuclear weapons can provide any assurances of nonproliferation.

We would add that world political conditions that motivate nations to reject nuclear weapons would also help.

The Government Information and Individual Rights Subcommittee held hearings on February 28, March 20, and August 20, 1979, concerning the ability of the government to classify, restrict, or assert ownership over privately generated ideas or data [Note X-10]. Floyd Abrams testified in his prepared statement that "although I was 'unpersuaded that there was any persuasive editorial justification' for The Progressive to publish its H-Bomb article, the country was still well served by the government's ultimate loss in the case." He pinpointed the difficulty with the Atomic Energy Act as lying with the definition of Restricted Data (as did we in our written statements to the subcommittee), and summarized his own view of the doctrine of classification at birth:

The doctrine is an extremely dubious -- and dangerous -- one, and...the government's assertion in The Progressive case of the power to punish individuals for disclosure of information they themselves have created is fraught with constitutional pitfalls.

Others have held that the Atomic Energy Act should not be amended. This apparently reflects both pragmatic and ideological opinions. Two prominent members of the House of Representatives have taken that position in the past: Melvin Price, chairman of the Committee on Armed Services, has said that "the unrestrained publication of weapons design information requires a restriction of the right to publish," and Edward P. Boland, chairman of the Permanent Select Committee on Intelligence, wrote that "certain narrow categories of speech are indeed dangerous to the vital interests of our government and people." As discussed in the next chapter, we agree with the underlying sentiments regarding the need for certain restrictions, but we do not agree that the Act does not need to be revised.

HOLLOW VICTORY?

As we noted earlier, in the Pentagon Papers case the government maintained that publication would pose a "grave and immediate danger to the
security of the United States." Subsequently, no one has asserted --
let alone demonstrated -- that publishing the Papers has had that
effect. As for the Morland article, publication will have similar
negligible effects on American national security. This is not to say
that the domestic effects of publication of the Pentagon Papers were
insignificant; on the contrary, they had far-reaching consequences.
Although Morland's article is unlikely to have as large an impact on
the domestic scene, the effect will not be unnoticed. One example is
the accelerated declassification of information on inertially confined
fusion (ICF), which we discuss in Chapter VII.

In another national-security case [34] (Marchetti), the government
demanded deletion of 339 sensitive items from Marchetti's book; the CIA
later relented on 171 of them. The situation was not much different in
Progressive: The government slowly and reluctantly agreed to declassify many of the documents.

From a legal viewpoint [CHEH-80], "the case proved to be a victory
for no one." The government was successful in convincing a court to
temporarily prevent publication, but the defendants lost the
opportunity to challenge the lower court's decision. "The court's
overall reasoning was so flawed...that its conclusions probably would
not have been upheld on appeal."

Although The Progressive won the right to publish the once-censored
article, one might well wonder whether the U.S. Constitution was
strengthened or weakened. Some news media did join in publishing once-
forbidden material, but others -- including most of the major
periodicals (notably excepting the Chicago Tribune) -- appeared
disinclined to test the law. Some student newspapers published our
Glenn letter in its entirety, and the Chicago Tribune printed most of
Hansen's letter, as did the Madison Press Connection (which has since
folded for unrelated reasons).

If the legal reach of Progressive is limited, perhaps it is just
as well. Some recent decisions by the Supreme Court have given rise to
a feeling that the current court is inclined to a restrictive view of
the First Amendment. Because the article involved the most destructive
weapon known, it was perhaps the worst case for testing the scope of
the Atomic Energy Act. Also, a large fraction of the public is still
under the misapprehension that secrecy offers significant protection
from nuclear annihilation. From the viewpoint of those who see free
discussion to be a source of national strength, this could be the wrong
time to push litigation that could lead to "legislation by the
courts."

Morland and others before him have attempted to nudge open the door
that protects the myth of secrecy. We would like to think that, if a
legal confrontation occurs again, this book will have helped to create
a systematic process that will lead to judicial decisions that are
realistic and in the national interest.

 **Remedies**

It isn't that they can't see the solution.
It is that they can't see the problem.
        - G.K. Chesterton, British author

We have recounted the history of the Progressive case, discussed the myths and disclosures surrounding hydrogen bomb secrecy, and analyzed the extent to which the First Amendment and national security conflict. We find no serious incompatibility between public safety and the right to know; we also argue that a more enlightened citizenry would be of positive benefit to national security. Here we consider in more detail what can be done to strengthen national security and keep the public informed about what their government is doing.

Opinions on government secrecy run the gamut from the more the better to belief that there should be no official secrets at all. We reject both extremes, believing that the problem must be dealt with pragmatically. The issues will probably stay unresolved for decades. But for a few of them, if they are carefully defined, there might be enough common ground that constructive changes could be generally accepted. We now suggest some practical remedies, mainly partial solutions, limiting ourselves to goals that seem relatively uncontroversial. Had Progressive run its course through the courts, some of the procedural and statutory problems left dangling when the government withdrew at the appeals court level might by now have been resolved.

The First Amendment need not and should not be arbitrarily suspended in the name of national security: Our future will be more secure if secrecy is minimal. The invocation of national security to justify the suppression of information should not be accepted at face value -- especially when there are possible political motivations, as in the case at hand. That is one reason why the district court should have appointed an independent, technically competent panel to advise on whether disclosure of Morland's article would be against the public interest. If national security is a factor in a court's consideration of prior restraint, then there should be a systematic evaluation of the security implications. We continue to think that such a panel would be useful to the courts in similar future disputes.

217

The logical line between governmental action and inaction is the boundary between official and public origin. Official documents are classifiable according to established rules, and those who leak properly classified material should be subject to appropriate and clearly defined disciplinary procedures. But it is futile to attempt to restrain material of public origin, and such material should therefore not draw comment from the government.

Executive secrecy in the United States (and in Canada and Britain) usually involves [F&W-74] (1) the exercise of executive privilege, (2) executive classification of documents, and (3) selective/distortive disclosing or leaking of information by the executive. Although traditional political controls may work satisfactorily in particular cases, for lasting changes in the way policy decisions are made there must be substantial restructuring of the secrecy system. A number of proposals for reform [Note XI-1] have been accumulated by Franck and Weisband [F&W-74], centering on the establishment of an "analytical vocabulary in dealing with the challenge of secrecy."

With that introduction we now embark on a survey of possible reforms -- reforms that could touch some public institutions as well as agencies of the federal government.

THE COST OF LITIGATION

The Progressive magazine risked much and lost a lot in its conflict with the secrecy system. The editors and publisher did much soul-searching in making their decision, which was not initially unanimous; they had to seek out legal and technical support, which was not immediately or automatically forthcoming, and they had to risk the future of the magazine and the jobs of its staff. Despite considerable free support -- legal intervention from the ACLU and amici, and technical advice and testimony from scientists -- it cost the magazine about a quarter of a million dollars and a loss of subscriptions.

If an organization like The Progressive could barely sustain the burden, not many individuals could afford to support their principles in such a conflict. The overwhelming resources of the federal government often make it difficult to exercise the individual rights granted (in theory) by the Constitution. Perhaps some civil servants would perceive the situation in opposite terms: an imposing array of uninhibited and well-financed intervenors against underfunded and overworked officials attempting to carry out the law. It seems to us, however, that the government has considerable advantage when public funds are pitted against private resources.

A proposal advanced by Sam Day, The Progressive's managing editor, was that the government should be required to reimburse the defendants in classification dispute cases where it fails to achieve a permanent injunction or a conviction. Judge Warren, in his final order in the case [180], denied compensation to The Progressive.

REFORM PRINCIPLES

Pertaining to the general problem of executive secrecy, of which atomic secrets are a subset, Franck and Weisband [F&W-74] proposed

-- that intelligence estimates be made available to a key group of legislators on a par with Cabinet members, these legislators to be given top security clearance;
-- that committees of the Legislature dealing with foreign affairs should have the power to summon and examine Executive officers and to secure the release of information and documents;
-- that Legislative committees dealing with foreign affairs should have extensive data-gathering and analyzing capability, rivaling that of the Executive Branch;
-- that the question of the Legislative Branch's information-getting prerogatives vis-a-vis the Executive could, at least in the United States, be resolved by litigation;
-- that overclassification by civil servants should, like underclassification, be a punishable offense;
-- that classification of documents or refusal to produce documents and data should in every case be subject to review either by a special tribunal composed of persons other than the classifiers, or by the courts, or by an ombudsman;
-- that all documents should be automatically declassified in a relatively few years (2 to 10), except in rare circumstances determined by an independent review board;
-- that the press should unilaterally terminate the vestiges of their "buddy" relation with government by refusing to participate in non-attributable briefings, not-for-quote "backgrounders," and other co-optive arrangements;
-- that legislation punishing disclosure of government information be amended, clarified, and narrowed;
-- that public-interest groups and affected individuals should have the right to be heard, and to meet the arguments on the other side, in key decisions affecting trade, the environment, and other matters which, though pertaining to foreign relations, are also of direct domestic concern;
-- that more members of the Executive establishment should be encouraged, or should seize the necessary courage, to resign over matters of conscience and take their case to the public.

In 1974 the House Subcommittee on Foreign Operations and Government Information was responsible for oversight functions involving the security classification system. The system was originally designed by Congress to protect vital national defense secrets and confidential dealings with foreign nations, while also ensuring the right of Congress and of the public to be fully informed on the policies of their government. On the basis of experience on that subcommittee, Representative William S. Moorhead devised his own list of reforms [F&W-74]. He noted a basic guiding principle: Our nation is strengthened whenever the people are informed on matters involving our international commitments and defense posture to the maximum extent consistent with overriding security requirements.

He also observed that proper use of classification categories was very important, and that downgrading and declassification should take place just as rapidly as possible.

For secrecy to be effective, Moorhead believed, there must be a sound mechanism for strictly limiting the classification authority of federal agencies and officials, and there must be strong, vigorous review and policing, to assure that the system does not abuse the people's right to know, does not compromise vital defense and foreign policy secrets, and does not flounder in its own bureaucratic excesses.

Moorhead and others have proposed the creation of an independent Classification Review Commission, which has never been established by congressional action. A similar entity (the Information Security Oversight Office, ISOO) was created, on paper, by executive order of President Carter.

INFORMATION SOURCES

In Grosjean the court held that "informed public opinion is the most potent of all restraints upon misgovernment." To become informed about government activities, the public must rely upon access to relevant information and, to some extent, upon the news media as a conduit and as a bellringer.

In order for the media and the public to gain access to reliable government information, avoiding speculations and inaccuracies, a number of reforms of the Freedom of Information Act are warranted [H&H1-77]. One would be to set up a procedure that would weigh pros and cons in an internal review of items denied release. Halperin and Hoffman have pointed out that the most significant FOIA loophole now is that the executive branch is not required "to balance the public's need for the information against the possible harm to national security."

A further step would be to establish a process of independent judicial review in disputed cases: The current FOIA does not permit the courts to consider benefits lost if access is not granted. As an alternative, it would make sense for FOIA exemptions to be based on classification criteria established by legislation rather than by executive order. In lieu of judicial oversight, a classification review board could hear FOIA appeals. While the present Information Security Oversight Office is supposed to review agency procedures and files with respect to National Security Information, it does not seem to have enforcement powers to ensure compliance with the FOIA.

One of the gains resulting from these changes would be increased confidence that classification serves a real purpose, with consequent reduction in the leakage of truly sensitive information. Nevertheless, it is interesting to note the view of Franck and Weisband [F&W-74] that, despite the access provided by the FOIA, "unauthorized information will remain democracy's principal antidote to unlimited, highly concentrated power."

The news media, as primary conduits to the public for information about government activities, play an important role in public discussions of matters that affect national security. Those reporters and editors who use multiple information sources and acquire a perceptive understanding of technical and societal issues can present balanced information that tempers possible public overreaction to threatening situations. Furthermore, good investigative reporters can and do uncover waste, abuse, and harm in actions of officials. With respect to government claims of national danger, greater skepticism by the media -- and also by the public, by scientists, and by the courts -- would make less likely such futile legal chases as the Progressive litigation.

What about the possibility that a free press will publish things that can cause harm, such as, perhaps, nondeducible details of destructive devices, or recipes for psychedelic drugs? For the more flagrant cases, and for deterring such offenses as libel, slander, and the revelation of legitimately classified data (other than that whose danger is so immediate and direct that prior restraint can be justified), there are statutes under which offenders can be prosecuted after-the-fact. Important also is journalistic responsibility, even though that is subjective and cannot be legislated. Bad judgment will sometimes occur -- a price a free society is willing to pay, and must: Without the freedom to be wrong, there can be no freedom to be right.

CLASSIFICATION REVIEW

For the classification system to operate reliably and well, it should be overseen by an impartial body, independent of both Congress and the executive branch. The interests of those two arms of government could be protected by adhering to a principle stated by Franck and Weisband [F&W-74]: "It [should not] be wholly within the power of either branch to make a determination [of secrecy or disclosure] binding on the other." Several types of third-party review have been proposed.

Halperin and Hoffman [H&H1-77] offer some carefully structured ideas that merit comment. They would assign existing classified information to one of three categories: presumptively classified, automatically released, and discretionary. A heavy presumption of classifiability would apply to details of advanced military systems, design and operating characteristics of military equipment, and details of military operations and plans. The kind of information that would be automatically released to Congress and the public includes general or conceptual information on combat missions, forces abroad, nuclear weapons abroad (including risks of seizure, and so on), financing of foreign operations, and the concepts and costs of new weapons systems (such as MX). Their discretionary category requires a balancing of concerns on a case-by-case basis.

Echoing Congressman Moorhead's earlier advice, Halperin and Hoffman have endorsed an independent classification review board to assist Congress in overseeing the administration of a legislated classification system. The board would be responsible for release of information that is more than three years old.

As President Carter put it when he signed Executive Order 12065 on June 29, 1978, "Experience has taught us that strong oversight is needed, both to make the classification system as open as possible and to safeguard properly classified documents." The ISOO, established by that order, was to be involved in coordinating and controlling many information security matters across the full spectrum of agencies of the federal government. What has been implemented in practice appears to be something much less comprehensive, with significant omissions. The CIA, we are told, held that the Interagency Classification Review Committee, predecessor to the ISOO, had no power to declassify documents, and the ISOO seems to be similarly impotent.

It was in recognition of the limitations of an agency that lacked congressional genesis that Representative Moorhead proposed a review commission as part of his 1972 classification system bill [F&W-74]. His bill would also have confined classification to "national defense information," with categories that would depend on the level of potential damage. The bill never became law.

Observe that there is a semantic distinction between "national defense" and "national security." In general usage, national security appears to extend beyond national defense. While the latter might be considered primarily focused on the homeland, actions in the name of national security could include covert and overt military expeditions to such places as Cuba, Vietnam, and Angola. The terminology chosen by Moorhead would have restricted the scope of classification to the narrower category.

Some features of Moorhead's proposal, at least in general concept, have since been incorporated into Executive Order 12065. For one thing, the three categories of classification (Top Secret, Secret, and Confidential) were adopted. In Moorhead's plan, classification authority was to be limited, and most documents were to receive phased, automatic downgrading over a three-year period; under the executive order it is six years. There would have been a procedural "savings clause" -- exemptions based on specific justification, approved by a classification review commission. Except for special exemptions, everything was to be declassified after fifteen years. The executive order is similar, except that classification is permitted for twenty years for domestic and thirty years for foreign data. Highly sensitive data, such as detailed specifications of nuclear weapons, would have continued to be exempt under Moorhead's proposal, as they are under the executive order.

Failure to implement others of Moorhead's recommendations, and the ineffectiveness and impermanence of a presidential order compared with an act of Congress, leave much to be desired in classification oversight. Lacking the enforcement powers that it might have had if Congress had created it, the ISOO has been ineffective.

The landmark report [DSB-70] of the Defense Science Board's task force contains the following recommendations: Each classified document should be marked with a "meaningful written justification" and a "time limit on the classification, as short as possible, which could be extended with detailed justification." Classification should be allowed only for major technological advances, countermeasures to weapons, and for support of national policy directives and regulations. Areas for continued classification, according to the DSB, should include international negotiations, plans for hypothetical emergencies, tactical and operational plans, intelligence information, specific research and development, and vulnerabilities of operational systems. These recommendations would best be implemented and monitored, in our opinion, by establishing a formal commission.

DECISION-MAKING PROCESSES

We do not know in detail the process that led to the government's decision to pursue the Progressive case, although to trace it would probably be interesting and instructive. Once that decision was made, however, an array of imposing officials participated: the Secretaries of Defense, Energy, and State supplied affidavits. Presumably the decision was made with the knowledge and at least tacit concurrence of the Attorney General and possibly President Carter (either directly or through the National Security Council). Secretary of Energy Schlesinger personally phoned key newspapers attempting to drum up support for the government's view.

We understand, however, that lawyers for the Justice Department found the case unappealing -- a potential loser, with the risk that portions of the untested Atomic Energy Act would be declared unconstitutional. DOE provided Justice with legal ammunition, in the form of affidavits that resoundingly declared the extreme sensitivity of Morland's article. Another unanswered question is who it was that decided to make public certain affidavits, such as those of Brown and Rosengren, which, as we have noted, reveal information the government was supposedly seeking to keep secret. According to newspaper reports, on several occasions Justice Department lawyers either asked to be excused from the case or threatened to remove themselves, especially after information far more sensitive than Morland's turned out to have been on open library shelves.

An ad hoc process of enforcement, while having the virtue of allowing decisions to be made quickly, has inherent in it the danger of serious mistakes. Had a commission for classification review been properly enacted and constituted by Congress, it could have evaluated the Morland article in more realistic terms, and perhaps would have averted the damaging and counterproductive conflict. The review could have been carried out by special panels assigned to the two technical issues: whether the concepts in Morland's article were still secret, and, even if they were, whether the article would add to proliferation risk.

Ignoring the Public Domain

One thing to be learned from the Progressive fiasco is that there should be no official action to try to suppress classified material that has become hopelessly public. Legal action should be taken for violating a secrecy statute only when the risk of additional disclosure is minimal. Attempted suppression draws attention to the material, and the implied confirmation increases its credibility. Pragmatically, of course, the government could not hope to police the entire body of public literature, American and foreign.

A government brief [21] in the Progressive case admitted that in a "context of...substantial misinformation," sensitive design data would "lack all credibility." This is precisely the point. Say nothing, and the secret might remain. Since this is so well understood in classification circles, we are surprised when it is officially violated. In Progressive, the government, for reasons unknown to us, ignored the likelihood that drafts had been widely distributed, with many impossible to recall. In any event, it would be a good idea if

Congress determined why that happened and enacted corrective legislation.

Safeguarding Classified Matter

The executive branch, being entrusted with safeguarding what it classifies, must have a viable, practical method of controlling dangerous information. Without violating the Constitution, administrative or legal actions can be taken against anyone who discloses, without authorization, data classified by the government.

In carrying out the custodial task, there are certain realities that must be taken into account. One of them is that sensitive documents may be "mistakenly declassified." A person in possession of such a declassified document is currently not obliged to surrender it: All that can be done at present is to hope that anybody who has one will responsibly safeguard it and will not disseminate its contents. A mechanism is needed for doing the best that can be done to ensure that such material is properly protected. If reclassification is to be considered (now explicitly forbidden under Executive Order 12065), it should include a two-step procedure: first, determination and declaration by the government that the document is subject to reclassification by virtue of having been erroneously declassified in violation of existing guidelines; second, determination by an independent board or commission that the government's claim is correct, and further, that the information is still protectible to a significant extent. If the board were to rule in favor of the government, the document would be reclassified. Otherwise it would remain unclassified.

In order to encourage more care in safeguarding classified information, greater accountability by government officials is needed. One example where responsibility should be improved concerns the release -- through negligence or by intention -- of sensitive information. Another is the failure to properly secure government documents, including the type of laxity that put UCRL-4725 onto the public shelves.

To carry out the reviews of reclassification and administrative enforcement, a classification review commission would be an appropriate vehicle, provided it were suitably set up by Congress. One of its virtues would be that it would have some credibility with the public, whereas executive decisions to reclassify would not.

THE JUDICIAL PROCESS AND TECHNICAL ISSUES

In view of the intimate and inherent role of the courts in interpreting the laws, we have a number of suggestions that apply specifically to judicial procedures. The courts are not now well equipped to deal with technological conflicts, and the "adjudicatory process is probably ill-suited to informed decision-making" about executive judgement in areas related to national security [CHEH-80].

As we point out earlier, just what would constitute "damage to our Nation" under the Stewart-Brennan opinion in the Pentagon Papers case is by no means clear. The government claimed in Progressive that its mere act of notifying the magazine and the court that damage would occur was sufficient to justify an injunction. Enforcement of the Atomic Energy Act should be based on substantive showing of cause and effect. Perhaps clarification will have to await litigation that is more definitive, but it would help if Congress supplied some guidelines.

If there were a classification review commission, its recommendations would enter importantly into determining whether publication would be dangerous. In addition the courts should make more use of panels of experts, agreed upon by both sides, when the subject matter is beyond their competence. We return to this point in another section.

The espionage statutes are relevant. There the principal thrust [F&W-74] is to "prevent the deliberate transmission of valuable information to an enemy. The basic ingredients of the offense are, thus, culpable intent and harmful effect; and they are set out in most, but not all, of the offenses." This legal philosophy should likewise apply to atomic weapons matters, but that is not now the situation with regard to §2274(b), which extends to members of the public. [Note XI-2]. In contrast to subsection (a) of §2274, under subsection (b) neither intent to harm nor harmful effect need be proven for conviction; in the Progressive litigation the government took the position that mere notification gave the magazine sufficient "reason to believe." Official information should remain protected under §2277, which prohibits disclosure by employees in classified programs. Employment contracts that restrict dissemination of government data are appropriate.

Ronhovde [RON-80], in his Congressional Research Service study, quotes from an article in the Harvard Law Review that would be "readily applicable to the Progressive case"; the article calls for "impartial guidance in evaluating executive claims of national security. Such guidance could be in the form of federal statutes providing injunctions or criminal punishment for enumerated kinds of publication."

Recurrently in national-security cases one or the other of the parties finds it would benefit from introducing as evidence certain sensitive material -- information that should remain classified. To meet that problem, there has arisen the practice of introducing evidence in camera that cannot be made public. In Progressive an incongruous situation arose: None of the defendants was allowed to attend the in camera hearings, nor were they given access to the written decisions and affidavits covered by the protective order, which prohibited external dissemination of in camera material under penalty of contempt of court.

This is not without legal precedent. There is need to ensure that defendants are not denied access to in camera materials pertaining to their case without well-substantiated cause. If there are valid reasons for keeping sensitive information from defendants, there should be a credible formal mechanism to assure that acceptable nominees with the necessary expertise can inspect the material and represent the defendant's interests: The proving of harm and the validity of classification should not be left to in camera submissions without adequate access by independent observers. In Rosenberg and Progressive (not unlike Marchetti and New York Times), the government greatly exaggerated the sensitivity of the data. Secrecy powers are too important, and have been too often abused, to allow a one-sided interpretation of what is properly classified or what is potentially harmful to the nation.

Advisory Committees

To avoid some of the quicksand associated with the subtleties and complexities of questions with a technical component, judges must have competent help. Technical jargon itself is a problem, being no less mysterious to the legal mind than the law is to a technologist. One answer to this communication dilemmma lies in accepting, in an advisory role, specialists who are not part of the adversary process -- who are not committed to being "expert witnesses" for either side.

That was the course proposed by the ACLU in its earliest Progressive brief [34]. It is not a new idea. Federal rules permit appointment of special "masters" in any pending action, and courts sometimes use them when technical matters beyond their own professional experience are involved. Another possibility is to involve some sort of classification review commission directly in judicial proceedings.

With either arrangement, the process could proceed in two stages. First, an appropriate, independent committee (either ad hoc or standby) would determine whether the challenged material could be independently derived by competent people who do not have access to classified sources. If the answer is yes, the court should permit the material to be published unless there is persuasive, authoritative counterevidence. If no, or if a yes determination is rejected by the court, the second stage would be invoked: The same panel would be augmented with additional experts. For example, if the matter involves proliferation and national defense, the expanded panel would be charged with determining the impact publication would have upon national security. If the decision is that it would not "surely result in grave, direct, immediate, and irreparable harm," publication should then be permitted unless the court found truly compelling reasons for ruling otherwise. We see such a process to be in the best interests of both national security and the First Amendment.

The government too should make use of an independent review panel. Review would be instituted in either of two situations. First: if the government decided that it was necessary to enjoin publication, it could first seek a temporary restraining order. Before proceeding with a request to the court for a preliminary or permanent injunction, however, the government would convene the panel and hear its recommendation. If the panel disagreed with the government, then the Justice Department should ask that the order be vacated. If the panel were to support classification, the court proceedings would continue (if the enjoinee remained adamant), presumably with a new panel as in the preceding paragraph.

The second situation, where the government tries to suppress publication without going to court, is the more common one. If the work in dispute was not sponsored by the government, and the differences between author and government become intractable, the author should have the right to appeal to the panel for prompt review and decision. If the panel decides in favor of publication, the government should accept that decision.

Work produced by government scientists could be adjudicated by the same process. However, if the work is government-sponsored, other considerations, such as condition-of-employment agreements, might settle the matter.

One major purpose of the panel would be to restrict the ability of the federal government to impose censorship by harassment and the threat of legal action. The panel could not abridge the right of the press to publish information in the public interest or to seek judicial remedy when the government classifies data. It is needed to ensure that a unilateral claim by the executive branch of the need for restraint is confirmed by independent authorities. In any event, such advisory committees will tend to keep classification disputes from going through unnecessary and costly litigation. On one hand, they can reinforce the need for legitimate, defensible classification; on the other, they can act as a buffer against capricious or politically inspired secrecy.

In summary, the difficulty the courts have in evaluating technical data makes it imperative that standards be articulated and that a process be established conducive to sound judgement. Part of the process would involve a more rigorous administrative determination in the first place that a given matter should be brought to court, and the remainder calls for judges at all levels to have a better way to evaluate technical issues. The result would be fewer unnecessary confrontations where official claims of sensitivity are used in trying to bypass the "heavy burden of proof" that should be met to justify prior restraint.

DEALING WITH CLASSIFIED INFORMATION

There are a few practical and useful rules that should govern the handling of sensitive information about atomic weapons. The criteria are easy to spell out, although marginal cases can be difficult.

1. Official approval should be required for the release of restricted information by someone who has been part of, or has had official access to, the classified effort that produced the information -- with appropriate penalties for violation. This, of course, is current government policy.

2. Published data from classified sources should not be publicly noted or acted upon, apart from appropriate penalties for unauthorized disclosure. Here "appropriate" must take into account any risk that legal prosecution might lead to disclosure of further sensitive information. This also, as we understand it, is current policy.

3. Information that parallels classified data but is privately generated without use of classified sources should not be publicly noted or acted upon by the government after publication. This too has been official policy. One of the mistakes in the Progressive case was neglect of the fact that copies of the draft had been distributed, a form of de facto publication.

4. Privately generated information that parallels classified data and is about to be published requires judicious consideration. If the government is alerted to impending publication in time, there might, at least in principle, be cases where it would be in the national interest to enjoin publication. Care must be taken to see that the cure is not worse than the disease, as it turned out to be in the Progressive affair.

The thinking behind these criteria is not complicated. The first one, concerning official data, is common sense. So is the second, since calling unnecessary attention to published sensitive data should obviously be avoided.

As for the third, there is no need for, nor benefit from, any legislation that attempts to deal with water over the dam. The reason that there should be no official comment on published thoughts in sensitive areas is that such comment can often reveal important nondeducible information regarding the credibility of the public speculation -- thus inadvertently breaching security.

The fourth expresses the need to walk the tightrope between revealing sensitive information by official reaction in public and permitting crucial data that might not be easily deduced by others to spread through inaction.

These criteria would not prevent the government, under existing regulations, from imposing sanctions against any research effort that goes well beyond the use of published information sources and can be shown to be harmful to the nation.

The fourth point superficially involves "born secret" aspects, but is really very different. "Meaningful and effective information controls," as Cheh points out, "require that the government recognize, as far as possible, which atomic energy information is or is not publicly available or readily derivable." Further, the Atomic Energy Act defines a broad category of information to be classified, whereas under our fourth guideline the government would have to show that the Pentagon Papers tests (or some clarification thereof) could be met.

Although the Atomic Energy Act has occasionally been cited to persuade somebody to refrain voluntarily from publishing (we have given examples), the case at hand is the first time that the born-classified concept has been invoked in court. Classification under a born-secret policy is not, in fact, explicit under the Act, but rather is an operational interpretation that has not yet been fully tested in the courts.

General Congressional Actions

Some changes to the secrecy provisions of the Atomic Energy Act are called for, even though they might not do much to alleviate the tendency of judges to issue restraining injunctions when the Justice Department asks that the court be "prudent." It is understandable that, out of concern for national security, both the government and the courts should lean toward injunctive restraints. Perhaps, however -- as was suggested by Supreme Court justices in both the Near and Pentagon Papers cases -- existing criminal statutes, permitting after-the-fact prosecutions, provide sufficient protection in most eventualities, if not all. Relevant case law, so far, is sparse, and Progressive did not clarify much of anything.

A "clear congressional mandate [with] legislated guidelines" would have considerable value [H&H1-77] in assisting "the delicate function of judicial review on national security matters." Halperin and Hoffman point to the "more congenial task" of implementing the legislated guidelines in place of "the independent development of judicial standards for balancing secrecy and disclosure values." As Cheh puts it, "Individual rights are best protected by legislation that is specif-

ically and narrowly tailored to an appropriate governmental objective."
The problem is that many who favor more restrictions on disclosure
would like to preserve the ambiguity of the current situation.

We agree with Halperin and Hoffman that "legislated reform...is a
constitutionally appropriate and politically viable approach.... [No]
satisfactory alternative is available." However, we do recognize that
opening the question could lead to reinforcing, rather than reforming,
the undesirable aspects of the status quo.

One further point: The terminology in the Atomic Energy Act needs to
be made clearer, with precise meanings spelled out. We have frequently
mentioned difficulties that arise from the all-encompassing definition
of Restricted Data. Criteria for judging intent and belief are not
explicit (perhaps an inherent problem, since such criteria are hard to
formulate), and the meaning of the terms "published information" and
"in the public domain" is not addressed at all. As stated by Cheh, "if
Congress intended to control privately developed atomic energy information, it did so in a highly ambiguous, equivocal, and uncertain way."

ATOMIC ENERGY ACT REFORMS

In 1946 the singular problems of atomic energy led to the original
Atomic Energy Act. Congress had concluded that the spread of
technology related to nuclear weapons posed such a potential risk to
the nation's security that the unusual, restrictive provisions of the
statute were justified. It chose the Act as the vehicle for "a program
for Government control of the possession, use, and production of atomic
energy and special nuclear material, whether owned by the Government or
others," as well as "a program for...the control, dissemination, and
declassification of Restricted Data, subject to appropriate
safeguards." In essence, atomic energy was designated, uniquely, as a
technology subject to special controls.

Over the last thirty years, however, a significant amount of information regarding nuclear weapons has, through declassification and
leaks, entered the public domain. Enough has become public that any
nation with the requisite industrial base can make workable atomic
weapons if it chooses to do so. Secrecy is no longer much, if any,
impediment to an industrial state, although it might remain a valid
means for delaying, to an unknown extent, less developed nations in
their acquisition of nuclear weapons.

As a result of historical evolution, therefore, some of the controls
in the Atomic Energy Act have become outmoded. In reality, data
restrictions on peaceful applications of nuclear energy have all but
disappeared, and the ability to keep the principles and technology of
nuclear weapons under wraps has largely faded away. Born secret has
become an anachronism.

The most important step to help solve the problems with the born-
classified interpretation of the Atomic Energy Act would be to define
Restricted Data so as to exclude information that has become public.
It should only cover "government information that the United States
affirmatively determines must be kept secret in the interests of
national security" [CHEH-80]. Care would be needed to ensure that
creative scientific insights are not made illegal: A sudden impulse, a
flash of genius, cannot readily be traced to public information.

To compensate for more specific deficiencies of the security classification system, many reform proposals have been made in the past. Some of the suggestions have not advanced far because various parties have been afraid either that the classification system would be emasculated or that repressive features would be introduced.

Broadening the Scope of the Act

In a trial balloon growing out of the Progressive case, Congressman Paul N. McCloskey, late in 1979, sought to stimulate debate by putting forward a possible amendment extending the scope of the Atomic Energy Act. If adopted, that amendment would have been a step backward, because it proposed extending classification to include the relevant "mind products" of people never connected with government programs. It did trigger some discussion, and was soon withdrawn. However, proposals along that line with more serious support might appear, and so -- at the risk of repeating ourselves -- we emphasize a couple of the more obvious reasons why broadening the scope would be wrong.

As McCloskey phrased it, the extended Act would apply to "privately generated restricted data" -- a felicitous description of an untenable concept. The phrase has no operational utility because attempting to control the spread of readily deducible ideas is useless, as well as potentially harmful to national security, for the following three reasons:

1. Privately generated data that require few resources to create can be duplicated by anyone with the ability and motivation. Thus there is little or nothing to be gained from trying to keep such ideas from those who have the resources to exploit them.

2. That being the case, broadening the coverage of secrecy could keep information only from the public, which is to say from scientists and others who would have no interest in using the information to the detriment of national security, but who need to be informed in order to (a) further the peaceful use of technology in solving urgent problems, and (b) provide intelligent input to policy decisions.

3. The responsibility for protecting classified data necessarily rests with those who have custody of it. Outsiders cannot realistically be presumed to have accurate knowledge of what is or is not officially considered sensitive, nor can they in fairness be held legally responsible for adhering to criteria they are forbidden to know. Inasmuch as the classification guidelines are themselves classified, it would be outrageous to make uncleared personnel legally responsible for divining what might or might not be officially considered Restricted Data.

Not only would there be no positive benefit to national security from extending the reach of the Atomic Energy Act, but actual damage could well be done. Predictable would be: (1) needless proliferation of the classification bureaucracy; (2) impediments in the free flow of scientific information, including some that is needed for solving the world's urgent problems; (3) inadvertent release of truly sensitive information in the course of coping with unnecessarily large quantities of potentially classifiable material; and (4) the potential for misuse of the classification process for political purposes in covering up official ineptness and in favoring one research approach over another for vested-interest reasons.

Other legislation might someday be suggested that would remove tests of intent to injure or of actual injury. Any such proposal should be resisted, as there would be difficult practical problems of implementation, apart from the obvious constitutional ones. Nor should existing provisions be weakened with substitution of "probable" injury, which would lead to a nebulous interpretation depending upon the prevailing climate of opinion. The prosecution must continue, as under the espionage statutes, to prove intent and actual injury by positive showing.

On the other hand, sufficient cause for a temporary restraining order might consist of "administrative" or "functional" notice that there would be serious damage to the nation. Though that would be acceptable for a TRO, substantive proof -- not merely administrative opinion -- should be required for a temporary or permanent injunction. This was forcefully stated by Justice Brennan in New York Times: "If the Executive Branch seeks judicial aid in preventing publication, it must inevitably submit the basis upon which that aid is sought to scrutiny by the judiciary."

In Great Britain there is an Official Secrets Act that gives the government power to control communication and publication over a broad spectrum of information relative to national defense or with impact on foreign policy. That sort of law would not only be an incursion upon American practices and protections, but would hamper the type of public discussion that is a national asset.

Task Force on Secrecy.

In 1970 the Department of Defense Science Board set up its Task Force on Secrecy. This task force had Frederick Seitz as its chairman and included Dr. Edward Teller as one of its nine members. The basic conclusion it came to was that DOD had too much secrecy, not too little [DSB-70]. In his memorandum to the Chairman of the Defense Science Board (Gerald F. Tape), Dr. Seitz stated: "The negative aspect of classified information...is not adequately considered in making security classification determinations. We may gain far more by a reasonable policy of openness because we are an open society." The summary of the report warns us that

it is unlikely that classified information will remain secure for periods as long as five years, and it is more reasonable to assume that it will become known by others in periods as short as one year through independent discovery, clandestine disclosure or other means.

Regarding what we have called deducible and nondeducible information, Dr. Seitz further stated:

Security classification is most profitably applied in areas close to design and production, having to do with detailed drawings and special techniques of manufacture rather than research and most exploratory development. [Emphasis added]

And most to the point, we find in Section 4 of the report this admonition:

It must be recognized that certain kinds of technical information are easily discovered independently, or regenerated, once a reasonably sophisticated group decides it is worthwhile to do so. In spite of very elaborate and

costly measures taken independently by the U.S. and the
U.S.S.R. to preserve technical secrecy, neither the United
Kingdom nor China was long delayed in developing hydrogen
weapons.

Any expectation that the basic concepts of thermonuclear weapons (as
opposed to technical details) could be protected for thirty years is
completely unreasonable, based as it is on confusing the secrets of
nature with the traditional type of military secret.

Positive Proposals

In view of the problems the born-secret interpretation of the Atomic
Energy Act have caused and can cause, remedial action is in order. At
the very minimum, the Act should be changed so that it no longer
applies to individuals or small-scale research efforts where there has
been no access to information from classified documents.

As the Progressive case has shown, action taken under the Act may
well conflict with rights granted by the First Amendment. Future
attempts to use the unusual injunctive powers that stem from the Act
might lead to further legal confrontations, with the consequent
unwanted release of sensitive information and ultimately perhaps the
declaration that portions of the Act are unconstitutional.

Here are some features that a revised Atomic Energy Act, or any
legal instruments that replace it, should have. We have discussed most
of them at some length earlier in the book. They point up five areas
where the Atomic Energy Act of 1954 is deficient.

1. Regardless of intent, the communication of information already
published should not be subject to criminal charges.

2. For a person to be punished for disclosing sensitive data, it
should be necessary to prove access to official, classified sources of
the data. As the Act is currently worded, a private citizen who
unknowingly disclosed Restricted Data could be held accountable simply
because of prior unrelated military or government service [Note XI-3].
(This capricious feature has never been invoked, however.)

3. Documents mistakenly released but not officially declassified
by the government should not be recoverable except through an
established, formal procedure such as we discussed earlier in the
chapter. The recall should be on the dual grounds that the information
is protectible and that its release was a genuine error (or malfea-
sance), demonstrably inconsistent with declassification criteria.

4. The out-of-date classification requirements for nonmilitary
nuclear energy applications currently in the Act should be dropped.
Most if not all information on peaceful applications of atomic energy
has been affirmatively declassified, so this would do nothing more than
recognize the current status. However, data regarding safeguards
against diversion or other damage by terrorists should still be
protected. Cheh [CHEH-80] would control dangerous technologies by
licensing research for "very limited and specific areas of militarily
important developing technologies."

5. Any definition of Restricted Data should be carefully worded so
as to exclude ideas that are deducible from public information, for the
reasons given in Chapter VII. Language for this approach has been
embodied in a bill introduced by Congressman McCloskey [Note XI-4];
another possible approach is given in Note XI-5.

OVERSIGHT OF THE CLASSIFICATION SYSTEM

Currently, oversight of the operation of the classification and declassification process is deficient. If a classification review commission were established, that would be a large step toward a safer and more equitable system. The commission could mediate disputes over classification and declassification, see to it that documents were declassified according to their prescribed schedule, ensure automatic, independent review of documents not declassified, and supply other appropriate supervision.

For permanency and independence, the commission should be created by Congress rather than by order of the executive branch. To prevent its operations from being nullified or frustrated by other agencies, it should be under the General Accounting Office, which has an outstanding reputation for independence and has long been involved in evaluating the classification system.

The tasks assigned by executive order to the Information Security Oversight Office would appropriately be taken over by the classification review commission [Note XI-6]. Included would be general management of the interagency classification network, with particular emphasis on attempting to ensure that declassification is carried out on schedule.

There are responsibilities [Note XI-7] now not mentioned in the executive order that should be carried out by the classification review commisssion, including the organization of expert panels and the balancing of risks and benefits of exposure of classified information.

Some of these tasks have in principle been implemented by the first directive of the Interagency Classification Review Committee [Federal Register, 43:194 (October 5, 1978)]. Despite that administrative structure, there is need for a Congress to set up an encompassing classification review process.

Additional roles that could logically be assigned include similar oversight over secrecy and enforcement in patents and cryptography.

These recommendations, which represent a distillation of ideas from many other analysts of the classification system, are minimal for adequate reform of the security classification system. With or without changes in the Atomic Energy Act, a standing commission to review and oversee classification procedures remains an urgent need.

SUMMARY OF SUGGESTED REMEDIES

The atomic energy law needs reform. In particular, "born secret" is a concept whose usefulness is over -- if it ever had any. Ruling it out would go a long way toward removing the current difficulties in enforcement.

Although the judiciary seems largely unaware of it, there is need for expert evaluation of the classification criteria in general, as well as of their application in specific cases. Panels of suitable specialists should be set up when needed. They should act in an advisory capacity only, with no judicial prerogatives.

If the proposed guidelines for dealing with classified information were consistently followed, the security of still-secret data would be improved, while needless or damaging litigation would be avoided.

Finally, Congress should authorize a review commission to help administer the Atomic Energy Act and also to play an important role in minimizing the inconsistencies between regulations and practice in managing classified data.

Epilogue

A man said to the universe:
"Sir, I exist:"
"However," replied the universe,
"The fact has not created in me
A sense of obligation."
                    - Stephen Crane

It is not clear whether the Progressive case had a winner. Certainly the government was not able to permanently enjoin the Morland article because of a combination of factors: a weak factual basis, a flimsy statutory and constitutional position, the futility and counterproductiveness of attempts to suppress the already public thermonuclear concepts, the government's own breaches of the secrecy system, and a security-classification structure that has gotten large and unwieldy.

To some extent the Department of Energy might have been the victim of historical circumstances, in that the statutory definition of Restricted Data is untenable and unenforceable. This also partly explains why there was a conflict of experts over what was really classified. Even if some information concerning nuclear weapons was already in the public domain, any variation or nuance could, as a technicality, be considered restricted.

Perhaps the winner in a sense was the government, which succeeded in deflecting a constitutional challenge to the Atomic Energy Act, and managed, for the first time, to convince a federal judge to issue an injunction on the basis of the Act. On the other hand, although The Progressive was financially drained, it ultimately won the right to publish. So where does that leave the public? With an ambiguous outcome, we think, that strengthens neither national security nor the Constitution.

Claims by both sides that Morland had found "the secret of the H-bomb" led the public, and initially the press, to see the national-security significance larger than life. The other side of that coin is that the First Amendment implications were not at first generally appreciated.

There are lessons to be learned. We have pointed to the need for changes in antiproliferation policy, for legislation to eliminate the

235

born-secret interpretation of the Atomic Energy Act, for permanent and
thorough oversight of the classification system by means of a standing
commission, and for Congress to streamline the classification and declassification review process. Needed also is an impartial process for
competent evaluation of the risks of publishing information about
atomic weapons. Such reforms would improve the protection of truly
sensitive data. Without them, there might well be further useless
legal conflicts over the Atomic Energy Act.

Meanwhile, the continued spread of nuclear weapons seems inevitable,
the arms race continues, and the likelihood of nuclear war grows. In
his farewell address, President Carter stressed that "the United States
and all countries must find ways to control and reduce the horrifying
danger that is posed by the world's stockpiles of nuclear arms."
    Nuclear weapons will not be brought under control unless the
realities of world politics are taken into account. Currently, for
example, the United States relies on its tactical nuclear arsenal in
Europe as an equalizer to counter the large conventional forces of the
Soviet Union, which is one of the reasons why the U.S. has not pledged
no-first-use of nuclear weapons. The phasing out of tactical nuclear
weapons in the European theatre would necessitate a greater reliance by
NATO on conventional alternatives.
    The Progressive case has particularly pointed up the need for an
understanding of nuclear-weapons proliferation and the forces that
drive it. With that comprehension could come a much-needed shift in
nonproliferation policy away from an overreliance on secrecy and
technology denial. Proliferation is primarily fueled by the arms race
between the superpowers, not by the availability of information. What
drives the arms race, in turn, is complicated -- but some elements are
known. A former chief scientific adviser to the British government,
Lord Zuckerman, sees the underlying considerations as not predominantly
military:
        I...submit that military chiefs, who by convention are the
        official advisers on national security, merely serve as a
        channel through which the men in the [weapons] laboratories
        transmit their views.
    Herbert York has commented on the motivations of those who keep the
arms race going, saying that they
        have had a deep long-term involvement.... They derive
        either their incomes, their profits, or their consultant
        fees from it. But much more important than money as a
        motivating force are the individuals' own psychic and
        spiritual needs; the majority of the key individual
        promoters of the arms race derive a very large part of
        their self esteem from their participation in what they
        believe to be an essential -- even a holy -- cause.
    In his often quoted farewell address as president, Dwight Eisenhower
in 1956 warned about undue influence of the military-industrial and
scientific-technological sectors, between which there is a synergistic
relationship:
        In the councils of government we must guard against the
        acquisition of unwarranted influence, whether sought or
        unsought, by the military-industrial complex. The

potential for the disastrous rise of misplaced power exists and will persist.... In holding scientific research and discovery in respect...we must be alert to the equal and opposite danger that public policy could itself become the captive of a scientific-technological elite.

The world view of people who have a personal stake in a continuing arms race is far too narrow to lead to effective nonproliferation policy, to say nothing of bringing the superpowers' arsenals under control. Nonproliferation should not be viewed as a way to exclude small countries from the nuclear-weapons club, but rather as part of a general process of nuclear arms reduction that is essential if there is to be a future for the human race.

The next few pages contain commentaries by some of the principals in the Progressive case. Their views are not always consonant with ours. That Morland (uniquely) regards the affair as largely a publicity stunt may particularly shock the reader. Yet it is not the motives of a roving freelance reporter that we find surprising, but rather the poorly thought-out response (whether overreaction or misguided attempt to exploit the situation) of the United States government.

Nevertheless the long-term results of the affair are more likely to be positive than detrimental. If needed changes come about, particularly in nonproliferation policy and the Atomic Energy Act, Howard Morland will have done us all a favor.

Commentaries

Howard Morland [© 1980],
author of the article that was temporarily restrained:

At least from the author's point of view, publication of "The H-Bomb Secret" in The Progressive was largely a publicity stunt, as cynical critics have charged. It is certainly not necessary for private citizens to know how the insides of an H-bomb look in order to understand that our survival as a society, and even as a species, requires the abolition of nuclear weapons. That fact is evident in the effects of nuclear weapons, their numbers in present stockpiles, and their physical size. They are too destructive, too numerous, and too easily transported for their use to be anything other than an act of suicide on a global scale. Even the threat of their use will eventually end in disaster. Disarmament is our only hope for survival, and unilateral disarmament is better than continuation of the present arms race. That conclusion does not need to be proven; it needs to be publicized.

There is a vast difference between objective truth, if there is such a thing, and political truth. Political truth is whatever is said most often and believed by most people. Publicity is its key, and those who promote and perpetuate the nuclear arms race in America have a monopoly on access to the mass media and hence a monopoly on credibility. They also have their hands deep in the public pocket. They claim to be the only ones who know what they are talking about, and editors and politicians believe them. The voice of sanity is like a whisper in a hurricane in contrast to the daily outpourings of right-wing rhetoric and money for more bombs and missiles. If there is any way out of this madness, those who advocate disarmament must first find a way to get equal time on the network news.

One way is to trick the bomb makers into bestowing some of their own credibility on their critics and then into making fools of themselves in a very public way, which is what we did. Even casual consumers of the news will now be slightly less prone to believe the government's nuclear weapon experts and slightly more prone to ask embarassing questions. We have won a small, but significant victory -- at a cost of $250,000 in legal expenses and fees.

238

There are also reasons why this particular piece of information, the H-bomb secret, needs to be in the public libraries of the world, anyway. The Department of Energy is asking for five billion dollars a year, twice the present amount, to build new warheads during the 1980s, as if we didn't have enough already. There is some reason to believe that much of the increase may be, in a subtle way, a disguised subsidy for the troubled nuclear power industry, or perhaps a pure garden-variety porkbarrel for local politicians. We can't know the answer as long as the bomb makers are making a secret product. However, being ripped off is a minor inconvenience compared with being killed, which is what we are all going to be if the bomb makers keep building their toys and dreaming up new games to use them in.

(These views and others are expanded in my book, The Secret That Exploded, published by Random House.)

Samuel Day, Jr., Managing Editor of The Progressive:

In publishing the Morland article, The Progressive knowingly disseminated information which the United States nuclear weapons establishment and its supporters believed would be injurious to the national interest and therefore should be kept "secret/restricted." In demonstrating that the information was already in the public domain, we showed that no legally significant injury could be caused by the article, thereby forcing the Government to abandon its attempt at censorship.

However, justification of publication does not rest solely on the fact that the information was indeed not secret, or that it could be readily ascertained by others, or even on the assertion of our First Amendment right to print anything we saw fit, subject to limitations imposed by the United States Supreme Court. The information merited publication because, whether secret or not, whether injurious to the United States or not, whether protected by the First Amendment or not, it offered an idea of value to the people of this country and the world.

The idea is that survival in the nuclear age may well depend on the ability of Americans to muster contempt for official secrecy. The nuclear weapons race which threatens to incinerate our planet derives its primary impetus from the nuclear weapons program of the United States, historically the leader in this field. The general outlines of the program are well known, as are many of the details, but the "secrecy mystique" which immerses it provides an essential nutrient. It excludes informed criticism, hides adverse impacts, fosters public acquiescence, obscures the terrible implications, removes the subject from the arena of political debate. A demystification which could impart to every man and woman a visceral feeling for nuclear weapons may well be the key -- perhaps the only key short of nuclear war -- to the stopping of the nuclear arms race. The Morland article was a start.

Many writers, including the authors of this volume, have advocated the puncturing of nuclear secrets. What made the Morland article unique -- and historically important -- is that it punctured them.

Erwin Knoll, Editor of The Progressive:

The authors of this volume recognize and articulate the inherent
conflict between secrecy and freedom: "Secrecy and the democratic
process are fundamentally inconsistent, since information and programs
protected by secrecy are effectively removed from public view and
discussion." Therefore, they suggest, the benefits of secrecy "must be
carefully evaluated, and balanced against the costs."
    This is, I believe, an inadequate response to a critical problem.
Freedom is an absolute value -- not one to be "balanced" or
compromised. Those who understand, as the authors clearly do, that
secrecy must undermine democracy have a special obligation to resist
secrecy regardless of the cost.
    A system of secrecy undoubtedly confers enormous benefits on those
who are privy to the secrets. Knowledge is power, and those who can
maintain a monopoly on knowledge can maintain a monopoly on power.
Disclosure can be awkward, embarrassing, inconvenient, even
threatening. There are occasions -- though I believe they are
extremely rare -- when disclosure may actually be dangerous. But the
dangers of disclosure are always problematic, while the dangers of
secrecy are always real.
    In the public uproar that attended the Progressive case, we had
ample opportunity to gauge the calamitous consequences of secrecy. We
discovered that many of our fellow citizens -- including highly
educated men and women deeply involved in public affairs -- were
profoundly ignorant of even the most elemental facts about nuclear
weapons and the nuclear arms race. Even more disturbing was the
discovery that many did not want to know; after a third of a century
in which the mystique of nuclear secrecy had been relentlessly
developed and sustained, they were convinced that their safety lay in
ignorance. Such delusions do not merely undermine the democratic
process; they undermine the prospects of survival itself.
    The Progressive case represented a small assault on the mystique
of secrecy. This book, for those who will be fortunate enough to read
it, will further undermine the secrecy system. But if democracy is to
be more than an empty word, if citizens are actually to have a voice in
public decisions that may entail matters of life and death, we must
confront the problem of secrecy head on -- not by "balancing" freedom,
but by insisting that freedom is our first concern.

Charles Sims, ACLU attorney defending The Progressive:

The legal issues in the Progressive case appeared at times to participants -- and may at first blush to nonlawyers -- to be encrusted with
legal technicalities that often make our law seem out of step with the
real world. A complicated multipart legal test -- whether publication
surely, directly, and immediately would cause grave and
irreparable harm to the nation and its people -- seemed an awkward
way to undertake an inquiry that scientific participants in the affair,
and others, would have approached quite differently. Will our country,
our national security -- they would have asked directly -- be better or
worse off if the Morland article is published? Will it make nuclear
proliferation, and therefore nuclear destruction, more likely? Worse,

the question that increasingly drew the lawyers' attention as the months went by -- Have these concepts been previously released in public, even accidentally? -- struck me as a hypertechnical approach which would apparently justify release of a governmental weapons document, UCRL 4725, which they knew should be kept secret.

This difference in approach stemmed from the fundamentally different methods of science and constitutional law. The defense lawyers began with an axiom: the First Amendment, and especially the never-breached rule against prior restraints. That axiom answered categorically many of the questions the scientists wanted to approach experimentally and pragmatically. Our experts, on the other hand, tended to take the facts and the risks they projected from the facts with a seriousness that precluded concern for the effect their recommended actions might have on legal rules constructed as barriers to official censorship, barriers that once breached have little practical effect.

The results of this conflict were predictable. The lawyers tended to minimize risks of publication -- after all, the framers of the First Amendment had instructed us to do so on the firm and unchallengeable assumption that the risks of disclosure were always less grave than the risks of censorship. The scientists tended to gloss over the damage that bad precedents inflict on legal rules, especially fundamentally antigovernmental rules like the First Amendment. As they saw it, if UCRL-4725 should not be left in the public domain, it should be reclassified, notwithstanding regulations and logic arguing against attempting to rebottle a genie already let loose.

The defendants' legal approach reflects these tensions, and should be examined with them in mind. Faithful, as a rule, to First Amendment axioms that permit constitutional defense of cases like this at all, the legal team nevertheless was constantly obliged to defend and rework points that give scientists too much practical concern. Disagreements were resolved, or resolved with difficulty, or effectively postponed or avoided. The processes of dispute, resolution, and conciliation -- rejected as a way of settling disputes between the parties before the court -- were in fact used extensively within our legal team.

From what we have heard, the tensions between legal and technical approaches played themselves out in the government's case as well, as the Departments of Justice and Energy struggled to impose their approaches on the legal strategy. The prevalence of the conflict, and the lingering sense that the resolution of the case has only intensified it, suggests what the widespread ambivalence of nearly all parties to the case seems to confirm: The two approaches reflect deeper underlying themes -- on the one hand, fears of the final erosion of the rule against prior restraint and of the gradual tightening of the national security state; on the other hand, fears of nuclear proliferation and perhaps a sense of collective scientific guilt over responsibility for nuclear terror.

More than the small mindedness of the district judge who happened to be assigned to the case, or the courage of journalists who finally relieved the participants in this case of the continued misery of fighting an ill-advised and an increasingly silly injunction, these themes provide the lessons to be learned. These conflicts are likely to continue. Attention to them can clarify how the legal strategy developed and how the actors in a future case will respond.

Hugh DeWitt: expert witness for The Progressive

At the beginning of the Progressive case in March 1979 the Dept. of Energy believed that the basic principles of operation of the U.S. thermonuclear weapons were truly secret. In fact, however, one of the crucial concepts, the idea of radiation implosion, had already become known to physicists working on the inertial confinement approach to fusion. This approach employs either high-intensity laser beams or charged-particle beams to deliver the required energy to compress and heat tiny targets containing fusion fuel to thermonuclear burn conditions. In the U.S. some target designs were and still are classified because of their relation to thermonuclear bomb design, notwithstanding the existence of published research describing the radiation implosion concept. Early in the Progressive case this source of published information about the classified concept was made clear to the court in several affidavits. As far as can be ascertained, Morland himself was not aware of this publicly available information when he wrote his article. The well-documented fact that the government's concept #2, the idea of radiation coupling or radiation implosion, was known in parts of the scientific community further weakened the government's case against The Progressive.

An early example of how the radiation implosion idea could be deduced by a competent physicist is illustrated by the March 17, 1979 affidavit of Dr. Kosta Tsipis, who worked at MIT and had never had a Secret clearance for nuclear weapons work, nor was he involved in inertial confinement fusion research. Yet in his affidavit he says:

> The concept of radiation pressure as the method for compressing the fusion fuel can be indirectly deduced from published accounts of the early work on the hydrogen weapons and their published aspect ratios. I personally arrived at this conclusion deductively in 1973 by combining the fact that the early fusion weapons were long cylinders and that extensive hydrodynamic calculations had to be performed before the Teller-Ulam design was considered feasible. But much more directly, a knowledgeable physicist could deduce the exact mechanism of igniting the fusion material by reading the literature on inertial confinement of fusion fuel pellets by lasers, for the purpose of extracting energy from the fusion process.

Since Dr. Tsipis had no access to classified literature, his deduction of the Teller-Ulam "secret" represented what could be done by any physicist with comparable ability and background.

The Tsipis affidavit was put into the in camera file as soon as it arrived at the Court, and the particular statement quoted above was not made public until the document was declassified and released from the Court Protective Order on Sept. 4, 1980. Thus Dr. Tsipis' affidavit, though not intended for immediate publication, was "born classified." Dr. Tsipis was never notified that his affidavit contained information that the DOE regarded as classified.

The connection between well known inertial confinement fusion ideas and thermonuclear weapon design concepts was made explicit by Dr. Ray Kidder at the Livermore Lab in his March 23, 1979 affidavit, which was written as a Secret document inside the Livermore Lab and remained Secret Restricted Data in the in camera file until it was released entirely (except for one word) on Sept. 4, 1980. In his affidavit, Dr. Kidder said:

> The concept of radiation implosion that is identified in the Morland article as the key secret of the hydrogen bomb is appearing with increasing frequency in the open scientific literature. Evidence to this effect is contained in the attached articles from Laser Focus (Sept. 1976); Science (Oct. 1976); and the Annual Progress Report on Laser Fusion Program (1977) of Osaka University, Japan. In addition, a classified letter (COK 77-160, Nov. 2, 1977) from Arthur D. Thomas (LLL Classification Officer) to J. A. Griffin (Director of the Division of Classification, DOE) establishes the fact that the Division of Classification of the DOE was advised in 1977 that the concept of the radiation implosion was no longer a secret.

If taken at face value, Dr. Kidder's affidavit should have completely destroyed the Government's case against the Progressive even before the Permanent Restraining Order against publication of the Morland article was handed down by Judge Warren on March 26. The Kidder affidavit caused the DOE officials in charge of the case much concern. It arrived at the Court one day before the March 26 hearing, and immediately two Government scientists, Drs. Jack Rosengren and William Grayson, wrote a long and tortuous affidavit dated March 26, 1979 in which they tried to refute Dr. Kidder's statements. In my opinion they failed completely.

The Thomas letter referred to by Dr. Kidder has been only partially released since it refers to work in another country. In the released portion there is a significant statement:

> There is the question of what role we should play with regard to influencing the directions taken by uncleared scientists (in the U.S. and elsewhere). Should the policy be to discourage [DELETED] target work and its publication; to continue to classify information we believe is important to the development of ICF because the concepts are used in weapons; or to consider the best way to declassify the pertinent ICF concepts in an ICF context? Whatever the decision, it is likely to be widely recognized and discussed publicly in a few years.

A significant event concerning the radiation implosion concept was the Rudakov disclosure in the summer of 1976, nearly three years before the Progressive case. Dr. L. I. Rudakov is a distinguished physicist in the Russian ICF program. During the course of a scientific visit to the U.S. in 1976 he gave seminars at several U.S. laboratories. He discussed Russian ICF research, and in particular he described a target design idea that they were developing. Obviously what Dr. Rudakov had to say to audiences of American scientists was not considered to be classified information in the Soviet Union. His seminars caused consternation among DOE officials, however, when it was learned that he was giving a coherent exposition of the idea of radiation driven ablation to compress ICF pellets. The Russian work was published in one of their standard physics journals, J.E.T.P. Letters 24, 206 (Aug. 20, 1976). During the Progressive case the Government argued that the Rudakov publication did not directly refer to weapons, although the connection was made explicit in the references quoted in Dr. Kidder's affidavit. The Rudakov incident is most instructive. Not only did the U.S. classification policies fail to keep a supposedly secret scientific idea from foreign countries, but in this case our policies drew particular attention to the fact that Rudakov's work in Russia was considered classified in this country. There were many bizarre and silly incidents during the Progressive case, but the Rudakov affair perhaps best illustrates the futility of trying to keep simple scientific concepts secret for an indefinite period.

Appendix A
Morland's Article and Erratum
[Courtesy of H. Morland and The Progressive]

The H-bomb secret

To know how is to ask why

Howard Morland

What you are about to learn is a secret — a secret that the United States and four other nations, the makers of hydrogen weapons, have gone to extraordinary lengths to protect.

The secret is in the coupling mechanism that enables an ordinary fission bomb — the kind that destroyed Hiroshima — to trigger the far deadlier energy of hydrogen fusion.

The physical pressure and heat generated by x- and gamma radiation, moving outward from the trigger at the speed of light, bounces against the weapon's inner wall and is reflected with enormous force into the sides of a carrot-shaped "pencil" which contains the fusion fuel.

That, within the limits of a single sentence, is the essence of a concept that initially eluded the physicists of the United States, the Soviet Union, Britain, France, and China; that they discovered independently and kept covered independently and kept tenaciously to themselves, and that may not yet have occurred to the weapon makers of a dozen other nations bent on building the hydrogen bomb.

I discovered it simply by reading and asking questions, without the benefit of security clearance or access to classified materials. There may be some missing pieces here and there — some parts of the puzzle that eluded my search — but the general accuracy of my descriptions and diagrams has been confirmed by people in a position to know.

Why am I telling you?

It's not because I want to help you build an H-bomb. Have no fear; that would be far beyond your capability — unless you have the resources of at least a medium-sized government.

Nor is it because I want India, or Israel, or Pakistan, or South Africa to get the H-bomb sooner than they otherwise would, even though it is conceivable that the information will be helpful to them.

It isn't so much because the details themselves are helpful to an understanding of the grave public policy

'A complete one-megaton bomb ...would fit under your bed'

questions presented by hydrogen weaponry — though they may well be essential.

I am telling the secret to make a basic point as forcefully as I can: Secrecy itself, especially the power of a few designated "experts" to declare some topics off limits, contributes to a political climate in which the nuclear establishment can conduct business as usual, protecting and perpetuating the production of these horror weapons.

The pernicious effects of hydrogen bomb secrecy are well illustrated by an incident that occurred in Washington five months ago.

On October 24, 1978, Representative Ronald V. Dellums, a member of the House Armed Services Committee, sent a letter asking the Department of Energy to explain publicly why it expects a shortage of plutonium in its nuclear weapons production program.

Would the neutron bomb, which was then going into production, require more plutonium than the standard tactical nuclear weapons it is designed to replace?

Had the shortage been induced by the plutonium requirements of a new generation of multiple-warhead ballistic missiles — the Navy's Trident (successor to Poseidon), and the Air Force's M-X (successor to Minuteman III)?

What were the weapons specifications that had led the Department of Energy to contemplate a massive industrial retooling: the rebuilding of its old plutonium production plant at Hanford, Washington, and the restarting of a standby reactor at Savannah River, South Carolina?

"Each of these options will involve both financial costs and environmental costs," the letter stated. "The American people need to know the reasons for the anticipated plutonium shortage in order to have informed opinions on the cost-benefit aspects of the plutonium shortage issue."

As chairman of the Subcommittee on Fiscal and Government Affairs, and as a Congressman whose California district includes one of the nation's two nuclear weapons laboratories,

Dellums had more than a casual interest in such questions.

Three weeks later he received the Energy Department's reply:

"...It is not possible to respond to most of the questions in an unclassified manner. The enclosure to your referenced letter contains 'secret/restricted data' and should be so classified." The enclosure was the list of questions. *It* is now a secret.

Had Dellums invoked the security privileges available to Representatives and Senators with a "need to know," he could readily have obtained the answers. But he did not choose to do so. The response he received demonstrates the lengths to which the keepers of the secrets are prepared to go in dealing with the public: They do not simply withhold the answers; *they can also confiscate the questions.*

Such tactics have served since the dawn of the atomic age to shield nuclear weapons policies from public scrutiny and debate, giving an advantage to those who formulate the policies and have a stake in their perpetuation. And yet the advantage is one gained mostly by default. It results as much from the self-imposed restraint of those who are not members of the classification elite as from the weapon makers' own complicated security system. The importance of looking behind "secret/restricted" curtains, the relative ease of doing so, and the value to be gained from the exercise are lessons we have still to learn.

The self-serving purposes of official secrecy — not the least of which is its paralyzing effect on the spirit of public inquiry — can best be understood by examining the most momentous official secret of them all: the mechanism of a hydrogen bomb.

O f all the world's nuclear weapons secrets, none has eluded publication more successfully than the secret of the H-bomb. In the twenty-five years since its first successful field test in the South Pacific, no description of how it works has ever been made public.

The diagrams that accompany this article are a close approximation of that process. They show the progression of events that occur during the detonation of a hydrogen weapon. The energy of an exploding fission bomb, the circular object near the top of each drawing, is transferred by means of radiation pres-

sure to the hydrogen part of the weapon. Radiation pressure — a term never mentioned in the open literature — is

Somebody talked

"Does anyone know the secret of the H-bomb?"

Howard Morland didn't really expect an answer when he threw the question out half-seriously one night a year ago in a dormitory at the University of Alabama at Tuscaloosa.

About thirty students had gathered to see his traveling slide show on atomic power and the arms race; in the discussion that followed he was explaining that his next project would be to find out more about nuclear weapons.

"Sure, I know," said a young man in the back of the room. "The secret is in the radiation reflectors."

The student went on to explain that he knew some of the people who worked at the big Union Carbide plant in Oak Ridge, Tennessee, where most of the components for hydrogen weapons are built, and that they had told him the reflection of x- and gamma rays was the key to how the weapons work.

The explanation made little impression on Morland at the time, and he didn't even bother to get the student's name. But later on it helped him crack what the weaponmakers consider to be one of their best-kept secrets.

Such chance remarks were part of the mosaic of information from which Morland, a thirty-six-year-old peace activist, constructed the report on these pages — a report confirmed by people who are knowledgeable about the hydrogen weapon program but are not at liberty to discuss it openly. He undertook the project on as-

signment from *The Progressive* to demonstrate that official secrecy in this area serves no useful public purpose.

A 1965 graduate of Emory University in Atlanta, Morland has had only a smattering of science education: two courses in physics, two in chemistry, and one in quantum mechanics. As a journalist, it was only this winter that he published his first article ("Tritium: the New Genie," in the February issue of *The Progressive*). What knowledge he has of military affairs comes largely from the two years he spent piloting Air Force cargo planes between California and Vietnam.

But Morland put his training and experience to use in an intensive six-month self-education project in which he read virtually every scrap of information available on the subject, visited every production plant to which he could gain access, and interviewed scores of scientists and engineers in and out of the weapons program.

Every technical fact was double-checked; none was printed unless it could be authenticated by at least two knowledgeable sources. His diagrams and descriptions received widespread review in the scientific community prior to publication. Copies also were submitted to the Department of Energy for verification as to technical accuracy. The Department declined to do this.

Morland's research was supported by donations to *The Progressive*'s arms race investigation fund. He also received research assistance from a colleague, Louise Franklin Ramirez.

the essence of what remains of the H-bomb secret.

This description and the details that follow are the result of six months' investigation of the nuclear weapon production complex in the United States. It is a mosaic of bits and pieces taken from employe recruitment brochures, environmental impact statements, books, articles, personal interviews, and my own private speculation. A number of reliable sources have confirmed that the information fragments are correctly assembled.

The simple facts are deducible from careful journalistic inquiry and from well-known physical principles. If weapons proliferation is to be controlled, the availability of this information must be recognized by policy makers, who presently prefer to believe the information is unique to the weapons states.

A discussion of nuclear weapons secrets might well begin with Albert Einstein's memorable comment: "There is no secret, and there is no defense." He offered as a corollary, "There is no possibility of control except through the aroused understanding and insistence of the peoples of the world."

Nuclear energy, Einstein concluded, "cannot be fitted into outmoded concepts of narrow nationalisms." But America had emerged from World War II as the sole possessor of nuclear weapons — and those who had capitalized on Einstein's mathematical genius had no use then for his political equations. Less than a year after the Hiroshima bombing, Congress passed the Atomic Energy Act, extending wartime information control into the indefinite future and creating the illusion that it was possible for one nation to keep nuclear secrets from another.

By that time, it was too late to keep the A-bomb secret from the world. The Army had already told where the factories were, what they did, who designed them, and who ran them. The disclosures came in a report by Princeton physicist H.D. Smyth, written before the weapon was ever tested, to protect the Army's bureaucratic flank in case the $2 billion Manhattan Project turned out to be a dud. It was published immediately after the war. Foreign scientists wishing to build fission bombs could learn from the Smyth Report about the materials required, the nature and the scale of operations needed to obtain the materials, the enrichment and production techniques that worked best, and the names of people to contact for further information. Atomic spies could read the Smyth Report like a manual telling them where to go and what to look for.

Smyth's exhaustive account, later regretted by the security-conscious Atomic Energy Commission, was the first of many flaps over secrecy.

On March 15, 1950, *Scientific American* went to press with an article by Cornell physicist Hans Bethe about thermonuclear fusion, the process that lights the sun and other stars. The AEC, sensitive about anything having to do with the H-bomb, ordered the presses stopped. Three thousand copies of the magazine were destroyed, and the presses were restarted with several sentences removed. At that time, the H-bomb had not yet been invented. The concept was still under study, and a feeble — and ultimately abortive — public debate was starting over the issue.

Publisher Gerard Piel charged the Commission with "suppressing information which the American people need in order to form intelligent judgments," but Bethe declined to complain about it. "These people can cause me all kinds of trouble," he said. To supplement his job teaching physics at Cornell, he had been doing consulting work for the AEC.

When the first prototype hydrogen weapon exploded in the South Pacific on November 1, 1952, the public had no idea how it worked, except that some of its energy came from hydrogen fusion. No one outside the U.S. and Soviet governments knew that five of its ten megatons of explosive energy had come from fission, not fusion, and that 5,000 square miles of ocean surface had, therefore, been contaminated with lethal levels of radioactive fission products. The evidence sank to the ocean floor.

Sixteen months later, when the second bomb went off, that part of the H-bomb secret was revealed. A hundred miles downwind, the entire population of Rongelap Island and the crew of a Japanese fishing boat called *The Lucky Dragon* were dusted with powdered coral containing enough radioactive fission products to blister their skin and make their hair fall out. One fisherman died. Japanese scientists analyzed the deadly ash on the fishing boat deck and concluded that the bomb was as much a uranium bomb as a hydrogen bomb. Half its energy had come from the fission of uranium-238, as had most of its deadly fallout.

The bomb designers had felt no obligation to warn the world that their new invention was anything more than a bomb with a super-powerful blast — that, in fact, its radioactive fallout could lethally poison a far greater area than its blast could destroy. Indeed, the hydrogen weapon had been publicized as a "clean bomb." Edward Teller and J. Robert Oppenheimer, weapon designers whom the press routinely called "brilliant," kept the faith with the nuclear weapon priesthood and kept their mouths shut. They would not divulge weapon design information merely to discuss such moral issues as fallout.

The dangers of fallout from nuclear testing soon became a national preoccupation, but when American and Soviet nuclear testing went underground in 1963, radioactive fallout ceased to be a public issue. Nuclear weapon production entered a golden age of public apathy. Multiple warhead missiles were designed and deployed

'...Workers...look like astronauts on a training exercise'

without serious complaint, and arsenals grew enormously. By removing their products from sight, the weapon makers were able to continue to refine their weapons without protest.

Few people remember that nuclear weapon secrets were the underlying issue in the witchhunts and blacklists of the Joseph McCarthy era. In ways sometimes subtle, sometimes direct, the continuing challenges to civil liberties in America today are traceable, in part, to widespread belief in the need for *some* secrecy. People assume that even if nothing else is secret, surely hydrogen bomb designs must be protected from unauthorized eyes.

The puncturing of that notion is the purpose of this report.

The hydrogen bomb secret is now more than twenty-five years old. Five national governments have built industries to produce H-bombs, and there is little reason to think that any other nation that wanted to build them would have trouble finding out how to do it. Pieces of the secret have been declassified and published in what weapon makers call "the open literature," which is accessible to you and me. But enough of the secret has been kept from the general public to perpetuate the mystery and discourage inquiry. Weapon makers can still hide behind their solemn duty to secrecy when hard questions are asked about what they are doing.

Congressman Dellums's questions are a case in point.

They concern a predicted shortage of plutonium in the weapons program — a shortage that calls for hundreds of millions of dollars to be spent upgrading production reactors and fuel reprocessing facilities in Washington state and South Carolina. Why?

Is the nuclear warhead and bomb production rate scheduled to increase dramatically? Do the latest weapon designs call for more plutonium than older designs? (Enriched uranium, which is used together with plutonium, remains abundant.) Is the plutonium shortage really a tritium shortage in disguise, caused by the neutron bomb's high requirement for tritium? (Tritium and plutonium production operations compete for space in the same South Carolina reactors.) Is the Energy Department's proposal really a

porkbarrel project for South Carolina, where nuclear weapons production is the state's largest industry? Or for Washington state, home of the powerful and military-minded Senator Henry M. (Scoop) Jackson?

The Department's assertion of secrecy protected it from having to provide public answers. The answers, as we shall see, would have raised profound questions of public policy.

Before considering technical details, it should be noted that for most people there will always be an H-bomb secret, just as there will

problems of nuclear waste disposal and the biological effects of radiation — can also understand the technology of nuclear weapons, if provided with the necessary information. The growing scientific and technical expertise which has strengthened worldwide opposition to nuclear power is equally vital to a revival of effective public concern over nuclear weapons.

Knowledge of the basic principles of hydrogen weapon design is helpful in understanding the structure of the nuclear weapon production system. It provides insight into the purposes of continued nuclear testing, the nature of

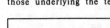

'Understanding the product is necessary to understanding the system'

always be, for most people, a radio secret and an automobile secret. Not everyone is interested in how things work. But millions of people in our highly technological society are amateur experts on gadgets as varied as the electric doorbell and the nuclear power reactor.

Anyone familiar with elementary principles of college physics — such as those underlying the technical

new developments in nuclear weaponry such as the neutron bomb, and the devastating effects of nuclear war.

Paying attention to the details is also a way of reminding ourselves that the weapons are real. The most difficult intellectual hurdle most people encounter in understanding nuclear weapons is to see them as physical devices rather than as abstract expressions of good or evil. The human mind

'No defense'

The following is from a letter from Albert Einstein, signed January 22, 1947, appealing for support for the Emergency Committee of Atomic Scientists:

"Through the release of atomic energy, our generation has brought into the world the most revolutionary force since prehistoric man's discovery of fire. This basic power of the universe cannot be fitted into the outmoded concept of narrow nationalisms. For there is no secret and there is

no defense; there is no possibility of control except through the aroused understanding and insistence of the peoples of the world.

"We scientists recognize our inescapable responsibility to carry to our fellow citizens an understanding of the simple facts of atomic energy and its implications for society. In this lies our only security and our only hope — we believe that an informed citizenry will act for life and not death."

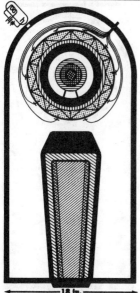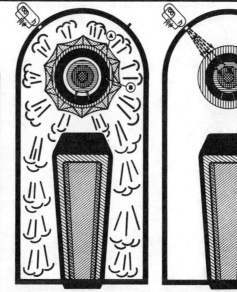

Figure 1. Schematic diagram of a 300-kiloton thermonuclear weapon before detonation. Concentric spheres near the top make up the primary system, or fission trigger. The rest is the secondary system.

Figure 2. High explosives in the primary system begin to burn, driving beryllium neutron reflector (A) and heavy Uranium-238 tamper (B) inward toward the fissile core. The space between the tamper and the core allows the tamper to develop momentum before hitting the core.

Figure 3. The fissile core is squeezed to more than double its normal density, going supercritical. Neutrons fired from a high-voltage vacuum tube start a chain reaction in the fissile material. The chain reaction concentrates first in the fast-fissioning Plutonium-239 (C).

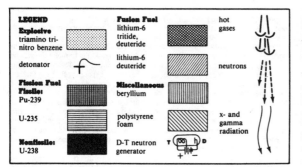

LEGEND			
Explosive triamino trinitro benzene		**Fusion Fuel** lithium-6 tritide, deuteride	hot gases
detonator		lithium-6 deuteride	neutrons
Fission Fuel **Fissile:** Pu-239		**Miscellaneous** beryllium	
U-235		polystyrene foam	x- and gamma radiation
Nonfissile: U-238		D-T neutron generator	

boggles at gadgets the size of surfboards that can knock down every building for miles around. But these are devices made by ordinary people in ordinary towns. The weapons are harder to believe than to understand.

There are three stages to the detonation of a hydrogen weapon: fission, fusion, and more fission. Although one event must follow the other for the weapon to work, they happen so rapidly that a human observer would experience only a single event — an explosion of unearthly magnitude. Within the bomb, however, fission — the splitting of uranium and plutonium nuclei — comes first.

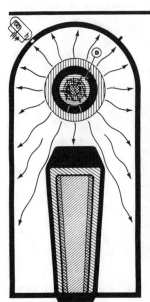

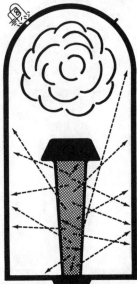

(Copyright ' 1979, Howard Morland.)

Figure 4. The chain reaction spreads to slow-fissioning Uranium-235 (D). Fusion fuel at the center of the core showers the core with neutrons, "boosting" fission efficiency. As the core expands to its original size, reaction stops, completing the first stage of the detonation. Energy release so far: forty kilotons. Prompt gamma rays and x-rays travel outward at the speed of light.

Figure 5. The weapon casing (E) reflects radiation pressure around the thick radiation shield (F) and onto the sides of the fusion tamper (G), collapsing the tamper inward. Heat and pressure of the impact start fusion in the tritiated portion (H) of the fusion fuel "pencil." The precise location of the tritium within the pencil depends on where the designer intends the fusion reaction to begin. Neutrons from this fusion activity breed tritium throughout the pencil.

Figure 6. Fusion fuel reacts virtually simultaneously throughout the pencil, releasing 130 kilotons of energy to complete the second stage. High-energy neutrons from fusion are absorbed by Uranium-238, which has so far served as a fission tamper, radiation shield, radiation reflector, and fusion tamper. Now it serves as fission fuel.

The mechanism for the first fission stage is a miniaturized version of the Nagasaki bomb. It has roughly the same explosive power as the World War II weapon, but it measures less than twelve inches in diameter. This fission "trigger" vaguely resembles a soccer ball, with the same pattern of twenty hexagons and twelve pentagons forming a sphere. Detonator wires are attached to each pentagonal or hexagonal face. When its full explosive energy is realized, this oversized cantaloupe becomes the source of the radiation pressure which ignites the fusion stage.

Weapon designers call this miniature

A-bomb the "primary system." The rest of the nuclear part of the weapon is called the "secondary system." In published accounts, the primary system is often referred to as the "trigger." By itself, it could level a small city, but in a hydrogen weapon it merely provides the energy necessary to ignite the second stage, which releases energy by fusing hydrogen to form helium. A fission bomb is the only force on Earth powerful enough to provide the compression and heat needed to detonate a fusion bomb.

The secondary system is the mechanism which captures the fission energy of the primary system and puts

it to work in the fusion process. The design of the secondary system is the H-bomb secret.

The challenge in designing a hydrogen weapon is to make the secondary system finish its task of fusion before the expanding fireball of the primary systems engulfs and destroys it. About a millionth of a second is all the time available for doing the job. Pure radiant energy, in this case the energy of x- and gamma radiation, is the only thing fast enough and manageable enough to be harnessed for that purpose.

X- and gamma radiation travel at the speed of light, more than a hundred

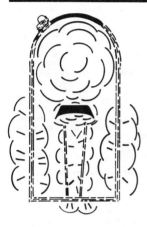

Figure 7. Uranium-238 fissions, adding another 130 kilotons of energy to the explosion and generating enough fission products to kill everyone within 150 square miles with fallout. This is the end of the third stage. A fireball begins to develop....

times faster than the expanding debris from an exploding A-bomb. If the primary system and the fusion fuel are located some distance apart, say twelve inches, the radiant energy of the primary system will have time to race ahead of the expanding nuclear debris and reach the fusion fuel first.

The cylindrical shape of most hydrogen weapons plays an important role in determining how this radiant energy will be distributed inside the casing. The primary system is located inside one end of a three- or four-foot-long hollow cylinder casing, and the fusion fuel is located inside the other end. The cylinder is normally eighteen inches in diameter, large enough to contain the soccer-ball sized primary system inside one end and leave a few inches to spare around the sides. A complete one-megaton bomb (having the explosive power of one million tons of TNT) would fit under your bed.

The cylindrical casing is more than just the package that holds the nuclear parts together. It is also a radiation reflector designed to capture radiation

from the primary system and focus it on the fusion fuel. It is the largest and heaviest component of any hydrogen weapon, and one of the most important.

The reflector-casing is usually made of uranium-238, a heavy, shiny, metal called "depleted uranium." In the last stage of the weapon's detonation sequence, the depleted uranium explodes with the power of many Hiroshima bombs, producing most of the weapon's deadly fallout. However, the first function of uranium-238 in the secondary system is to serve not as an energy source but as a finely engineered energy reflector.

All the major components of the secondary system are made by Union Carbide, the chemical company, in the foothills of the Great Smoky Mountains of Tennessee. The 500-acre bomb factory where the work is done still bears the code name, Y-12, assigned it by the World War II designers of the atomic bomb. The Oak Ridge buildings where scientists enriched uranium for the Hiroshima weapon now house the world's most sophisticated H-bomb production line. When an American hydrogen weapon explodes, most of the explosive power comes from components made at Y-12. Half the equipment in the country's far-flung nuclear weapon production complex is concentrated there.

Few residents of Oak Ridge and nearby Knoxville are aware that such products come from their peaceful valley. A chemistry professor who occasionally lectures at Y-12 told me he didn't know what went on at the plant; he sometimes wondered, but he didn't think it was the production of bombs. A woman whose husband is an Oak Ridge radiologist expressed outright disbelief that Oak Ridge was still in the weapons business. And yet the weapons role of the plant is not secret; it just isn't mentioned in public.

Much of the H-bomb secret is in a form that can't be written down. It exists in the hand-and-eye coordination of the skilled workers who operate machine tools at the Y-12 plant, or in the quality of the machines themselves. One of the high-precision tasks is the squeezing of large blocks of

uranium-238 metal into thin sheets and the machining of those sheets to make radiation reflectors.

The raw material for this process arrives by truck or rail from Fernald, Ohio, where gaseous uranium-238 hexafluoride has been chemically reduced to pure metal blocks. At Y-12, the blocks are fed like cordwood to a giant rolling press which flattens them into sheets five-and-a-half feet wide and one inch thick. The sheets are then fed through smaller presses which reduce their thickness to as little as five-thousandths of an inch. When a sheet has reached the proper thinness, the weapon part is cut from it the way cookies are cut from a sheet of dough. The rough-cut parts are then machined to final dimensions.

A graduate student at the University of Alabama, who knows people who work in Oak Ridge, told me the reflector-casing is composed of thousands of finely machined reflecting surfaces. Jack Case, Union Carbide's manager for the plant, says some parts made at Y-12 are so thin and delicate that special techniques for "fixturing," or attaching rough-cut parts to a lathe, had to be developed. Normal fixturing techniques would mar the parts or allow them to sag and be distorted by their own weight. Y-12 pioneered in the use of chemical adhesives and suction in fixturing. The reflector-casing may be composed of many thin pieces of uranium-238 sandwiched together into an exotic metal plywood.

Radiation reflectors for the H-bomb arsenal enter the Oak Ridge Y-12 plant as great blocks of uranium-238 metal and emerge as finely engineered canisters the size of household garbage cans. When war comes, the canisters will reflect and focus the radiation that sets off hydrogen fusion.

Fusion is called a thermonuclear process because heat makes it happen. Temperatures of several hundred million degrees Celsius are needed to start the process. However, the *rate* of fusion is determined by the *density* of the hydrogen fuel. In a weapon, the rate of fusion must be extremely rapid. For a useful amount of fusion fuel to fuse in the allotted millionth of a second, it must first be greatly compressed. Without tremendous compression, the fusion fuel would not fuse fast enough to add much energy to the explosion before it was scattered uselessly by the expanding fireball of the primary system. In a hydrogen weapon, radiation pressure is what compresses the fusion fuel sufficiently to make the device destroy a city's suburbs as well as its center.

Radiation pressure, the principle by which the secondary system works, is normally too weak to be detected by human senses. You cannot feel the physical push of a flashlight beam, for instance. There are no examples in the human environment of radiation intense enough to move solid objects with more than barely measurable force. But the primary system of a hydrogen weapon is a nuclear power plant that generates twenty million kilowatthours' worth of thermal energy in a few billionths of a second, all inside a lump of metal compressed to the size of a baseball. Its radiant energy can exert enormous force on an object located only inches away.

In fact, the radiation pressure inside the weapon casing can theoretically be as high as a million million times greater than atmospheric pressure — about eight billion tons per square inch. Physicists would describe the radiation as a "gas of photons," a dense cloud of highly energetic pulses of electromagnetic energy, pushing violently against anything it touches. For the briefest moment, the inside of the weapon becomes an x-ray oven, similar in principle to a microwave oven, but with unearthly temperatures and pressures.

As any science student can tell you, heat is the enemy of compression. The greatest densities are achieved when a substance is compressed cold: Heat tends to make it expand. Because fusion fuel in a weapon must therefore be compressed *before* it reaches ignition temperature, the fusion fuel of the secondary system is not exposed directly to radiation from the primary system. It is protected on the end nearest the primary system by a large radiation shield.

Around the sides of the fusion fuel is a tapered cylinder called the fusion tamper. Radiation from the exploding fission trigger is reflected around the large shield, or pusher, in the center of

the weapon and onto the sides of the fusion tamper. The fusion tamper then collapses inward with enormous force, driven by the pressure of x- and gamma radiation from the primary system. The fusion tamper compresses the fusion fuel and simultaneously heats its perimeter to ignition temperatures.

An important part of nuclear weapon design is the judicious use of empty spaces inside the weapon. The empty space between a raised hammer and a nail allows the hammer to strike the nail with much greater force than could be mustered if the hammer were

pressing the fuel; the empty space between the fusion tamper and the fuel is used to produce maximum compression. In addition, the delicate ceramiclike fusion fuel must be firmly cradled and supported from all sides during the weapon's possibly rough ride to the target.

A key ingredient in the design of this aspect of the secondary system is the polystyrene foam that keeps the fusion fuel centered inside the fusion tamper. By holding the fuel and the tamper apart, the foam allows the tamper to develop momentum before it strikes

'Continued...testing...is a paradox unless you know the secret'

placed against the nailhead before pressure was applied. In a hydrogen weapon, the fusion tamper serves as a hammer that strikes the fusion fuel simultaneously from all sides, com-

the fusion fuel. Polystyrene foam is thus both a packaging material and an empty space, protecting the hydrogen fuel during weapon delivery and collapsing into nothing during detonation.

The price of secrecy

Ten years ago the Pentagon appointed a nine-member "Task Force on Secrecy" to investigate the effectiveness of the nation's security system. This was one of its findings:

"With respect to technical information, it is understandable that our society would turn to secrecy in an attempt to optimize the advantage to national security that may be gained from new discoveries or innovations associated with science and engineering.

"However, it must be recognized, first, that certain kinds of technical information are easily discovered independently, or regenerated, once a reasonably sophisticated group decides it is worthwhile to do so.

"In spite of elaborate and very

costly measures taken independently by the U.S. and the U.S.S.R. to preserve technical secrecy, neither the United Kingdom nor China was long delayed in developing hydrogen weapons.

"Also, classification of technical information impedes its flow within our own system, and may easily do far more harm than good by stifling critical discussion and review or by engendering frustration. There are many cases in which the declassification of technical information within our system probably had a beneficial effect and its classification has had a deleterious one."

One of the task force members was Dr. Edward Teller, father of the U.S. hydrogen bomb.

The foam is made in Kansas City, Missouri, by the Bendix Corporation, in a factory that manufactures most of the non-nuclear parts for nuclear warheads and bombs.

Only the heavier isotopes of hydrogen serve as fuel in a hydrogen weapon. Hydrogen-2 and hydrogen-3, known respectively as deuterium and tritium, are the fuel which explodes with the force of many trainloads of TNT. Tritium is expensive and highly radioactive. For practical reasons, most of the tritium is stored in the weapon as lithium-6, a less expensive, non-radioactive material which is converted instantly to tritium once the fusion process begins. Conveniently, lithium-6 bonds chemically with deuterium to make a gray powder, called lithium-6 deuteride, that is much easier to manage than either pure deuterium or tritium in gaseous form, although it must be kept dry.

The fusion fuel in a hydrogen weapon, except for a small amount containing tritium, is made at the Oak Ridge Y-12 plant. Metallic lithium-6 is chemically bonded with deuterium, obtained from the Department of Energy's Savannah River plant (operated by DuPont), and compacted into a chalk-like solid, resembling a large aspirin tablet in consistency. The pressed powder is then baked and machined to final dimensions. The result is a ceramic material so unstable chemically in the presence of moisture that it must be assembled in "dry rooms."

Dry-room workers in the Y-12 plant wear air-conditioned waterproof body suits with sealed fish-bowl helmets to keep their body moisture from causing the lithium-6 deuteride to decompose spontaneously. When viewed through the windows of their dry rooms, they look like astronauts on a training exercise.

When the charge of lithium-6 deuteride for a single weapon is assembled, it makes a column one or two feet high and several inches in diameter. It is tapered to fit inside the fusion tamper the way the core of a carrot fits inside the carrot.

When this charge of fusion fuel is struck simultaneously on all sides by the imploding fusion tamper, it is compressed and heated. Fusion begins in the perimeter where some tritium is present. The lithium-6 is converted to tritium throughout the charge, while the exploding perimeter further compresses the center and the bulk of the fusion fuel fuses and explodes.

The third and final stage in the explosion of the weapon is virtually an afterthought. In fact, it is optional, although in most hydrogen weapons it is a highly desired option — it provides roughly half the total energy release of the weapon and most of the fallout. In this third stage, the uranium-238 casing which was used to capture and focus the radiation undergoes fission as a result of bombardment by the high-energy neutrons released by the second-stage fusion process.

The result can be an explosion a thousand times more powerful than the blast that destroyed Hiroshima.

Do we need to possess this technical information? Yes. Without it, there is little hope of understanding the vast industrial complex that turns out three new nuclear weapons a day. The only book about modern nuclear weapon production, *The Great American Bomb Machine,* written eight years ago by Roger Rapoport, illustrates the point. Because of an inadequate understanding of thermonuclear weapon technology, Rapoport completely overlooked the Oak Ridge Y-12 plant, the most important factory in the system. The significance of the role of Union Carbide and the Energy Department's Oak Ridge Operations Office cannot be explained without knowledge of the importance of lithium-6 deuteride and uranium-238 to nuclear weapons manufacture. Understanding the system's product is necessary to understanding the system.

Another example:

Continued nuclear testing underground in Nevada is a paradox unless you know the secret. Underground nuclear explosions are never higher in yield than a few kilotons, despite unofficial acknowledgement that our latest strategic nuclear weapons are in the 100 to 500 kiloton range. The widespread belief that the weapon makers are testing only the primary systems, or triggers, is incorrect.

The primary system can be tested without an actual nuclear detonation. The fissile material, plutonium-239 and uranium-235, can be replaced with electronic sensing devices, and the high-explosive charges detonated. Instrument readings and high-speed photographs tell the designers most of what they need to know about the primary system. Such tests are conducted frequently, above ground, at the nuclear weapons laboratories in Los Alamos, New Mexico, and Livermore, California. The explosion is about as powerful as that of an ordinary mortar shell (but far more dangerous, because it scatters a cloud of uranium-238 and beryllium dust).

The secondary system, on the other hand, cannot be tested without the intense radiation that comes only from an exploding fission weapon. The primary system must actually be detonated with a nuclear yield in order for the secondary system to be tested. The fusion fuel in the secondary system can be replaced with electronic sensing devices. The second and third stages of the explosion need not occur, but the primary system must explode in all its fury if useful information is to be had about the rest of the weapon. Hence the weapon makers' compulsion for underground testing.

As refinements in radiation reflector

'People who make the weapons enjoy talking shop'

design have allowed more of the energy of the primary system to be captured and focused, smaller fission explosions have become adequate as triggering events. One result of fifteen years of underground tests is a reflector that will set off half a kiloton of secondary fusion explosion with as little as half a kiloton of fission energy. Enter the neutron bomb. The neutron bomb radiation reflector has to be made of high-density metal other than uranium-238, so there will be no dirty fission explosion following the fusion. The metal is probably tungsten alloyed with nickel, iron, and, perhaps, rhenium. Underground testing was part of its design procedure.

Unofficial sources say that a neutron weapon with a total energy yield of one kiloton, one-twentieth of the Nagasaki weapon, must contain more radioactive tritium than a full megaton weapon of more conventional design. The reason is that the deliberately weak neutron weapon is unable to generate much of its own tritium; more of it must be provided ready-made. Since the country's only supplier of tritium is also the sole present supplier of plutonium-239, an increase in orders for tritium is one plausible explanation for the plutonium shortage about which Congressman Dellums inquired.

How could I, a journalist with no formal training in nuclear physics, learn things the Government has kept out of public print for a quarter of a century? It was surprisingly easy. People who make these weapons enjoy their work. Like most of us, they enjoy talking shop. They also promote their activities in order to raise funds from Congress and to recruit employes. They learn to talk and write without using classified words, but they can't live in a vacuum. In fact, any persistent investigator with the time, inclination, and determination to learn the underlying scientific and technological principles, to pierce the jargon and euphemisms of the industry, to examine the voluminous public record, to look and listen carefully, and to put two and two together, can discover the findings and inventions of others.

In the business of nuclear weaponry, as in science and technology itself, no

secret, once discovered, can long endure, as Einstein observed. Attempts to limit knowledge may succeed temporarily, but ultimately they are no match for a determined investigator.

The more practical effect of secrecy is to discourage and inhibit public participation in the formulation of public policy — in this case not only nuclear weapons policy but also a broad spectrum of related policies (national security, energy, environmental protection, natural and human resource allocation) with which it is inextricably intertwined.

secret, once discovered, can long endure, as Einstein observed. Attempts to limit knowledge may succeed temporarily, but ultimately they are no match for a determined investigator.

of nuclear fission bombs became available long ago in the Smyth Report. Subsequent Atomic Energy Commission declassifications and the accumulation of mountains of data and experience with the growth of the worldwide nuclear enterprise have eliminated the secret of fission bomb construction. Credible designs and instructions for these have been prepared by college-level physics students.

The building of a hydrogen bomb, which can be ignited only by a fission weapon, is a different matter. It would take millions of dollars worth of spe-

'The effect [of secrecy] is to stifle debate about...nuclear policy'

Since World War II, the process of secrecy — the readiness to invoke "national security" — has been a pillar of the nuclear establishment. As Representative Dellums's recent experience demonstrates, that establishment, acting on the false assumption that "secrets" can be hidden from the curious and knowledgeable, has successfully insisted that there are answers which cannot be given and even questions which cannot be asked.

The net effect is to stifle debate about the fundamentals of nuclear policy. Concerned citizens dare not ask certain questions, and many begin to feel that these are matters which only a few initiated experts are entitled to discuss. This self-imposed restraint only entrenches further those who are committed to the nuclear arms race.

The secret of how a hydrogen bomb is made protects a more fundamental "secret": the mechanism by which the resources of the most powerful nation on Earth have been marshaled for global catastrophe. Knowing *how* may be the key to asking *why*.

Is it dangerous to tell how a hydrogen bomb is made? No. For one thing, the information falls far short of providing a blueprint for nuclear weapon construction. The general features

cialized equipment and hundreds of trained technicians to build a hydrogen bomb — a feat beyond the capability of all but the most industrially sophisticated nations.

Whatever insights these descriptions may provide to nations seeking to perfect their thermonuclear capability — Israel and South Africa, for example — they are at best a trifling addition to the information already available. No government intent upon joining the nuclear terror club need long be at a loss to know how to proceed. Nothing you or I could learn would long elude the nuclear physicists and engineers whose participation would be essential to such as enterprise.

The risks of proliferation of hydrogen weapons, such as they are, must be weighed against the public gain that may come from greater awareness of how and why they are already being produced.

Whether it be the details of a multimillion dollar plutonium production expansion program or the principles and procedures by which nature's most explosive force is being packaged in our midst, we have less to fear from knowing than from not knowing. What we do with the knowledge may be the key to our survival. ∎

Errata

Pressure *generated* by radiation — not the direct force of radiation pressure — is the key to the design of the hydrogen bomb. That somewhat esoteric distinction has apparently been the focal point of *in camera* hearings and court filings in the case of *The United States* vs. *The Progressive,* the prior restraint case that delayed publication of my article, "The H-Bomb Secret," for more than six months.

In my description last month of how the H-bomb works, I stated that the physical pressure of radiation reflected off the inside wall of the bomb casing compresses the fusion fuel package directly. That statement omits an important intermediate step: X-rays from the fission bomb that serves as the H-bomb trigger are absorbed by an exotic, high density polystyrene-type foam. The foam is transformed into a highly energized plasma which explodes and compresses the fusion fuel package.

Exploding styrofoam is thus an important element in the H-bomb detonation sequence which is entirely missing from my account. My account incorrectly attributes the compression effect to radiation pressure.

In the diagrams accompanying my article, I showed an empty space between the carrot-shaped fusion fuel package and the bomb casing that surrounds it. That empty space should be filled with hard foam material that explodes when it absorbs x-rays, as shown here.

This information was released for public filing on September 24, when a Government brief authorized the restoration of certain passages that had been previously deleted from the public version of the August 31 brief of defendants Erwin Knoll, Samuel H. Day Jr., and myself.

The pertinent passages, on Page 47, are as follows: "Essentially, the x-rays produce a plasma of energized matter which pushes on the fusion fuel tamper in much the same way that boiling water produces steam which pushes on the blades of a turbine. But Morland's discussion of the role of radiation coupling in the compression of fusion fuel is as inaccurate as if he said that boiling water turns the blades of a turbine — he leaves out the steam.... Morland's discussion of the role of radiation pressure is entirely incorrect...."

Even though the quotation is from the defendants' own legal brief, none of the defendants had seen that statement before September 24. A wall of secrecy separates the defendants and their attorneys. The defendants' attorneys were obliged to obtain security clearances in order to read the secret documents the Government was showing to the judge. The defendants refused to apply for security clearances on the grounds that a security clearance is a secrecy agreement which would interfere with the defendants' ability to write about nuclear matters in the future. Thus the defendants have been informed of such discussions about the technical deficiencies of the article only after the censor has approved.

The Government had no obligation to show any secret documents to the judge. The introduction into the court record of technical information that

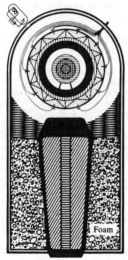

(© 1979, Howard Morland)

was not included in my article was initiated by the Government for reasons that are still not clear. It seriously hampered the defense, which may have been part of the reason it was done, and it ultimately resulted in the disclosure of more information that the Government is supposedly trying to keep secret.

In addition to the matter of exploding styrofoam, there are probably technical errors in my description of the fusion fuel capsule of the secondary system. It probably does not contain any tritium, but it probably does contain, at the center, a one- or two-inch diameter rod of highly enriched uranium or plutonium running its length. That rod of fissionable material is compressed to supercriticality as the fusion fuel capsule surrounding it is compressed in on it by the exploding styrofoam. It then becomes the second A-bomb trigger which is often mentioned but incorrectly described. It heats the fusion fuel capsule from the inside while the styrofoam compresses it from the outside. The Uranium-238 which contributes up to 90 per cent of the total explosive energy of the bomb is probably not located in the bomb casing, but rather is probably confined to the casing of the fusion fuel capsule, where its fission by high energy neutrons can further add to the heat and pressure which promote fusion.

Finally, the fusion fuel inside the plutonium core of the primary system is probably a mixture of tritium and deuterium gas under high pressure.

The whole affair illustrates that the secrecy provisions of the Atomic Energy Act are unenforceable, in addition to being an unwarranted interference with the First Amendment rights to unfettered public discourse. When the Government tries to suppress discussion of information that is in the public domain, at the very least it must confirm the accuracy of the information it is trying to suppress. Furthermore, if this case is typical, the Government will eventually reveal publicly more of its "secrets" than are already out if it attempts to take private citizens to court in order to silence them.

Howard Morland

Appendix B
The Glenn Letter

[Text of letter dated April 25, 1979, to Senator John Glenn]

The Government has released classified information that identifies the nature of the design concept upon which U.S. thermonuclear weapons are based. The release occurred in the course of a legal proceeding to prevent publication of an article by Howard Morland about the H-bomb in the Progressive magazine. We ask for a Congressional investigation into why the Government has released classified information it claims to be trying to protect.

The U.S. Government has alleged that publication of Morland's article would breach national security because it assembles certain facts about thermonuclear weapons that the Government regards as Secret/Restricted. During the course of the litigation, and in spite of efforts to alert the Government, several potentially sensitive affidavits were made public. The documents released by the Government collectively identify the design concept on which U.S. thermonuclear weapons are based, and reveal that this design concept is far superior to all other known configurations. It is now clear that the Government's management of this information has resulted in a breach of its own security.

The Government's position is that information in the Morland article could significantly decrease the development time and effort necessary for a non-thermonuclear country to achieve thermonuclear status. The utility of this information, according to the Government's arguments, follows from the historical experience of the U.S. thermonuclear weapons program. In view of the large amount of relevant scientific information currently available, we doubt the correctness of the Government's argument. However, we will describe that argument in order to provide a framework for the discussion that follows.

The successful detonation of any thermonuclear weapon, the argument goes, requires that a variety of competing processes be delicately balanced under physical conditions that are extreme even compared with those found at the center of the sun. There are many design ideas and concepts that can be aimed at achieving this delicate balance. Determining which of these design concepts work, how easy they are to implement, and how efficient they are relative to each other is a major activity in any weapons program. Since each design idea might itself require an enormous industrial and scientific effort, an identification of which design concept should be most favored could dramatically reduce the amount of redundant effort necessary to achieve a militarily useful weapon.

In the context of that argument, consider the current situation. In Edward Teller's 1976 Encyclopedia Americana article on the H-Bomb, a possible solution as to how a fission trigger and fusion materials might be arranged relative to each other within the casing of a thermonuclear weapon is outlined in a diagram. In an affidavit submitted amici curiae by Marsh, Stanford and DeVolpi to a federal court through the A.C.L.U., this configuration was identified as conceptually similar to a diagram which the Government wants to suppress in the Morland article. Teller's peculiar geometrical arrangement of separated elements requires that the weapon casing play an essential role in achieving thermonuclear ignition in a high-yield device, and is unique among possible design concepts.

A further significant piece of information was released through a two-part affidavit submitted by T.A. Postol. He attempted, in the second part of his affidavit, to demonstrate how certain concepts discussed in the Morland article would follow from principles of elementary physics and pieces of public information. As the Government wants to suppress this reasoning, the second part of the Postol affidavit was classified. Both the classified and

256

unclassified parts were accompanied by a detailed list of references which included specific page numbers to these concepts. The Government refused to delete these page numbers from the unclassified affidavit, in spite of the fact that the inclusion of the page numbers was called to their attention.

In an alarmingly detailed affidavit solicited by the Government from Jack Rosengren, it is stated that Morland's diagram (and hence Edward Teller's diagram through the unclassified Marsh, Stanford, DeVolpi affidavit) reveals "the nature of the particular design used in the thermonuclear weapons in the U.S. stockpile," and further declared this configuration to be "the basic design concept(s)" on which U.S. thermonuclear weapons are based. This affidavit was made available to the media. The Rosengren affidavit further identifies this design concept as one that is particularly practical in that it is easier (relative to other configurations) to implement successfully and is far more efficient than any other known type of design. The general correctness of the Morland article is further confirmed by the deposition of Harold Brown, which was also placed in the public domain. It is inexplicable that these affidavits were not classified, if one accepts the Government's arguments as to the sensitivity of the contents of the Morland article.

The nature of the design concept on which U.S. thermonuclear weapons are based, and the efficiency of this design concept relative to others, appear to have been closely guarded secrets. Although we regard much of this information as already in the public domain, the consistent protection of this information by the Government would have dictated that the Teller diagram never be published, the Marsh, Stanford, DeVolpi reference to that diagram be classified, Postol's references be classified, and no statements that either draw attention to, or rule out, any thermonuclear design concept be allowed.

Thus it seems that those entrusted with handling classified information associated with this court case have already released much of the information that the suit was brought to protect. Further, even if the Morland article is not eventually published, the bootleg copies that will inevitably get into circulation (some already having reached Australia) now have their credibility certified by Government imprimatur.

Another particularly disturbing aspect of the Government's handling of this information pertains to the possible use of classification and declassification for political purposes. The Government's confirmation of the general accuracy of te Morland article might be a conscious attempt to influence the outcome of the case by increasing the apparent sensitivity of Morland's information in hopes of establishing a legal precedent for prior restraint. Such use of the classification process for political purposes is not in the national interest. The United States is currently facing a wide range of policy decisions associated with the use of technology with respect to foreign countries. Among these are issues of technology transfer, strategic arms limitation, proliferation of fission weapons, and a comprehensive test ban treaty. The power to selectively classify documents that contain information that is, and properly should be, in the public domain, is an effective tool for influencing policy discussion and public opinion.

A timely example of the influence that selective declassification has had on public policy pertains to the status of the S.A.L.T. treaty. Until six months ago, State Department spokesmen were not permitted to validate that national technical means of verification included satellite photoreconnaissance, yet alone to discuss well known and readily appreciated features of such systems. (While it may be true that such information is readily available to technically knowledgeable individuals, it is not available to the general public, who must ultimately make judgements about S.A.L.T. through their legislators.) It is not surprising that the public wants a S.A.L.T. treaty but is afraid to support it when Government officials are unable to explain how it will be enforced.

If individuals are allowed to selectively classify and declassify information for the purpose of influencing public policy debate, it should be recognized that they are being given power to deprive the American people of information they need to intelligently chart their future. While governments obviously have legitimate classification needs, it is imperative that these powers be used responsibly or we risk destroying the democratic society we wish to preserve.

The resolution of the conflict between the Progressive and the U.S. Government is clearly a judicial matter; however, the inept or improper handling of sensitive information by servants of the American people is a matter that transcends the concerns of a legal conflict. We believe that this deplorable mishandling or misuse of secured information should be investigated at a Congressional level.

All of the signatories have read an early version of the Progressive article and have filed affidavits with the court. We are all members of the professional staff at Argonne National Laboratory; however, this letter has no official connection with the Laboratory, with the University of Chicago, nor with the U.S. Department of Energy.
[Signed by Theodore A. Postol, Gerald E. Marsh, George S. Stanford, and Alexander DeVolpi]

Appendix C
Selected Passages from the Atomic Energy Act

(REVISED, 1954: 42 U.S.C)

§ 2011. Atomic energy is capable of application for peaceful as well as military purposes. It is therefore declared to be the policy of the United States that --
(a) the development, use, and control of atomic energy shall be directed so as to make the maximum contribution to the general welfare, subject at all times to the paramount objective of making the maximum contribution to the common defense and security; and
(b) the development, use, and control of atomic energy shall be directed so as to promote world peace, improve the general welfare, increase the standard of living, and strengthen free competition in private enterprise.

§ 2012. The Congress of the United States makes the following findings concerning the development, use, and control of atomic energy:
(a) The development, utilization, and control of atomic energy for military and for all other purposes are vital to the common defense and security.
(c) The processing and utilization of source, byproduct, and special nuclear material affect interstate and foreign commerce and must be regulated in the national interest.
(d) The processing and utilization of source, byproduct, and special nuclear material must be regulated in the national interest and in order to provide the common defense and security and to protect the health and safety of the public.
(e) Source and special nuclear material, production facilities, and utilization facilities are affected with the public interest, and regulation by the United States of the production and utilization of atomic energy and of the facilities used in connection therewith is necessary in the national interest to assure the common defense and security and to protect the health and safety of the public.
(f) The necessity for protection against possible interstate damage occurring from the operation of facilities for the production or utilization of source or special nuclear material places the operation of those facilities in interstate commerce for the purposes of this chapter.
(g) Funds of the United States may be provided for the development and use of atomic energy under conditions which will provide for the common defense and security and promote the general welfare.
(i) In order to protect the public and to encourage the development of the atomic energy industry, in the interest of the general welfare and of the common defense and security, the United States may make funds available for a portion of the damages suffered by the public from nuclear incidents, and may limit the liability of those persons liable for such losses.

§ 2013. It is the purpose of this chapter to effectuate the policies set forth above by providing for --
(a) a program of conducting, assisting, and fostering research and development in order to encourage maximum scientific and industrial progress;
(b) a program for the dissemination of unclassified scientific and technical information and for the control, dissemination, and declassification of Restricted Data, subject to appropriate safeguards, so as to encourage scientific and industrial progress;

(c) a program for Government control of the possession, use, and production of atomic energy and special nuclear material, whether owned by the Government or others, so directed as to make the maximum contribution to the common defense and security and the national welfare, and to provide continued assurance of the Government's ability to enter into and enforce agreements with nations or groups of nations for the control of special nuclear materials and atomic weapons;

(d) a program to encourage widespread participation in the development and utilization of atomic energy for peaceful purposes to the maximum extent consistent with the common defense and security and with the health and safety of the public;

(e) a program of international cooperation to promote the common defense and security and to make available to cooperating nations the benefits of peaceful applications of atomic energy as widely as expanding technology and considerations of the common defense and security will permit; and

(f) a program of administration which will be consistent with the foregoing policies and programs, with international arrangements, and with agreements for cooperation, which will enable the Congress to be currently informed so as to take further legislative action as may be appropriate.

§ 2014. The intent of Congress in the definitions as given in this section should be construed from the words or phrases used in the definitions. As used in this chapter:

(c) The term "atomic energy" means all forms of energy released in the course of nuclear fission or nuclear transformation.

(d) The term "atomic weapon" means any device utilizing atomic energy, exclusive of the means for transporting or propelling the device (where such means is a separable and divisible part of the device), the principal purpose of which is for use as, or for development of, a weapon, a weapon prototype, or a weapon test device.

(g) The term "common defense and security" means the common defense and security of the United States.

(h) The term "defense information" means any information in any category determined by any Government agency authorized to classify information, as being information respecting, relating to, or affecting the national defense.

(i) The term "design" means (1) specifications, plans, drawings, blueprints, and other items of like nature; (2) the information contained therein; or (3) the research and development data pertinent to the information contained therein.

(y) The term "Restricted Data" means all data concerning (1) design, manufacture, or utilization of atomic weapons; (2) the production of special nuclear material; or (3) the use of special nuclear material in the production of energy, but shall not include data declassified or removed from the Restricted Data category pursuant to section 2162 of this title.

(aa) The term "special nuclear material" is defined by §2014(aa) as follows:
(1) plutonium, uranium enriched in the isotope 233 or in the isotope 235, and any other material which the Commission, pursuant to the provisions of section 2071 of this title, determines to be special nuclear material, but does not include source material; or (2) any material artificially enriched by any of the foregoing, but does not include source material.

§ 2161. It shall be the policy of the Commission to control the dissemination and declassification of Restricted Data in such a manner as to assure the common defense and security. Consistent with such policy, the Commission shall be guided by the following principles:

(a) Until effective and enforceable international safeguards against the use of atomic energy for destructive purposes have been established by an international arrangement, there shall be no exchange of Restricted Data with other nations except as authorized by section 2164 of this title; and

(b) The dissemination of scientific and technical information relating to atomic energy should be permitted and encouraged so as to provide that free interchange of ideas and criticism which is essential to scientific and industrial progress and public understanding and to enlarge the fund of technical information.

§ 2162. (a) The Commission shall from time to time determine the data, within the definition of Restricted Data, which can be published without undue risk to the common defense and security and shall thereupon cause such data to be declassified and removed from the category of Restricted Data.

(b) The Commission shall maintain a continuous review of Restricted Data and of any Classification Guides issued for the guidance of those in the atomic energy program with respect to the areas of Restricted Data which have been declassified in order to determine which information may be declassified and removed from the category of Restricted Data without undue risk to the common defense and security.

(c) In the case of Restricted Data which the Commission and the Department of Defense jointly determine to relate primarily to the military utilization of atomic weapons, the determination that such data may be published without constituting an unreasonable risk to the common defense and security shall be made by the Commission and the Department of Defense jointly, and if the Commission and the Department of Defense do not agree, the determination shall be made by the President.

(d) The Commission shall remove from the Restricted Data category such data as the Commission and the Department of Defense jointly determine relates primarily to the military utilization of atomic weapons and which the Commission and Department of Defense jointly determine can be adequately safeguarded as defense information: Provided, however, That no such data so removed from the Restricted Data category shall be transmitted or otherwise made available to any nation or regional defense organization, while such data remains defense information, except pursuant to an agreement for cooperation entered into in accordance with section 2164(b) of this title.

(e) The Commission shall remove from the Restricted Data category such information concerning the atomic energy programs of other nations as the Commission and the Director of Central Intelligence jointly determine to be necessary to carry out the provisions of section 403(d) of Title 50 and can be adequately safeguarded as defense information.

§ 2164. (a) The President may authorize the Commission to cooperate with another nation and to communicate to that nation Restricted Data on -- (1) refining, purification, and subsequent treatment of source material; (2) civilian reactor development; (3) production of special nuclear material; (4) health and safety; (5) industrial and other applications of atomic energy for peaceful purposes; and (6) research and development relating to the foregoing:

Provided, however, That no such cooperation shall involve the communication of Restricted Data relating to the design or fabrication of atomic weapons: And provided further, That the cooperation is undertaken pursuant to an agreement for cooperation entered into in accordance with section 2153 of this title, or is undertaken pursuant to an agreement existing on August 30, 1954.

(b) The President may authorize the Department of Defense, with the assistance of the Commission, to cooperate with another nation or with a regional defense organization to which the United States is a party, and to communicate to that nation or organization such Restricted Data (including design information) as is necessary to -- (1) the development of defense plans; (2) the training of personnel in the employment of and defense against atomic weapons and other military applications of atomic energy; (3) the evaluation of the capabilities of potential enemies in the employment of atomic weapons and other military applications of atomic energy; and (4) the development of compatible delivery systems for atomic weapons....

(c) In addition to the cooperation authorized in subsections (a) and (b) of this section, the President may authorize the Commission, with the assistance of the Department of Defense, to cooperate with another nation and -- (1) to exchange with that nation Restricted Data concerning atomic weapons: Provided, That communication of such Restricted Data to that nation is necessary to improve its atomic weapon design, development, or fabrication capability and provided that nation has made substantial progress in the development of atomic weapons; and (2) to communicate or exchange with that nation Restricted Data concerning research, development, or design, of military reactors....

(d) The President may authorize any agency of the United States to communicate in accordance with the terms and conditions of an agreement for cooperation arranged pursuant to subsection (a), (b), or (c) of this section, such Restricted Data as is determined to be transmissible under the agreement for cooperation involved.

§ 2274. Whoever, lawfully or unlawfully, having possession of, access to, control over, or being entrusted with any document, writing, sketch, photograph, plan, model, instrument, appliance, note, or information involving or incorporating Restricted Data—

(a) communicates, transmits, or discloses the same to any individual or person, or attempts or conspires to do any of the foregoing, with intent to injure the United States or with intent to secure an advantage to any foreign nation, upon conviction thereof, shall be punished by imprisonment for life, or by imprisonment for any term of years or a fine of not more than $20,000 or both;

(b) communicates, transmits, or discloses the same to any individual or person, or attempts or conspires to do any of the foregoing, with reason to believe such data will be utilized to injure the United States or to secure an advantage to any foreign nation, shall, upon conviction be punished by a fine of not more than $10,000 or imprisonment for not more than ten years, or both.

§ 2275. Whoever, with intent to injure the United States or with intent to secure an advantage to any foreign nation, acquires, or attempts or conspires to acquire any document, writing, sketch, photograph, plan, model, instrument, appliance, note, or information involving or incorporating Restricted Data shall, upon conviction thereof be punished by imprisonment for life, or by imprisonment for any term of years or a fine of not more than $20,000 or both.

§ 2276. Whoever, with intent to injure the United States or with intent to secure an advantage to any foreign nation, removes, conceals, tampers with, alters, mutilates, or destroys any document, writing, sketch, photograph, plan, model, instrument, appliance, or note involving or incorporating Restricted Data and used by any individual or person in connection with the production of special nuclear material, or research or development relating to atomic energy, conducted by the United States, or financed in whole or in part by Federal funds, or conducted with the aid of special nuclear material, shall be punished by imprisonment for life, or by imprisonment for any term of years or a fine of not more than $20,000 or both.

§ 2277. Whoever, being or having been an employee or member of the Commission, a member of the Armed Forces, an employee of any agency of the United States, or being or having been a contractor of the Commission or of an agency of the United States, or being or having been an employee of a contractor of the Commission or of an agency of the United States, or being or having been a licensee of the Commission, or being or having been an employee of a licensee of the Commission, knowingly communicates, or whoever conspires to communicate or to receive, any Restricted Data, knowing or having reason to believe that such data is Restricted Data, to any person not authorized to receive Restricted Data pursuant to the provision of this chapter or under rule or regulation of the Commission issued pursuant thereto, knowing or having reason to believe such person is not so authorized to receive Restricted Data shall, upon conviction thereof, be punishable by a fine of not more than $2,500.

§ 2278. Except for a capital offense, no individual or person shall be prosecuted, tried, or punished for any offense prescribed or defined in sections 2274 to 2276 of this title unless the indictment is found or the information is instituted within ten years next after such offense shall have been committed.

§ 2280. Whenever in the judgment of the Commission any person has engaged or is about to engage in any acts or practices which constitute or will constitute a violation of any provision of this chapter, or any regulation or order issued thereunder, the Attorney General on behalf of the United States may make application to the appropriate court for an order enjoining such acts or practices, or for an order enforcing compliance with such provision, and upon a showing by the Commission that such person as engaged or is about to engage in any such acts or practices, a permanent or temporary injunction, restraining order, or other may be granted.

Appendix D
Executive Order On
National Security Information

1-101. Except as provided in the Atomic Energy Act of 1954, as amended, this Order provides the only basis for classifying information. Information may be classified in one of the three designations listed below. If there is reasonable doubt which designation is appropriate, or whether the information should be classified at all, the less restrictive designation should be used, or the information should not be classified.

1-102. 'Top Secret' shall be applied only to information, the unauthorized disclosure of which reasonably could be expected to cause exceptionally grave damage to the national security.

1-103. 'Secret' shall be applied only to information, the unauthorized disclosure of which reasonably could be expected to cause serious damage to the national security.

1-104. 'Confidential' shall be applied to information, the unauthorized disclosure of which reasonably could be expected to cause identifiable damage to the national security.

1-201. Top Secret. Authority for original classification of information as Top Secret may be exercised only by the President, by such officials as the President may designate by publication in the Federal Register, by the agency heads listed below, and by officials to whom such authority is delegated in accordance with Section 1-204:

The Secretary of State
The Secretary of the Treasury
The Secretary of Defense
The Secretary of the Army
The Secretary of the Navy
The Secretary of the Air Force
The Attorney General
The Secretary of Energy
The Chairman, Nuclear Regulatory Commission
The Director, Arms Control and Disarmament Agency
The Director of Central Intelligence
The Administrator, National Aeronautics and Space Administration
The Administrator of General Services (delegable only to the Director,
  Federal Preparedness Agency and to the Director, Information Security
  Oversight Office)

1-202. Secret. Authority for original classification of information as Secret may be exercised only by such officials as the President may designate by publication in the Federal Register, by the agency heads listed below, by officials who have Top Secret classification authority, and by officials to whom such authority is delegated in accordance with Section 1-204:

The Secretary of Commerce
The Secretary of Transportation
The Administrator, Agency for International Development
The Director, International Communication Agency

1-203. Confidential. Authority for original classification of information as Confidential may be exercised only by such officials as the President may designate by

262

publication in the Federal Register, by the agency heads listed below, by officials who have Top Secret or Secret classification authority, and by officials to whom such authority is delegated in accordance with Section 1-204:

The President and Chairman, Export-Import Bank of the United States

The President and Chief Executive Officer, Overseas Private Investment Corporation

1-204. Limitations on Delegation of Classification Authority.

(a) Authority for original classification of information as Top Secret may be delegated only to principal subordinate officials who have a frequent need to exercise such authority as determined by the President or by agency heads listed in Section 1-201.

(b) Authority for original classification of information as Secret may be delegated only to subordinate officials who have a frequent need to exercise such authority as determined by the President, by agency heads listed in Sections 1-201 and 1-202, and by officials with Top Secret classification authority.

(c) Authority for original classification of information as Confidential may be delegated only to subordinate officials who have a frequent need to exercise such authority as determined by the President, by agency heads listed in Sections 1-201, 1-202, and 1-203, and by officials with Top Secret classification authority.

(d) Delegated original classification authority may not be redelegated.

(e) Each delegation of original classification authority shall be in writing by name or title of position held.

(f) Delegations of original classification authority shall be held to an absolute minimum. Periodic reviews of such delegations shall be made to ensure that the officials so designated have demonstrated a continuing need to exercise such authority.

1-205. Exceptional Cases. When an employee or contractor of an agency that does not have original classification authority originates information believed to require classification, the information shall be protected in the manner prescribed by this Order and implementing directives. The information shall be transmitted promptly under appropriate safeguards to the agency which has appropriate subject matter interest and classification authority. That agency shall decide within 30 days whether to classify that information. If it is not clear which agency should get the information, it shall be sent to the Director of the Information Security Oversight Office established in Section 5-2 for a determination.

1-301. Information may not be considered for classification unless it concerns: (a) military plans, weapons, or operations; (b) foreign government information; (c) intelligence activities, sources or methods; (d) foreign relations or foreign activities of the United States; (e) scientific, technological, or economic matters relating to the national security; (f) United States Government programs for safeguarding nuclear materials or facilities; or (g) other categories of information which are related to national security and which require protection against unauthorized disclosure as determined by the President, by a person designated by the President pursuant to Section 1-201, or by an agency head.

1-302. Even though information is determined to concern one or more of the criteria in Section 1-301, it may not be classified unless an original classification authority also determines that its unauthorized disclosure reasonable could be expected to cause at least identifiable damage to the national security.

1-303. Unauthorized disclosure of foreign government information or the identity of a confidential foreign source is presumed to cause at least identifiable damage to the national security.

1-401. Except as permitted in Section 1-402, at the time of the original classification each original classification authority shall set a date or event for automatic declassification no more than six years later.

1-402. Only officials with Top Secret classification authority and agency heads listed in Section 1-2 may classify information for more than six years from the date of the original classification. This authority shall be used sparingly. In such cases, a declassification date or even, or a date for review, shall be set. This date or event shall be as early as national security permits and shall be no more than twenty years after original classification, except that for foreign government information the data or event may be up to thirty years after original classification.

1-502. Documents classified for more than six years shall also be marked with the identity of the official who authorized the prolonged classification. Such documents shall be annotated with the reason the classification is expected to remain necessary, under the requirements of Section 1-3, despite the passage of time. The reason for the prolonged classification may be stated by reference to criteria set forth in agency implementing regulations. These criteria shall explain in narrative form the reason the information needs to be protected beyond six years. If the individual who signs or otherwise authenticates a document also is authorized to classify it, no further annotation of identity is required.

1-504. In order to facilitate excerpting and other uses, each classified document shall, by marking or other means, indicate clearly which portions are classified, with the applicable classification designation, and which portions are not classified. The Director of the Information Security Oversight Office may, for good cause, grant and revoke waivers of this requirement for specified classes of documents or information.

1-505. Foreign government information shall either retain its original classification designation or be assigned a United States classification designation that shall ensure a degree of protection equivalent to that required by the entity that furnished the information.

1-601. Classification may not be used to conceal violations of law, inefficiency, or administrative error, to prevent embarrassment to a person, organization or agency, or to restrain competition.

1-602. Basic scientific research information not clearly related to the national security may not be classified.

1-603. A product of non-government research and development that does not incorporate or reveal classified information to which the producer or developer was given prior access may not be classified under this Order until and unless the government acquires a proprietary interest in the product. This Order does not affect the provisions of the Patent Secrecy Act of 1952 (35 U.S.C. 181-188).

1-604. References to classified documents that do not disclose classified information may not be classified or used as a basis for classification.

1-605. Classification may not be used to limit dissemination of information that is not classifiable under the provisions of this Order or to prevent or delay the public release of such information.

1-607. Classification may not be restored to documents already declassifid and released to the public under this Order or prior Orders.

2-201. Classification guides used to direct derivative classification shall specifically identify the information to be classified. Each classification guide shall specifically indicate how the designations, time limits, markings, and other requirements of this Order are to be applied to the information.

3-204. After the termination of a Presidential administration, the Archivist of the United States shall review and declassify or downgrade all information classified by the President, the White House Staff, committees or commissions appointed by the President, or others acting on the President's behalf. Such declassification shall only be undertaken in accordance with the provisions of Section 3-504.

3-301. Declassification of classified information shall be given emphasis comparable to that accorded classification. Information classified pursuant to this and prior Orders shall be declassified as early as national security considerations permit. Decisions concerning declassification shall be based on the loss of the information's sensitivity with the passage of time or on the occurrence of a declassification event.

3-303. It is presumed that information which continues to meet the classification requirements in Section 1-3 requires continued protection. In some cases, however, the need to protect such information may be outweighed by the public interest in disclosure of the information, and in these cases the information should be declassified. When such questions arise, they shall be referred to the agency head, a senior agency official with responsibility for processing Freedom of Information Act requests or Mandatory Review requests under this Order, an official with Top Secret classification authority, or the Archivist of the United States.... That official will determine whether the public interest in disclosure outweighs the damage to national security that might reasonably be expected from disclosure.

3-401. Classified information constituting permanently valuable records of the Government, as defined by 44 U.S.C. 2103, and information in the possession and control of the Administrator of General Services, pursuant to 44 U.S.C. 2107 or 2107 note, shall be reviewed for declassification as it becomes twenty years old. Agency heads listed in Section 1-2 and officials designated by the President pursuant to Section 1-201 of this Order may extend classification beyond twenty years, but only in accordance with Sections 3-3 and 3-402. This authority may not be delegated. When classification is extended beyond twenty years, a date no more than ten years later shall be set for declassification or for the next review. That date shall be marked on the document. Subsequent reviews for declassification shall be set at no more than ten year intervals. The Director of the Information Security Oversight Office may extend the period between subsequent reviews for specific categories of documents or information.

3-402. Within 180 days after the effective date of this Order, the agency heads listed in Section 1-2 and the heads of agencies which had original classification authority under prior orders shall, after consultation with the Archivist of the United States and review by the Information Security Oversight Office, issue and maintain guidelines for systematic review covering twenty-year old classified information under their jurisdiction.

3-404.   Foreign government information shall be exempt from automatic declassification and twenty year systematic review. Unless declassified earlier, such information shall be reviewed for declassification thirty years from its date of origin.

3-501. Agencies shall establish a mandatory review procedure to handle requests by a member of the public, by a government employee, or by an agency, to declassify and release information. Requests for declassification under this provision shall be acted upon within 60 days.

5-301. There is established an Interagency Information Security Committee which shall be chaired by the Director and shall be comprised of representatives of the Secretaries of State, Defense, Treasury, and Energy, the Attorney General, the Director of Central Intelligence, the National Security Council, the Domestic Policy Staff, and the Archivist of the United States.

5-303. The Committee shall meet at the call of the Chairman or at the request of a member agency and shall advise the Chairman on implementation of this order.

5-502. Officers and employees of the United States Government shall be subject to appropriate administrative sanctions if they:

(a) knowingly and willfully classify or continue the classification of information in violation of this Order or any implementing directives...

6-102. 'Classified information' means information or material, herein collectively termed information, that is owned by, produced for or by, or under the control of, the United States Government, and that has been determined pursuant to this Order or prior Orders to require protection against unauthorized disclosure, and that is so designated.

6-103. 'Foreign government information' means information that has been provided to the United States in confidence by, or produced by the United States pursuant to a written joint arrangement requiring confidentiality with, a foreign government or international organization of governments.

6-104. 'National security' means the national defense and foreign relations of the United States.

Notes

Note I-1. According to Morland [90], drafts of his article were sent only to the following reviewers: Theodore Postal (Argonne, Ill.), Randy Forsberg (Brookline, Mass.), and Ronald H. Siegel (Cambridge, Mass.). Three copies of Postol's draft were made for the other Argonne reviewers.

Note II-1. Rear Admiral H.C. Eccles [Christian Science Monitor (April 3, 1980)]:

[MX] is part of the policy of nuclear deterrence and as such its merits and demerits are usually argued in language and logic so esoteric and so speculative that informed, honest, and patriotic men can reach, and plausibly support, opposite conclusions. Each makes a personal, intuitive, and unquantifiable evaluation of the inherent critical risks. Therefore we must cut through the confusion of argument to reach the critical issues.

National Security. National security is both the security of the state itself as a sovereign political entity and the security of the institutions of the nation. These institutions grow out of and protect the values of the people of the nation. Thus, national security should be seen as: External security -- national political sovereignty, territorial integrity, and access to economic resources. Internal security -- economic sufficiency, freedom of enterprise, of expression, of elections, and of the judiciary.

Each category of security and of freedom has its own constituency of special interests which is in continuing competition with other interests for economic and political preference and power. Since resources are always limited, this complex competition makes it impossible to formulate and carry out a no-risk national security policy.

Fundamentals of nuclear action. In conventional war, a major command error can be overcome by extraordinary effort by that command itself or in another area of the field of action. Nuclear weapons are so swift and so destructive that their use leaves no room for error in the commander-in-chief's decision process or the operation of the command and control system. Time and timing are critical: time available to make the decision, time required to carry out the decision, timing of the various phases of the action, particularly the time required to change targets in response to unanticipated developments.

In nuclear warfare, mistakes are irretrievable. Thus, nuclear weapons command and control is a system of absolutes. Once the weapon is loose, the decision cannot be reversed.

The weak link in this vital system is the sense of moral responsibility for making the critical decision to initiate the use of nuclear weapons. This cannot be resolved by scientific analysis. It is the ultimate expression of one's deepest sense of human values. It must be made in a few critical minutes during which the commander-in-chief comes to the shocking recognition that, right now, he must decide the life or death of tens of millions of his fellowmen.

266

Any decision to use a nuclear weapon would require the imposition of authoritative control over most of the normal activities of the nation to prepare for the vast physical destruction and social, economic, and political disruption which certainly would follow even a limited nuclear exchange. Even the imminent threat of such exchange can create panic. No one can foresee the consequences of the news that the president has gone to a sheltered command post while 200 million of his people are exposed to extinction.

Repeated studies show that even a relatively small nuclear exchange would produce catastrophic long-range harm as well as immediate damage and casualties. There is no effective civil defense in the US nor is there any evidence that one will be adequately funded and competently managed.

The concept of counterforce nuclear warfare as a means to assure national security is being challenged. Recent events have shown the fallibility of the presidential decision process. The reliability of the operation of the command and control system under stress is seriously questioned. The cumulative effect of these and of the secondary issues is to diminish rather than enhance both the external and internal elements of national security.

Therefore, we should abandon the MX missile system program, continue to depend on the present general system of nuclear weaponry to provide deterrence against nuclear attack, make every effort to reduce nuclear weaponry, and accept an acknowledged risk in so doing.

Note III-1. Many of the diverse and interesting issues about arms limitation are discussed in Opportunities for Disarmament, edited by J.M.O. Sharp, Carnegie Endowment for International Peace, Washington, D.C. (1978), and in "Arms, Defense Policy, and Arms Control," in the summer 1975 issue of Daedalus (Journal of the American Academy of Arts and Sciences).

Note III-2. A good reference to the technical (and institutional) issues is the book edited by A. Chayes and J.B. Wiesner, ABM: An Evaluation of the Decision to Deploy an Antiballistic Missile System, The New American Library, NYC (1969). That book presents in great detail examples of technical data that can be important to policy discussion. In one of the contributions, Steven Weinberg dealt with the technical aspects of the protection afforded the U.S. deterrent by the proposed ABM system (then called "Safeguard"). To make his assessment, Weinberg had to look into ABM effectiveness, cost, and its defensive (vis-a-vis offensive) nature and appearance. This called for examination of high- and low-altitude penetration aids that could be employed by incoming offensive missiles. He also considered a counter-strategy of attacks upon the missile-site radars. This type of detailed analysis, entailing offensive and defensive strategies, undoubtedly would have been classified if the Atomic Energy Act were applicable to weapons-delivery systems.

The "Command and Control" chapter by Bill D. Moyers likewise required independent evaluations: the hair-trigger problem for prompt or delayed response, the permissive-action-link safety features against inadvertent detonation of a nuclear warhead, and the role of presidential control. Both the underlying philosophy and the manner of implementation continue to be urgent candidates for public attention -- probably to a very fine technical detail when it comes to safety decisions, hardware, and decision-making on the subject of the accidental or intentional initiation of nuclear warfare.

Leonard S. Rodberg wrote on "ABM Reliability," a subject that requires knowledge of radar readiness, missile and component reliability, and the performance of various computers. J.C.R. Licklider looked with more detail into computer hardware and software reliability, in terms of military applications. Hans A. Bethe contributed a chapter on "Countermeasures to ABM Systems," discussing the "kill" radius, weapons effects that cause destruction, penetration aids and their effect on the radar, and possible blackout by precursor explosions. One appendix contains technical notes, formulas, and numbers on missile trajectories, payload ratios, nuclear-weapons scaling laws, and hard-point kill probabilities.

None of that information, in the detail that was needed, was inaccessible to the Soviets. Even so, had it not been for the reputation of Bethe and other contributors (and the implied sponsorship of Senator Edward M. Kennedy), it is doubtful that such a book would have survived any classification review, considering the sensitivity of the material contained in it.

Note III-3. After a Titan II missile exploded in Arkansas, a Chicago Tribune [September 22, 1980] editorial asked, "Are they safe?"

Of course the're not safe. They are the most unsafe contraptions ever

devised by man. The shattered Titan II in Arkansas carried a warhead
that was consciously designed to vaporized the concrete, steel, flesh,
and bone of a considerable part of Moscow. If it can do it to Moscow,
it can also do it to Chicago, Little Rock, or Bee Branch, Ark.

Fortunately, however, Bee Branch seems not to have been threatened
with a thermonuclear explosion. If we can accept the word of Pentagon
officials (have we any choice?) the explosion of the rocket's fuel could
not have produced an explosion of the warhead itself.

Note III-4. Additional information may be found in a recent treatment by Louis
Rene' Beres, Apocalypse: Nuclear Catastrophe in World Politics, The University of
Chicago Press, Chicago (1980).

Note III-5. A history of false war alerts has been compiled by James Coates of the
Chicago Tribune [2 November 1980]:

WASHINGTON -- The chairman of the Joint Chiefs of Staff has faced a
critical task four times since Oct. 3, 1979 -- deciding in seconds
whether American satellites were recording actual Soviet sneak attacks
or just issuing a false alarm of nuclear war.

Four examples were cited: an October 3, 1979, detection of orbiting space junk
"misread...as a submarine-launched missile;" a wrong tape fed to a computer on November
9, 1979, causing it to appear as though land- and sea-based missiles were launched from
the Soviet Union; a Russian training exercise of March 15, 1980, that wrongly appeared
to launch a missile towards the United States; and a June 3, 1980, computer error that
"flashed a false warning of Soviet attack."

The last event prompted the Senate Armed Forces Committee to investigate whether
there was a risk of accidental nuclear war because the complex network of satellites,
radar, and computers was prone to false alarms.

...an investigation...concluded that the U.S. has had 151 false alarms
from its supersensitive warning system in 18 months.

Four times...the chairman of the Joint Chiefs was alerted and had to
decide whether to order an alert and summon the President.

[Senator] Hart acknowledged..."there will never be a guarantee that
false alerts won't happen in the future."

Note IV-1. Specifically, the charge was that the article "involves or incorporates
Secret Restricted Data pursuant to the Atomic Energy Act, 42 U.S.C. §2280...."
Violation of §2274(b) was alleged.

Note IV-2. From the government brief [4]:

Such a disclosure will increase the number of nations capable of
constructing thermonuclear weapons and decrease the time it takes for
these nations to develop such weapons. If this occurs, the nuclear
nonproliferation and strategic arms limitation policies of the United
States will suffer serious and perhaps irreversible setbacks,
jeopardizing the security of the United States.

Note IV-3. From the government brief [4]:

In hearings before the Joint Committee on Atomic Energy...Congress was
advised that the Restricted Data definition "has been interpreted...by
the [Atomic Energy] Commission to mean that all information in these
fields at birth, that is, when there is a new discovery, development, or
article, is instantly classified.... Despite some objection...to this
interpretation, Congress declined to modify it, thus giving occasion for
application of the "venerable principle that the construction of a statute by those charged with its execution should be followed...especially
when Congress has refused to alter the administrative construction."

Note IV-4. The government also said [59] that

the information, to the extent it is referenced in any public document,
has never been confirmed by the Government....

It is not simply the filing of this suit that confirms the accuracy
of the article. The manuscript itself is, and professes to be,
qualitatively different from other publications in this area because it
purports to tell the "secret" of the H-bomb, while other sources contain
speculation, implication, and suggestion....

Affidavits executed by Morland...reveal a substantial amount of the
Restricted Data contained in the article that by process of reference
has now been confirmed by the United States as describing the operation
of the hydrogen bomb....

The unique context in which these affidavits would be produced is one
in which they will serve as a roadmap enabling the informed reader to

select from "the vast collection of good and bad ideas and hints" (Rosengren Aff., paragraph 4) concerning thermonuclear weapons the correct information concerning the design and manufacture of the hydrogen bomb.

Note IV-5. Quotes from government affidavits attesting to the accuracy and sensitivity of the Morland article:

Charles N. Van Doren [6]. Van Doren, head of the Nonproliferation Bureau of the Arms Control and Disarmament Agency, stated:

In my judgment there is no question that the article contains a substantial amount of sensitive Restricted Data relevant to the manufacture of thermonuclear weapons, which to the best of my knowledge and belief has not previously been available in unclassified form.

The publication of that data would provide to states that have not developed nuclear weapons, as well as to any state that had developed a fission device, a substantial amount of otherwise unpublished information that in my judgment would be highly likely to facilitate and accelerate any efforts by such a state to design and develop thermonuclear weapons -- thus deserving our strong national security interest in preventing and delaying any such efforts.

Of all the manuscripts purporting to be unclassified that I have reviewed in my twelve years in this field, this one, if made public, appears to be the most flagrant example of deliberate dissemination of sensitive weapons design information, and the most likely to damage U.S. interests in preventing the spread of nuclear weapons capabilities.

Thomas R. Pickering [7]. On behalf of the nuclear nonproliferation policy of the Department of State and the National Security Council, Assistant Secretary of State Pickering charged that Morland's manuscript contained "detailed information related to the design and manufacture of advanced types of nuclear weapons." In particular, he referred to data on both "boosted fission weapons and thermonuclear weapons." Further:

The principal effect of this publication would be to secure an advantage for foreign nations by significantly reducing the difficulty in progressing from design of simple fission weapons to advanced, high-yield weapons. Both the time to make this progression and the uncertainty in achieving a successful progression would be reduced. In my opinion, the decade it might take some countries to develop thermonuclear weapons could be reduced to a few years.

Pickering emphasized the advantage to foreign states of more rapid and more certain acquisition of thermonuclear weapons and that a larger number of states would be able to develop them. He added:

The greater the availability of nuclear weapons to states in conflict, the more likely will be their use. Moreover, the likelihood that the United States and the world will suffer from nuclear catastrophe through accidental or unauthorized nuclear strikes will increase with the number of nuclear weapon states. For these and other reasons a fundamental tenet of United States foreign policy has been to prevent this proliferation of nuclear weapons. The successful pursuit of this policy has been based on achieving a reasonable amount of time both for diplomacy to be effective and for the United States to develop the incentives which judgment and the security of the United States as well as international security is seriously injured by any activity that makes nuclear weapons acquisition more rapid, more likely, and more widespread.

Duane C. Sewell [8]. From the Defense Program branch of DOE came the official statement of classification status by Assistant Secretary of Energy Sewell:

It is my determination based on my familiarity with the entire body of knowledge having to do with nuclear weapons, that information contained in the Morland manuscript is information which is classified as "Secret Restricted Data" and this data has not been declassified.

The manuscript contains essential principles of the operation of the hydrogen bomb; the disclosure of such information could in my judgment materially aid non-nuclear weapon states in their development of nuclear weapons. My classified affidavit provides this information in greater detail.

The danger to the security interests of the United States, by the disclosure of this information, which involves the design and operations of thermonuclear weapons, is immediate, clear, and irreparable.

The publication of these basic principles of thermonuclear weapon design would materially reduce the research and development time required by countries to achieve a thermonuclear weapon capability, and thereby induce additional countries to decide to go forward with a nuclear weapon program.

John A. Griffin [9]. Griffin, the DOE's director of classification, determined that a significant portion of the manuscript contains information which the law requires to be classified as Secret Restricted Data. Those portions...are primarily concerned with basic concepts underlying the design and operation of thermonuclear weapons, as well as the manner in which these concepts are applied....

To my knowledge the Restricted Data information contained in the Morland manuscript concerning the design and operation of a thermonuclear weapon is not in the public domain.

The publication of these basic principles of thermonuclear weapon design would materially reduce the research and development time required by countries to achieve a thermonuclear weapon capability, and thereby induce additional countries to decide to go forward with a nuclear weapon program.

Spurgeon M. Keeney, Jr. [22]. The acting director of ACDA gave his opinion that the article 'could significantly contribute to the ability of certain foreign nations to progress from fission to thermonuclear weapons in a considerably shorter period of time than would otherwise be the case.'

Jack W. Rosengren [23]. Because Rosengren was the primary technical witness brought in by the government, extensive excerpts of his affidavit are repeated here:

I am a member of the Senior Research Staff of R&D Associates, an independent company that conducts technical studies for government and private organizations. I am also a consultant with the Department of Energy on classification policy. I received my Doctorate degree in Physics from the University of California at Berkeley, and taught Physics as an Assistant Professor at the Massachusetts Institute of Technology. I am a nuclear physicist by training, and thoroughly familiar with the design and construction of thermonuclear weapons. Prior to working at R&D Associates, I was at the Lawrence Livermore Laboratory, responsible for the physics design of the first Polaris warhead and an early Minuteman warhead. Later, I was the Associate Director for Nuclear Weapons Design at Livermore, then Deputy Director for Science & Technology at the Defense Nuclear Agency. In addition, I have been a member of the Foreign Technology Panel (Bethe Panel), which evaluates intelligence on foreign weapon tests, and the (former) Committee of Senior Reviewers of AEC/ERDA/DOE.

My appraisal of the article is that it contains a significant amount of information which is properly classified as Secret Restricted Data. While certain bits and pieces of the information contained in the article have been previously disclosed in scattered sources, the article nevertheless contains information that has never been released anywhere before. It provides a more comprehensive, accurate, and detailed summary of the overall construction and operation of a thermonuclear weapon than any publication to date in the public literature.

There are many feasible and grossly different possible designs for thermonuclear weapons. These differ in crucial ways from one another. Some are awkward and extremely difficult to design successfully. Some require scarce materials in impractical amounts. Some cannot be made to operate efficiently. There are bits and pieces of information in the open literature that apply to one or more of these different types of designs.

Once a nation has produced a fission weapon, gaining the required know-how to design a practical thermonuclear weapon presents a greater obstacle to the development of a thermonuclear weapon that the problem of acquiring the additional material (thermonuclear fuel) that is required to construct such a weapon.

James R. Schlesinger [26]. As Secretary of Energy, Schlesinger had primary cabinet-level responsibilities for the nuclear weapons research and development programs and for maintaining security of weapons information and supporting nonproliferation goals. Thus his conclusions regarding the article reflect the official stance:

Publication, communication, or disclosure...would irreparably impair the national security of the United States by making available to foreign nations Secret Restricted Data pertaining to the design and operational characteristics of a thermonuclear weapon. Such information would materially aid foreign nations by enabling them to develop such weapons in a shorter period of time than otherwise would be possible. This result would be contrary to the non-proliferation policy of the United States, including that adopted in the Treaty on Nonproliferation of Nuclear Weapons, and would increase the risks of thermonuclear war.

Robert N. Thorn [26A]. The acting director of Los Alamos Scientific Laboratory, one of two U.S. thermonuclear weapons development laboratories, stated that

the Article...is perhaps as suggestive of the process used in thermonuclear weapons as the original outline on the subject by Teller and Ulam. The original conceptualization of this process led rapidly to successful efforts by the United States in this area. There can be no doubt that some of the concepts discussed are essential to the development of thermonuclear weapons. It has taken present thermonuclear weapon states from 2-9 years to go from a fission explosion to a thermonuclear weapon....

I am familiar with the publicly available literature on this subject... I believe that the Restricted Data contained in the Morland Article is not publicly available, either in literature or conversation.... Had data of the nature contained in the Morland Article ever been made public, I feel confident that it would have come to my attention.

Roger E. Batzel [26B]. The director of the Lawrence Livermore Laboratory, the other national thermonuclear weapons establishment, made the following affirmation:

In spite of some minor technical errors, [the Morland article] contains or strongly suggests key concepts for the functioning of the hydrogen bomb. Once the key concepts were discovered by researchers from the United States, it took only a matter of months to translate it into practice. The experiences of other countries in their development of thermonuclear weapons reaffirms the crucial nature of these concepts....

I believe that the Restricted Data contained in the Morland Article is not publicly available, either in literature or unclassified conversation. Previous publications contain some correct hints mixed with incorrect ones, but in no way come so near to describing the operation of thermonuclear weapons.

Note IV-6. The first point evolved from the standards set in the per curiam decision of the Pentagon Papers case (New York Times). As cited in the brief [52A], "any system of prior restraints of expression comes to this Court bearing a heavy presumption against its constitutional validity." The government "thus carries a heavy burden of showing justification for the imposition of such a restraint." The brief added that "the government's affidavits are replete with conclusions, conjecture, and speculative language," and gave a variety of examples:

The government has acknowledged that it must meet the test of New York Times. While contending that it has met that test...the government has failed to prove the grave, direct, immediate, and irreparable damage that it must establish to convince this Court to impose the extraordinary remedy of prior restraint.

On the public domain issue, the defendants suggested that the government had to show that the article incorporates "Restricted Data," that its publication constitutes communication, transmission or disclosure, that the information in the article "will be utilized" to injure the United States or to secure an advantage to a foreign country, and that the defendants have "reason to believe" the information will be so utilized.... [It must also be shown that] the "information" in the article is "Restricted Data"..."not available elsewhere"...[and that the] information in the article "has never been made publicly available."

The affidavits submitted by the defendants convincingly demonstrate that every pertinent item of information in the article had its source in the public domain.

Note IV-7. From Morland [38A]:

I read the literature, I asked questions and I speculated. Obviously, a competent physicist should be able to duplicate my efforts in considerably less time than it took me. He could do it in this country, France, Britain, China and the Soviet Union or anywhere that knowledgeable nuclear weapons specialists gather for conferences, vacations and so forth. In other words, by any reasonable measure, the information is already in the public domain. I have not looked at any classified documents of any kind or nature nor do I know of any classified information which has been given to me by any public information office of the Department of Energy or anyone else.

Note IV-8. Robert D. Richtmyer [39], Henry Pierre Noyes [40], Charles Schwartz [41], Edward Cooperman [42], Roger Dittman [46], Ralph S. Hager [47], and Calvin G. Andre [48] agreed:

The basic physical concepts underlying the design and operation of thermonuclear weapons, as well as the general manner in which such concepts may be applied, are known to many physicists and other scientists and persons, both within and without the government in this country and elsewhere....

Government policy designed to preserve secrecy with respect to such matters not only is unsucccessful, but tends to inhibit scientific research by erecting barriers between people in closely related fields.

Note IV-9. Hugh Edgar DeWitt [56]. Although Dr. DeWitt was employed at Livermore, he had never directly worked on nuclear weapon design, despite his clearance for access to Secret Restricted Data. Yet he was "familiar with weapons designs concepts and technical information used in weapons designs." Consequently, he was able to state:

The basic conceptual "secret" of the hydrogen bomb is described in the first two portions of the article...very qualitatively the Teller-Ulam idea which led to [the] first successful hydrogen bomb explosions by the United States in the early '50's. This "secret" has been regarded for over 25 years as highly classified. Yet there is by now enough information in open publications that a capable physicist could deduce the basic idea for himself without access to classified literature. An intelligent and resourceful reporter could probably do the same thing, and I understand that this is in fact what Morland has done. Edward Teller, one of the inventors of the hydrogen bomb, has an article in the Encyclopedia Americana, 1977, titled Hydrogen Bomb.

Some portions of DeWitt's affidavit were deleted to satisfy government objections regarding sensitive information. The remainder continued:

If this article by Morland is not published, I expect that it will be only a short time before another reporter working independently for a different publication will uncover the same information and write a very similar article. In short after more than 25 years the H-bomb secret is not so secret anymore....

On the question of whether the publication of the Morland article will aid a nuclear weapons design group in another country to design a workable hydrogen bomb...the answer is probably yes, but by only a few days. Such a group of weapons design physicists would first have to have successfully designed and tested a fission device, and they then would have to go through the enormous labor of calculating the exact specifications of a workable device for causing fusion reactions. No such technical details are in the Morland article.

It is known that four other countries beside the U.S. have independently invented hydrogen bombs. Of the present nuclear powers only India has not gone on to the fusion bomb stage of development. If the Indian government sets its mind to make a hydrogen bomb, the Morland article might help them, but I repeat, only for a very short time.

Note IV-10. Ray E. Kidder [75A]:

The basic principles of operation of the hydrogen bomb as set forth in the Morland article are deducible from information widely available to the public by a person having an unexceptional knowledge of physics and without access to classified information.

Most details of design of the hydrogen bomb described in the Morland article that are not deducible from the public record are not of such a nature that their disclosure would significantly influence the national security.

Note IV-11. Tsipis's affidavit [55] continued (a portion originally censored is indicated by angle brackets < >):

Although the [article] correctly identifies the general method by which energy from the fission trigger <can be coupled to the fusion fuel> and cause its detonation, it is not nearly enough to permit another nation to develop and manufacture such a fusion device. Detailed knowledge about the necessary hydrodynamic calculations and processing of materials are two of the numerous technical issues a nation bent at developing a weapon of this type would have to master, in addition to the general design described in the article....

If the nation in question had no previous knowledge or experience in fusion physics, the information in the article objected to by the D.O.E. could facilitate the initiation of appropriate research and development and offer guidance to the developers of the device on the general design that could lead to successful results and the choice of materials to be used in the manufacture of the weapon...[and] would also focus the attention of the designers of another nation on those parameters of the design that would most likely be critical in manufacturing a successful device.... The total time necessary for another nation to arrive at a successful device could be foreshortened by the...article.

Note IV-12. Other excerpts from DeVolpi's affidavit [63]:

Any test of direct, immediate, or irreparable harm by publication must take into consideration the proliferation that has already existed, the influence of United States policy in failing to stem the tide of proliferation, and whether or not the aggregate of present policies is conducive to further proliferation....

Examples arise in analyzing the continuing production and testing of nuclear weapons, particularly with regard to impact on proliferation. In my opinion, the U.S. Government has failed to set appropriate examples of national self-restraint, such as a moratorium on production and testing of nuclear weapons. The Government has argued that various technical factors have influenced its decision to continue the manufacture and testing of nuclear explosive devices. Without the capability for independent evaluation -- by means of universal, unclassified principles -- of technical factors related to design concepts, it is difficult to analyze Government claims regarding the need for continued nuclear-explosive testing. An unnecessary limitation of public debate regarding these practices could result in policies that tend to promote, rather than retard, proliferation.

In considering the redeeming public interest value of articles such as Morland's, the affidavit says:

The balancing of public safety and environmental impact against national defense is another issue that should be openly debated, as attempted in the Progressive article. Paragraph 3 of the Affidavit by Harold Brown mentions his official responsibilities concerning the safety, security, and deployment of nuclear weapons. It is my opinion that the capability for independent assessment of fundamental weapons principles as they affect public safety must be retained by the public at large. As a specialist in the safety of nuclear reactors, I am keenly aware of the necessity for open, widespread knowledge of inherent and engineered safety features in operating reactors. Special concern for the security and safety of nuclear-weapons -- their production, transportation, and storage -- is not unwarranted in view of the potential for massive devastation by nuclear weapons. It is too important a topic to leave entirely behind closed doors. Without independent vigilance, the abiding public interest in safeguards and accident-prevention for nuclear weapons cannot be protected from facile attention by officials. Because the design and operation of nuclear weapons are governed by established physical principles, it is not necessary for functional details to be divulged in order to make an assessment of the potential for incidents involving nuclear weapons.

Note IV-13. Other excerpts from Bethe's [72] affidavit:

I have read the manuscript. There are sizeable portions of the text which in my judgement should be classified as Restricted Data, because the processes described in the manuscript, despite a number of technical errors, correctly describe the essential design and operation of thermonuclear weapons. The concepts described in the manuscript are as fundamental and necessary to the design of a thermonuclear weapon as those originally formulated by Dr. Edward Teller and Dr. Stanislav Ulam....

I have concluded that the design and operational concepts described in that manuscript are not expressed or revealed in the public

literature nor do I believe they are known to scientists not associated
with the government weapons programs.

Note IV-14. Dr. Harold W. Lewis is a member of the Defense Science Board and the
nuclear panel of the U.S. Air Force Scientific Advisory Board; he has been a consultant
to LASL and is "thoroughly familiar with the design and construction of all types of
nuclear weapons, including thermonuclear devices." His affidavit [67] reads in part:

In my judgment, the Morland article contains thermonuclear weapon design
concepts which are not openly or publicly available and which are
fundamental to the development of such weapons.

In my opinion, the public literature and the excerpts from it
attached to the Morland Affidavit I do not provide [a basis for the
thermonuclear weapons design and operation concepts revealed in the
Morland article]. In my opinion, the Morland article reveals classified
concepts which were developed other than through simple assembly of
information available in public literature.

Note IV-15. To counter the "public domain" argument of The Progressive, the
government stated [66]:

Although a minor proportion of the Restricted Data in the article is
available in unrelated and scattered public sources, the preponderance
of the Restricted Data is not available to the public in this form....
In sum, its publication would provide a more comprehensive, accurate,
and detailed summary of the overall construction and operation of a
thermonuclear weapon than any publication to date in the public
literature. (Rosengren Aff., P. 3)....

The affidavits of the Cabinet Officers of the United States, charged
with maintaining United States security and preventing nuclear
proliferation, fully establish that publication of this Restricted Data
would lead to the proliferation of nuclear weapons (Vance, Pickering,
Schlesinger and Keeney affidavits).

Note IV-16. The Fund for Open Information and Accountability, Inc. [80]:

There is no "secret" of how to make an "atomic" or plutonium implosion
bomb.

The massive destruction possible through existing and potential
atomic fission bombs makes a mockery of the government's claims herein
that the threat of thermonuclear holocaust will be increased by
publication of the Morland article.

The Court must take judicial notice that there is a secret which
the government is trying to keep from the American people and the world.
That secret is that there are no scientific secrets to prevent nuclear
and thermonuclear proliferation without the total and massive nuclear
disarmament and a cessation of the development of nuclear weaponry.

Note IV-17. Rosengren and Grayson described [109A] their own previous affidavits
as follows:

The Government affidavits filed in camera present material that is
classified as Secret, Restricted Data, and Secret, National Security
Information....

Therefore, considering this authorship, the design statements made in
the Government Affidavits can be taken to be authoritative and
definitive as to the nature of U.S. thermonuclear weapons....

Note IV-18. A research assistant, Thomas Kirkman, at the University of Wisconsin
was retained by The Progressive to research the public literature on thermonuclear weapons. At the library of the University of Wisconsin he found information also contained
in the Morland article; those references were deleted from his affidavit [129].

Note IV-19. Defendants' arguments followed these lines [124]:

I. The preliminary injunction should be vacated because the recent
developments in this case demonstrate that the information in the
Morland article already is in the public domain.

A. The Government has the burden of proving that the three "central"
concepts prescribed in the Morland article are not in the public
domain.

B. Since the Court entered its preliminary injunction, there have
been a number of developments which have a decisive impact on this
case.

II. If the Court cannot grant the defendants' motion to vacate the
preliminary injunction solely on the basis of documentary evidence, it
should require testimony on the issues of fact before it.

Note IV-20. DeVolpi [134] said:

I believe the court erred in finding that the Morland article contained technical details. Comparison with UCRL-4725 shows that the Morland article does not contain technical details that would be helpful to a nation in constructing fusion weapons, whereas UCRL-4725 does contain technical details that would readily assist certain foreign nations in designing and constructing fusion weapons, if they chose to acquire that capability.

The government rebutted [142] that there was still value in the Morland article despite UCRL-4725:

The Morland article provides a tutorial framework to connect the generalities of the open publications to the very specific but disconnected bits of information in [UCRL-4725].

Note IV-21. Taylor [135] stated:

Although UCRL-4725 contains no diagrams, it describes or directly infers the basic design principles used in thermonuclear weapons....

The information in UCRL-4725 describes the results of situations in which the Teller-Ulam concepts are being used. I believe that a reasonably competent physicist who has read encyclopedia articles and other publicly available literature which describes nuclear weapon behavior could extract the Teller-Ulam concepts from UCRL-4725.

Note IV-22. Sewell's affidavit [146] read in part:

Some of the articles submitted [by the defendants] suggest certain design concepts related to thermonuclear weapons. Those portions of the public articles dealing with weapon design concepts are speculative in nature, somewhat obscure and quite brief, in the majority of cases consisting of one or two sentences in a several page article. Therefore, my determination that the Morland article contains Secret Restricted Data is not affected by these articles.

Note IV-23. The following points not previously noted may be found in the index to the government's 124-page brief [166]:

[IB.] The District Court's determination that information in the Morland article is properly classified as restricted data required issuance of the injunction.

[IIB]. The public literature cited by defendants has not caused the secret of the H-bomb to become public knowledge. [DELETED]

[IIC.] Morland's ability to obtain the H-bomb secret does not demonstrate that the restricted data can be derived from unclassified sources and does not require that the protections afforded by the Atomic Energy Act be abandoned.

[IID.] The possiblity that UCRL 4725 and UCRL 5280 have been compromised as to some nations does not vitiate the Atomic Energy Act's protection against universal disclosure of the similar technical principles in the Morland article.

[IIIA.] Congress may constitutionally restrain the disclosure of nuclear weapons secrets.

[IIIB.] The prohibition against the communication of restricted data in 42 U.S.C. §2274(b) is neither vague nor overbroad....

Note IV-24. From the index of The Progressive's reply brief [167]:

[IIA.] Scientific information is protected speech under the First Amendment.

[IIC.] If the Act is not vague or overbroad as the Government seeks to apply it here, the Government still must prove the constitutional standards of extraordinary harm under the New York Times rule.

[IID.] The Government cannot avoid its problem of proof of harm under the New York Times standards by applying a balancing test.

[IVA.] The Act and the construction placed on it by the Government create an incredibly sweeping system of automatic peacetime censorship.

[IVB.] Vagueness and overbreadth merge under the Act to preclude fair notice.

[IVC.] The Government's analysis of the Act ignores its glaring defect -- the deterrence of constitutionally protected speech.

[IVD.] The Act's overbreadth is clearly substantial, and becomes gross under the Government's construction of it.

[VIA.] This Court should review the record de novo in determining the public domain issue.

[VIB.] The Government's failure to respond to defendants' experts and public domain evidence underscores the doubt and weakness in its proof.

[VIC.] The Government ignores the vital point that Morland and many others have learned the three concepts.

[VID.] The detail in the Morland article is not authoritative because of the many inaccuracies therein.

Note IV-25. From the Joint Reply Brief of Appellants, September 26 [169, 168]:

II.   The...Atomic Energy Act...only authorizes issuances of an injunction consistent with general equitable principles and First Amendment standards.

[IIA.] The Act requires the Government to establish "reason to believe."

[IIB.] The Government has not shown "reason to believe."

[IIC.] Even when a violation of the Act is shown, Congress still intended Courts to exercise discretion to deny an injunction under the First Amendment and established equitable principles.

[IID.] In the absence of the required statutory showing, there is no inherent authority to impose prior restraint.

[IIIA.] It is the Government's burden to prove that the injunction will be effective, and it has not done so.

[IIIB.] The Government's proposed "public domain" test was announced in a case involving judicial review of classification decisions, not prior restraint. But even under that wholly inapposite test, defendants should be free to publish.

[IIIC.] The Morland article is not more comprehensive, accurate and authoritative than any other publication. Its accurate information is publicly known, and much of the article is inaccurate. Publication of inaccurate information cannot justify prior restraint.

[IIID.] A competent scientist would learn most of he information defendants are enjoined from republishing by reading currently available public literature which bears the Government's stamp of authenticity.

Note IV-26. Marsh said [133]:

Although the concepts presented in the Morland Article would not significantly reduce the time and effort necessary for a non-thermonuclear country with a fission weapon capability to achieve thermonuclear status, this is not true of the information contained in UCRL-4725. This does not mean that release of UCRL-4725 would necessarily induce any country to develop fusion weapons. On the contrary, the technical aspect is only one facet of the issue. A country must still have the motivational and political factors that predispose to weapons acquisition, and further be willing to embark on an ambitious testing program.

Note IV-27. The Committee for Public Justice et al [173] expressed its common interest in insuring that the availability of information to the public at all levels be maximized so that there can be informed public debate of every phase of government decision-making. This covers even technical data about atomic and hydrogen weapons, including their cost, quantity and the dangers in their deployment and use. Information about nuclear weapons is vital so that the public can evaluate government decisions about developing new weapons or limiting the arms race or increasing peaceful uses.

Note V-1. See S.M. Ulam, Adventures of a Mathematician, Charles Scribners Son's, New York (1976); a different perspective is found in Blumberg and Owens [B&0-76].

Note V-2. Before and after the Progressive case, professor Winterberg published diagrams of H-bomb concepts. His 1952 copyrighted conceptual design ["The Truth of the So-called Secret of the Hydrogen Bomb" (in German), Atomkernenergie 34:A28 (1979)] for igniting an autocatalytic fusion burn consists of separate stages in which compression of lithium-6 deuteride is induced by focused shock waves from the fission trigger. His updated design ["The Concept MIRV and the Neutron Bomb" (in German), Atomkernenergie 36:225 (1980)] makes use of radiation coupling.

Note V-3. Gerald Marsh had this to say in the public version of his affidavit [133] comparing relative sensitivity:

The [Morland] article is in part conceptually in error. UCRL-4725, in striking contrast, subsumes everything accurate in the Morland article and accurately (and certifiedly so) goes beyond it, both conceptually and technically.

Without going into detail, the following list (by no means exhaustive) demonstrates the type of information found in UCRL-4725 that could be useful in designing or constructing a fusion weapon. This should be contrasted to the information contained in the Morland article that would not be of any material benefit. [DELETED]

Note V-4. After reviewing UCRL-4725, DeVolpi made the following observations [134]:

Comparison with UCRL-4725 shows that the Morland article does not contain technical details that would be helpful to a nation in constructing fusion weapons, where UCRL-4725 does contain technical details that would readily assist certain foreign nations in designing and constructing fusion weapons, if they chose to acquire that capability....

In sharp contrast to the Morland article, UCRL-4725 is replete with valuable technical details regarding selection and properties of materials, measurements of weapon yields under widely varying conditions, and methods of calculations. [DELETED] Various calculational methods and their specific relationship to weapons tests are described. [DELETED] None of these details is in the Morland article....

The UCRL report has substantial information on the results needed, achievable, and obtained from expensive overt programs of nuclear explosive testing. Inasmuch as the first thermonuclear explosion test took place about four years before the report, the information contained in the report distills key data derived from up to six or seven years of fusion weapon research and eleven years of fission weapon development. A great many nuclear explosives (hundreds) had been tested to reach this level of knowledge in 1956. [DELETED]

The kind of information derived from these tests is clearly necessary information for the designing and optimization of the thermonuclear weapons for strategic arms. Discussion of conceptual information, as in Morland's article, would provide no assistance to foreign nations, in sharp contrast to the knowledge that results from weapons testing revealed in UCRL-4725.

Each of the three central concepts that the government claims to be Secret Restricted Data revealed by the Morland article has been publicly disseminated in UCRL-4725. [DELETED]

Note V-5. From an expurgated version of defendants' brief [169] that was made public after the case was settled:

From the [Glenn letter] the scientist would learn that the diagram accompanying Edward Teller's 1976 Encyclopedia Americana article has been identified by a public affidavit filed in this case "as conceptually similar to a diagram which the government wants to suppress in the Morland article."

The scientist would learn that the Teller diagram suggests "a possible solution as to how a fission trigger and fusion materials might be arranged relative to each other within the casing of a thermonuclear weapon," and would learn that "Teller's peculiar geometrical arrangement of separated elements requires that the weapon casing play an essential role in achieving thermonuclear ignition in a high-yield device, and is unique among possible design concepts."... The scientist would therefore know already, and could confirm by looking at the Teller diagrams, that the fission trigger and the fusion fuel are physically separated from each other, and that the weapon casing plays an "essential" role in transferring the energy from the fission trigger to cause "ignition" in the physically separated fusion fuel. The scientist would thus know the concept of "separate stages" and would know much of the information embodied in the concept of "radiation coupling."

By reading the Glenn letter further, the scientist would learn how to find, from public documents filed in this case, the specific pages of designated books and articles which the government has classified as revealing Restricted Data.... These books and articles are publicly available.... By reading them the scientist would learn specific formulas and mathematical computations confirmed by government action to be relevant in a weapons context. But even a lay reader would learn the importance of "thermal radiation."... Specifically the reader would learn that the "initial radiations from a nuclear weapon" include "the

X-ray radiations from the extremely high temperatures of the bomb vapors," and that the energy "may be radiated out as X-rays before the bomb begins to blow apart."... The reader would learn that "X-rays in this range of a few tens of millions of degrees Kelvin are rather 'soft' [and] they are absorbed in the air immediately around the bomb," which means "the air around the bomb is heated to very high temperatures" because of "the high temperatures created by these X-ray emissions."

The scientist would know that some form of energy would have to leave the fission trigger and "ignite" the fusion fuel before the expanding debris and fireball of the fission trigger reached the fusion fuel and blew it apart. He or she would know that soft X-rays are among "initial radiations," and since soft X-rays travel at the speed of light, they would reach the fusion fuel before the debris and fireball, which travel much slower than the speed of light.... Obviously, this would lead the scientist to think about the relationship between the "casing" and the "soft X-rays," and how that relationship could "ignite" the fusion fuel.

By reading the references noted in the footnotes to the Postol affidavit...the scientist would be directed to consider the importance of "radiation pressure," discussed three times by Reif...and "vapor pressure," discussed by Wannier.... The scientist would then know what Morland knew when he wrote his article: that the "radiation pressure" of "soft X-rays" from a "physically separate" fission trigger can be utilized with the weapon "casing" to "ignite" the fusion fuel.... The scientist would thus know, without reading the Morland article, most of what Morland said about "separate stages" and "radiation pressure," two of the three concepts the government seeks to suppress in this case.

Note V-6. In addition to three draft copies sent to Postol, Forsberg, and Siegel for review, at least sixteen copies of the final typescript were sent out by Morland [89].

Note VI-1. On the basis of an in camera affidavit [8A] by Duane Sewell, the government [2] concluded that "this information could provide nations with thermonuclear capabilities in the near future."

Note VI-2. A joint affidavit [62] by three of the authors of this book contained these remarks:

The danger of proliferation of nuclear weapons is real and serious; the remedies to this danger are in dispute. The practices of secrecy and technology denial are only two facets of a needed comprehensive antiproliferation program. The undersigned are in agreement that agents of the Executive Branch should not be permitted to distort, distract, or divert attention from significant political components in antiproliferation programs by overemphasizing secrecy where other, less restrictive strategies are available to meet legitimate national needs.

To acquire thermonuclear capability, the five nations that have developed such weapons have shown that a country must have:

(a) the requisite substrata of advanced industrial and scientific national capacity,

(b) the motivational and political factors that predispose to weapons acquisition, and

(c) a detectable, self-revealing program of nuclear explosive testing.

Given in any country the existence of capability, motivation, and the willingness to reveal intentions through testing, it is our opinion that the availability of the Morland article might be of negligible or at most minor consequence to the speed with which additional nations could succeed in developing thermonuclear weapons.

Note VI-3. An affidavit by Alexander DeVolpi [63] summarized a recently published analysis of U.S. nonproliferation policy:

Advanced industrial nations...are already in a position, if they so choose, to carry out the development of fusion weapons, especially weapons of high yield, and they can only do this if they can openly test such devices. It is for this reason that a moratorium on nuclear weapons testing would be a major, substantive step towards retarding potential proliferation. The failure of the government to lead by example or to execute bilateral agreements in this regard is far more contributive to proliferation risk than public discussion of weapons concepts found in Morland's article. The bridge between concept and execution in nuclear weapons design is much greater than the Government has acknowledged in its Affidavits, and the suppression of information at this level acts only to perpetuate the questionable policies enunciated by the Government.

Furthermore, in reference to Paragraphs 7 and 8 in Brown's Affidavit dealing with proliferation, it should be emphasized that information of the sort gathered by Morland is clearly subject to independent discovery either by compilation from public source documents or by inductive reasoning by scientists in technologically advanced nations. The decision by such nations not to proceed with development of fission or fusion weapons is rooted primarily in the self-defeating nature of such armaments and other motivational disincentives. In addition, there are safeguards and technical barriers that deter other nations, less technologically advanced, from acquiring materials or fulfilling fabrication of fission weapons that are needed to trigger the thermonuclear devices discussed by Teller and Morland.

Note VII-1. The following paragraphs are from a statement President Carter made on issuing Executive Order 12605:

The public is entitled to know as much as possible about the Government's activities. Classification should be used only to protect legitimate national security secrets and never to cover up mistakes or improper activities.

While some material must be classified, the Government classifies too much information, classifies it too highly and for too long. These practices violate the public's right to know, impose unnecessary costs, and weaken protection for truly sensitive information by undermining respect for all classification.

The new order will increase openness in Government by limiting classification and accelerating declassification. At the same time, it will improve protection for information that needs to be kept secret.

The standard for classification has been tightened. No document is to be classified unless its release reasonably could be expected to cause identifiable damage to the national security. Insignificant damage is not a basis for classification. In addition, the number of agencies and officials with classification authority is being reduced. Delegation of such authority shall be held to a minimum.

All documents should be declassified as early as national security permits. Under the new order, most documents will be declassified after no more than 6 years. Only agency heads and officials with "Top Secret" classification authority may classify for a longer period and only by indicating why classification will remain necessary despite the passage of time. With a few exceptions, the documents given extended classification will be declassified after no more than 20 years. The millions of documents classified under prior orders that are over 20 years old will be reviewed and -- in almost all cases -- released as quickly as possible.

In addition, I have created an Information Security Oversight Office to provide overall supervision. This Office will have authority to review agencies' procedures and files. It can overrule their regulations and their decisions on classification of individual documents, subject to appeal to the National Security Council.

Note VII-2. In a letter titled, "Classification and Nonproliferation Studies," John Griffin advised all national laboratories (September 5, 1978):

Much, if not all, of the officially declassified information was declassified at a time when the main threat to the United States was considered to be a overt foreign national nuclear weapons production effort.

Although information, standing alone, is unclassified, there is the possibility that evaluations (or assessments) could add information that, when taken together, could be classified as National Security Information. Of particular concern are evaluations of (1) clandestine separation of special nuclear material, (2) clandestine fabrication of nuclear weapons, and (3) methods of concealing such clandestine activities....

When knowledgeable authority, in a U.S. Government-supported study, offers proliferation alternatives based on modifications or

extensions...for clandestine facilities, it does not fall within the
scope of the declassified technology.

Significant alternatives or modifications to previously declassified
technology or information which are authoritatively suggested for
avoiding detection...are in a similar category as the foregoing.

In addition to the above, some Restricted Data information which has
not been officially declassified has made its way into the open
literature.   Such publication does not provide justification for
repeating the information on an unclassified basis. The detailed
identification of unclassified sources of such information [a
bibliography of unclassified references] is classified as National
Security Information in the same manner as are upgrading notices.
Elaboration may be Restricted Data.

Note VII-3. According to material from the Government Information and Individual
Rights Subcommittee:

This 1952 statute -- replacing several acts of a temporary nature dating
to 1917 -- authorized the Commissioner of Patents and Trademarks to
order that an invention be kept secret and withhold the grant of a
patent "for such period as the national interest requires." To violate
a secrecy order could bring two years imprisonment and a $10,000 fine.

The National Security Agency, military services, Department of
Energy, NASA, and even the Department of Justice can notify the
Commissioner to issue a secrecy order. Such orders have covered voice
scramblers, rocket propulsion, missile guidance, cryptographic devices
and means of escaping detection by radar. In 1979 the Patent Office
issued 243 new secrecy orders. In the last year it has renewed 3,300
secrecy orders -- some of them 30 years old.

Until the national emergency declared by President Truman was terminated in 1978, secrecy orders could be issued for the duration. Now they
can be issued for only one year, but are renewable annually if the
defense agency that requested the order determines that it should be
continued.

A patent applicant under secrecy order has the right to seek "just
compensation" from the agency that caused the order to be issued: for
damage caused by the order itself and/or for the use of the invention by
the Government. He can apply for compensation during a period that
begins when he is notified by the Patent Office that a patent on his
invention would issue but for the secrecy order, and ends six years
after a patent issues. The Patent Office said it understands that 29
administrative claims for compensation have been filed with the
Department of Defense since 1945.

Note VII-4. The Defence Science Board [DSB-70] concluded:

Security has limited effectiveness. One may guess that tightly controlled
information will remain secret, on the average, for perhaps five years. But
on vital information, one should not rely on effective secrecy for more than
one year. ...never in the past has it been possible to keep secret the
truly important discoveries....

Note VII-5. A news article "Should inertial-confinement fusion be classified?" in
the August 1980 issue of Physics Today contained the following statements:

[The argument goes that] public disclosure of inertial-fusion principles and
technology could...lead to proliferation of thermonuclear weapons throughout
the world.

According to [Fred] Mayer, "The science of inertial-confinement fusion
would progress much faster if most of the physics was declassified."

"A particular example," according to Ronald Martin (Argonne), "is the
tradeoff between target performance and ion kinetic energy, which the
accelerator designers would like to be as high as possible. Statements
about target design, even though based on only preliminary calculations, are
hard to debate because of classification issues, and could lead the
accelerator development program in unnecessarily restrictive directions."

Coordination of nonproliferation policy within the Federal government is
the responsibility of the State Department, although the Department of
Energy took over the AEC's role of classification watchdog. In the last
year or so, the State Department has been becoming more and more visible in
the inertial-fusion arena.

An objection commonly voiced regarding the State Department's intervention in inertial-fusion affairs is that the State Department was, until recently, apparently operating in a technical vacuum as far as ICF was concerned, having no fusion experts on its staff and not soliciting technical advice from the inertial-fusion community.

These objections are not raised against DOE procedures.

Ray E. Kidder wrote:

With the understanding that ICF targets do not involve fission, actinides, high explosives (HE), or thermonuclear yields greater than one ton HE-equivalent, there is no difficulty or ambiguity in distinguishing an ICF target from a nuclear weapon. It is therefore possible to maintain the ne-cessary classification of nuclear weapons, while at the same time declassi-fying ICF. Classification can be decided on the basis of context, the nu-clear weapons context being readily distinguishable from the ICF context.

With regard to computer programs, it is proposed that the physics and difference equations, input, output and data of ICF codes be unclassified. The flow charts, source programs, and compiled programs...need not be unclassified, especially those generated at the weapons laboratories.

Note VIII-1. The currently classified Foster and Moe reports: See testimony of John S. Foster before the Energy Research Advisory Board, 3 May, 1979; also Nature 281:414 (1979)].

Note IX-1. In a defense statement orignally classified by the government [169], The Progressive said:

On April 25, 1979, four physicists wrote to Senator John Glenn to point out that in the course of these proceedings 'the government has released classified information that identifies the nature of the design concept upon which U.S. thermonuclear weapons are based' and that 'those [government officials] entrusted with handling classified information associated with this court case have already released much of the infor-mation the suit was brought to protect.'

The government classified the [entire] letter as containing 'Secret Restricted Data' about nuclear weapons, the same level of classification applied to the Morland article. Thus, in the government's opinion, publication of the Glenn letter would cause the same degree of injury to the national security as would publication of the Morland article. However, seven college newspapers, with a combined circulation of 67,000 persons, published the letter in full and informed their readers that the government had classified the letter as containing Secret Restricted Data about nuclear weapons. By placing its stamp of authenticity on the letter, the government has thereby informed any foreign scientist who wants information about nuclear weapons to read the letter with care and pursue any leads suggested by the letter.

Note IX-2. DeVolpi reported his first-hand experience about accessibility of declassified reports at the Los Alamos Scientific Laboratory (LASL):

I have visited LASL on about six occasions. On December 5-6, 1977 I attended an unclassified Specialists' Meeting...at the National Security and Resources Study Center at LASL. The open public library is on the first floor of the Study Center. The conference halls on the second floor are reached through the first floor entry, which leads directly to the open library. It is not necessary to pass through any security gate or identification check to reach either the open library or the conference hall during such unclassified meetings.

It would have been a simple matter for anybody attending our Specialists' Meeting [many of whom were foreign nationals] to peruse the documents in the library and unnoticed to make copies of interesting reports. In particular, if a scientist had a special interest in the type of non-weapons research reported in UCRL 4725, for example regarding nuclear propulsion, it would have been quite appropriate to copy all of UCRL 4725.

I have made two official trips to Europe, visiting laboratories and attending conferences. Upon returning from each trip, I was interviewed by an agent of the CIA requesting information regarding observations I may have made about the status of weapons research or nuclear technology in European countries. It is reasonable to expect that such debriefing of foreign scientists also takes place routinely upon their return from the United States.

Inasmuch as the LASL library at the National Security and Resources Study Center is a unique facility for declassified weapons data and pertinent information on fusion research, any serious researcher or foreign agent is likely to plan to go to that library. Since there are no restrictions in access to the library, no record of access would necessarily be available. In view of Rotow's success in finding UCRL 4725 within a half hour, any researcher who is looking for weapons, nuclear propulsion, or fusion data is likely to have encountered that report. Consequently, it is extremely likely that the document has already been compromised.

Note X-1. There have already been several legal analyses of various aspects of the case. Some cited in Chapter X are [RON-80], [ABR-80], [CHEH-80], [ENN-80], and [HEN-80].

Note X-2. The temporary injunction was the first ever issued to stop publication of a newspaper or magazine for national security reasons. There had been one involving a book, however -- the Marchetti case, in which a permanent injunction was sustained. That case differed in that it involved contractual arrangements between the government and an employee.

Note X-3. Judge Warren wrote into the court record the following findings of fact [85]: The correct defendants were charged; the history of the article was placed on the record; the offical determination of classification by Griffin and Sewell was noted. He found that government warnings -- that the article contained Restricted Data whose publication would be harmful to the United States -- were, in fact, conveyed to Morland; The Progressive did refuse to voluntarily accept censorship; and a hearing had been held, resulting in issuance of a TRO. The judge concluded that "the article in question contains concepts that are not found in the public realm, concepts that are vital to the operation of the bomb."

On the question of proliferation potential, Judge Warren ruled:

Publication...would be extremely important to a nation seeking a thermo-nuclear capability, for it would provide vital information on key concepts. Once basic concepts are learned, the remainder of the process may easily follow. The article could provide sufficient information to allow a medium-size nation to move faster in developing a hydrogen weapon.

Note X-4. Let us examine Warren's conclusions in detail:

"With Reason to Believe." Under a juridical requirement of scienter (intent), we understand that "reason to believe" requires more than mere administrative showing of notice -- much more than the "self-evident" status ascribed by the government [166]. (However, the Rosenberg decision indicates the legal criteria under the statute would be satisfied by administrative notice.) Moreover, the fact that the government has applied a classification label is not supposed to be determinative of whether information is actually related to national defense; "reason to believe" should be established for the defendant's actual state of mind, rather than being based on administrative notice of document classification.

"Will be Utilized." From the viewpoint of a careful semantic selection, "will" is a very strong probabalistic condition, stronger for example than "surely" and much stronger that "could" or "may." "Likely" implies something over 50 percent probability of occurrence, while "could" and "may" mean only that a nonzero, but possibly small, probability exists.

"To Injure the United States." An appropriate defense against this facet of the charge would be a balancing of long- and short-term interests, with deference to individual judgment. One person's view of injury to the United States may be another's path to its salvation. Consider the Vietnam conflict. Protests against American involvement were categorized by some as "injurious" to U.S. interest, yet it is arguable that early disinvolvement would have been beneficial to the United States.

"Secure an Advantage to Any Foreign Nation." This phrase is vague and potentially arbitrary in application. After all, something that secures an advantage to a foreign nation might also benefit the United States. Not all international relationships are zero-sum games, where one's gain is the other's loss. It is mutually advantageous for nations to cease nuclear weapons proliferation. Should not redeeming virtues of Morland's work weigh against claims of possible foreign advantage?

Note X-5. A person could, of course, submit a private work product to DOE for clearance. However there are undoubtedly many cases where the individual has good reason to believe that the work contains only public information, expecting that the delay and nuisance caused by submission would be pointless. In other cases, anyone who had submitted an article that was declared to contain Restricted Data would have to accept deletions or blanket classification, and charges of political motivation might arise if DOE or any other federal agency were a target of criticism in the article that was censored.

Clearly, universal application of that sort of DOE review is impractical, and therefore hypothetical. Each time an article was submitted for review, the response could inadvertently give clues about classified information. Thus DOE would have to lean toward overclassification. As word got around that the law was being rigorously enforced, the process would predictably be saturated by clearance-review requests from anybody who wrote anything "concerning" nuclear weapons or nuclear reactors. In addition, there are situations that are difficult to police: publications take place in foreign media, Americans submit articles overseas, and foreigners publish in American journals. Finally, repetition of the sort of thing that happened (unexpectedly) with our letter to Senator Glenn and (perhaps deliberately provoked) with Hansen's letter to Senator Percy could run security officials ragged: If copies are sent to publication outlets in parallel with submission to DOE, a decision to classify could trigger comic-opera episodes of attempts to garner the copies.

Note X-6. When the Supreme Court in Near struck down the injunction as violating the First Amendment, it added that "subsequent punishment for...abuses as may exist is the appropriate remedy."

Note X-7. Further references by the government to technical information may be found in its terminology: "nuclear weapons design data"; "designated technical information that describes the workings of the H-bomb"; and "technical information describing the design, construction and utilization of nuclear weapons." The latter phrase would be acceptable for use in this case; the implied meanings an associations of the others merely muddle the issues.

Note X-8. Two of the authors have looked over the twenty-two Appendix C documents contained in the court's protective order of September 4, 1980 (not to be confused with Appendix C of this book). All Restricted Data and NSI have been deleted from those documents. Brackets or boxes surround material that is considered sensitive by the Department of State or ACDA -- statements or phrases that, under the agreed-upon court order, cannot be "attributed to the government" if quoted.

Almost all technical phrases used by to the government, as well as the counterarguments to defendants' expert affiants, have been bracketed. Essentially all of the technical phrases are to be found in documents now publicly available. None of the material is still classified, and we think that no harm to the nation would ensue if the government let its counterarguments be attributed to it. Because it seems to be pushing the "never confirm or deny" principle a little hard here (if that is the motivation), future readers, if any, of the "Appendix C" documents might get the impression that the government did not want to fully reveal the logical weaknesses of the arguments it employed in camera. (The agreement expressly did not prohibit FOIA requests for those documents, but it did note that the government remained free to oppose such requests.)

We can give two isolated but specific examples of this protective order censoring information that is not otherwise legally classifiable. The public version of Duane Sewell's first affidavit [8] says, "Dissemination of the material contained in the Morland paper would in my judgment materially shorten development time of thermonuclear weapons [DELETED]." This deletion is unfortunate, inasmuch as the public has a legitimate interest in knowing the time shortening estimated by the highest official with administrative responsibility for carrying out atomic data restrictions.

In the second example, brackets surround a numerical value in the following otherwise unclassified statement made in a government brief [166]: "Assistant Secretary of State Pickering identified [ ] nations, some located in sensitive geographical areas, that are now believed to be capable of producing a fission (atomic) weapon." Although some marginal value might be conceded to the State Department's withholding (which it has done as NSI) the names of the nations it believes to be capable of making fission weapons, it is difficult to understand the rationale for also placing under court pro-tective order the total number. On the contrary, it is important, and perhaps suffic-ient, for public or congressional evaluation of administration policy to know how many nations there are that the U.S. government has reason to believe could make fission weapons now.

Note X-9. The availability of UCRL-4725, as well as numerous other erroneously declassified documents, was of considerable importance during the appeals hearing. The government maintained that it was extremely unlikely that the documents had been compromised. This is not in accord with the following quote taken from a letter from F.C. Gilbert, Acting Assistant Secretary for Defense Programs, to Senator John Glenn and dated June 29, 1979, well before the appeals hearing in September:

(3) Notwithstanding paragraph (2), any information which is published and which, but for such publication, would be Restricted Data within the meaning of paragraph (1) shall be treated as Restricted Data for purposes of the initial publication thereof but not for purposes of any subsequent publication.

(4) For purposes of this subsection, the term "publish" and "publication," when used with respect to any information, refer to any act which has the effect of making such information public.

The bill would also require "that if private citizens are to be punished for violations of the Act, they have a specific intent to injure the United States or help a foreign nation, and are not subject to prosecution merely because DOE thinks they should have 'reason to believe' they will harm the U.S. or help a foreign nation" [emphasis added]. ["Additional views of Congressman McCloskey," attached to the House Government Information and Individual Rights Subcommittee report concerning the classification of private ideas [HR-80]].

Note XI-5. Another approach would be to use language that emphasizes excluding deducible data from the definition of Restricted information. To do that §2014(i) and (y) could be amended so that the term "design" includes the detailed information contained therein or the government-sponsored research and development data pertinent to the information contained therein.

Also the term "Restricted Data" would be confined to all nondeducible data describing design, manufacture, or operation of nuclear weapons. The use of special nuclear material in the production of energy would also be excluded from Restricted Data.

A major difficulty with this approach becomes apparent when attempts are made to explicitly define "nondeducible." What may be deducible to one person my not be to another. It is for this reason that the alternative form in Note IV-4 is preferable.

Note XI-6. ISOO tasks to be taken over by a classification review commission:

1. Issuing and maintaining guidelines for systematic review of twenty-year-old classified information.

2. Compiling a list of specific categories of documents for which systematic review for declassification has been postponed.

3. Listing information over ten years old that has been exempted from mandatory review for declassification.

4. Compiling copies of complaints and suggestions received from persons within or outside the government with respect to the administration of the information security program, including appeals from decisions on declassification requests.

5. Making available copies of annual reports on implementation of Executive Order 12065.

6. Reporting on agency-implemention regulations and guidelines for systematic declassification.

7. Receiving copies of onsite reviews of the information security program of each agency that handles classified information.

Note XI-7. Additional responsibilities of a classification review commission:

1. Reviewing and having veto power automatically over any efforts to achieve a permanent injunction under §2280 of the Atomic Energy Act.

2. Providing the Congress and the public with such other information as may be of use in evaluating declassification progress under Executive Order 12065 and implementing directives.

3. Acting as a board of appeal in classification disputes under both the Atomic Energy Act and the Freedom of Information Act.

4. Having available a panel of experts to assist courts in cases involving classified materials.

5. Maintaining visible classification accountability by any agency of the federal government.

6. Ensuring that appropriate classifications practices are followed, including meaningful written justifications, assigned time limits until declassification, and proper authorization.

7. Evaluating and deciding the need and practicality of reclassifying mistakenly declassified documents.

8. Publishing unclassified guidelines for declassification.

9. Reviewing classified guidelines for consistency with all policy objectives.

10. Reimbursing nongovernment parties for loss of property value due to government classification of a private work product.

11. Balancing the risks and benefits of public exposure of classified information.

A current update on the possible distribution of any of these documents through the Technical Information Center (TIC)...shows that [thirty documents] were introduced into the TIC system for distribution, but only one of those appears to require [classification] upgrading (tentatively, pending headquarters review) because it may have nuclear proliferation aspects.

...we feel very strongly that publication of the material in this declassified interim report at this time would give a misleading impression of the true situation, and could affect the Government's position in the Progressive H-Bomb secrets case.

Note X-10. The February hearing examined the Invention Secrecy Act, and in March the Progressive case was covered. Witnesses appearing before the Subcommittee included Representative Paul N. McCloskey; Assistant Secretary for Defense Programs Duane Sewell; Floyd Abrams, an expert on constitutional law who had prepared a brief for the appeals court during the Progressive case on behalf of the New York Times et al.; and the executive associate director of Lawrence Livermore Laboratory, Richard Wagner. There was also a panel consisting of George Davida from the University of Wisconsin-Milwaukee; David Kahn, whose writings include "Cryptology Goes Public" in the Fall 1979 issue of Foreign Affairs; and Admiral B.R. Inman, director of the National Security Agency. In addition, we submitted written testimony to the Subcommittee, as did Ray Kidder and Hugh DeWitt of Lawrence Livermore.

Congressman McCloskey pointed out in his written statement that

nine reputable individuals, six government employees and three private citizens have therefore been able to generate communications in good faith which the government subsequently chose to classify.

The six government employees apparently believed that DOE was involved in classification procedures for political purposes rather than in checking bona fide attempts to protect nuclear secrecy....

If, indeed, a Harvard student, a newspaper reporter and an untrained nuclear amateur can generate articles gathered from publicly available sources, which the government feels must be kept secret because those articles threaten the peace of the world, the law is no longer adequate to protect the national security.

Note XI-1. [F&W-74]: One should understand the difference, and its importance, between "secrets" and "information"; the difference between "the right to know" and the "right to participate"; the distinction between access to "official data" and access to "written opinions or advice of officials"; the distinction between the "intelligence community" and the "community of policy-makers"; and the legal difference betwen "the right to know" and "the right to divulge." There is also a difference between "true" and "false" secrets -- the latter referring to information classified to protect not the national interest but the government's political interest. Sharpening these distinctions can lead to fewer disputes.

Note XI-2. Subsection (a) of §2274 at present forbids the communication, transmission, or disclosure of Restricted Data, whether lawfully or unlawfully in possession, to another "with intent to injure the United States or with intent to secure an advantage to any foreign nation." Subsection (b) applies if there is "reason to believe such data will be utilized to injure the United States or to secure an advantage to any foreign nation." If a person disregarded notification of an administrative determination to the latter effect, that person could perhaps be held in violation of subsection (b), even if there was no intent to injure the nation and even if no injury resulted. Congressman Paul N. McCloskey has introduced a bill before Congress that would delete subsection (b) entirely.

Note XI-3. §2277 applies to any person with some previous or contemporary connection to the government; any unauthorized communication or receipt of Restricted Data "knowing or having reason to believe that such data is Restricted Data" is forbidden.

Note XI-4. The bill proposed by Congressman McCloskey [HR-8422, 96th Congress; HR-1406, 97th Congress] contains the following wording to replace part of §2014:

(1) Except as provided in paragraph (2), the term "Restricted Data" means all data describing--

(A) the design, manufacture, or utilization of atomic weapons; or

(B) the production of special nuclear material.

(2) The term "Restricted Data" shall not include any information which is declassified or removed from the Restricted Data category pursuant to section 142. Such term shall also not include any information which is, or is derived from information which has been published.

Glossary

AMICI CURIAE. Literally, friends of the court. Filings made in court by intervenors who are not litigants.

ANTIPROLIFERATION. Used to describe actions or policies that oppose propagation of nuclear weapons.

BOOSTER. A thermonuclear fusion component that amplifies the yield of a fission explosive.

CHAIN REACTION. A series of nuclear fissions, each one stimulated by a neutron emitted in a previous fission.

CLASSIFIED. Having distribution restricted under the Atomic Energy Act or other authorization. Classification labels include Top Secret, Secret, and Confidential.

CLEARANCE. Government authorization for access to classified information. A Q-clearance represents standard DOE approval, but a Sigma clearance level is needed for nuclear weapons data.

CONCLUSORY. Presenting unsupported conclusions; used by each side in the Progressive case to characterize the other side's affidavits.

CRITICAL MASS. The smallest accumulation of fissionable material that will sustain a self-perpetuating neutron chain reaction; its value depends on density, isotopic composition, chemical form, and surroundings.

DECLASSIFIED. Officially declared no longer classified. A document may be declassified in part or in toto.

DIVERSION. The diverting, from a legitimate channel, of fissile material for illicit weapons manufacture. Could apply to clandestine or overt actions by a country nominally committed to a nonnuclear-weapons policy. Could also apply to collusion that puts the material in the hands of a nongovernmental entity. Overt diversion would probably only occur at a time of international tension.

ENRICHMENT. The process of increasing the fissile fraction of uranium by means of isotopic separation.

FAST NEUTRON. A neutron moving with relatively high velocity, with kinetic energy usually in or above the kilovolt range.

FISSILE. Fissionable in thermal reactors -- that is, can be fissioned by thermal neutrons. This does not exclude fissionability by fast neutrons.

FISSILE FRACTION. The fissile-isotope fraction of a mixture of fissile and nonfissile fissionable material.

FISSION. The splitting of a nucleus into two or more lighter ones called "fission products," invariably accompanied by other nuclear radiation.

FISSIONABLE. A fissionable nucleus is one that will, with some probability, undergo fission upon absorption of a neutron. A nucleus that is fissionable but not fissile requires a fast neutron to cause it to split.

FISSION EXPLOSIVE. A device that uses a nuclear chain reaction to produce an explosive release of blast, heat, and radiation.

FERTILE. Actinide isotopes that are not fissile, but can become so upon absorption of a neutron. They are fissionable, and some can sustain a fast-neutron chain reaction (with a large critical mass).

FUSION.   The process of combining light nuclei into heavier ones.   It is accompanied by release of large amounts of thermonuclear energy.

GUN-TYPE NUCLEAR WEAPON. A device in which subcritical masses are driven together by high explosive to produce a nuclear explosion.

HORIZONTAL PROLIFERATION. Propagation of nuclear weapons to nations that did not previously have them.

IMPLOSION-TYPE NUCLEAR WEAPON. A device in which high explosives surrounding a subcritical configuration of fissionable material compress it into a condition of supercriticality, thereby producing a nuclear explosion.

ISOTOPE. A material whose atoms have a specific number of neutrons as well as of protons. A chemical element can consist of several isotopes, whose atoms have the same number of protons but different numbers of neutrons, and hence have different masses, even though chemically very similar.   For example, plutonium has the relatively stable isotopes Pu-236, Pu-238, Pu-239, Pu-240, Pu-241, and Pu-242, the numerical suffixes specifying the combined number of protons and neutrons.

MILITARY-GRADE MATERIAL. High quality, weapons-grade, fissile material.

MODERATOR. A component -- usually water, heavy water, or graphite -- of some nuclear reactors.   The moderator causes the neutrons to slow down, thereby increasing their chances of being absorbed by a fissile nucleus.

MULTISTAGE WEAPON. A weapon consisting of a primary fission trigger, secondary fusion package, and massive, usually fissionable, casing.

NATIONAL SECURITY INFORMATION. A category of restricted data defined by Executive Order 12065.

NEUTRONS. Neutral particles which, together with protons, comprise the nucleus of an atom.

NONNUCLEAR-WEAPONS STATE. A nation that has not claimed or demonstrated posession of nuclear weapons.

NUCLEAR EXPLOSION. Same as fission explosion: an energy burst derived from a supercritical mass.

NUCLEAR WEAPON. A weapon that has explosive or radiation dispersive effects caused by a fission explosion; the name implies configuration -- and deliverability -- appropriate for intended application.

NUCLEAR-WEAPONS STATE. A nation that claims or has demonstrated possession of nuclear weapons.

OVERT DIVERSION. See diversion.

PENTAGON PAPERS. The set of documents comprising a history of U.S. decisio - making on Vietnam policy ("United States-Vietnam Relations 1945-67, Department of Defense Study") that became subject to the Supreme Court decision in New York Times.

PERMANENT INJUNCTION. A court order indefinitely forbidding the particular action enjoined.

PREDETONATION. The premature initiation of the chain reaction in a nuclear weapon, leading to reduced yield ("fizzle") because the imploding material did not have a chance to reach its most explosive configuration before it began to "disassemble." Predetonation is caused by excessive numbers of inherent neutrons, as from sontaneous fission in the nuclear material, combined with too-slow "assembly" by the chemical high explosive.

PROCEDURAL SAFEGUARDS. Safeguards measures not inherently technical in nature that rely upon auditing the fissile material and maintaining its security.

PROLIFERATION. An increase in the number of nuclear weapons, usually horizontal (involving more states), unless vertical (involving more weapons) is specified.

PROLIFERATION POTENTIAL. Usually, the capability of a country to acquire its first nuclear weapons; somtimes used to refer to the capability to add to an existing nuclear arsenal.

PROLIFERATION RESISTANCE. Factors or actions that impede proliferation.

REACTIVITY CHANGE. Change in neutron multiplication factor of a fissile assembly resulting from a change in physical condition, such as mass, density, reflector, poison, etc.   For a weapons-type assembly, a certain reactivity increment is needed to bring the system above critical.

REACTIVITY WORTH. The reactivity change induced by a unit-mass change in the amount of fuel in a nuclear reactor.

REACTOR. A facility containing a controlled nuclear fission chain reaction.

REACTOR GRADE. The fissile quality of a particular reactor fuel; the quality can range over a wide latitude, depending upon the degree of burnup; generally considered to contain more than seven percent even isotopes of plutonium.   See weapons grade.

RECLASSIFIED. Information that has been classified after having once been declassified (either intentionally or mistakenly). Reclassification is currently forbidden by Executive Order 12065.

RECYCLE. The reuse as reactor fuel of unburned uranium and plutonium from spent fuel, after separation from fission products at a reprocessing plant.

REPROCESSING. Chemical treatment of spent reactor fuel to separate the plutonium and uranium from the fission products and/or from each other.

RESTRICTED DATA. Information concerning nuclear weapons that is defined under the Atomic Energy Act to be subject to special controls in communication, transmittal, disclosure, or publication.

SAFEGUARDS. Quasi-technical and nontechnical methods of controlling fissile materials at all stages, primarily by surveillance, physical security, and accounting; includes regulations, procedures, and equipment designed to prevent or detect diversion.

SENSITIVE. An informal term that has no legal standing, used to describe information or documents that are or should be classified.

STRATEGIC. Major weapon quantities or systems usable for large-scale warfare. (The term is not used in this book in the sense of 'significant' quantities of fissile or special nuclear material.)

SUPERCRITICAL. Having more than enough reactivity to support an exponentially increasing chain reaction.

TECHNICAL SAFEGUARDS. Measures used for technically assisting in the auditing of fissile materials at any stage by means of monitoring, detecting, sealing, and measuring.

THERMAL NEUTRONS. Slow-moving neutrons, with kinetic energies generally below 1 eV.

THERMONUCLEAR PROCESS. A nuclear fusion process that requires the reactants to be at extremely high temperatures; the source of the sun's energy.

VERTICAL PROLIFERATION. An increase in the number and quality of nuclear weapons and related delivery systems in the nuclear-weapons states.

WEAPONS GRADE. Applied to fissionable material with a very high fissile content -- over 93 percent for plutonium -- well suited for efficient fission-explosive use; sometimes called military grade.

Acronyms and Abbreviations

ABM	Antiballistic missile
ACDA	Arms Control and Disarmament Agency
ACLU	American Civil Liberties Union
AEC	Atomic Energy Commission (U.S. -- superseded by ERDA)
ANL	Argonne National Laboratory (U.S. DOE)
CIA	Central Intelligence Agency (U.S.)
CTBT	Comprehensive Test-ban Treaty
DOE	Department of Energy (U.S.)
ERDA	Energy Research and Development Agency (U.S. -- superseded by DOE)
FAS	Federation of American Scientists
FOIA	Freedom of Information Act
GAC	General Advisory Committee (AEC)
GAO	Government Accounting Office
ICBM	Intercontinental ballistic missile
ICF	Inertially confined fusion
INFCE	International Nuclear Fuel Cycle Evaluation
ISOO	Information Security Oversight Office
kT(TNT)	kiloton (TNT equivalent)
LASL	Los Alamos Scientific Laboratory (of U.S. DOE)
LLL	Lawrence Livermore Laboratory (of U.S. DOE)
MARV	Maneuverable Reentry Vehicle
MIRV	Multiple Independently Targetable Reentry Vehicle
MX	Missile Experimental
NATO	North Atlantic Treaty Organization
NPT	Non-Proliferation Treaty
NSA	National Security Agency
NSI	National Security Information
RD	Restricted Data
SIPRI	Stockholm International Peace Research Institute
SLBM	Submarine-Launched Ballistic Missile
SRAM	Short-range attack missile
SRD	Secret Restricted Data
TRO	Temporary Restraining Order
UCRL	University of California Radiation Laboratory (U.S. AEC)

Progressive Case Legal References

The docket number for the initial proceedings in Progressive is 79-C-98. On appeal the numbers are 79-1428 for repeal of the injunction and 79-1664 for the motion to vacate.

The reader is cautioned that in spite of much effort on the part of the authors, the following list of references is missing some information and may contain errors. There should, however, be internal consistency between the list as given and references made within the body of the book.

Documents originally filed in camera are marked with the symbol #. Some documents were "sanitized," that is, filed publicly after approved deletions; these are marked *. Documents originally filed in the public record are unmarked below. Conference calls and other material for which a formal written record does not exist are marked with +. Documents that were originally in camera but have been subsequently declassified have the identifying symbol x. Public documents not in our possession are marked with -. Dates associated with the documents below are generally the date of affirmation or filing, whichever is listed first. Numbers at end of reference in angular brackets < > correspond to 72 in camera documents listed by Government in Appendix A of [181]. A document marked by the letter C indicates that it is included in Appendix C of [181].

HEARING FOR TEMPORARY RESTRAINING ORDER

[1]   Complaint: United States of America, Plaintiff, v. The Progressive, Inc., Erwin Knoll, Samuel Day, Jr., and Howard Morland, Defendants (March 8, 1979).
[2]   Application for temporary restraining order (March 8).
[3]   Motion of the United States for preliminary injunction (March 8).
[4]   Plaintiff's statement of points and authorities (March 8).
[4A]   x Morland article (March 8), <1>.
[4B]   x DOE Analysis of Morland article <4C>.
[5]   Affidavit of James S. Cannon (March 1).
[6]   Affidavit of Charles N. Van Doren (March 1).
[7]   Affidavit of Thomas R. Pickering (March 1).
[7A]   # Affidavit of Thomas R. Pickering (March 7). <3>
[8]   Affidavit of Duane C. Sewell (March 7).
[8A]   # Attachments to affidavits of Griffin <11C>, Rathjens and Sewell <2C> (March 8).
[9]   Affidavit of John A. Griffin (March 7).
[10]   Affidavit of Lynn R. Coleman (March 7).
[11]   Affidavit of George William Rathjens (March 8).
[13]   Affidavit of Frederick J. Erhardt (March 8).
[14]   Admission of service, Earl Munson, Jr. (March 8).
[15]   + Certificate of service on Howard Morland (March 9).
[15]   + Certificate of service on Howard Morland (March 9). (3/9) (15 March).

[16]   Notice of hearing (March 9).
[17]   - Memo disqualifying Judge Doyle (March 9).
[18]   Temporary Restraining Order (March 9).
[19]   + Order (RWW) for hearing on motion (March 9).
[20]   Marshall's return of service of S&C; Morland, The Progressive,
            Day and Knoll served 3/9 (March 12).
[21]   Supplemental memorandum of law for plaintiff United States
            (March 12).
[22]   Affidavit of Spurgeon M. Keeny, Jr. (March 12).
[23]   Affidavit of Jack W. Rosengren (March 13).
[24]   Supplemental affidavit of John A. Griffin (March 13).
[25]   Affidavit of Marian L. Olson (March 12).
[26]   Affidavit of James R. Schlesinger (March 13).
[26A]   Affidavit of Robert N. Thorn (March 12).
[26B]   ? Affidavit of Roger Batzel (March 12).
[27]   Amended motion for protective order (March 12).
[28]   Memorandum of points and authorities in support of the motion
            for amended protective order (March 12).
[29]   + Conference call (March 14).
[30]   Protective order for in camera filing (March 14).
[30A]   Protective order (unsigned, for Doyle) (March 14).
[31]   Transcript of proceedings on hearing for temporary restraining
            order (3/9) (March 15).

HEARINGS FOR PRELIMINARY INJUNCTION

[32]   Appearance as attorney for defendant Howard Morland of Thomas
            P. Fox (March 15).
[33]   Order, extending restraining order of 3/9 to 5:00 PM 3/26
            (March 15).
[33A]   Order, Re: seating priority (March 15).
[34]   Memorandum of points and authorities on behalf of the American
            Civil Liberties Union and the Wisconsin Civil Liberties Union
            as amici curiae (March 16).
[35]   + Conference call (March 15).
[36]   Declaration of Cyrus R. Vance (March 14).
[37]   Affidavit of Harold Brown (March 14).
[38]   Affidavit I of Howard Morland (March 19). <7>
[38A]   x Affidavit I of Howard Morland (March 21). <7>
[39]   x Affidavit of Robert D. Richtmyer (March 16).
[40]   Affidavit of Henry Pierre Noyes (March 12).
[41]   Affidavit of Charles Schwartz (March 12).
[42]   Affidavit of Edward Cooperman (March 13).
[43]   Affidavit of Erwin Knoll (March 16).
[44]   Affidavit of Samuel Day, Jr. (March 16).
[45]   Affidavit No. I of Theodore A. Postol in opposition to motion
            for preliminary injunction (March 15). <5>
[46]   Affidavit of Roger Dittman (March 13).
[47]   Affidavit of Ralph S. Hager (March 20).
[48]   Affidavit of Calvin G. Andre (March 20).
[49]   x (Same as document 52A).
[50]   x (Same as document 55,56).
[51]   Brief of Jermemy J. Stone, director, Federation of American
            Scientists, as amicus curiae, (March 22).
[52]   + Order (RWW) re: seating priority (March 21).
[52A]   Defendants' memorandum brief in opposition to the government's
            application for a preliminary injunction (March 21).
[52B]   x Defendants' in-camera brief. <12>
[53]   x (Same as document 63).
[54]   # Griffin's supplemental affidavit II with enclosed affidavits
            (March 22). <11?>
[55]   x Affidavit of Kostas Tsipis (March 17). <9>
[56]   x Affidavit of Hugh Edgar DeWitt (March 20). <10>
[57]   x Affidavit II of Howard Morland in opposition to motion for
            preliminary injunction (March 19?). <8>

[58]   x Affidavit No. II of Theodore A. Postol in opposition to prelim-
          inary injunction (March 15). <6>
[59]   Memorandum of United States in support of objections to public
          filings of defendants' affidavits (March 21).
[60]   Motion of ACLU for leave to file affidavits (March 21).
[61]   Order (RWW) granting leave to amici (ACLU) to file affidavits
          (March 22).
[62]   Affidavit/declaration of Gerald E. Marsh, George S. Stanford,
          and Alexander De Volpi submitted on behalf of the American
          Civil Liberties Union and the Wisconsin Civil Liberties Union
          as amici curiae (March 20).
[63]   x Affidavit/declaration of Alexander De Volpi submitted on behalf
          of the American Civil Liberties Union and the Wisconsin Civil
          Liberties Union as amici curiae (March 20).
[64]   Objection to plaintiff's motion to delete portions of defen-
          dants' affidavits and documents (March 22).
[65]   Defendants' memorandum in opposition to government's request to
          prevent public filing of defendants' affidavits (March 23).
[66]   Reply brief for United States (March 23).
[67]   Affidavit of Harold W. Lewis (March 22).
[68]   # Reply brief for United States <14C> with affidavits of Jack W.
          Rosengren and William Grayson (March 23). <13C> <18>
[69]   Motion of The Progressive, Inc., Erwin Knoll and Samuel Day,
          Jr. to vacate the temporary restraining order, deny plain-
          tiff's motion for preliminary injunction and dismiss the
          complaint because the issue is now moot (March 22).
[70]   x In camera hearing (RWW). No one to reveal anything that hap-
          pened in court -- on pain of contempt of court. Transcript
          filed (March 23).
[71]   Order (RWW). Documents held in camera to remain in camera
          pending further order of the court (March 23).
[72]   Affidavit of Hans A. Bethe (March 22).
[73]   (Same as document 72).
[74]   x Affidavit II of Ray E. Kidder (March 23). <17>
[74A]   Affidavit II of Ray E. Kidder (March 23).
[75]   x Affidavit I of Ray E. Kidder (March 23). <16>
[75A]   Affidavit I of Ray E. Kidder (March 23).
[76]   x Affidavit of Samuel Day, Jr. (II) (March 25).
[76A]   x Affidavit III of Howard Morland in opposition to motion for
          preliminary injunction (March 25). <15>
[76B]   # Affidavit II of Earl Munson (March 26).
[77]   # Joint supplemental affidavit of Jack W, Rosengren and William
          C. Grayson (same as document 68 without reply brief).
[78]   Motion of The Progressive, Inc., Erwin Knoll, and Samuel Day,
          Jr. to vacate the temporary restraining order and to deny
          plaintiff's motion for preliminary injunction because of the
          plaintiff's interference in the defendants' preparation of
          its defense (March 26).
[79]   Affidavit of Earl Munson, Jr. (I) in support of motion to
          vacate temporary restraining order and to dismiss motion of
          plaintiff for a preliminary injunction (March 26).
[80]   Motion for leave to appear and participate as amicus curiae,
          Fund for Open Information and Accountability, Inc. (March 26)
[81]   Preliminary injunction (March 26).
[82]   Memorandum and order (March 26).
[83]   + Hearing on preliminary injunction (March 26).
[84]   Posthearing amicus curiae brief, Federation of American Scien-
          tists (March 27).
[85]   Findings of fact and conclusions of law (March 28).
[86]   Answer of Howard Morland (March 29).
[87]   Answer of the defendants, The Progressive, Inc., Erwin Knoll,
          and Samuel Day Jr. (March 29).
[88]   # Letter from defendant Morland per court's order of 3/26
          (April 3). <21>
[89]   # Supplemental affidavit of John Griffin (April 3). A. D. Thomas
          letter <19C>

[90]   # In camera accounting by The Progressive per court's order of
          3/26 (April 4). <20>
[91]   Plaintiff's response to defendants The Progrssive, Knoll, and
          Day's motion to vacate the temporary restraining order, deny
          plaintiff's motion for preliminary injunction, and dismiss
          the complaint because the issue is now moot (April 6).
[92]   Plaintiff's opposition to defendants The Progressive, Knoll,
          and Day's motion to deny plaintiff's motion for preliminary
          injunction because of the plaintiff's interference in the
          defendant's preparation of its defense (April 12?).
[93]   Affidavit of Elizabeth Gere Whitaker (April 9).

APPEALS TO THE DISTRICT COURT

[94]   Joint notice of expedited appeal (April 10).
[95]   x Transcript of proceedings, before RWW on 3/26 (April 12). <28C>
[96]   Motion of The Progressive, Inc. and Howard Morland for modifi-
          cation of the protective order dated March 14, 1979 and for
          other relief (April 19).
[97]   Affidavit (III)of Earl Munson, Jr. in support of motion for
          modification of protective order for affirmative relief
          (April 19). <22>
[98]   Motion for order requiring defendants and their counsel to
          provide to the plaintiff all documents in their possession
          that contain restricted data, or alternatively, to maintain
          such documents in a secure container approved by plaintiff
          (April 23). <23C?>
[99]   Memorandum of points and authorities in support of plaintiff's
          motion for order requiring defendants and their counsel to
          provide to the plaintiff all documents in their possession
          that contain restricted data, or alternatively, to maintain
          such documents in a secure container approved by plaintiff
          (April 23).
[100]   Affidavit of Robert E. Cattanach. Exhibit attached (April 20).
[101]   Defendant's motion for access to in camera submissions and for
          modification of protective order (April 23).
[102]   Memorandum of law in support of defendants' motion for access
          to in camera submissions, and for modification of protective
          order (April 20).
[103]   Affidavit of Mark H. Lynch (April 19).
[104]   Affidavit of Morton H. Halperin (April 24).
[105]   x Affidavit III of Samuel Day, Jr. (April 24).
[106]   Motion to postpone discovery, plaintiff (April 26).
[107]   Brief in support of plaintiff's motion for a protective order
          postponing discovery (April 26).
[108]   # Affidavit IV of Earl Munson, Jr. (May 1) <26C>
[109]   Plaintiff's response to motion of The Progressive, Inc., and
          Howard Morland for modification of the protective order and
          for other relief, and defendants Day and Knoll's motion for
          access to in camera submissions and for modification of the
          protective order (May 1).
[109A] Affidavit of Jack W. Rosengren and William C. Grayson
          (April 30).
[110]   Defendants' opposition to plaintiff's motion to postpone
          discovery (April 30).
[111]   Memorandum of The Progressive, Inc. and Howard Morland in
          support of: (1) defendants' motion to dismiss because of
          government interference in the case; (2) defendants' motion
          to modify protective order; (3) defendants' motion for
          assistance from the United States government in the
          preparation of its defense; and in opposition to: (4)
          plaintiff's motion to strip defendants' files or require
          security; (5) plaintiff's motion to postpone discovery
          (April 30).
[112]   Motion and notice of hearing on motions, defendants (April 27).
[113]   # Affidavit of John A. Griffin with attachment (May 3). <27>

[114] * Stipulation for supplemental record (May 2). <31>
[115] # Affidavit of Dimitri Rotow (May 10). <24>
[116] # Defendants' motion to reconsider and vacate the preliminary
          injunction with affidavit of Earl Munson, Jr. (May 10). <25>
[116A] * In camera affidavit of Earl Munson, Jr. in support of motion
          to retain jurisdiction but remand the record to the United
          States District Court for a limited hearing and, in the
          alternative, for judicial notice (May 7).
[117] # Hearing (JWB) on motions. Transcript in camera (?).
[118]   Plaintiff's opposition to defendants' motion to dismiss the
          action and the preliminary injunction (May 16).
[119]   Modification of protective order (RWW) (May 15).
[120]   Stipulation for supplemental record (II) (May 15).
[121] + Certified copy of order U.S. Court of Appeals, Seventh
          Circuit -- briefing (May 21).
[121A] # Defendants' letter to court (May 25).
[122] + Conference call (May 30).
[122A] + Letter from Thomas Fox to court (May 30).
[123] * Defendants' supplemental motion to reconsider and to vacate the
          preliminary injunction issued March 26, 1979 (June 5). <29>
[124] * Memorandum in support of defendants' motion to reconsider and
          to vacate the preliminary injunction (June 5). <30C>
[125] x Stipulation (I) in connection with defendants' motion to recon-
          sider and to vacate preliminary injunction (June 5). <31>
[126] x Defendants' motion to present oral testimony in support of its
          motion to reconsider and to vacate the preliminary injunction
          issued March 26, 1979 (June 5). <33>
[127]   Defendants' motion to vacate the court's order postponing
          discovery (June 5). <34>
[128] x Memorandum of points and authorities in support of above motion
          (June 5). <32>
[129] x Affidavit of Thomas Kirkman (June 5). <35>
[130] x Affidavit of Mark H. Lynch (June 4). <36>
[131] x Affidavit III of Ray E. Kidder (June 4). <37>
[132] * Supplemental affidavit of Ray E. Kidder (May 31). <38C>
[133] * Affidavit II of Gerald E. Marsh (June 1). <39>
[134] * Affidavit III of Alexander De Volpi (June 1). <40>
[134A] x Letter from M. Lynch to Warren with DNA 4501F extracts. <50>
[135] x Affidavit of Theodore B. Taylor (June 1). <42>
[136] x Affidavit of Charles S. Sims (May 31). <41>
[137] * Affidavit II of Dimitri A. Rotow (June 4). <45>
[138] * Affidavit II of Hugh Edgar Dewitt (June 5). <43>
[139] * Affidavit III of Hugh Edgar Dewitt (June 4). <44>
[140] x Stipulation regarding UCRL-5280 (June 8). <72C>
[141] # Plaintiff's opposition to defendants' motion to reconsider and
          to vacate the preliminary injunction (June 11). <46C>
[142] # Joint supplemental affidavit of Jack W. Rosengren and William
          C. Grayson, Jr. (June 11). <47C>
[143] x Supplemental affidavit of Hans A. Bethe (June 11). <48>
[144]   Affidavit of Louis Cucchiara (June 10).
[145] x Supplemental affidavit of James R. Schlesinger (June 11). <49>
[146]   Affidavit of Duane C. Sewell (June 10). Griffin Supplement.
          <56C>
[147]   Affidavit of J. Arthur Freed (June 7).
[148]   Opposition to defendants' motion to present oral testimony in
          support of its motion to reconsider and to vacate the
          preliminary injunction issued March 26, 1979 (June 11).
[149]   Opposition to defendants' motion to vacate the court's order
          postponing discovery (June 11).
[150] # Defendants' proposed findings of fact and conclusions of law on
          defendants' motion to reconsider and vacate (June 12). <51>
[151] # Affidavit V of Earl Munson, Jr. (?). <52>
[152] x Joint brief of appellants Knoll, Day, and Morland (June 15).
          <59?>
[153]   Memorandum and order (RWW) [denying defendants' motion to
          reconsider] (June 15).

[154]   x Memorandum and order (RWW) [denying defendants's motion to
           reconsider] (June 15). <54>
[155]   # Oral argument (RWW) and motion taken under advisement (June 15).

APPEALS TO THE CIRCUIT COURT

[156]   Notice of appeal (defendants) (June 15).
[157]   Joint notice of expedited appeal (June 15).
[158]   x Motion for an order making public the portions of the district
           court's in camera opinion of June 15, 1979 that do not
           reveal restricted data (July 27). <57?>
[159]   x Declaration of Bruce J. Ennis (July 27). <55>
[160]   Memorandum of law in support of the motion of defendants Erwin
           Knoll, Samuel Day, Jr., and Howard Morland for an order
           making public the portions of the district court's in camera
           opinion of June 15, 1979 that do not reveal restricted data
           (July 27). <63>
[161]   Order (RWW) [court will make public unrestricted portion of
           opinion]
[162]   * Motion of expedited briefing schedule and oral argument
           (September 6).
[163]   x Memorandum of defendants Knoll, Day, and Morland in opposition
           to plaintiff's motion that entire argument be conducted in
           camera (September 6). <58>
[164]   x Brief of appellant, The Progressive, Inc. (June 15). <60>
[165]   x Joint Brief of Appellants Knoll, Day and Morland on Consoli-
           dated Appeal from Preliminary Injunction and from Order
           Denying Motion to Vacate Preliminary Injunction. (July 13).
           <61C>
[165A] * Supplemental brief of appellant, The Progressive, Inc.
           (July 13). <62C>
[165B] x Appendix for the Appellant, The Progressive, Inc. <67C>
[166]   * Brief for the appellee (August 7). <64>
[167]   * Reply brief of appellant, Progressive, Inc. (August 28).
[168]   x Joint reply brief of appellants Knoll, Day, and Morland
           (August 31). <65C>
[168A] x Appendix of Appellants Knoll, Day, and Morland. <68C>
[169]   Joint reply brief of appellants Knoll, Day, and Morland
           [Bracketed portions were originally required to be filed in
           camera but were released for public filing by Government
           Reply of September 24, 1979] (September 26). <69C>
[170]   Brief of Fusion Energy Foundation as amicus curiae (?   ).
[171]   Appendix to brief of Fusion Energy Foundation as amicus curiae
           (?).
[172]   Brief for Chicago Tribune Company, the Reporters Committee for
           Freedo m of the Press, and the Freedom to Read Foundation as
           amici curiae (?   ).
[173]   Brief for the Committee for Public Justice, Pen American Cen-
           ter, Authors League of America, Inc. as amici curiae (?   ).
[174]   Brief of the The Nation, Columbia Journalism Review,
           Playboy, National Journal, New York, New West, Juris
           Doctor, Inquiry, Working Papers, New York Review of
           Books, New Republic, New Engineer, Focus Midwest,
           Village Voice, St. Louis Journalism Review, Black
           Scholar, Rolling Stone, Editor & Publisher, The Witness,
           Sojourners, Texas Observer, American Lawyer , Cleveland
           Magazine, Seven Days, Transaction, I.F. Stone's Weekly,
           American Booksellers Association, Inc. and Council for Peri-
           odical Distributors Associations, as amici curiae in support
           of defendants-appellants (May 21).
[175]   Brief on behalf of Scientific American as amicus curiae
           (May 21).
[176]   Brief of the New York Times Company, American Society of
           News paper Editors, Association of American Publishers, Inc.,
           National Association of Broadcasters, Association of American

University Presses, Inc. and the Globe Newspaper Company as
amici curiae (May 21).
[177] x In-camera to Supreme Court (October 1979). <70C>
[178] x Motion to Supreme Court (?   ). <71C>
[179]   Report to the court, attorneys for plaintiff (in camera
filings) (December 26).
[179A]   Certificate of service (December 28).
[179B]   Affidavit of Duane C. Sewell (December 26).
[179C]   Affidavit of Robert T. Duff (December 26, 1979).
[180]   Protective order (September 4, 1980).
[181]   Stipulation (September 4).
[182]   Memorandum and order (September 4).
[183]   Transcript of proceedings (September 4).

General References

[ABR-80] Floyd Abrams, Statement Before Subcommittee on Government Information and Individual Rights of the Committee on Government Operations (20 March 1980).

[BRO-68] Harold L. Brode, "Review of Nuclear Weapons Effects," Annual Review of Nuclear Science,8:153 (1968).

[B&O-76] Stanley A. Blumberg and Gwin Owens, Energy and Conflict: The Life and Times of Edward Teller, G.P. Putnam's Sons, New York (1976).

[CHEH-80] Mary M. Cheh, "The Progressive Case and the Atomic Energy Act: Waking to the Dangers of Government Information Controls," The George Washington Law Review, 48(2):163 (January 1980).

[COX-75] Arthur Macy Cox, The Myths of National Security: The Peril of Secret Government, Beacon Press, Boston (1975).

[C&C-80] Andrew Cockburn and Alexander Cockburn, "The Myth of Missile Accuracy," The New York Review, p. 40 (20 November 1980).

[DEV-79] Alexander DeVolpi, Proliferation, Plutonium and Policy: Institutional and Technological Impediments to Nuclear Weapons Propagation, Pergamon Press, New York (1979).

[DSB-70] Report of the Defense Science Board Task Force on Secrecy (unpublished); Office of the Director of Defense Research and Engineering, Washington, DC (1 July 1970).

[ENN-80] Bruce J. Ennis, "The United States v.The Progressive: The Case Against The Government," speech to the American Physical Society Forum on Science and Society, Washington, DC (30 April 1980).

[F&W-74] Thomas M. Franck and Edward Weisband, eds., Secrecy and Foreign Policy, Oxford University Press, London (1974).

[GRI-78] John A. Griffin, "Classification and Nonproliferation Studies," letter to national laboratories (September 5 1978).

[HEN-80] Nat Hentoff, The First Freedom: The Tumultous History of Free Speech in America, Delacourt Press, New York (1980).

[HOL-79] David Holloway, "Entering the Nuclear Arms Race: The Soviet Decision to Build the Atomic Bomb, 1939-45," Working Paper No. 9, International Security Studies Program, Smithsonian Institution (1979).

[HR-80] House Report No. 96-1540, 96th Congress, 2d Session, "The Government's Classification of Private Ideas," Thirty-Fourth Report by the Committee on Government Operations together with Additional Views (December 22, 1980).

[H&H1-77] Morton H. Halperin and Daniel N. Hoffman, Top Secret: National Security and the Right to Know, New Republic Books, Washington, D.C. (1977).

[H&H2-77] Morton H. Halperin and Daniel N. Hoffman, Freedom vs. National Security: Secrecy and Surveillance, Chelsea House Publishers, New York (1977).

[LAPP-79] Private communication.

[LOV-80] A. B. Lovins, "Nuclear weapons and power-reactor plutonium," Nature, 283:817 (28 February 1980).

[MCP-75] John McPhee, The Curve of Binding Energy, Ballantine Books, New York (1975).

[M&M-80] Gerald E. Markowitz and Michael Meeropol, "The 'Crime of the Century' Revisited: David Greenglass's Scientific Evidence in the Rosenberg Case," Science and Society (Spring, 1980).

[NIZ-74] Louis Nizer, The Implosion Conspiracy, Faucett Publications, Greenwich, Conn. (1974).

[RON-80] Kent N. Ronhovde, "The Progressive Case: Legal Issues," Congressional Research Service, Library of Congress (February 14, 1980).

[SIP-79] Stockholm International Peace Research Institute, Nuclear Energy and Nuclear Weapon Proliferation, Taylor and Francis Ltd, London (1979).

[TAY-75] Theodore B. Taylor, "Nuclear Safeguards," Annual Review of Nuclear Science, 25:406 (1975).

[TEL-74] Edward Teller, Encyclopedia Americana, Volume 14, p. 654, New York City (1974).

[WIS-78] David Wise, "The New Secrecy," Inquiry, p. 20 (October 16, 1978).

[YORK-76] Herbert York, The Advisors: Oppenheimer, Teller, and the Superbomb, W. H. Freeman & Co., San Francisco (1976).

Index

A-bomb (see Nuclear weapons)
ABM, 19, 34f, 41, 122, 123, 165f, 267
Abrams, Floyd [ABR-80], 194, 196, 215, 282, 284
Abuses (see Classification)
ACDA, 60, 111, 213-214, 283
ACLU, 7, 67, 190, 191, 193, 197, 218, 226, 240; proposed panel (see Advisory panel)
Advisory: committees, 217, 223, 224, 226f; panel, 7, 68, 71, 226;
  -see also: Remedies
AEC, 135
Affidavits: by amici, 66, 112, 114, 271
  -on behalf of defendants (see: Andre, C.; Cooperman, E.; Day, S.; DeVolpi, A.; DeWitt, H.; Dittman, R.; Hager, R.; Kirkman, T.; Marsh, G.; Morland, H.; Munson, E.; Noyes, H.; Postol, T.; Richtmyer, R.; Schwartz, C.; Taylor, T.; Tsipis, K.)
  -on behalf of the government (see: Batzel, R.; Bethe, H.; Brown, H.; Grayson, W.; Griffin, J.; Keeney, S.; Lewis, H.; Pickering, T.; Rosengren, J.; Schlesinger, J.; Sewel, D.; Thorn, R.; Vance, C.; Van Doren, C.)
  -see also: Briefs
Agee, Philip, 166
Agnew, Harold, 47
Alamogordo, 26, 119
Amchitka, 141
American Civil Liberties Union (see ACLU)
American Society of Newspaper Editors, 10
Amici curiae, 7, 57, 218
Amin, Idi, 61, 113
Andre, Calvin G.: affidavit, 272
Antiballistic Missiles (see ABM)
Antiproliferation (see Proliferation)
Appeals, 8, 208f, 275, 276
Arms control, 20-23; disarmament, 238; issues, 236, 267, 276; verification (see Testing)
Arms race, 238, 240, 276
Atomic Energy Act, 11f, 42, 44, 51, 57-81, 110, 131-137, 154f, 156f; applicability, 188f, 190, 282; challenges, 10, 182, 183f,

235; charges, 188; effectiveness, 179; constitutionality, 200, 211, 223; enforcement, 134, 189; excerpts, 258-261; injunctions authorized, 134; provisions, 132-137, 190, 225, 228, 284; penalties, 134, 164; reforms, 215, 229, 230, 232, 233, 284f; violations, 184, 268
  -see also: Criminal violations; Restricted Data
Atomic weapons (see Nuclear weapons)
Australia, 97, 152, 179
Authoritativeness, 107, 274, 276

Batzel, R. E., 47f, 213; affidavit, 48, 107, 271
Baxter, Sir Phillip, 97
Beckerly, James, 128
Beres, Louis Rene, 268
Bethe, Hans, 52, 70, 72, 111f, 113f, 123, 135, 197, 267; affidavits, 70, 111, 114, 273; diagram, 99f, 108; letter, 70; statement, 99f
Black, Justice Hugo, 202, 206
Blumberg, S. A., and Owens, G. [B&O-76], 87, 128, 276
Bohr, Nils, 26, 152
Boland, Edward P., 215
Bombers (see Weapons)
Booster (see Thermonuclear weapons)
Born classified (born secret): doctrine, 12, 59, 80, 81, 136, 196, 268; implications, 136, 154, 157, 191f, 215
Bradbury, Norris, 47
Brennan, Justice William J., 197, 198, 199, 201, 205, 231
Briefs and stipulations: amici, 67, 80, 134, 137, 190, 191, 197, 204, 206, 207; defendants', 63, 74, 76, 77, 78, 79, 82, 89, 97f, 106, 136, 142, 209, 271, 274, 275, 277, 281; government's, 59, 60, 66, 71, 73, 75, 76, 78, 106, 107, 111, 112, 115, 136, 137, 181, 186, 188, 200, 209f, 223, 268, 275; stipulations, 214
  -see also: Affidavits

Brode, Harold L. [BRO-68], 66, 111, 113, 117
Brown, Harold, 180-181; affidavit 111, 113, 117, 172, 273, 278
Burden of proof (see: Criteria for damage; Legal; Prior restraint)

Carter, President Jimmy, 47, 126, 129f, 137, 221, 236, 279
Cases: Aspin, 187, 209; Cannikin Papers, 140, 165f, 196; CIA censorship, 166f; Gorin, 196, 198; Green, 196; Grosjean, 220; Halperin, 187, 209; Heine, 63, 193, 196, l98; Knopf, 187; Lesar, 194; Marchetti, 11, 12, 67, 166f, 216, 282; Mink, 196; Near, 199, 201, 283; Nebraska, 197; New York Times (see Pentagon Papers); Progressive (see Progressive case); Reynolds, 196; Rosenberg, 71, 144, 161-164, 201, 210, 282; Schenck, 196; Snepp, 212; Totten, 196; Watterman, 196
Censorship, 166-168, 227, 241, 283
Chayes, A., and Wiesner, J. B., 267
Cheh, Mary [CHEH-80], 133, 138, 141, 154, 188, 190, 192, 194, 195, 196, 198, 201, 202, 216, 228, 229, 232, 282
Chesterton, G. K., 217
Chicago Sun Times, 103, 184
Chicago Tribune, 8f, 10f, 40, 116, 152, 170, 183, 216, 267, 268; brief, 80
Christian Science Monitor, 267
Chronology of events, 4-9
CIA, 111, 117f, 132, 166ff, 171, 212, 216, 222, 281
Civil defense, 37, 122
Civil suit (see Progressive case)
Classification, 279; accountability, 218; appeals, 285; at birth (see born classified); authority, 220; categories (Confidential, Secret, Top Secret), 132, 138, 165f; complaints, 285; criteria, 233; derivative, 140f, 165; duration, 138, 279; guidelines, 139, 221, 233, 279; implementation problems, 156, 191f; misuses, 13, 158, 170, 279; oversight, 233, 285; patents, 141; policy, 159, 171f, 218; political motives, 169, 283; prohibited practices, 139f, 220, 279; procedures, 285; reclassification, 105, 139f, 283f; regulations, 285; reports, 285; review, 220, 221f, 224, 234, 267, 282f, 285; selective, 168; unclear, 137, 141; volume of, 141, 142f
    -see also: Cryptography; Declassification; Glenn letter; Hansen letter
Classified information: confirmation, 179-181; deducibility, 149-151; dissemination, 227; leaking, 143, 158, 176; privately generated, 227, 232; protection, 151, 187, 227; safeguarding, 224
    -see also: Born classified; Restricted Data; Secrecy
Coates, James, 268
Cockburn, Andrew & Alexander [C&C-80], 39
Committee for Public Justice: brief, 50, 80, 276

Committees, advisory (see: Advisory committees; Remedies)
Conant, James B., 2
Congress: House subcommittees, 141, 210, 214, 215, 219, 280, 284; Senate subcommittees, 142, 186, 213, 214, 268
Congressional: action, 222, 228; bills, 232; hearings, 214f
Comprehensive Test Ban Treaty (CTBT) (see Test Ban)
Concepts, 275, 276; versus details, 114, 118f, 127, 144, 150f, 154, 277; compression, 87, 89ff, 102, 108, 276; deducibility, 48, 91-96, 108f, 144, 149-154, 272, 284f; radiation coupling or pressure, 57, 64, 88ff, 108, 174, 209, 242, 276, 277; separate or multiple stages, 57, 64, 88ff, 108, 153, 174, 276, 277
    -see also: Teller-Ulam
Constitutionality, 195ff
    -see also: Atomic Energy Act; First Amendment; Prior restraint
Cooperman, E.: affidavit, 272
Cost of litigation, 218
Counterforce, 39
Court action: conclusions of law, 189; denial of motion, 108; findings of fact, 190; protective orders, 192, 283
    -see also: Injunction; Temporary Restraining Order
Cox, Arthur Macy [COX-75], 126, 131, 132, 160, 165, 176, 177f
Crane, Stephen, 235
Criminal violations: alleged, 8f, 64, 211, 212f; dropped, 188, 190, 194, 224, 240
Criteria for damage, 7, 76, 81, 139, 177, 198, 200f, 271, 273; direct, 60, 76, 77, 80, 202; grave, 60, 76, 77, 80; immediate, 60, 76, 77, 80, 203; irreparable, 60, 76, 77, 80, 190, 203f; surely, 190, 198, 204
Criticality, nuclear, 84
Cruise missiles (see Missiles)
Cryptography, 132, 140, 141f

Daily Californian, 7, 9, 106, 170, 182, 183
Data: communication of, 196, 225; deducible (see Concepts); Restricted (see Restricted Data)
Day, Anthony, 6
Day, Samuel, 3, 5, 218; affidavit, 65; brief, 152; Commentary, 239
Decision-making processes, 223
Declassification, 133, 137, 189, 220, 233, 279; mistaken, 103; no published guide, 137; procedures, 137f, 139f; selective, 172ff
    -see also: UCRL-4725; UCRL-5280; Los Alamos
Deducibility (see Concepts)
Defense: outdated, 15-23, 110
    -see also: ABM
Defense Department (see DOD)
Defense Science Board [DSB-70], 148, 152, 153, 222, 231, 274, 280

Denaturing, isotopic, 43-45
Denial of Technology, 25, 144-149
Details (see Concepts)
DeVolpi, Alexander, 4, 7, 9, 305; affidavits, 68, 69, 75, 79, 102, 104, 112, 121, 168, 184, 186, 273, 275, 277, 278, 281; book by, 43, 69, 86, 87, 113, 116, 128, 147, 305
DeWitt, Hugh, 7, 67, 82, 181f, 213, 284; affidavits, 71, 114, 272; Commentary, 242-244
Diffie, Whitfield, 141
Disarmament (see Arms control)
Disincentives to proliferation, 127-129; technology denial, 127; secrecy, 127f; institutional actions, 128.
Disputes: constitutional, 188f; factual, 190f, 192ff; statutory, 188f, 192ff
Dittman, R.: affidavit, 272
DNA-4501F, 101f, 209
Documents: 'Appendix C,' 213f, 283; in camera, 213f
    -see also: DNA-4501F; UCRL-4725; UCRL-5280
DOD: Task Force on Secrecy, 40
DOE, 82, 170f, 181f, 184, 186, 241, 282; warhead production, 239
Drell, Sidney, 64

Eccles, Rear Admiral H. C., 22, 42, 266f
Einstein, Albert, 51, 78
Eisenhower, President Dwight, 236
Ellsberg, Daniel, 160, 180
Emerson, Thomas: brief, 49, 145
Encyclopedias: Americana (see Teller, E.); Merit Students (see Bethe, H.)
Energy Department (see DOE)
England, 123; weapons program, 111, 119; Official Secrets Act, 218, 231
Ennis, Bruce, 77, 153; speech, 193, 282
Enrichment, 45
Environmental issues, 45f
Espionage, 118f, 144; penalties, 162; statutes, 63, 131, 140, 162, 225
Executive Order 12065, 12, 22f, 131, 137-140, 156, 214, 222, 279; excerpts from text, 262-265; infractions, 143; prohibitions, 139; reclassification, 224
    -see also National Security Information
Explosion, possible clandestine, 125

Federation of American Scientists (FAS), 155; brief, 51; letter on testing, 47; post-hearing suggestion, 208; proposed panel, 207
Fermi, Enrico, 2, 149
Fifth Amendment: vague, 190, 195, 208, 275f; due process, 195, 208, 209; fair notice, 195; property rights, 195
First Amendment, 6f, 62, 170, 188, 189, 190, 196f, 200, 206, 209, 211, 212, 216, 217, 232, 239, 241; overbroad, 195, 198, 208, 275f
Fission, 83ff; chain-reaction, 83, 86; discovery of, 15, 26, 83; triggers (see Thermonuclear weapons); weapons (see Nuclear Weapons)
Flugge, S., 26
FOIA, 137, 161, 165f, 180, 194, 220, 283
Forsberg, Randy, 267
Foster, John S., 281
France: weapons program, 112, 116, 119, 122, 149; power program, 129
Franck, T.N. and Weisband, E. [F&W-74], 131, 139, 141, 142, 143, 158f, 166, 176, 217, 218f, 221, 284
Fuchs, Klaus, 118, 144, 162
Fund for Open Information and Accountability: brief, 71, 112, 161, 274
Fusion: process, 84, 94, 153; heavy ion, 80; inertial confinement, 45, 155, 242, 280; laser-driven, 80
    -see also: Thermonuclear weapons
Fusion Energy Foundation, 50, 52, 176; brief, 50, 52, 80, 170; Fusion magazine, 75, 102
Fygi, E. J., 141

GAC (General Advisory Committee); 1949 report, 2, 29
GAO (Government Accounting Office), 156, 186, 233
Germany: atomic bomb, 26; rockets, 148
Gilbert, F. C., 283
Gillette, Robert, 6
Glenn, Senator John, 283; letter to, 7, 105f, 108, 168, 170, 181f, 213, 216, 256f (text), 277, 281; subcommittee hearings, 104
Goffman, John, 64
Grayson, W. (see Rosengren, J. W.)
Griffin, John, 175, 243, 279; affidavit, 67, 82, 132, 133, 137, 154, 270
Groves, Major General Leslie, 44, 152, 161
Guidelines: on classification, 221, 279; on proliferation, 279

H-bomb (see Thermonuclear weapons)
Hager, R. S.: affidavit, 52, 272
Haig, General Alexander, 16f
Halperin, M. and Hoffman, D. [H&H1-77, H&H2-77], 35, 52, 131, 132, 140, 160, 168, 171, 180, 196, 220, 221, 228, 229
Hand, Judge Learned, 193f
Hansen, Charles, 8, 99, 106, 108, 134, 182;letter from, 8, 10f, 106f, 183, 211, 212; charges by, 171f, 183
Heisenberg, Werner, 26
Hellman, Martin, 141
Hentoff, Nat [HEN-80], 155, 282
Hiroshima, 1, 27-29, 119
Holloway, David [HOL-79], 28, 29, 54, 144, 146
Honolulu: weapons storage, 155
Hydrogen bomb (see Thermonuclear weapons)

ICBM (see Missiles)
In camera, 58, 191, 225

Inertially confined fusion (ICF) (see Fusion)

India & NPT, 123, 129; nuclear explosion, 117, 204, 272

Injunction, 110, 179, 241; motion to vacate, 108; permanent, 282; preliminary, 6, 12, 57ff, 63ff, 282; requirements, 189, 192f
-see also: Court action

Intent (scienter), 225

Interagency Classification Review Commission, 143, 222, 233

International Fuel Cycle Evaluation (INFCE), 128

Invention Secrecy Act, 141
-see also: Patents

ISOO, 220, 221f, 233, 279, 285

Jackson, Justice Robert H., 201

Joliot-Curie, M., 26

Judicial process, 198, 200, 224f

Justice Department, 194, 198, 200, 205, 207, 211, 212, 214, 223, 241; brief, 52

Keeney, S.M., Jr.: affidavit, 270, 274

Kahn, David, 142, 284

Kaze, Toshikazu, 27

Kendall, Henry, 173

Kennedy, Senator Edward M., 267

Kerr, Donald, 47

Kidder, Ray E., 7, 70, 88, 155, 242-243, 281, 284; affidavit, 67, 82, 272

Kirkman, T.: affidavit, 274

Kissinger, Henry, 144

Kistiakowsky, George, 52

Knoll, Erwin, 3, 6, 65; affidavits, 3, 49, 65 ; brief, 51; Commentary, 240

Lapp, Ralph, 30, 135, 197

Lasers (see Enrichment; Thermonuclear power)

Launch on warning, 36

Legal: action, 179; evidentiary hearing, 191, 108, 274; injury, 190; intent, 225; issues, 57, 208, 240; precedents, 211f; proof, 190, 191, 193; reason to believe, 188, 190, 192, 193, 212, 276, 282; strategy, 241
-see also: Disputes, factual

Leipunskii, A.I., 26

Lewis, Anthony, 11, 24, 167

Lewis, Harold W.: affidavit, 71, 274

Licklider, J. C. R., 267

Lilienthal, David, 29

Livermore, 155, 172, 184, 213, 284

Los Alamos 10, 47, 118, 184; library, 79, 103, 152, 185f, 281f

Lovins, Amory, 44

Madison Press Connection, 8, 183, 216

Manhatten Project, 26, 30, 54, 86, 119

Marchetti, Victor (see Cases)

Markowitz, G. E. and Meeropol, M. [M&M-80], 86, 128, 162, 164

Marsh, Gerald E., 7, 9; affidavits, 68, 74, 79, 104, 168, 184, 276, 278

McCloskey, Paul N., 88, 99, 171, 182, 230, 232, 284

McGrory, Mary, 170

McPhee, John [MCP-75], 93, 120, 171

Milwaukee Sentinel, 75, 102

Mink, Patsy, 165f

MIRV - see Missiles

Missiles, 18; accuracy, 39f; cruise, 38f; 116; ICBM, 20, 33f, 116; MARV, 116; Minuteman, 116; MIRV, 36f; MX, 22f, 34, 267; Nike, 41; Polaris, Poseidon, Trident, 18, 32f, 36, 116; satellite destroyers, 116; Titan, 267
-see also: ABM

Moe report, 281

Mooney, M.M., 191

Moorhead, Rep. William S., 219f, 222

Morland, Howard, 3f, 154, 186, 212, 222, 237, 278; affidavits, 50f, 51, 63, 64f, 89, 134, 141, 267, 271; article, 4f, 89-100, 90, 179, 245-255 (text), 267, 269, 270; authoritativeness of, 107, 276; book by, 239; Commentary, 238; Errata, 212, 255 (text); proliferation risk from article, 110-118, 269

Motivations, political, 69

Mountbatten, Lord, 110

Moyers, Bill D., 267

Munson, Earl, 173ff; affidavit, 101

MX (see Missiles)

Nagasaki, 27, 120

National security, 267, 284; and Pentagon Papers case, 189; distinctions, 222; information, 196; infractions by government, 178; policy (see Policy, national security); reasons for injunction, 188, 189

National Security Information (NSI) 11f, 131, 138-140; definition, 11, 138f; reclassification, 224
-see also: Executive Order 12065

NATO, 236

Nature Magazine, 44, 281

Need to know, 43-56

Neutron Bombs (see Nuclear weapons)

Neutrons (see Fission)

New York Times, 9f, 11, 26, 102, 113, 135, 160, 188, 197; brief, 49f, 80, 284

New York Times case (see Pentagon Papers case)

New Yorker magazine, 111, 113, 123

News media, 207, 216 220, 241

Nizer, Louis [NIZ-74], 201

Nonnuclear-weapons states, 110

Nonproliferation (see Antiproliferation)

Noyes, H. P.: affidavit, 272

Nuclear: chain reactions, 148; criticality, 84; explosives (see Nuclear weapons); power, need for, 129; reactors, as source of weapons material, 43-45, 126; reprocessing, 126; warfare, 267
-see also: Nuclear weapons; Nuclear-

weapon states; Test ban; Testing
Nuclear Regulatory Commission (NRC), 194
Nuclear-weapon states, 115f, 148, 237;
    fission weapons, 116; potential, 17, 107,
    116, 117, 148; prerequisites, 44, 72, 88,
    112, 113, 117f, 119, 127; thermonuclear
    weapons, 116
Nuclear weapons: accidents, 42; command
    and control, 41f, 267, 268, 273; computer
    error, 42, 268; effects, 18, 19;
    efficiency, 43-45, 86, 121; enhanced
    radiation, 116, 121, 276; explosion,
    possible clandestine, 125; explosive
    yield, 43f, 86, 89, 120; functional
    elements, 86f; initiator, 86; neutron
    bomb, 116, 121, 276; materials, 88f, 126-
    128, 146; policy, 39-42, 236, 276;
    predetonation, 86; production, 239;
    reflector, 87; reliability, 42, 46, 121f;
    safety, 41, 267, 273; tamper, 86; types,
    84f
    -see also: Arms race; Fission; Fusion;
    Missiles; Proliferation; Testing; Thermo-
    nuclear weapons

Official Secrets Act, 231
Oppenheimer, J. Robert, 30, 44, 50
Overclassification, 176ff

Panofsky, Wolfgang K. H., 47
Patents, 131, 141, 280, 284
Peninsula Times Tribune, 183
Pentagon Papers, the, 159
Pentagon Papers case 11, 58, 59, 67, 72,
    80, 81, 110, 135, 180; 188, 189, 190, 197,
    198f, 201, 211, 216, 271; history, 11,
    160f
    -see also: Criteria for damage
Percy, Senator Charles, 106, 171
Photoreconnaissance, 20, 31f, 125, 132;
    detection of possible nuclear explosion,
    125
Physics Today, 280
Pickering, Thomas: affidavit, 67, 73f,
    111, 114, 117, 269, 274, 283
Piel, Gerard, 136
Pitzer Panel, 166
Plutonium, 83; reactor-grade, 43, 127,
    146
    -see also: Fission; Denaturing
Poseidon (see Missiles)
Polaris (see Missiles)
Policy: national security, 202
    -see also: Nuclear weapons; Prolifer-
    ation
Postol, Theodore, 4, 6, 8, 173f, 184, 267,
    305; affidavits, 65f, 82, 92, 102, 145,
    173f
Power (see Nuclear; Thermonuclear)
Predetonation, 86
Preliminary injunction (see Injunction)
Press reaction, 9-11
    -see also: News media
Price, Rep. Melvin, 215
Primary, the (see Thermonuclear weapons)

Prior restraint, 7, 13, 48, 61f, 73, 135,
    197f, 208; heavy burden of proof, 185,
    209
Progressive, The, 3, 197, 218
Progressive case, 188ff; and CTBT, 46f;
    beginnings, 6, 242; end, 8f, 183, 194,
    210f; sequels, 212; implications, 177,
    216; mooted, 74, 184; outcome, 216, 235,
    238; participants, 159; precedents, 11,
    134, 211, 214, 216
Proliferation, 47, 48f, 53, 54f, 236, 274,
    283; antiproliferation policy, 115, 128-
    130, 177, 215, 236, 268, 269, 270, 273,
    278; and nuclear power, 126f; concerns,
    241; DOE guidelines, 139; material
    safeguards, 127; Non-Proliferation Act,
    210; Non-Proliferation Treaty, 60, 111,
    123; rate, 114, 149, 269, 270, 271, 272,
    273, 276, 278, 282, 283; risk, 110-130,
    205, 269, 270, 271, 273, 276, 278;
    vertical, 121
    -see also: Disincentives; Nuclear
    weapons states
Protective Order, 12, 58, 213
Public: domain, 97, 100, 182, 192, 209,
    239, 271, 274, 275, 277, 278, 282; ignore
    public domain, 97, 109, 128; need to know,
    43-56, 282; right to know, 31-43
Publication of sensitive data, 284f

Rabi, Isador, 2
Radiation coupling (see Concepts)
Rathjens, George, 5f, 52, 171
Reactors (see Nuclear)
Reagan, President Ronald, 130
Reason to believe, 188, 190, 192, 193,
    212, 276, 282
Remedies 217-234, 236; ignore public
    literature, 97, 109, 128
    -see also: Advisory committees
Restricted Data, 11f, 44, 48, 131f, 195,
    235, 229, 239, 275; confirmation, 169,
    172f, 268; definition, 133, 138; leaks,
    143, 158, 176
Richtmyer, R. D., 272
Right to know, 31-43
Rodberg, Leonard S., 267
Ronhovde, Kent [RON-80], 194, 211, 225,
    282
Rosenberg, Julius and Ethel (see Cases)
Rosengren, Jack: affidavit, 61, 72, 102f,
    172, 175, 180-181, 270 (excerpts);
    and Grayson, W., 64, 73, 102, 108, 120f,
    243, 274
Rotow, Dimitri, 103, 140, 214, 281;
    affidavit, 185
Rudakov, L.I., 243

Sakharov, Andrei, 30, 40f
SALT, 20, 21f, 23, 40f, 123, 129
Satellites (see Photoreconnaissance)
Schlesinger, James R., 6, 47f, 223, 274;
    affidavit, 48, 102, 111, 186, 200, 270f,
    274
Science magazine, 125

Scientific American, 51, 80, 101, 136, 197; brief, 49, 51, 80, 135f, 145, 204, 206
Schwartz, Charles: affidavit, 272
Secondary, the (see Thermonuclear weapons)
Secrecy, 284; executive branch, 70, 158; government, 131-157, 218, 274; implementation problems, 156, 191f; inhibiting effects, 156, 157; limitation, 208f; misuse, 13, 143, 158f, 170, 191f, 274; myth, 193, 216, 239, 240; overreliance on, 128, 280; restrictive effects, 1-3, 154-156, 143, 212; role, 2, 12, 131f, 143, 145f, 150, 159
   -see also: Born classified; Classification
Secrets; H-bomb, 239, 242; metastable nature, 148, 152; spilled, 180f
Sewell, Duane, 210, 213, 284; affidavits, 67, 75, 82, 102, 200, 269, 275, 278, 283
Siegel, Ron, 5, 267
Sims, Charles, 77; Commentary, 240
SIPRI, 44, 116
Soviet Union, 21, 25, 40f, 54, 123, 144, 162, 176; weapons program, 2, 26, 46f, 87, 89, 112, 116, 118f, 124f, 144, 146f, 153, 154
Stanford, George S., 5, 7, 305; affidavit, 68, 168, 278
State Department, 13, 82, 111, 213-214, 283
Statutes (see Atomic Energy Act; Espionage)
Stewart, Justice Potter, 158, 190, 198
Stone, Jeremy, 52f, 173, 207; brief, 52f
Supreme Court, 7, 212, 216
   -see also: Cases
Szilard, Leo, 26

Tamm, Igor, 146
Taylor, Theodore, 52f, 75, 93, 52, 86, 93, 120, 125, 171, 177, 184-185; affidavit, 75, 184, 275
Technical information, protection of, 209f, 275, 283
   -see also: Born classified; Classification; Classified information; Secrecy
Technology: denial, 25, 144-149; influence on social change, 15-23
Teller, Edward, 30, 87, 125, 128, 154, 171; diagram, 8, 65, 66, 68, 89, 91ff, 98, 99, 102, 106f, 108, 168, 171, 173, 272, 277; Teller-Ulam concept, 47, 95f, 106, 111, 150f, 154, 175, 184, 185, 242, 272, 273; statements, 30, 99, 177f
Temporary Restraining Order (TRO), 6, 57ff, 61, 188f
Terrorists, 113f, 117, 126
Test ban, 17, 32, 46f, 54, 122-125; CTBT, 123-125; verification, 123
Testing, 46, 116, 119-122, 147f, 277; in the atmosphere, 49, 122, 154; necessity of, 47, 48, 118, 119-122, 125, 147f, 149, 273; on Mars, 47, 124f; underground, 122, 165f

Thermonuclear power research, 45, 155
Thermonuclear weapons: boosting, 87, 119; computations, 147f; decision to develop 2, 29f, 55, 168; design & fabrication, 120, 128, 147; history, 87, 95f, 116, 118, 154; primary, the, 88, 93; process, 86ff; production, 239; relevance of information, 48; secondary, the, 88, 94; time to develop, 68, 70, 72, 111ff, 114f, 149, 190; trigger, 86, 88, 95, 114, 119, 121, 276
   -see also: Concepts; Fusion; Testing
Thomas, Arthur D.: letter, 154, 243
Thorn, Robert N., 47f, 107; affidavit, 47f, 271
Trident (see Missiles)
Tsipis, Kosta, 242; affidavit, 68, 71, 113, 242

UCRL-4725, 8, 48, 57, 74f, 76, 79, 103ff, 120f, 140, 184f, 204, 209, 214, 241, 275, 277, 281, 283
UCRL-5280, 74, 75, 76, 79, 104f, 120, 140, 184f, 275
Ulam, Stanislaw, 47, 64, 276
   -see also: Teller, Edward
Uranium 45, 83, 120
   -see also: Fission

Vance, Cyrus R.: affidavit, 111, 115, 274
Van Doren, Charles N.: affidavit, 67, 269
Victory, hollow, 216f

Warren, Judge Robert, 107, 109, 113, 134, 153, 241; decisions 7, 9, 57-81, 72, 73, 75, 113, 114, 115, 187, 189f, 192f, 194, 199, 206, 207, 208, 218, 282; statements by, 61f, 72f, 75, 113, 114, 115, 148f
Washington Post, 102f, 175, 188, 197
Weapons: bombers (B-1, B-52), 37-39, 46; F-15, 25; nerve gas, 20, 25; oversight, 42; particle beam, 50
   -see also: Concepts; Missiles; Nuclear weapons; Thermonuclear weapons
Weinberg, Steven, 267
White, Justice Byron R., 190, 199, 201
Winterberg, Frederick, 101, 276
Wise, David [WIS-78], 137f, 142

X-rays: in H-bombs, 88, 90, 91, 98, 101, 102, 106, 277f

York, Herbert [YORK-76], 29, 86, 87, 147, 162, 236

Zuckerman, Lord, 15, 236

About the Authors

All four authors are physicists at Argonne National Laboratory, which is near Chicago, Illinois. Theodore Postol is on leave of absence from the Solid State Science Division and the other three work in the reactor safety program. Collectively the authors have had a wide range of experience with nuclear data, primarily civilian but some of it weapons-related. George Stanford has a Ph.D. in experimental nuclear physics from Yale University, Alexander DeVolpi in physics from Virginia Polytechnic Institute, and Postol in reactor engineering from Massachusetts Institute of Technology. Gerald Marsh has his M.S. from the University of Chicago, and has done further work in the field of his side interest, general relativity. DeVolpi is the author of a recent book, Proliferation, Plutonium, and Policy: Institutional and Technical Impediments to Nuclear Weapons Propagation (also published by Pergamon Press). All of the authors have taken part in individual and organized activities to promote control of the arms race.

KF
228
U5
B67
1981

Born secret : the H-bomb, the
 Progressive case and national
 security / A. De Volpi ... [et al.].
 -- New York : Pergamon Press, c1981.
 xiii, 305 p. ; 24 cm. -- (Pergamon
policy studies)

    Bibliography: p. 297-298.
    Includes index.
    ISBN 0-08-025995-2. -- ISBN 0-08-
027529-X (pbk.)

1. United States, appellee.   2. The
Progressive.   3. Liberty of the press--United
States.   4. Atomic weapons information--Law and
legislation--United States.   5. Hydrogen bomb.
I. De Volpi, Alexander, 1931-

MUNION ME   820130   820127 CStoC
C000702   KW /UPG   A*   82-B350
                                80-28841